Virgin Mary's Bayside Prophecies

Volume 6 1980 to 1994

A gift of love

Library of Congress Card No.: 98-84412

ISBN: 1-891981-00-5

Printed and bound in the United States of America

These Last Days Ministries, Inc.
P.O. Box 40
Lowell, MI 49331-0040

Ph. 616-698-6448
Fax 616-698-2260
http://www.tldm.org
Email tldm@tldm.org

1998

Acknowledgments

First and foremost, we are most grateful to God the Father in Heaven for sending, the Virgin Mary under the title Our Lady of the Roses, Mary Help of Mothers, to us with His words of warning and prophecy for these end days.

We thank Our Lady for delivering the words of the Eternal Father to warn us, to save us, to guide us, to love us, and to protect us from the coming judgments, if we will only listen and act upon these instructions.

We thank Veronica Lueken for being Heaven's voice box and accepting Our Lady's Mission to bring the Bayside Prophecies to the world. We thank her for accepting all the sufferings that came with it. Heaven gave her the title: "Veronica of the Cross."

We thank Mrs. Ann Ferguson, Veronica's close personal friend and secretary, who played a major role behind the scenes to help bring the Bayside Prophecies to the world.

We thank Veronica's husband, Arthur, who lovingly cared for her and help shield her from the attacks of the devil and the world.

Next, we thank the shrine workers for transcribing and printing the messages for the entire world. The address of the shrine is: Our Lady of the Roses, Mary Help of Mothers, P.O. Box 52, Bayside, N.Y. 11361.

Next, I want to thank all the generous souls whose prayers, Holy Hours at home and before Our Lord's Most Sacred Heart in the Most Blessed Sacrament, and their financial support, made this book and These Last Days Ministries possible.

And finally, I want to thank our full and part time Ministry family: Marilyn, Fannie, Irene, Gail, Mike, John Paul, Jeannette, and Michael for their dedicated hard work and prayers that made it all happen.

Explanation of front cover pictures

Picture #1

On September 14, 1971, a man took a picture of Our Lady's statue with a Polaroid instant camera on the spot, no negative. In an eerie supernatural scrawl across the whole face of the picture are these words: "Jacinta 1972". You can see different letters and numbers by turning the picture 90° to the right and to the left so the side are pointing down.

Jacinta 1972 . . .

Our Lady - "I ask that the photograph given from Heaven, 'Jacinta 1972', be propagated, made known worldwide; for within this photograph lies the date, the month, the hour, the year, of the coming Chastisement. Search it well, My children: for those who are given the grace will find the answer to the puzzle. 'Jacinta of Fatima - Jacinta 1972.'" (10-6-79)

Jesus - "The photograph 'Jacinta 1972' was given to mankind as a puzzle for the human race to figure out, and I say and repeat again to you: if not solved in due time I will set the answer upon the world Myself. Jacinta 1972." (5-27-78)

One of the greatest gifts to mankind . . .

Veronica - The world must recognize the importance of the 'Jacinta 1972' picture. Our Lady asked that all read and examine the picture well. It is one of the greatest gifts given to mankind in these latter days, a manifestation from Heaven. All who are in the light will recognize and interpret the photograph 'Jacinta 1972', and they will not be taken unawares." (12-7-78)

The date for the Chastisement . . .

Our Lady - "My child, the picture 'Jacinta' must be read now by all of earth's children. You will give them this direction, My child. If it is in the will of the Eternal Father that they be graced to receive the truth, they will observe carefully and examine the photograph miraculous 'Jacinta 1972'. You will read the wording 'Jacinta' and search for lines and figures and numbers. Within the miraculous picture is given the date by God the Father for the chastisement of mankind. All will be conditional to the response of mankind.

"You must well remember the words of My Son to the world in relation to this miraculous picture: 'Consider this picture as a puzzle for the human race to figure out. If not solved in due time, I, Jesus, will set the answer upon the world My self?' Within this picture, My children, is the date, the month, the year, the hour, of the Chastisement as planned by God the Father." (11-25-78)

Picture #2

At the August 21, 1974, prayer vigil, Veronica holding up the Shrine Crucifix for Our Lady to kiss.

Picture #3

This miraculous picture taken in 1988 reveals two statues of Our Lady. The lower one is the Shrine statue. Another statue with almost real-to-life features appears miraculously above it.

Picture #4

Luminous cross appears over American Flag . . .

Our Lady Herself explained this picture. A large cemetery-like cross brimming with light appears over the American flag. It represents a heavy cross that will send upon the United States. However, with the suffering many will return to the light and save their souls.

Our Lady - "My Son's hand grows heavy. I cannot hold it back much longer. Your country shall receive the cross, My child! Now you understand My child the photograph. The Cross to many shall be their salvation. The Cross, My child, as you observed upon the photograph was a cross of light, beaming with life." (5-15-76

Our Lady - "The cross, My child, that was placed upon your flag has full meaning now to you, for your country, America the Beautiful, shall fall unless there is now a complete reversal... not a renewal, My child, but a reversal of the ways that have set you into darkness." (5-29-76)

Picture #5

Mr. 666, the Antichrist . . .

Miraculous picture taken on November 20, 1982, at Our Lady of the Roses Shrine with a Polaroid camera by Michael D. of Michigan. In the picture appeared 3-6's for 666, the Antichrist.

The true meaning of Mr. 666 . . .

Our Lady - "We still hope to gather our stray children and therefore, We reveal to you now, the secret of the ages.

"The true meaning of Mr. 666, known as the Antichrist: 6 is for the 6 who are coming, 6 is for the 6 days of suffering, 6 is for the 6 who will be punished.

"Man is wise but through the ages the true meaning becomes lost.

"This, My child, We give to you." (2-11-71)

The coming of the time of 666 . . .

Our Lady - "The Eternal Father through His prophets upon earth have given you in writing, your Bible, a clear and simple plan for redemption. And it has been made known to you all by John the plan of the end days and Lucifer being loosed upon earth... the coming of the time of 666. 6 is for the six who are coming and are here now. 6 is for the six days of terrible suffering. And 6 is for the six who will be punished and re - chained." (8-4-79)

Introduction

In 1917 the Virgin Mary gave warnings and prophecies to three children in Fatima, Portugal. Many of these prophecies have already occurred with 100% accuracy. At Bayside, New York, Mother Mary, under the title Our Lady of the Roses, Mary Help of Mothers, explained in great detail the Fatima prophecies and the soon coming events upon mankind.

Veronica Lueken, the seer of Bayside, was a wife and mother of five children. She lived on Long Island, New York. The story of her heavenly visitations goes back to the year 1968 when St. Theresa began appearing to her and dictating sacred poem-messages. St. Theresa prepared Veronica for the first heavenly visitation of Our Lady in 1970. Before this Veronica had not received any manifestations from Heaven.

Our Lady Herself appeared to Veronica in her home on April 7, 1970, informing her that She would appear on the grounds of the old St. Robert Bellarmine Church in Bayside on June 18, 1970. Our Lady said there will be a miraculous spring and Our Lady will appear over the old church building and then the Bishop cannot deny Her appearances. It will be called the "Lourdes of America."

Our Lady asked that vigils of prayer be held there (now temporarily held at the Vatican Pavilion site in Flushing), and that full directions be given to the clergy of the parish to prepare for Our Lady's first visit there. Our Lady also requested that a Shrine and Basilica be erected on this Her chosen Sacred Site, which is to be named "Our Lady of the Roses, Mary Help of Mothers." She promised to come on the eve of the great feast days of the Church, which dates would be given to Veronica to disseminate the messages given to her throughout the whole world. Our Lord and Our Lady promised to continue to come to the prayer vigils until the Second Coming.

Our Lady requested that the Rosary be recited aloud by the crowd during the whole of the Vigil. All are requested to kneel in the presence of Jesus. Veronica described what she saw and repeated the Messages word for word and all was recorded on an audio tape. The tapes were later transcribed and sent around the world.

This book will give you great wisdom and comfort in a troubled world. With these new prophecies you will discover how to prepare your family and loved ones for the days just ahead. You will be free from the anxiety and worry of the things to come. This is the second most important book you could read, along with the Holy Bible, in these last days before that glorious day when

Jesus returns to the earth.

You will discover a new peace and serenity in this troubled world. You will see how much the Virgin Mary and Jesus love you. Most of all you will discover how to protect yourself from the great misfortunes coming in the near future.

These Bayside Prophecies come directly from the Eternal Father in Heaven. He is telling what is going to happen in North America and the world. In the Bible we learn God always warns a nation or a people before He chastises them.

In Genesis, Chapter 3, verse 15 God tells the serpent: "I will put enmities between thee (satan) and the woman (Mary), and thy seed (demons and condemned souls) and her seed (Jesus): she shall crush thy head, and thou shalt lie in wait for her heel". God was saying that Mary, under the direction of the Holy Trinity, would lead the fight against the devil until She would crush his head, his rule, and he, the snake, satan would lie in wait knowing the plan.

The Eternal Father sends the humble Virgin Mary to guide and save us from the forces of evil in the momentous days ahead. The Saints longed to live in these days and witness the many great miracles to come. We are seeing Bible Prophecies happening that were written approximately 2,000 years ago.

There are some blank pages near the end of the book for notes. Also, there are some order forms for sacramentals and more materials on the Bayside Prophecies.

Consider this a great blessing that God has placed this book in your hands. Call upon the Holy Ghost to enlighten you as you go through this book. Prayerfully read it and discover the great wisdom, knowledge, grace, and peace it will bring to you.

Gary Wohlscheid
President of TLDM

"My Son's hand has now been withdrawn and the tribulation is coming upon mankind."

Tenth Anniversary of Our Lady Coming to Bayside, NY - June 18, 1980

Veronica - There's a beautiful blue illumination coming out from beyond the trees. The illumination of blue cascading, oh, like rays of beautiful sunshine from the trees high up into the sky. Our Lady is coming closer. She's traveling in very fast, coming from a great distance, because now Our Lady is coming down.

She's dressed in the most beautiful white gown. Oh, the brilliance and the brightness... so beautiful! Our Lady has on a white mantle. There is a trim of about a half-inch of gold all about Her mantle. Our Lady has on Her head a most beautiful golden crown. It's not the Fatima crown. It has - it's very delicate in appearance and gold. It has a - it's circular, setting down high on Our Lady's forehead. Our Lady has Her mantle - the mantle is coming halfway down over Her forehead, and the crown is just about on the edge of Her mantle.

Our Lady has Her hands joined in prayer, and about Her fingers the beautiful Rosary with the golden Our Fathers and the translucent Hail Mary's are entwined about Our Lady's hands. Oh, She's so beautiful!

Our Lady is looking about Her. She's smiling She has a soft, sad smile. It's quite windy. Our Lady's long gown is caught about Her feet. And now I can see that Our Lady has on a pair of the most beautiful sandals. They're gold. They're strapped with one strap about Her ankle. As the wind is blowing, I can see Her sandals; they go down to the edge of Her toes. And just on the edge is the most delicate golden rose on each foot.

Our Lady now is taking the crucifix from Her Rosary and extending it out, like this, and making the sign of the cross: In the name of the Father, and of the Son, and of the Holy Ghost. Our Lady is placing the crucifix to her mouth and

1

kissing Her Jesus. Now Our Lady is placing Her first finger to Her lips, which means to listen and repeat.

Our Lady - "My child and My children, and especially My child Veronica, do I speak to you now to console you for your past sufferings, and I must bring you additional news of salvation for many.

The Cross will not be lifted

"My child, the cross will not be lifted from you. Your mission as a voice box will be shortened; however, the Mission from Heaven will continue, as those whom We have called to assist in the Mission have, I assure you, My child and My children, adopted themselves well into their roles. Heaven finds them fully capable of now accepting the responsibility, as you will grow weaker and unable to come from your bed.

"Do not be saddened, My child, at this news; it is truly a great grace for mankind. There will be many victim souls throughout the world. Remember, My child, I told you many years ago that I could not promise you a life without suffering upon earth. Therefore, you will continue with great patience and understanding.

"There will be many sent to assist in the Mission from Heaven. Do not be concerned of the acceptance of mankind at this time. It is all in the plan of the Eternal Father in the salvation of souls during these days of the Antichrist.

"You must make it known to all that I, your Mother, as a Medatrix between God and man, will continue to guide you in the remaining days ahead. The Eternal Father, My Son, and the Spirit of life shall guide you all in the remaining days ahead.

A very crucial period of tribulation

"You are entering now into a very crucial period of tribulation. Your world, your country, your nation, the United States, will find much suffering and death. My children and My child, how often have I wandered among you bringing you the warnings from Heaven, and how many have listened and acted upon My counsel?

"Yes, My child, there have been many years of suffering, demanding patience and perseverance for many in the Mission from Heaven. You will all continue to go forward, remembering always that there lies ahead a great chastisement for mankind, the Ball of Redemption. Many will die in the great flame of the Ball of Redemption. Only a few will be saved.

"Already the Eternal Father has marked His own, and the forces of evil under the title of 666 have marked their own. The war of the spirits accelerates. You will soon understand that the Eternal Father has now taken away all restraint, and you will all be now subjected to the great test.

"My child, in your weakened condition, I will not ask you to bring forth again the many minor chastisements, the great War, and the Ball of Redemption, for there is a time for your relief, and We are extending this for a short time. In your state of incapacity, My child, you will still accomplish much work. Pray constantly, My child. The test is great, but the reward will far exceed all earthly sufferings and tests.

For those who will fall away

"You must make it known now to all of the workers in the Mission from Heaven these words. For those who will fall away and do not flourish in grace, I say unto you now, to all workers: If you lose your way and stop your mission, I repeat unto you the words of My Son: If the workers have been told the truth and they do not hasten to return, it is their own punishment that they have accepted. I repeat: If the workers have been told the truth and they do not hasten to return to the Mission, it will be their own punishment that they have chosen.

'Veronica of the Cross'

"My child, do not be concerned of your disability. Remember Theresa did not give you the knowledge of Our name for you, as We rightly called you 'Veronica of the

3

Cross.'"

Veronica - Now Our Lady is taking Her Rosary and She's placing the crucifix out, like this, and making the sign of the cross: In the name of the Father, and of the Son, and of the Holy Ghost.

Our Lady - "I bless you all, My children, for the Eternal Father in My Son and the Spirit of light.

"Remember: Do not become prideful, nor arrogant, nor be - let your guard down in conceit, for pride is a sin. Remember always that the closer you approach to Heaven, the greater the armies of Lucifer will come after you seeking to take you away from the road, the narrow road that leads to the Kingdom."

"Among you now, My children, as you hear My voice, two will be removed. However, do not be concerned; they are saved. Do not, My child, ask Me to give you any further information, for it cannot be made public knowledge at this time.

"You will continue to pray for your cardinals. your bishops, your priests, My Son's Church, His House upon earth. By your example many will be saved. By your prayers and example there is salvation for others. Continue now with your prayers of atonement. They are sorely needed, for the world is in great spiritual darkness. Satan has poisoned many minds.

"You will all now go forward as apostles of My Son, disciples of the latter days, under the banner of 'Our Lady of the Roses, Mary, Help of Mothers.' Many will come to join you. The Message from Heaven has now reached all corners of the earth. Many voices are sending out the news, the good news to mankind.

"It is just about time now, My child, for the world now to be tested. My Son's hand has now been withdrawn and the tribulation is coming upon mankind. Many will be taken and spared the terrible sorrows ahead.

Destroy the family and you destroy your country

"Pray constantly your Rosary, your beads of prayer to Heaven. Remain unified in your family lives. The institution of your country - the great foundation is based on family life. Destroy the family and you destroy your country. The enemies - the enemy is already within your country. Watch and pray well, My children."

Veronica - Our Lady is now going back; She's rising higher into the sky. She's now taking Her crucifix and making the sign of the cross. She's turned to the right: In the name of the Father, and of the Son, and of the Holy Ghost.

Our Lady now is directly standing over us high in the sky. She's going back into the sky, moving without Her feet moving. She's floating, actually being carried like on the wind. There's no way I can explain it to you. If only you could see it. Our Lady is just carried - though She is as solid as you and I - Our Lady is carried back as though She was weightless.

And now She's turning to the left, Her left side, and making the sign of the cross with Her Rosary: In the name of the Father, and of the Son, and of the Holy Ghost. Now Our Lady is placing Her hands together in prayer, like this, and She's nodding.

Our Lady - "Continue now, My child and My children, with your prayers of atonement."

Veronica - "It's amazing to watch the coloring developing as though it's coming from within the trees; and it's going upward high into the sky. Now from a great distance - I say a great distance - I recognize now Jesus coming forward; and He is coming from a great distance because He is - He's a small figure, almost statue - like in appearance, as He approaches. Now He's coming very fast.

The light is opening up all about Him. Jesus comes through the sky, which is dark, but there seems to be a white, glass - like translucent, very iridescent light that is separating the sky about Him, almost round, host like in shape.

Now Jesus is coming through the sky, and the light about Him is so brilliant that I'm certain that, without the grace of

God in the Providence of the Eternal Father, I would surely be blinded, or perhaps die from the brilliance. It is beyond any human words to explain this light. It's brighter than any flashing light or anything that I have seen upon earth, and it has a depth, though a glass like translucency to it.

Jesus is coming down slowly now. He's coming very close down to Our Lady's statue; in fact, I have never seen Him descend so low by the trees there.

Jesus has on a burgundy cape, and His gown is an off white, an ecru color - almost like - oh, I don't know exactly the color to call it. It's like a beige. The material seems to be rough like, almost sack - like type of material; and the gown is very long and belted about His waist with a - a sash like type of belting. It looks almost like it could be a piece of leather or skin. It's not material; it looks like some type of animal skin, like leather, but a light coloring, a light tan like, not a brown, not a deep brown, but a light tan. I can see the sash very clearly.

Jesus has on brown leather sandals. His feet are not bare. The sandals now cover - the strap covers the wounds on His feet. I can see a protrusion slightly from His feet - the wounds on His insteps. Now Jesus has the - about His neck, His cloak is held by a golden - it appears to be gold braiding. It's tied. And His cape is also blowing. It must be very windy.

Now Jesus' hair is down His back. I can see well now because He's turning to the right. Now He's turning back towards us and He's placing His hand out, like this, and making the sign of the cross: In the name of the Father, and of the Son, and of the Holy Ghost. Now He's placing His hand across His chest, like this, on His Heart. And Jesus is looking all about Him. Now He's placing His first finger to His lips, which means to listen and repeat.

Jesus - "My child and My children, I will not proceed with a long discourse, especially, My child, for your comfort. But the world has received countless warnings from Heaven. These warnings have been sent to every nation of the world.

"There is little time left now for mankind to restore itself,

6

to be pleasurable and a joy to the heart of the Eternal Father. Instead, mankind, your generation, has become perverse, degenerate, self seeking, proud, arrogant; and science, man of science, now seeks to create life and fly above the Creator. You do not learn from the past, but over and over again you repeat yourselves.

"Remember the first trial in Heaven. Lucifer was cast out of the Kingdom of Heaven. Let this all be a lesson to mankind, who seeks to go above His God, with the advance in knowledge, seeking to go above His Creator, caring more for the creature than the Creator. I say unto you, your God, that heavy trials now shall beset mankind.

"Your country, the United States, and most countries in your world have allowed satan to enter into the highest positions of your government, your medias of communication, and even into My House, My Church upon earth. Therefore, there is no other recourse left to Heaven but to cleanse you of your errors.

Only a few will be saved

"As in the past We sent to you voices crying in this wilderness of evil: Straighten yourselves out; make way for the Lord, for the hand of punishment shall come upon you! As in the past you all continue in your lives of pleasure, neither caring nor seeking the truth. Therefore, I say unto you as your God: many will die. Only a few will be saved.

"My Mother has set Herself to hold off a just chastisement upon mankind for many years, but your time has run out. Her warnings have gone by unaccepted, unnoticed, and rejected, even by My clergy! Her tears fall upon your generation. The saints in Heaven, sacrificed upon earth, have cried out now for reprisal upon this degenerate generation. 'How long, O Lord,' do they cry, 'shall you permit this perverse generation to exist?' And I say unto you now: your time is running out!

"Do not speculate on the dates, but be prepared. My Mother has spent countless years among you, preparing you. If you are not ready now, then you will never be ready! And

7

it will come upon you at a time that you least expect. You have been given your armor, instructed well by My Mother. Therefore, you will follow the way of the Lord! You will listen to the counsel of My Mother or you will fall!

"Your nation, the United States of America, has been now - the proud eagle has been plucked by satan; and as such shall be cleansed by trial and suffering and war. Humanism and modernism has set you on the road to satanism. Your country and many countries of the world now have adopted the worship of false idols.

"Satan, the master of deceit, has poisoned many minds. Satan, the ruler of the world of darkness has now entered into the highest places of governments, and even within My House, My Church upon earth. But I shall cleanse them, as I have cleansed them in the past.

The tribulation is at hand

"My voice cries out to you all now to be prepared, for the tribulation is at hand. All who have listened to My Mother's counsel and are of well spirit - have no fear. My words to you are consolation. I do not seek to place fear into your hearts. I console you with the knowledge that you will be saved. Remember in the days ahead, remember My words of consolation to you all: you will say 'MY JESUS, MY CONFIDENCE!'

The day, the hour of the tribulation

"My children, you will read and re read the messages from Heaven given through My Mother to you. Read them well, for much has been over looked in the past. You will receive great knowledge, and you will be able then to know the day, the hour of the tribulation.

"Continue the prayers of atonement, the Rosary. Wear your scapular; it was given for great reason. One day you will all understand. Pray, My children; a constant vigilance of prayer must go throughout your country and the world. Prayer now is the only means with action for saving the souls in your country and your country - men, for destruction is about to come upon you.

"Remember, My children, in the days ahead, your great comfort is the knowledge that there is no death. Life will continue beyond the veil for all. Many will be asked to sacrifice in the name of the Lord. But how great a sacrifice is this? Very little, in comparison to the great reward that lies for him over the veil.

"Pray, My children, for strength. It will take great courage to remain in the fold in the days ahead; but your courage shall be the cross and the knowledge of the truth.

"Remember, do not become a worshiper of the creature, but of the Creator; for the creature is the world, and the world is satan. The Creator is your God, and His world is the Kingdom of Paradise. This choice will be yours to make. Each and everyone of you will have to make that choice soon. No man shall be lost unless he is lost of his own free will.

"Remember, My children, those who have been given graces, much is expected of them. You must continue to go forward. Do not slacken in your work, your mission. Do not become complacent nor content in your own salvation, for that will be pride, and pride can make you fall. Therefore, in all charity, reach out for your brothers and your sisters. Your lives must remain free from contamination of worldly pleasures and seeking, for the world has now been given to satan."

Veronica - Now Jesus is placing His hand out in front of Him now, and making the sign of the cross: In the name of the Father, and of the Son, and of the Holy Ghost.

Now Jesus is looking all about Him, and He's now placing His first finger to His lips.

Jesus - "Veronica, My child, remember My Mother's counsel to you. You will not be cured, My child. The waters will not be for you. The cross cannot be lifted.

"You understand, My child, the words of My Mother to you several days ago. Remember them when you find the cross is heavy. It is the will of the Eternal Father that you

9

must accept, My child. You will find great joy in the knowledge that suffering has merits far beyond what man can understand in the salvation of souls.

"Theresa has directed you will in the past, My child, and you will soon be seeing her again."

(Pause)

Veronica - I'm not afraid, I have no fear.

"You shall see nations disappear from the earth in seconds."

Eve of the Feast of St. Theresa of the Child Jesus
- October 2, 1980

Veronica - The sky about the trees is becoming a very pink and blue combination of colors that I have never observed before. The colors are absolutely beautiful! And high over Our Lady's state the sky is opening, and it's becoming a most beautiful clear day. There are no words to describe the beautiful brilliance of the light!

And coming forward as the light is opening wider and wider, directly above Our Lady's statue now - the circlet of light is becoming so wide that it's now extending beyond our heads towards the rear... Directly in the center of the circlet are Our Lady and Jesus. Oh! They are so beautiful!

Our Lady has on a white gown. The white is so brilliant. And also She has on Her waist a very beautiful blue sash. The color of it is a sky blue. And all about Our Lady's mantle, approximately a half inch wide, is a border of gold. I cannot see Our Lady's feet this evening because Her gown is quite long.

Jesus is standing at Our Lady's right side now. He's moving about and looking to the right and the left. If you will observe carefully now, Jesus is making the sign of the cross, like this: In the name of the Father, and of the Son, and of the Holy Ghost.

Our Lady and Jesus are looking about Them. Our Lady is moving over to Her left side, that would be our right side, just slightly above the tallest limb of the tree. Our Lady now is taking from about Her waist Her beautiful Rosary, the Rosary with the golden Our Fathers and the translucent Hail Marys. Our Lady now is extending the crucifix, the beautiful crucifix. Oh, it is so brilliant that I am certain without Heaven's grace I would be blinded by the brilliance of the crucifix. And Our Lady now is extending it out to the people, and making the sign of the cross: In the name of the

11

Father, and of the Son, and of the Holy Ghost.

Now Our Lady is turning to the right and nodding to Jesus, and They are both now returning over, directly overhead, above Our Lady's statue. Jesus is touching His lips with His first finger: that always means to listen.

Jesus - "My child and My children, this is a moment of trial for many throughout your earth, and a time of grace for many as they are tested in trial.

The tribulations have started

"Remember always as I repeat to you that God is, God was, God always will be. Yesterday, today and tomorrow is forever. The tribulations of the world have started, and the course of mankind continues on the road to great trial because your generation has given itself over to all manner of sins of the flesh, that will condemn many to hell.

"There is only one way to restore your world to peace, and that is by following the way of My cross. You cannot change My words to bring them in line with mankind's own egotistical ways. You will find that humanism and modernism shall bring much suffering upon mankind.

"My Mother has directed you well through countless appearances upon earth, and how many have listened to Her counsel? And how many have acted upon it? I say unto you now: You have become a degenerate generation that asks for a just chastisement from the Eternal Father.

"Do not be affrighted, My children of the light. Know that My words are for those who have fallen into the web of Lucifer and his agents.

"Be known it to you that is has been written of and spoken of as 666, the masters of deceit. Satan has entered into the highest places of your government, of each nation of the world, to sow confusion, discontentment, atheism, communism, satanism and all manner of evil

Jesus shall destroy the church of man

"I give you a final warning from the Eternal Father. You

will turn back and restore the earth. You will turn back and restore My Church upon earth. You shall not set up a new church of man, for I shall destroy it. You shall see nations disappear from the earth in seconds.

"O My children... you're My children. You must stand alone, just as you, My child, must continue to kneel alone, and stand alone in the world, as the agents of hell come forward to destroy you."

Veronica - Our Lady now is nodding to Jesus, and touching Her first finger to Her lips.

Our Lady - "My child, We have allowed you the test of great suffering. You cannot understand at this time the countless numbers of souls who have returned to the Faith. You cannot realize at this time the numbers of souls that will not fall into the abyss because of the legions of light that the Eternal Father has gathered upon earth, in His heartfelt fatherly efforts, accounting with the free will of mankind, to restore the earth and mankind as it was in the beginning.

"What was to happen in the future shall be now. The merciful heart of the Eternal Father reaches out to all mankind, but unless you follow the directions from Heaven, you cannot be saved. And only a few then shall be counted as saved.

"My child, you have been given explicit instructions for the procedures. The world will understand in time the Mission from Heaven. To all who follow Our legions throughout the world, the legions of light, you will unite under a common banner called 'Faithful and True', and you'll then prove to the world what a true soul can do!

"My child and My children, because of the suffering that We watch, souls longing for relief, We shall not give you, My child, a long discourse this evening. But you will now go forward with the instructions given by My Son."

Veronica - Our Lady is now taking Her Rosary, the beautiful Rosary with the golden Our Fathers and the white Hail Marys... but as Our Lady is turning and looking about now, and extending Her crucifix, all of the colors of the rainbow radiate from them like pearls, the Hail Mary beads.

They're absolutely beautiful! And Our Lady is extending now the crucifix on Her Rosary, and making the sign of the cross: In the name of the Father, and of the Son, and of the Holy Ghost.

Our Lady - "My child now, you will read few photographs this evening, but you will now start the plan as I have directed you. Begin, My child, with a firm Act of Contrition."

Veronica - O my God, I'm heartily sorry for having offended Thee. And I confess to all my sins, because I dread the loss of Heaven and the pains of hell; but most of all because I love Thee my God. Who are all good and deserving of all my love. I firmly resolve, with the help of Thy grace, to confess my sins, to do penance and to amend my life. Amen.

My God, I believe, I adore, I trust and I love Thee. I beg pardon for all those, (put me in the rain*) who do not believe, do not adore, do not trust and do not love Thee.

O My Jesus, forgive us our sins, save us from the fires of hell; lead all souls to Heaven, especially those who are in most need of Your mercy.

Over to the right side, directly over the tallest limb of the trees, on the right side, St. Michael is coming forward. And following him - oh! it's Theresa. Oh! Oh, Theresa is dressed in her Carmelite habit. And behind her, I recognize her - St. Rita! Oh! St. Rita of Cassia. Oh! I know her. Oh, and there are many saints coming forward.

Our Lady now is touching Her lips, as She goes forward to them nodding. The light is becoming so brilliant about them. Jesus now also is crossing over to the right side, directly over - They don't walk, They float. It's absolutely beautiful! They just float across the sky like They're weightless! Yet Our Lady and Jesus look as solid as you and I.

Theresa's shower of roses

Oh, now They're - Theresa is taking roses, like this, and she's throwing the rose petals down, like this.

Our Lady is now crossing over with Jesus to the top, I would say - oh, about - I can't measure it in feet, but Our Lady and Jesus are rising a little higher, and They're being followed now by St. Rita and St. Theresa, and many other saints. And I can see now some Popes coming forward. I can tell by their habits. They're beautiful. They're white and gold, with high mitres on their heads. And one I recognize because his hair is very white. That must be St. Pius X. Yes, it is. He's nodding. Oh, they're so beautiful, the light is so brilliant! Our Lady now is touching Her first finger to Her lips.

Our Lady - "My child now, you will take three photographs and then continue with the procedure directed."

Veronica - Do not be concerned, Our Lady said, the waters will not make you ill. They are curative.

Our Lady asked Veronica to remove the protection of the umbrella. As She explains above, the rain will not make people ill.

"Bless them with the ... curative waters from the springs of the world."

Eve of the Feast of Our Lady of the Rosary - October 6, 1980

Veronica - There are blue streams of light coming down from the sky, high above Our Lady's statue. Directly over Our Lady's statue, the sky is opening up. It makes it appear that it's a clear day. Oh, the sky is just beautiful! It's a pale blue. And it seems to be just evaporating away all the darkness. And directly in the center of the beautiful pale blue sky, I see Our Lady coming forward. She's a small figure now because She's traveling in from a distance.

Now as She's coming closer, I notice that Our Lady has upon Her feet very delicate slippers. They're not sandals, they're actually slippers, fully closed. And on each tip of the slipper there's a - what appears to be a golden rose, but so tiny I would call it a rosette.

Our Lady has on a brilliant - the light is very brilliant this evening. She has on a brilliant white skirt. Her gown is extremely long. And it must be windy, because the gown is being blown back and forth. And I can see the beautiful small rosettes on Her feet. Our Lady has a blue sash about Her waist, and Her mantle covers completely Her head, down halfway over Her forehead. The mantle is a beautiful white, as white as snow, and it's trimmed all about the edge in a narrow border of gold, approximately a half inch wide.

Our Lady now is taking from about Her waist Her beautiful Rosary, the Rosary with the golden Our Father beads. And the Hail Mary beads are white. But as Our Lady is turning now and looking about Her, they are taking on all the colors, or reflecting all the colors of the rainbow; pinks and blues, and a lavender; but they're pastel shades that I have never seen before upon earth. They're a coloring that is beyond description; and not being able to paint or draw, I'm certain, I could never even place it upon a paper or easel.

Our Lady now is taking Her crucifix, the beautiful golden

large crucifix, and making the sign of the cross: In the name of the Father, and of the Son, and of the Holy Ghost.

Our Lady is kissing the crucifix, like this. And She's turning now to the right, and making the sign of the cross: In the name of the Father, and of the Son, and of the Holy Ghost.

Now Our Lady is turning to Her left, our right, and She's going across the sky until She's directly now over the tall tree; and She's bending now down, and extending the crucifix out quite far from Her waist, and making the sign of the cross: In the name of the Father, and of the Son, and of the Holy Ghost.

Our Lady now is returning to the center of the sky, and She says:

Our Lady - "Look backward, My child. See the numbers who have come with afflictions. You will not forget them, My child. But go forward now and bless them with the waters, the curative waters from the springs of the world."

(Pause)

Veronica - All about the trees, bordering the extension of the trees, you can see, if you look closely, a beautiful pale blue light, extending upward past Our Lady's statue. Now it's joining with an opening in the sky that's becoming very bright, round and circular, Host - like in shape. The Host area is becoming now a clear white. There was an intermingling of a beautiful pink, sort of a pale fuchsia pink coloring, and a very light pale blue, not a sky blue, but a misty blue, but beautiful blue coloring intermingled with the pink. But that's now like evaporating. It's the only way I can explain it.

And coming down now from high in the sky, They're coming through very fast, Our Lady and Jesus are coming side by side now. They're almost down very very low over Our Lady's statue.

Jesus has on a burgundy colored - it's deep velvet; I can see it very clearly. Now He has on a deep velvet cape, and it's tied with a golden rope - like material into a bow, though,

17

to hold the cape about His neck. Now the cape, as He's turning and looking at the people, I notice that the cape does have a - oh, a headpiece. Cowl? Our Lady is saying, "cowl", "cowl". Oh, I don't know what it means but Our Lady said a "cowl".

Now Our Lady is looking about Her, and She's touching - oh, She's looking towards Jesus, and He has nodded. And She's touching Her first finger to Her lips, which means to listen.

Our Lady - "My child and My children, I delayed a discourse with you, My child, Veronica, due to the urgency of the peoples in their infirmities. We behold them, and the merciful heart of the Father extends to them the graces: there will be cures, there will be conversions.

"My child and My children, your task is heavy, but remember: If the worker is laid low, he will be graced, for heavy is the work upon you. But if the worker is laid low, he will be graced.

The great beast of hell

"My child, it saddens Me to bring up anew a subject of great concern to Heaven. There is emerging again the great Beast of hell onto earth. He has been present among you now, under his banner of 666, for quite a number of years, building his forces for this moment.

"I have asked you for the salvation of all souls. For mankind there will be no peace without prayer and penance and atonement.

"A great catastrophe is approaching your country, North America.

"My child, weep with Me, pray with Me. Have mercy in your heart for the sinner. No man is without sin, and therefore charity must not grow cold among mankind. You are the creation of the Eternal Father, and as such you are brothers and sisters upon earth, with a destiny similar to all mankind. Sooner or later, you will fulfill this destiny by coming over the veil. Sadly, many are coming to Us unprepared, and not warranting entrance into the Eternal Kingdom of Paradise.

The sin of omission condemns many

"The sin of omission shall condemn many to hell, be they layman or Hierarchy. I repeat: not the sin of commission, but the sin of omission will commit many to hell. Among them there will be also mitres.

"My child, because of your weakened condition, I cannot at this time take you upon an extended trip that I planned, down into the abyss, to view and give to mankind the unholy sight of the abode of the damned. You will regain your strength, My child, in time, where you will be able to come out of the abyss with Me, without a fatality. My child, once in the past, I took you by the hand down into the abyss, and you viewed the creatures of darkness and the prince of darkness in his abode.

"We proceeded on, My child, in the past to purgatory. Oh, how My heart bleeds for the loss of the knowledge of the existence of purgatory and hell among the children! How many shall be saved? Only a few!

"O My child and My children, continue to send the urgent warning from Heaven throughout the world. You cannot slacken your pace, but must go forward with perseverance.

"You will have now, My child and My children, additional torment and irritation from the followers of 666 and the church of satan. There are many who come as angels of light among you. I have asked all of the immediate workers within the confines of the circle of light to confine themselves to their homes, allowing only the entrance of their immediate families and the close workers within the circle for reason! For the souls of whom knock upon your door will be evil. Do not test My words, My children, for the penance is heavy for disobedience to the Eternal Father.

Satanists seek sacrifices for their altar

"I will not describe the scenes of abomination witnessed

by Heaven now going on at this very moment as I and My Son are among you. Those who have given themselves over to worship the prince of darkness prepare a great feast and seek now sacrifices for their altar.

"I ask parents to be prudent in allowing their children to be on the streets after dark without protection, for they shall disappear and not be seen again.

The desecration of churches

"The world will soon learn that there exists now another unseen world of evil that is closing in now, for satan knows that his time is growing short. As I told you in the past, My child and My children, sin is insanity, and it is only now the beginning. Unless you pray and make atonement to the Eternal Father, you will see abominations and the desecration of churches, and murders will abound until those who remain upon earth will envy the dead.

"Do not scoff when I have given you, and do give you knowledge, My children, of the existence of a cult of satan. Sadly, will you learn too late and seek out the interlopers in this world, as your children are found without blood.

"My child, your second mission will now be extended. You will find there is reason to rejoice, for his deception shall now be exposed. You will, My child, be most careful now. It is a great test.

"I have asked you, also, to bar your doors to all but your immediate family and the close workers of the circle. Allow no one within your home for reason. You are now on a list for extinction. Others I shall not outwardly name, My child, for I do not wish to hinder their mission or to place fear in their hearts. I do assure all who will be part of this mission that they will be guided, and they will confuse and confound the church of satan.

"Yes, My child, much is asked of you, but you will receive additional strength to continue. When you find a moment of discouragement, you will say, 'My JESUS, MY CONFIDENCE.'

Theresa to assist you

"Be careful, My child, that you do not leave your home for any reason alone; that you do not allow entrance to your home on ground level. And I will send forth from Heaven an army of angels. Tusazeri shall guide you, and I shall have, with the permission of the Eternal Father, Theresa to assist you in the Mission.

"I do not wish to use a name, My child, but Heaven sends among you in the circle of light graces: graces for perseverance and graces for miracles, miracles that will confuse and confound the enemy. Those who have heckled and doubted shall be put to shame and confusion. For nothing remains hidden in the darkness, but must come forward into the light to be exposed at a certain time. Now, My child, you will understand why you found the trial so long and so strenuous.

The paws of the bear

"You will pray for your Holy Father, Pope Paul, in Rome, John Paul II. You will pray for all the clergy, the cardinals, the bishops; for, without your prayers, many cannot escape the paws of the Bear. Sadly, many in the world will sell their souls to get to the head, and many will turn their backs on My Tabernacle.

"I ask for victim souls for the merciful Father, to do penance as victim souls to repatriate those who, without their prayers, will wind up, My child, at the end of their lifetime in the abode of the damned. For the souls now are falling into hell as fast as the snowflakes fell during your winters, and as numerous as the rains will come.

Internal strife in the government

"Your country, the United States, My child, shall have great trial - the winter and the wars. There shall be internal strife in your government and your streets will become running with blood. It is not a sight, My child, not a pretty sight! Oh! Oh!

"That carnage, My child, that you view, shall extend not only from the cities into the country, but from coast to coast in all of North America and the world.

"Man in his arrogance and his growth of knowledge has now the capacity to destroy himself in moments. The Eternal Father knows the future, and He knows the past and all beginning. And your future is now. What was to happen in the future, My children, shall be now."

Veronica - Now Our Lady is looking over to Jesus, and He is extending His hand out, like this, and making the sign of the cross: In the name of the Father, and of the Son, and of the Holy Ghost.

He's now bringing His cloak about Him. It's very windy and He's touching His first finger to His lips:

Jesus - "My child, I will not add to the discourse of My Mother. Suffice it now to say that all fair warning has been given to mankind.

"You will continue to pray and make atonement to the Eternal Father: a life of full dedication to Heaven. For if you cast aside the Mission and go out into the world, you will be lost. And remember the admonition from Heaven to all in the Mission from Heaven: If the worker has been told the truth and he does not hasten to return, it is his own punishment that he has chosen.

"My child, I would advise you now to repair home, and go immediately to your home. Do not be concerned of an incident, for We are watching, and it will be diverted from you."

Veronica - Now Jesus is looking all about Him, and He's now motioning to His lips: "My final word, My children, is to warn all mankind at this time, that they must guard their families well - the children, with sacramentals. For there are mysterious forces now and false miracles that will abound upon earth, even to deceive the elect. Therefore, to protect your children, they must use all the armor available from Heaven. We do not wish to see and watch future broken hearts of parents as they bury their dead children.

"My child, you will receive additional discourse at home

22

from My Mother, but it will not be a public message at this time, for your safety and the benefit of all concerned and involved with the Mission from Heaven."

Veronica - Yes... I understand. Yes... the children.

The Old Catholics: A Schismatic Organization

Jesus - "Beware of those who start a new church among you. A Roman Catholic Church must have a legally ordained Roman Catholic Bishop, and the Old Catholic Church is not with Rome. It is a schismatic organization, and all who join these interlopers shall gain immediate excommunication by Heaven and through the legal Hierarchy of Rome. The Old Catholic Church is schismatic, and is not, and shall not use the name Roman Catholic Church. Later, My child, when you gain your strength, We will extend this message to mankind. For many shall come as angels of light and deceive the elect.

"I ask you all not to abandon My Church. Do not judge My Church by the priest, for in his human nature he can err. But I assure you, I am using him, as a legally ordained priest, to bring you My Body and Blood. Do not go seeking elsewhere, for you will lose your baptismal right, and you will no longer be accepted as a Roman Catholic, and you will not enter into the highest place of Heaven, the Kingdom of Paradise.

"My child and My children, you will understand, for My Mother will later give you full enlightenment upon this matter."

Veronica - Now Jesus is extending His hand out, like this, and He's making the sign of the cross: In the name of the Father, and of the Son, and of the Holy Ghost.

Jesus - "I bless you all, My children, in the name of the Father, the Eternal Father in Heaven, and the Spirit of Light. Go forward under the banner of 'Faithful and True.'"

23

"...Warn the world that they now have within their balance, the balance of life for Our Vicar John Paul II"

Eve of the Queenship of Our Blessed Mother - May 30, 1981

Veronica –The sky is shimmering with light. The light is very pale blue, but very translucent, and in patterns of waves cutting through the sky, directly upwards, high in the sky, over Our Lady's statue. There is a Host - like circle of light now forming, and it is widening. Oh, it's so brilliant, my eyes are absolutely pierced by the light. And directly in the center of the light, Our Blessed Mother.... oh, She's so beautiful! Oh, She's so beautiful! Our Lady is coming forward through the light. She's descending slowly, and She's looking about Her.

Our Lady has a most brilliant white gown with a blue sash about the waist. Her Rosary is tied to the right side of the sash. Our Lady's mantle is a brilliant white, whiter than sugar, whiter than snow. And there is a light that is cascading from within Our Blessed Mother. There is no way I can describe it. But it seems to be coming from within Her, going right out through Her clothes. And actually Our Lady is now surrounded by a tremendous light! And She's coming forward much closer now down, descending directly above Her statue.

The trimming of gold about Our Lady's mantle is approximately - I can see Her very well now - about an inch and a half wide. It looks like pure spun gold. I would say that, I don't think I have ever seen pure spun gold, but I know it's pure spun gold. It is absolutely brilliant!

Now Our Lady is looking about Her. It's a little windy, because Our Lady's skirts are being caught in the slight draft.

Oh, Our Blessed Mother has on sandals. The sandals - I can't see Her ankles because Her gown is so long, but I can see that there are two straps upon Her sandals; they're golden. The sandals are open, I can see Our Lady's feet. But on the edge of the sandal, the one in the center, there are three straps. Now I can see as Our Lady's turning about a bit - She's looking in both directions - I can see that the sandal has three straps through the feet. And in the center there is a small - it looks like pure gold - rosette, a small rose upon Her feet. Our Lady is absolutely beautiful! She looks very, very young. Oh, I couldn't even tell you Her age.

But Our Lady now is taking from about Her waist, Her Rosary. Oh, the beautiful Rosary with the - oh, they're very - extremely large, the beads. Our Lady has - the Our Father bead is a gold. It must be pure gold. I never saw anything like that. And Her Hail Mary beads are white. But they're really not white, because, as Our Lady's turning now - She's taking the beads in Her hands - they seem to be - have more colors, like all the colors of the rainbow are catching the light that seems to be cascading from - oh, all over about Our Lady... a tremendous stream of light, almost forming an oval pattern, almost like a medallion, a medal pattern about Our Lady.

And now Our Lady is taking the crucifix. The crucifix is a beautiful golden crucifix, pure gold. Oh, it's brilliant. It would really hurt your eyes to try to look at it but for the grace of God.

And Our Lady now is extending out the crucifix, and making the sign of the cross: In the name of the Father, and of the Son, and of the Holy Ghost.

Now - oh, over to the right - oh, he's so big. He is so immense, Michael is. I didn't notice him because of the brilliant light; but I see now, beyond the tree, Michael covers the whole sky! He is immense! Our Lady looks almost, like childlike, with him behind Her. He's covering the whole sky.

And Our Blessed Mother now is cutting across, She's cutting across to our left side - that would be Her right side - and She's also extending the crucifix on Her beautiful Rosary, like this, and making the sign of the cross: In the name of the Father, and of the Son, and of the Holy Ghost.

Now Our Lady is smiling - a very soft smile, but there's a

25

great sadness upon Her face tonight. And Our Lady is looking down, and nodding, yes. There are graces now falling from Heaven. Our Lady says there are graces now being given.

Now She's crossing the sky; and Our Blessed Mother is going quite fast now across to our right side. She's just above now - approaching the extension limb of the tree, and Our Lady is leaning over with Her beautiful crucifix, and making the sign of the cross: In the name of the Father, and of the Son, and of the Holy Ghost.

Our Lady is nodding again. And now She's turned, and She's coming across the sky, and She's pointing upward though with Her crucifix. She's pointing upward with the crucifix over to the left side of the sky. And I see forming there a large black cross. It's a very somber - looking black cross. I don't feel so very good, Blessed Mother. What is that?

And now under the black cross there is a ball, a large ball forming, the world. But I see, I see flames now, there are flames. It seems like there's fire - oh, terribly, terrible fires all about the ball. The heat is so... stifling. Ah! Ah! ah...ah...ah. Now Our Lady is nodding over to my right side, taking my eyes to the right.

And now I see St. Peter's. I see everyone waiting. I - I - I... I see everyone waiting in St. Peter's. They're all hushed. Something's happening. I don't know what's happening there, Blessed Mother. Oh... there's a hush, some kind of an announcement being made. Oh, I don't know what it is. Now Our Lady - I can't see the - the square is fading away.

And Our Lady now is motioning that She is going now over above the statue, and I am to follow Her. Now Our Lady is placing Her Rosary, like this, in Her hands, and She's touching now Her first finger to Her lips.

Our Lady - "My child and My children, especially My child, Veronica, I have, with permission of the Eternal Father, been unable to spare you from this scene, and have brought you here in your weakened condition that you may warn the world that they now have within their balance, the

26

balance of life for Our Vicar John Paul II.

"I come to you as your Mother, your Mother of hope, your Mother of perseverance, your Mother of love, your Mother of all nations. I ask you, I plead with you to listen to My counsel.

"Man of free will has cast doubt, looking for the answer with scientific minds and humans with theological knowledge, but man is forever seeking and never coming to the truth.

"Your world, My child and My children, has not progressed back to the Eternal Father. Should you receive now one chastisement so sorely due to you for your disobedience to Our Vicar... do you as a nation, do you, all nations of the world, deserve the continuance of the struggle of Our Vicar for your salvation, or shall you, through your own actions, force the hand of the Eternal Father upon you by abandoning you to your sin? Your nation, the United States, and all nations of the earth - none shall escape the fires.

Prayers needed to save your Vicar

"But, My child, as you well know in My discourse with you the past weeks, satan will seek to stop the prayers, the acts of atonement and sacrifice that will be needed to save your Vicar. A victim souls must take his place. My child, do not be affrighted, you cannot be this victim.

"Yes, My child and My children, there are many mysteries of faith that will be known to you when you come across the veil.

"As a nation, as a country, to all nations of the world, I say to you as Your Mother, that as you have sown, so shall you reap. How many years have I traveled across your earth, crying with tears of pity and frustration, that the great Chastisement be withheld from mankind, because of the many souls that will be lost to Heaven. How many have listened to My counsel and prepared? Have you become so blinded by your lives of luxury and worldly pursuits that you can no longer recognize what is happening about you! Murders abound. Blood flows in the street. Hunger shall be

27

set upon your country. Many shall die. And why? Because you have turned your back upon My Son... the only One now who can save you from what is fast coming upon you.

"My child, do not be affrighted. Through countless years have you seen this scene.

Veronica - Oh! Oh! (Veronica sighs heavily) Oh! (Pause) I - I don't know. The people are killing each other in the streets here! And I see such terrible blood... and the people have gone crazy. Oh, it's horrible! Blessed Mother, please!

Our Lady - "My child, I have asked all to go forward in these final days before the great Chastisement as disciples of My Son, first and uppermost in their lives. For he who gives his life shall be saved. He who walks away and abandons himself to the world shall be lost.

"I told you, My child, to shout it from the rooftops, that many will die in the great flame of the Ball of Redemption. Only a few will be saved. There will be nations disappear within a matter of ten minutes and less.

Earthquakes, famine, starvation

"Earthquakes in your country, the United States, extending up through Canada, earthquakes in places never before known to exist, or the possibility of. And they will know it comes but from the hand of God. Famine, starvation, your crops will rot. The heat will burn, the cattle will starve. And why? Because you refuse to turn back, complacent in your arrogance.

Restore the altar railing

"I have asked you to get down on your knees. Clergy in My Son's House, His Church, restore the altar railing, that man may be on his knees. For many shall crawl on their knees in desperation seeking to flee, but nowhere shall they escape the flames. Restore My Son's Church while there is time. Return the railings. Have the people make atonement upon their knees to their God.

"Why must you be like immature children, to be punished before you will be obedient to your God? Can you say, O clergy in My Son's House, and those who profess with mouths and barren hearts allegiance to Our Vicar in Rome - when he dies, you have killed him, because of your disobedience.

"My child, I realize the great strain and responsibility placed upon your at this time, but you cannot make known what I am about to tell you. Only when this permission is given." (Pause)

Veronica - Ah! Ah! (Veronica sighs heavily) Yes, I understand. Prayer, atonement and sacrifice. Yes, I understand.

Our Lady - "My child, you will instruct those about you to send out all of the messages from Heaven. And you must now gather the information given to compile the conversations with My Son. I ask as your Mother to continue upon the Mission. Do not abandon Me and My Son as We try to save you.

"The mores of the world are but vanity and foolishness, a temporal way of life. Beyond the veil is forever. Tomorrow could be forever for many.

An epidemic uncontrollable by science

"Pray always a constant vigilance of prayer. Protect your children. Tears shall be shed, for many children shall die in an epidemic uncontrollable by science.

"Man has reached to the stars for power. Self-gratification, glory, money - for what? They are but a shell that must one day be destroyed. And the spirit? What shall happen to your spirit? No consideration for your next life is given by Our errant children upon earth. One day may be too late. You must now live each day as though you were to go over the veil tomorrow, for so suddenly will many be taken from upon the earth.

Syria has the key

"My child, one part only can be made known, given to you. Syria has the key to the solution of world peace or the third world war. It will be the destruction of three-quarters of the world. A world aflame, with also the Ball of Redemption.

"Your country, the United States, and many nations of the world now are under the domination of a godless government. As such, without prayer, atonement and sacrifice. I say unto you now, as your Mother, that you, too, proud and arrogant a nation that you be, the United States shall fall. Many shall suffer.

"My child and My children, I have always promised to protect you and all who call to Me. But the powers, the forces of evil, have been allowed to enter even into My Son's Church. The smoke of darkness - darkness of the spirit covers the world. Already many have reached the point of no return. Pray, My child and My children, a constant vigilance of prayer.

"My child, I shall not burden you now with a long discourse on the offenses of mankind that has now been played, the scene before the final curtain, before the eyes of the Eternal Father as He sets judgment upon mankind.

Not the end of the world

"Continue, My child, as you have been, accepting for your Vicar now all manner of illness, sufferings of the heart, penance and atonement. For unless We have others who offer full dedication in that manner, giving their wills to the Eternal Father for the salvation of souls, your world will face within a short time the final destruction. Not the end of the world, My children or My child, but a destruction such as mankind has never experienced before, nor shall it ever again so few will be left.

"Pray a constant vigilance of prayer. Protect your children. Guard their souls well. And do not cast off the sacramentals. Do not care more for the acceptance of mankind.

Do not be guided, or misguided, by the derision of the multitudes against you. For, remember My words again, My children: Only a few will be saved!

"For many earth - years I traveled about, and many received graces far beyond ever known in the history of mankind, in Our final effort to save man from his own self.

"My children, I bless you all."

Veronica - Our Lady is extending Her Rosary with the crucifix, like this.

Our Lady - "I bless you all: In the name of the Father, and of the Son, and of the Holy Ghost.

"Your homes will now be your fortress against evil. For once you go without your door, can you say that you'll live forevermore? Or shall you return to that door?

"The forces of evil are gathering to do final battle upon earth. He who has ears to listen must awaken now from his slumber, or be forever lost.

"My child, you must now take three photographs, and retain the knowledge in them. They will give you firm consolation and conviction in what I have spoken to you of, that must temporarily remain a secret."

Veronica - Pink as you remember is Jesus' color. Whenever He's approaching, the sky always lights up the most beautiful pink. I don't think I've seen much of that color pink. It's very pale, but it's a really - I guess you'd call it a true pink. I don't know the different shades, but it's just beautiful.

Now all about the trees, the sky is becoming - oh, can't you see it - it's such a deep pink now. And - oh, Jesus is coming through the sky. The sky is opening up. Oh, do you know the sky just seems to roll away, and it's so clear - it's so clear, right as Jesus is coming forward, behind Him. It's like looking through a glass. The sky is absolutely - I never saw the sky like that behind Jesus. It's like He's coming through a glass. It's really - I don't even think it's the sky behind Him. I don't know what it is, but it's not stars. And it's not like the sky about us, but there's like a glass, like a partition or something.

Jesus is coming now down much faster. Oh, and He's - oh, Our Lady now - I see Our Lady now; She is coming also. I don't know where They were before, because I didn't see about the sky - how They went back in. But Our Lady is coming forward now, and She's now coming closer to Jesus. Jesus is just above the tree behind Our Lady's statue there on the excedra. Oh, I can't measure distance, but He must be standing at least about eight feet above the tree.

And now Jesus has on a robe - you know a robe, with a - I can only see a part now. He hasn't turned. Oh, He's turning now. He's looking over to the right. And it does have a hood on it; it's a cape. It has a gold tassel - like cording about the neck. And the cape look like it may be like a velvet. It's very regal looking, the cape Jesus has on. And His gown is not a white; it's like a - oh, like a beige color.

And Jesus has though - about His waist the belting is a deep brown. It matches His sandals. Jesus has on, they look like skin. I don't know what kind of skin, but they almost look like leather. They have also two, like straps, that go across down through His feet. And I can see, as the wind is blowing. I can see Jesus' ankles now. Oh, do you know He still has those marks, because the upside down V - like formation of the straps to His ankle exposes His insteps, and He still has the wounds on His feet. I can see them through the, you know, the division of the straps. I can see them. They're very sore - looking. The right foot, His right foot especially, it looks very sore across the instep, and on His left foot, that looks very raw, too.

Now Jesus is holding up His hands. Oh, my goodness! His hands look just like when I saw them years ago: they're very raw and sore - like where the nails went through; the spikes - not nails, they were spikes. And He's holding them up now.

Now They're both looking about. Our Lady is smiling very softly, and She's saying something, but I can't hear what She's saying to Jesus. And He's nodded. And now They're coming back. They had moved over to our left side - that would be Their right side - but They're coming back now. They're just directly over the statue. And Jesus is saying something to Our Lady; I can't hear. Oh, He's now turning, and He's nodding. And He's placing His first index finger to His lips, that means I must listen - repeat.

Jesus - "My child and children of the world - I refer to you as My children, for you are truly always in My heart. My Mother has asked that I refresh your memory in relation to the dire urgency of your times.

"As a generation that has given itself over to all sins of impurities of the flesh, seeking in an arrogant manner the plaudit of the world, and making others in servitude to him - I say unto you, as your God, that your world cannot exist in this condition.

"Many years My Mother has traveled in diverse places, among many tongues and nations, to caution you and counsel you. Her heart, the purest heart in all the women of the world, Our star of Heaven, your Mother, has tirelessly pursued Her urgent pleadings with mankind to turn back, as they slowly go forward, faster and faster, to their own destruction.

"How long, the voices of those who are persecuted and must die, are saying - the voices rise to heaven, join with the saints: 'How long, O Lord, shall you continue to find excuses upon excuses as these generations of degenerates have progressed into a spiritual darkness and depravity far worse than even during the time of Noah or Lot? How long, O Lord, shall many more martyrs shed their blood?'

"My children, voices cry out to Heaven to stop the carnage, the inhumanity of man to his brother. But I say unto you, as your God, that you have a free will to correct all the wrong or extend it until you destroy yourselves.

"My child and My children, the course ahead for all who will to stay in the light will not be easy. It will be one requiring sacrifice, full dedication and placing GOD IS, in front of them always. For God is, God was, God always will be. First always - yesterday, today and tomorrow. This generation shall pass away, but My words shall not. For the end is fast coming upon mankind, the end of time as you know it, and your nation shall fall. All because of your rejection of your God. All because you choose to ignore in disobedience your God. All because you have given yourself to the mores of the world and satan, as I have cautioned you and warned you through countless years upon earth.

"Times - the time is here. The sand is running out. And what are you going to do now? Shall you all burn? My child and My children, those who remain in the light, those who pray a constant vigilance of prayer, and remain free from the contamination of the world, protecting their homes which will be their fortress in the days ahead - this is no time to seek change or to go out into new pursuits. You will now spend your time being ready for what is to come upon your.

Murders will abound

"The days are numbered for your country. Murders will abound. You will see insanity among mankind, for sin is insanity. Brother against brother, children against parents, slander and scandal, murders, abortion. What manner of sin can I not count and list for you that does not stand in lieu of judgment?

"My child, shout it from the rooftops unto your last breath, for as such will the gates of Heaven be open to all. The road to Heaven is not easy. It is a road of sacrifice. Too few stay on that road, because they do not understand the value of suffering.

Hell is overflowing

"You are but pilgrims upon earth. You were placed here to do honor to your God. And now how many are honoring satan - Lucifer, the adversary. If I could open to you now and show you hell. It is overflowing. But no man shall enter hell, and be cast into damnation unless he wills this, of the free will given to him through the Eternal Father.

"Love, you cry, love and brotherhood - and who truly knows the meaning of love? What is love? Love is giving. Love is caring. Love is sacrifice. Love is believing.

Believe and you will be given the way. Pray and the doors of Heaven will be opened to you. Ask and you shall receive.

"Seek man to answer your decision, give you the decision, answer your problems... you are lost. No man has the key to eternity. God has. No man shall come across with you and plead your cause over the veil. You will enter as you came in, with nothing but what you have merited upon earth.

"I have been discoursing with My Mother, My child, that We may not place upon you at this time additional strain. However, know that no heavier a burden will be placed upon your shoulders than you can bear.

"For to whom much is given, much is expected, and discipline and obedience means suffering and sacrifice. Unquestioning love, unquestioning obedience, that is the only way to Heaven. Accepting all suffering, and offering this for good cause. Too few know, My child. I know Theresa has given you the full discourse on the value of suffering, that one day you will release to the world when you complete your second book. That will be left for My Church.

"The sufferings now upon earth, My child and My children - all who are now disciples of the end days, remember one day your names will be written in Heaven. Is this not worth suffering for, persevering for, and waiting for, My children?

"Understand: there is a Heaven, there is a purgatory, and, sadly, Lucifer's kingdom of hell. Man will take this from your minds. In that manner will you fall faster. Therefore, you will continue reading and rereading the counsel of My Mother in the many visits to you upon earth. For soon you will be reduced to praying, and prayers alone; and then your test of faith will come.

Obedience - the greatest test of all

"My child, in relation to your great test of the past several months, know, My child, that every one was to be tested,

35

and every one, My child, was you. And the greatest test of all was obedience, My child. But your mission in that respect is ended. You will not be given another trial again like that, My child. For the strength allowed you must now be given to compiling the conversations We had many years ago.

"My Mother will continue to direct you and all who now have joined the armies of the world. My Mother will continue, and I will continue to protect you. When you have doubts and lack of confidence, you will say, 'My Jesus, My Confidence.' Just call and I will listen. Believe and I will show you the way.

"Count not upon the frailties of human relationship, because they die and wither away. Whereas My Mother, in Her Immaculate Heart, will always be there to counsel you, to guide you; because no purer a love has ever been given to mankind, than expressed when She submitted to My persecution upon earth, and saw that I was to leave. Knowing the will of the Father, She accepted this, and in that way became truly the Mother of the world.

"My child, you will continue now, My children, with your prayers of atonement. They are sorely needed. Pray for your Vicar. My child, you will keep the second part of the message secret at this time."

Veronica - Now Jesus is extending His hands out, like this, and He's making the sign of the cross, like this: In the name of the Father, and of the Son, and of the Holy Ghost.

Jesus - "I bless you all, My children, for the Father, the Spirit of light, that you may continue your mission for the salvation of souls."

Veronica - Now Our Lady and Jesus are backing - They're just floating backwards, They don't walk. They just seem to be weightless, but Jesus and Our Lady look solid, not like the other people I saw. They look so solid that, that - as though human, Our Lady and Jesus, you know. And now They're going back. And Jesus is smiling. Oh, He's smiling. He's got His beard - it's very well cut. You know, sort of... (Veronica gestures with her hand to her chin to describe the appearance of His beard). I guess He thinks that's funny - it's embarrassing. He's got a nice beard... and it's like this, you know, sort of...

And Jesus' hair is very long. His hair is coming down now to His shoulders, but it - the light from His robe make His hair look like a reddish - brown - I guess reddish - brown. Jesus is nodding.

Our Lady now is smiling. Oh! I notice Our Lady has changed Her crown. Now before - She's changed into Her crown - She only had Her mantle on before; but Our Lady has that Fatima crown on Her head now, the round one, with the cross on the top. And Jesus is nodding.

Jesus - "You understand, My child, the reason. Remember about the secret."

Veronica - Our Lady is wearing the Fatima crown, that's all I can say, Jesus said. Oh, They're smiling.

Jesus - "Continue now, My child, and I counsel you to stop not on route home, but repair immediately to your home."

Veronica - One? I can take one more picture, one picture, Perry. One picture, Jesus said. Take one picture. (Pause)

(In a child like tone of voice) I don't like witches! Oh! (Pause) Oh! They do look human, but they sure act funny! (Pause) Oh, I'm not afraid of them, m - much. (Pause) Oh, that's why the altar railings have to come back. That way they don't get... that's right. That's terrible! They just carry them away. (Pause) They can't carry them away. Oh! Oh, if they got their hands up where the priest can watch them. The altar railings must come back.

"...Wars are a punishment for man's sins"

Eve of Trinity Sunday - June 13, 1981

Veronica - The sky all about the trees is now becoming alight with a most beautiful blue cascading light. The light, at first appearance, seems to be coming from within the trees itself, lighting up the sky - but no, as it's growing brighter, I can well see now that the lights are cascading in a pattern combined with long streams of blue, pale blue light, and also circular almost Host - like balls, I would say, of light. They are floating across the sky directly above Our Lady's statue, Host - like in formation.

Now directly, if you'll look high in the sky, Our Lady is coming through the sky. Oh, She is so beautiful! Our Lady is wearing a pure white gown and She has on gold sandals.

And now Our Lady is coming in much faster. She's not walking, She's absolutely floating. So beautiful!

Her gown is a pure white - oh, as white as snow, as white as sugar. I have no explanation, human - wise, to tell you of the brightness of Our Lady's gown.

She has all about Her head a most beautiful mantle of white, going completely across Her head and down to the edge of Her gown at Her feet. And the mantle has a trim of about an inch and a half of gold. I really believe it's a real gold, because it certainly looks like pure spun gold.

Now Our Lady has Her hands up in prayer, like this (Veronica folds her hands together in prayer). And in Her hands, I just noticed. Our Lady has Her Rosary, the beautiful Rosary with the very huge beads - the golden Our Father beads and the white Hail Marys. And the crucifix dangling quite low towards Our Lady's belting.

Our Lady, this evening, has on a gold belting. It's like a gold cloth with a tassel that comes down at Her waist.

And Our Lady's hands are still in prayer, as She's coming closer in that position.

I see Our Lady now standing upon the world. There is a large globe; I know it's the world. I see outlines like you do

38

on the globes you use in schools.

A huge gathering of ships

And Our Lady is looking all about Her. Now Our Lady is taking Her hands and She's pointing to the sky, over to Her right, our left. And I see in the sky, on the left, a huge gathering of ships. I see the water. There's no land in sight, but there are many ships. And the sky is becoming very dark. It gives me a very ominous feeling. I can't explain it, but they're all ships... I - I'm trying to recognize them, I'm not familiar with ships, but they look like - they're not tankers, but they look like battleships.

Now - oh... oh! One of them has - it's flying a hammer and a sickle - a flag, a red flag with a hammer and a sickle. Oh! And now the scene, it's just evaporating, fading away.

And Our Lady is motioning over now to Her left side, which is our right side, and I see a map of Africa. And I see the Mediterranean, and I see ships going out - I can see them coming out of a channel. I recognize the Mediterranean. And they're heading down... I - oh, they seem to be cutting a pattern across the sky now over to those battleships. Now everything is becoming fading; I can't see anymore on either side.

And Our Lady now is taking Her crucifix from the beautiful Rosary now, and extending it out, and making the sign of the cross: In the name of the Father, and of the Son, and of the Holy Ghost.

Our Lady - "My child, it was urgent that I call you here this evening. And you will be given the strength to bring forth the message so necessary at this time.

The fall of nations

"As I had discoursed with you this week, My child, you understand now that there is an urgent call for prayers, for your world now stands before a precipice overlooking a fall - this fall being far beyond what man can ever anticipate. I speak, My child, not of the spiritual fall, because that has

39

precipitated the present crisis of mankind, but I speak of the fall of the nations.

"I have traveled throughout your world for many earth-years pleading your cause before Heaven for an extension of time for Our errant children. I have prayed with you, I have interceded for you, and now I must come to you with a torn heart. See, My child, My heart, filled with thorns. I accept the burden of My Son for a generation that has given itself over to satan."

Veronica - Oh! Oh! On Our Blessed Mother's chest, I see a heart, a human heart beating, I can feel it beating. But it is just filled with huge oversized thorns. And I - I see also a dagger, like some type of a huge saber - like knife being thrust into it. And it's bleeding... it's bleeding, Her heart is bleeding. Oh! (pause)

Now Our Lady is motioning for me to look up. Oh!

Our Lady - "See, My child, the sufferings endured for the salvation of your generation. Were it not for the few who have given themselves to be victims to the Eternal Father for the salvation of mankind, your country, the United States, and most nations of the world - and I would tell at this time a fact, My child, that every nation of the world shall feel the catastrophe.

"I have asked you all to make atonement to the Eternal Father, to live a life of prayer. You must be in the world, but not of the world. My Son has asked much of many of you who hear My words and will read My counsel. But for those who have received much, much is expected of them. The test is great.

To be a disciple of My Son

"To be a disciple for My Son, the test of love and obedi-ence is great. No man or woman chosen for the path to Heaven shall go without test. You will be tested as metals in the fire. If you love your mother, your father, your sister, your brother, your wife, your husband, your children before, and place them between the border of spiritual salvation or destruction of the soul; if you place them first before My

Son, you cannot be a disciple for Heaven, and your salvation shall be in the balance. The road to Heaven is a narrow one. The roses are given at the end of the road, My child and My children.

"I ask those who can now - are enabled to hear My voice, I plead with you, as Your Mother, to listen to Me and follow this direction, or you will receive a great chastisement. You must now go down upon your knees and make atonement, sacrifice and do penance for your country, for your nation, and for the countries of the world. You are upon now the brink of great destruction. That is why, My child, I took you to the corner, the edge of the chasm, and showed you.

"You understand, My child and My children, that wars are a punishment for man's sins.

"Clergy in My Son's House, I, Your Mother, I come to you as the Mother of the world, Your Mother, known to you by many names - Mary Immaculate, of the Immaculate Conception - I have appeared to many, in all nations of the world, in order to save your world from destruction.

A godless nation

"Without My Son you are lost. A godless nation shall fall. A nation that has been eaten away and rotted by sin shall fall. A nation that has turned itself back and regressed to a state of animal living bordering on all sins of the flesh and impurity; given over to all manner of seeking things of the world; power, lust, envy, hate, murders, abortions, worship of false idols; loving money, power, and lacking the instinct of survival when survival can only be reached by pleading for them to the merciful heart of the Eternal Father.

"My child, you will continue with lessened energy to see that all of the messages of Heaven are dispersed as fast as possible.

"Minds have become clouded, as some will give themselves over to pursuits of the world, and their minds become clouded and do not understand the Message from Heaven. The danger, My child, to this, and, My children, is that you can fall away and be forever lost.

41

"For I repeat again: What is there tomorrow for you? Will you see another day for you? Will you know another sigh for you? How do you count your time upon earth? Through science? Through your physicians of the world?

"O My children, how foolish you have become. Running hither and yon, gaining great knowledge, but you cannot stop the deaths that abound throughout your world. You cannot stop the increased murdering of your children: father against son, mother against daughter. And now all restraints gone for the protection of your children and your home life - the disintegration within the home because GOD IS does not have any place in your home today.

"It is always a great sorrow to My heart, My children, that you are truly like little children, never learning until you are punished. You are traveling the same road as in the past. You do not learn from your past.

"But, My children, I repeat again: Throughout the world's whole population, only a few will be saved. To be saved you must now withdraw from the world, which has been given to satan. You must earn your daily bread it is true; but the Bread of life is still My Son, first and foremost.

"In your pursuit of worldly living, have you sold your souls to get to the head? Corruption and dishonesty abound in your country, the United States, and many - most countries, nations of the world. This corruption will not go unpunished.

"Your country, My child, must turn back to God, because the time is running out. You cannot compromise with the enemies of your God, nor can you compromise with the enemies within My Son's House, His Church. Conform and you will die on the vine. I say unto you, all clergy, cardinals, bishops and lay people in My Son's House, His Church: Conform and you will die on the vine!

"The Eternal Father in the Trinity, the giver of all life and the taker of life - however, satan now has great rule over your world. All will be tested.

The coming cataclysm

"In the coming cataclysm - I do not refer, My child, to a minor warning, I refer to a great minor chastisement for your nation - many will die. The good - some good will die also, but they will be martyred for their Faith.

"My child and My children, much cannot be in discourse with you at this time. But I must stress the urgency of your remaining in My Son's Church regardless of the turmoil. I stress again this urgency for the salvation of your soul. You must not tear it asunder. You cannot run hither and yon setting up a new church, for to divide is to conquer, and that is the plan of satan against My Son.

"The adversary, the prince of darkness, knows that his time is growing short. He will do great battle now with the children of God. Prepare now for you will see days ahead such as have never taken place within your country, My child. That is why I stress the urgency of this message. There will be much suffering. No class shall be excluded. Those who do not suffer shall be damned to hell. For they have sold their souls to get to the head.

"In time this puzzle will be explained to you fully, all who hear My voice and will read the Message from Heaven. For the future is now, and it will unfold before your very eyes.

"Life, as you know it, will have no value. Death shall be commonplace among you: murder, death by murder, in the name of mercy - death, murder.

"My child and My children, only you as an individual can save your soul now and the souls whom you love and whom you have the charity to reach out for. For those with great graces, they can be shared. You have a great obligation now to go forward as disciples of My Son.

"If you proceed ignoring My counsel, and My direction, you will see many nations disappear from your world within moments. Hunger and starvation, famine, disease, pestilence.

"My children, how sad I am that too few have followed My counsel to read the revelations of St. John to the world, the Apocalypse. Read them, My children. Ask My Son, ask the Eternal Father and the Holy Spirit to enlighten you, and the pages will become clear to you. The pages will open up like the scroll, and you will have full understanding of the days ahead. What was hidden from mankind for many years is being revealed in order to save the world from its own destruction.

"Pray, My children, a constant vigilance of prayer. Pray for your Holy Father in Rome; pray for your bishops, pray for your priests; pray for your government leaders, for satan has clouded many minds.

"I do not come to place fear in your hearts, My children, to prepare you for what is to take place. Know that the merciful heart of the Eternal Father is with you. He does not wish to see you destroy yourselves, because the destruction of many in their physical bodies means the destruction of their eternal souls. For many will then be taken in the plan of satan before they have time to come back, do penance, make atonement, and prepare for coming over the veil.

"Retain your sacramentals, My children. Feed on the Bread of life, My Son in the Eucharist. He will sustain you in the days ahead. Cast Him aside, and you will be lost.

No dead body shall ever be restored to life

"You cannot, in your scientific minds, and no man of science will ever have the secret for the restoration of the dead to the living. Life only goes over the veil; it begins a life anew. No dead body shall ever be restored to life, until the final judgment at the end of all time. Unto that time, there is a Heaven; there is a purgatory, a place of purging - cleansing; and there is, sadly, a hell, the abode of the damned, the kingdom of Lucifer, the adversary to My Son. The battle rages now for souls, My children.

"Understand that you are living in the latter days. Do not have your minds clouded by those who are skeptic, those who will reason with all man's scientific intellectual knowledge, which is as nothing. For soon, as their minds seek a way out, without prayer, satan will come in, and many will

44

die."

Veronica - Our Lady now is looking all about Her. She's looking all about Her, and now She's pointing up to Her right sky - that's to the left of us - high up in the sky, I see forming again two - they're two hearts. Oh! On - oh! on the right side, Her right side, the heart is the same as Our Lady had on Her chest. It's a human heart, I know it. And it's all like thorns around it; and, also, there's a knife through it. Oh, my goodness! And then there's a heart, it's almost like an entwining of rings like; and there's another heart right next to it. Our Lady is saying, " the Sacred Heart of My Son." And that is covered completely with thorns. They're very sharp. I can reach out and touch them. They're very large. I don't know - I never saw a thorn so big, not even on a rose bush; they're not that big. Oh, I've cut my hand.

Now Our Lady - it's growing very dark, and I can't see them anymore. Our Lady now is nodding, and She's placing Her first finger to Her lips.

Our Lady - "My child now, you will continue with your prayers of atonement. You will be sustained for the arrival of My Son, but then you must repair to your home. You will not be able, My child, to leave your bed until My next visit with you on the anniversary.

"O My child, be consoled. I repeat again: For those who have received great graces, much is expected of them. And the value of suffering has been explained to you, My child.

"Continue now, My child, with your prayers of atonement."

Veronica - The sky all about the trees is a beautiful light pastel shade of pink. Of course, you must understand that pink is Jesus' color. So when the pink starts cascading above the trees, it's a signal from Heaven that Jesus is coming.

Now directly over Our Lady's statue, the sky is opening up. I - oh, it's amazing! Oh, I hope someone else can see this, it's so fantastic. The sky is opening up just like, it's like - oh, just a mist blowing away, and the sky is opening up into a circular pattern. And it's so clear above - Jesus is coming forward now. He just - the whole sky was closed, but it opened up, and - and He's coming right through as though He was stepping through a sheet of glass. I can't explain it, because the light is so brilliant. It's circular in pattern, like out - like actually spanning out from Jesus. The light is emanating, I believe, from within Jesus, because that's the way it looks now.

Now Jesus is coming forward. He has on a - oh, it's - I don't know what color it is - Jesus' gown, it's a very long. He has it like tight about the waist, with a cord - like - made of some kind of skin. I don't know, it looks like leather, but lighter in color, like a very light brown. But I don't believe it's any type of cord. It looks like a piece of skin, tying like, cinching in His gown at the waist.

And it has a - I see it very clearly... Jesus is smiling. He has a round neckline about the gown. It seems to be very simple in the way it's made. But His robe - Jesus' robe is a very deep, plush - looking, velvet type of burgundy color. It's burgundy, I believe that's the color. It's between a rose and a red. Oh, I can't explain it, but His robe look like velvet - beautiful! And He has it tied at His - right under His chin, between His chin and the upper part of His gown by a gold cording.

And it's very windy, because there is a - I think it's called a cowl. Does Jesus say a cowl? C - O - W - L? From the back of His neck... that's a hat, like the cape part of His - of His like long - like mantle, like Our Lady wears a mantle; but He has on like more of a heavy type of cloak.

And Jesus is looking all about Him. The light is very brilliant, but I can see His hair is quite long. Jesus' hair reaches down below His shoulders. And it always appears - I don't know if it's the reflection from the burgundy of His robe, but His hair looks like a reddish - brown. It's a beautiful shade of - it must be brown, but the light cascading from His robe makes it look like, sort of reddish - brown.

And Jesus' eyes are - oh, I can't explain His eyes. His eyes are beautiful.

See with Our Lady, Our Lady talks, but it's like She's

talking, like with Her lips moving. But Jesus looks - just looks at me, and there's not a movement of His face, and there's no way to explain it - He's talking right into me.

Now He's moving over, to be directly over Our Lady's statue, but beyond the first tree. And He's looking all about Him. Now He's placing His hand up, like this. And Our Lady is coming forward. I didn't notice where She was before. But She's coming forward from behind Jesus. And She's standing now - She's going over to Jesus' right side.

Our Lady has on now, over Her beautiful white mantle that extends to Her feet with the gold trim on it, She has the beautiful Fatima crown. I've learned to recognize it from the way it's rounded with the cross on the top. It's the Fatima crown, all of gold, Our Lady has on Her head.

And She's standing right next to Jesus with Her hands together, like this, in prayer, and the beautiful large Rosary beads just dangling from Her fingers.

Our Lady looks very much petite next to Jesus, because, you know, Jesus is quite tall. I would say He's about six feet tall. And Our Lady only comes up to His shoulder now as the way She's standing there. Our Lady is just motionless standing with Her hands in prayer, like this.

Now Jesus is turning, and He's moving back a little. He floats back. Our Lady and Jesus seem to be weightless, yet they look as solid as you and I, except for that brilliant light. The light is tremendous.

Now Jesus is placing His first finger to His lips, which means to listen and repeat.

Jesus - "My child and My children, My Mother goes untiringly throughout your world in these latter days counseling you to prepare you for the days ahead.

"My child, in the early part of your mission, I directed you in the path, to the path of recovery of souls. My words, My child, I repeat anew. What was to happen in the future shall be now. It was for you to try to prevent this by getting out the Message in great haste.

"My child, I am fully aware of the energies and the ceaseless work entailed upon you in your weakened condi-

47

tion. However, We understand, My child, and shall not place a more heavy a burden than you can carry at this time. The strength will be given you from Heaven.

"My child and My children, I will not, at this late date, continue with a lengthy discourse, giving you all countless reasons for the necessity for a just intervention from Heaven upon mankind for the salvation of souls. My Mother has prepared you well. You have been counseled to wear your sacramentals and to restore the Faith in the hearts of the multitudes.

All clergy shall be accountable

"All clergy, cardinals, bishops, parish priests and laymen, shall be accountable for the fall of all souls within their self - imposed dedication of protection, which has been cast aside; as many have been blinded by a life of too much luxury and ease.

"As I told you in the past, through prophets and the word, that it will be easier for a camel to go through a needle's eye than for a rich man to enter Heaven. For his richness has been directed from satan for the destruction of his soul.

"Charity is known to few. Charitable people are few, My child and My children. Blessed are the poor and the peacemakers, for they shall be truly called children of God.

Faster than the snowflakes

"The more you give yourselves to the world and the pursuits of the flesh, and the pleasures of the flesh, the farther you fall out of grace and lose the road. Souls are falling into hell faster than the snowflakes that cascaded upon you in the worst part of your winters.

"No, My child, have no despair or fear at this time. You shall not be making the trip into the abyss with My Mother at this time. But, My child, you know full well that even many mitres shall fall into hell unless there is a victim soul or victim souls willing to do penance and make atonement. Prayer, penance and atonement by all for them.

"Your priests, priests in My House, My Church upon earth, do not have a special passport to Heaven. In their human nature they have the same struggle and must carry the cross. However, many are casting aside the simple way for a most complicated life, using man of science and intellectualism to destroy his own soul.

"The way to Heaven is a simple way. It cannot be compromised; it cannot be modernized; it cannot be cast aside or a new religion started. For your religion will be of man, of humanism, and modernism, and satanism, and all the 'isms' that destroy mankind in the end.

"My child and My children, you will all keep a constant vigilance of prayer going throughout your country and the world. Proceed with great haste to send the Message throughout the world. Hasten, hearken and listen, for I shall not warn you again. You are now on the edge, the edge of doom for many. For the end shall come upon many suddenly, without warning. Are you ready for this, My children?

"I do not come as a prophet of doom to you, and neither will the voices crying out with the truth come as prophets of doom. But they will be disciples of the end days, bearers of light and the truth. Listen and you will be saved. Believe and you will be given the way. Close your ears, harden your hearts, and turn away and you are lost.

"Protect your children and your homes, for many tears shall be shed by parents. Wear your sacramentals. Do not be influenced by those who have lost their way and seek to take other with them. You must be different in this world of satan. Receive his mark and you are lost. Receive the mark of the cross and you are saved.

"The test will soon be placed heavily upon many. You will pray a constant vigilance of prayer, and when you grow despondent or despairing, you will say, MY JESUS, MY CONFIDENCE.

"My ears are never closed. Our hearts are open to you. Believe and you will be given the way. Seek and you will find. The truth is a simple way, and you must live this simple way, and stay out of the world and its entanglements with satan."

Veronica - Now Jesus is placing His hand in front, like this, and making the sign of the cross: In the name of the Father, and of the Son, and of the Holy Ghost.

Now Jesus is turning His head to Our Lady and is saying something. I just - I can't hear Him; it's like a - almost a whisper, like a rustle of the trees.

But They are now turning to the right, and Our Lady is leading the way. They're going across the sky. Now Our Lady is turning. She has Her hands up in prayer again, like this, and the Rosary is dangling from Her fingers now, quite down the front of Our Lady's gown. I can see the beads.

Now Jesus is over by the tree on the left side, and He's placing His hand out, like this, and making the sign of the cross: In the name of the Father, and of the Son, and of the Holy Ghost.

Now Our Lady is nodding to Jesus, and They're turning over to - They're cutting across the sky now. They float just effortlessly; it's just beautiful to see. They go clear across the sky, but without even moving Their feet. Oh!

Now Jesus and Our Lady are over by the third tree from... from the flag. Now Jesus is bending over. He has to mount the branches of the tree, and He's making the sign of the cross: In the name of the Father, and of the Son, and of the Holy Ghost.

Now Jesus is placing His hand across His chest. Now They're turning over to Their right, and They're coming across the sky now. And now as Jesus and Our Lady are standing above the statue, They are both simultaneously, both together, They're pointing to Their right side, that would be the left side of the sky.

And I see a huge globe forming, a huge globe. It must be the world. And there's a big cross on the top of it, but there are flames all about the globe. There are flames. They just seem to be coming out of the globe. And the cross is becoming very dark, very black. Oh! Now it's fading away; it just seems to evaporate, like the mist.

And Our Lady is - I can hear from here. Our Lady is

heaving a very deep sigh (Veronica sighs deeply).

And Jesus now is touching His finger to His lips.

Jesus - "You see, My child, the great trial that is to come upon mankind. The second part of Our message to you must still remain a secret, My child; you understand that.

"Continue now with your prayers of atonement; they are sorely needed for all."

"Many mitres shall fall into hell"

Eleventh Anniversary of Our Lady Coming to Bayside, NY-
June 18, 1981

Veronica - The sky all about the trees is becoming alight
with the most beautiful blue light that's pinpointing, it's not
cascading.... there are direct lights from the trees, line - like
in pattern - that's the only way I explain it - and it goes
straight up through the center of the sky, and as though they
were almost like fingers pointing from the trees. But they're
a pale blue. Now they're becoming deeper in blue. It's
almost as though the lights, which I would say the streams of
light are about a good - oh, four or five inches in thickness -
they're separated like banners. Yes, I would say that as
they're becoming deeper blue, deeper in color, they're like,
not confetti - no, like banners, streams of banners coming
down, cascading from the center of the sky.

Oh, now the sky is opening up in a round circular pattern
that - it's as though, beyond the sky, there is... well, we know
there's another world. But it's absolutely beautiful!

Now as the sky is opening up, I can see that they weren't
just lights, they're like banners, and they're held by beautiful
cherubims(?), young angels.

Now there are no faces. They have on beautiful gowns.
But they're very young angels. I know they are childlike in
appearance. And they have on gowns of all pastel colors;
pink predominating, with blue and white, and a lavender
shade, but it's a beautiful light pale. They're all pastel colors. Oh, they are so beautiful!

What they are doing now, they're circling... they're - oh,
they're circling Our Lady.

Our Lady is coming forward. She just came through the
opening in the sky. It's a Host - like opening. It's becoming
wider and wider. Now it's covering the whole area, even
now opening up over our heads.

Oh, it's just beautiful. It's as though the night has rolled
away and there's the most beautiful clear blue sky. And

there are over Our Lady's head, high in the sky, there are beautiful stars, thousands of twinkling stars. They are twinkling, because they are actually, not glowing, but they're glittering.

Oh, Our Lady is beautiful! Our Lady has on a white mantle, but oh! oh, I notice now on Her white mantle She has the gold trim. But She has the most - oh, it's beautiful gold, spun gold... it's a round crown a Fatima crown on Our Lady's head, but it seems as though the gold has diamonds set into it.

Our Lady is all aglow like the stars. Oh, She's so beautiful! And She - Our Blessed Mother has on the long gown. Oh, it's white as snow or sugar - so brilliantly white, I have no way to describe it in human language.

Our Blessed Mother has on the sandals - Her sandals are very delicate. Her feet look tiny from here. And the sandals are gold. They are a gold spun - like material. I don't know what they're made of, but they have these beautiful metallic - oh, they must be spun gold rosettes. I would call them rosettes because they're very, very tiny on the tip of Her sandal. It's not up near the ankle. I can't see our Lady's ankles because Her gown is so long, but I can see Our Lady's very - Her feet look very small and tiny under the gown. And the sandal, being golden, is brilliant in the light.

And all about Our Lady, the angels now are waving, they are weaving and waving these banners that are a most beautiful blue color. I don't think I have ever seen this color blue here on earth. It is absolutely beautiful. I've never seen anything like this, except that, perhaps, like the old fashioned maypole dances where the children would go with the banners. That's what it's so similar to: as though there was a celebration for Our Blessed Mother.

Now Our Lady is coming forward, and She's very, very close now. And the angels are separating. They're moving without moving their legs, but they're floating off to the side closer to the trees now. Our Lady is directly over Her statue and She's smiling. It's a sad smile. But Our Lady looks so beautiful, and so young! Oh!

Now Our Lady has about Her waist Her beautiful Rosary, the Rosary with the golden Our Fathers and the beautiful white Hail Mary beads. Oh! Now Our Lady is taking the crucifix of Her Rosary and making the sign of the cross: In the name of the Father, and of the Son, and of the Holy Ghost.

Our Lady is taking the crucifix now and placing it to Her lips, like this, and then touching it to Her heart, like this. Then She's crossing Her hands across her chest, like this, shoulder to shoulder, the fingers are.

Now Our Lady is motioning, She's placing Her hand upward, to look up high. Oh! Oh, there's Michael. Oh, St. Michael! Oh, he's tremendous. He's tremendous! Oh, but do you know what he's doing? He's got a chalice, a large golden chalice in his hand, and He's holding the chalice now and turning it down, and there's like blood pouring out of the chalice...blood! Oh, my goodness! Oh! Oh my!

Now Our Lady is motioning to me, and She's touching Her lips with Her first finger, which means to listen.

Our Lady - "My child and My children, how heavy is my heart in the midst of a time when joy should be in the hearts of all mankind, but We find now increasing sorrow and suffering.

"O My children and My child, how My heart is torn as I look upon your nation and other nations of the world that are fast approaching their annihilation.

"O My child and My children, how many earth - years have I traveled to and fro, My voice relentlessly crying out to you to do penance, atonement and make restitution to your God for the many offenses that you have committed against the Commandments, which the Almighty Father has handed down to you in order to guide you, so that you will not lose your way and will come to Heaven. However, as it was in the past, so it is today in your generation, that you have learned nothing from your past, and continue along the same path to your own destruction.

The true meaning of love

"My child and My children, if I could take you with Me and give you the eyes to see and the ears to hear, you'll understand why I have cried out to you in the past to protect your soul, your children's souls, your families, and accept as a victim soul the graces given to you from Heaven to reach out with to save others. For charity and love of heart knows no bounds, no restrictions, but in giving does one really bring forth the true meaning of love.

"Your world which cries for peace, the words come from the mouths of those who are lying. For while, they cry peace, they make provisions for destruction. Peace will not be restored to mankind until My Son in the Trinity is restored to your homes and the hearts of your families.

"Man upon earth has given himself over to perversion, for sin has become a way of life. And the children - O My child and My children, how I cry for your children. For would not it be better at this time, My child, for the second part of the secret to become a reality for the salvation of the young souls?

"Do not be affrighted, My child. I ask all to be long suffering, as the Eternal Father has been long suffering. For eternity is forever beyond the veil. The Eternal Father, the creator of all mankind, will struggle to bring back one of His lost sheep, never wishing even one to be lost to Him.

"Therefore, My child and My children, how generous of heart is the Eternal Father that this reprieve had been given to you. But the Son, who is My Son, the Son of the Eternal Father, your God, can no longer restrain mankind who has a free will.

The eyes of the world are on North America

"Therefore, as errant children, who learn only by experience and punishment, shall a great chastisement be set upon your nation and many nations of the world. The eyes of the world are on North America, and the eyes of all creatures possessed by demons of hell are on North America. And should North America join them, North America shall fall.

"Little do your news medias enlighten you to the truth. I cannot, My child, give you in discourse a full and open knowledge for mankind of the deceit and the misdirection in your country by leaders who have cast away the knowledge of God and the supernatural in your country and throughout the nations of the world.

"O My child, years upon earth, and what has happened? What has happened among My children? Purgatory is over-flowing. Satan, the adversary, the prince of darkness, has many now forever lost in hell. And who brings Our children to the knowledge of hell, of its existence?

"But I tell you now, as your Mother, that woe to the man who commits scandal and chooses of his own free will, to cause the fall of a young soul. For better that he had died in his mother's womb or a millstone be put upon his head, about his neck, and cast into the sea, before he brought scandal to the little ones.

The plague among the children

"My child and My children, I have counseled you on the approaching plague among the children. Because of the sin of man, this cannot be avoided, this cannot be held back, My child.

"I understand the great emotional strain this knowledge has brought to you, My child. But you will continue to shout it from the rooftops. The strength will be given you. Every message from Heaven must be duplicated and sent out in great haste. The time is growing short. The enemy is at your door!

Yes, My child and My children, My voice has not weak-ened, but My heart is more torn. For how many years have I traveled throughout your world pleading with you, as a lov-ing Mother, to listen to Me. And how many have listened to this counsel from Heaven? How many have hardened their hearts, closed their ears, so involved in worldly pursuits and pleasure.

"Pride, arrogance, lust, money, murders - all manner of corruption is set upon mankind because he will not listen. I will not say cannot listen - he will not listen. Therefore, he who will not listen must receive a just chastisement, so his ears will be forcefully opened, and he will bend his knee... to his God.

Bar your doors

"O My children, listen to Me now: your children, protect them. Bar your doors to all but your immediate family and your closest workers within the circle of light. I tell you again this for reason.

"Yes, My child, the trials of the past shall not be placed upon you again, but you understand now the full power that satan has been allowed in these latter times. It is a testing ground for all, and all will be tested like metals in the fire.

"I understand, My child, your grief at this knowledge. However, My child, you must accept the will of God, for it is for the eventual victory over satan.

The world is your family

"You must not become affected nor your Mission slackened by concern over a human being, My child. The world is your family. There are thousands of sheep straying with no leadership, no knowledge, misdirection, misguidance, even in My Son's Church upon earth.

"We see all manner of confusion, experimentation. There is no unity now in spirit. For man in the clergy has taken upon himself to set up My Son's Church to his own pursuits, his own man - given knowledge of intellect, without the spirit. For much of this intellect is being directed by satan and not by God.

"Awaken from your slumber, clergy in My Son's Church, for you will also be counted among the least. In pride and arrogance you have refused My counsel from Heaven. You have turned away from Me. You have persecuted those I have sent to you. Your pride and arrogance shall make you fall. Many mitres shall fall into hell. Is this what you want?

"For ears that hear, for those who hear My counsel, learn

by it, for the time is growing short. There will be many victim souls in these latter days, My child and My children. Persecution shall be great among the children of God, for the world will claim its own. And if you are not of this world, the earth, you will not be recognized. For the world you must live in is beyond the realm of human mankind. It is the world of the spirit, which all must enter sooner or later.

The heavy rains

"The knowledge of the supernatural has been taken from mankind. Therefore, satan has full access to your souls. And many are falling into hell faster than the snowflakes in your cold winters, and the heavy rains that destroy your towns.

"In the past the Eternal Father has sought to bring you back with minor chastisements, but to what avail? Now you ask and have brought upon yourself the time for greater chastisement. Many signs have been given from Heaven to guide you, and how few there were, My child and My children, who listened. Were it not so I would tell you. For were it not so, your world and the state of the souls within your world would not be in such darkness, were it not so.

"Yes, My child and My children, GOD IS shall be always before you, as God was, and God always will be.

"Man is no master of death. He can only inflict death upon the body. But with satan beside him, he can inflict death to your soul, your spirit, and you will be forever lost.

"Only you now, you, My children of reasoning, of the age of reasoning, must now make a full inventory of the graces you have gathered. For in an instant death will come upon your land, and many shall be claimed. Will you be ready? Have you prepared your children? Have you prepared your households? Many parents shall cry. Families shall be torn asunder. Blood shall be in the streets.

"O My children, and the nation of the United States that I have placed My mantle upon to protect you, a country of so greater in abundance materialistically, but now, sadly, My child and My children, falling fast to satan: immorality and all manner of licentious living, given over to murders, abortions, adultery, homosexuality, pagan worship. O My child, the list would grow longer and longer. In all justice to mankind and in all honor to your God, can you say that you do not warrant a just punishment?

"My child and My children, you will all continue to keep a constant vigilance of prayer.

The enemy is at your door

"My child, shout it from the rooftops to your last breath. The enemy is at your d - o - o - r! (Veronica sighs heavily) Oh! (Pause) Yes.

"My child, I cannot take you into the abyss at this time. You must complete the listing of conversations with My Son. When this is completed, My child, you will understand.

"Many workers shall be sent to you. Therefore, I wish, My child, that you concentrate now on completing the gathering of the conversations with My Son."

Veronica - Now Our Lady is taking the crucifix from Her beautiful Rosary now, and making the sign of the cross: In the name of the Father, and of the Son, and of the Holy Ghost.

Our Lady is turning now to Her right, and She's holding - extending Her crucifix, like this, high over the trees.

Our Lady is now rising a little higher so that She can go over to our left side, Her right side, and She's blessing with the beautiful crucifix: In the name of the Father, and of the Son, and of the Holy Ghost.

Now Our Lady is turning. And it must be windy because Our Lady's skirts are being caught in the breeze. And Our Lady now is floating across the sky. She doesn't walk. Her feet don't move. She's just carried as though She's weightless. Yes, Our Lady looks just as solid as you and I, but She's carried weightless, but beautiful. The light is so brilliant about Her that it's absolutely gorgeous. Ohh!

Now Our Lady is going over to our right side, Her left side, and now She's extending Her Rosary and the crucifix very, very far out in front of the trees, and making the sign of the cross: In the name of the Father, and of the Son, and of the Holy Ghost.

Now Our Lady is turning, and She's pointing up with the crucifix, like this, to the sky, and there is that large ball, a globe again. I know it's the world, I just know it's the world. And there's a big black cross now over the world. And I see coming out of the globe the flames again - the flames.

And now the globe - in some portions of the globe, I don't recognize it. The - the globe seems to be spinning faster and faster and faster. But as it's turning I can see there are sections that are black, absolutely black - something's happened, something's happened.

And now the globe is spinning, it's turning very slowly. It's, it's one of those like - what do you call them atlas', like where you could see the full impression of every country of the world. And some are absolutely blacked out. Oh... oh, they're blackened. It's, it's - it gives me a - I can't explain it - a very terrifying feeling to watch it.

Now it's fading; the whole - the whole sky is closing in over the ball, which is that huge globe of the world. And now I can't see it any longer.

And Our Lady is now nodding. As She's nodding - oh, that's so much better, Blessed Mother, to see the light. It was so dark over there with that world, so dark. And the cross is so black over it.

Our Lady - "The suffering, My child; that is the suffering that will be set upon the world."

Veronica - Oh! Our Lady has that most beautiful crown, as She's bending down now to talk. Her voice is coming in a very soft whisper now, and...

Our Lady - "Do not be affrighted, My child. All that is rotten must fall. The cleansing will be great to mankind. But all who have stayed in the light and gathered their graces shall be saved. That will give you great consolation, My children and My child, during the trials ahead. All who have gathered their graces and remained in the light will be saved.

"Now, My child, you will take one set of photographs,

but you must not interpret them publicly, My child."

Veronica - All about the trees, the sky is becoming illuminated with a beautiful pastel pink light. It's a solid covering now of the sky. They're not cascading like rivulets, or as usually forms, but the sky is becoming lighted, absolutely lighted with a beautiful pastel pink.

And directly over Our Lady's statue, high in the sky, the coloring, the pink is a solid pink now.

Now Jesus - oh, Jesus is coming right through the sky, through the center of the pink lighting. And He's holding His hand now on His chest. And now He's taking His hand away, and I can see - oh my, He's got a real heart. I've never seen a human heart, but I know it's a human heart. And it's pulsating, it's pulsating.

And oh my! And Jesus - oh, I know it's His Sacred Heart. It's pulsating though, and it's bleeding. Oh, His Heart is bleeding. Oh my!

And now as I'm watching, there are thorns now. It's like looking right inside of Him, through His - His garment. There are thorns all around His heart. Oh my!

Now Jesus is looking about Him, and over to the right side; He's looking about everyone. The pink glow is fading now. The sky is becoming lighted behind Him.

Oh, Our Lady is coming forward. I don't know where She came out of; I didn't see Her behind Jesus. But now She's coming forward. And She's coming over on Her - His right side, that's our left side.

Our Lady is standing now, She's standing next to Jesus with Her hands joined together, like this. She's so beautiful. She's so beautiful. And Our Lady's Rosary is hanging, it's hanging directly from Her fingers.

Now Jesus is looking about. I can't see that heart now. It seems to have disappeared, slowly like. It's just like vanishing, like in a mist. Oh my!

Now Jesus is turning to His left, and coming over directly above our Lady's statue. And He's touching His lips with His first finger.

Jesus - "My child, My Mother has given you full discourse on the state of your country and the nations of the world. It will not be necessary for Me to set forth more details on what is to come upon your country and many nations of the world.

"Many reprieves have been given to mankind, but now the Eternal Father has deemed it most necessary to bring some of His straying sheep back to the fold forcefully - unhappily, My child, I say this - but forcibly, by a chastisement.

These final moments of your generation

"You will all continue with a constant vigilance of prayer. Pray for your leaders, and the world's leaders in the governments in all of the universal nations of the world, and those men who have been given the power to govern lives or destroy them. Pray that the knowledge of your God will reach out among mankind in these few moments - I should say, My child and My children, these final moments of your generation.

"You cannot count time, My child and My children, for your earth time is not akin to the counting of time in Heaven. So do not speculate on dates, but be prepared for it will come upon you fast, without any knowledge to many. Do not be caught unawares.

"My Mother has counseled you well, and if you have not heeded Her warnings, Her counsel and direction, then you are fully accountable for your fall.

A keeper of the eternal flame

"Prayer, the power of prayer cannot be understood fully by mankind. And prayer also commands sacrifice and atonement, and love. But so few know the true meaning of love. Love is in giving. Love is in caring. But love above all is God, your God. For no man knows the full meaning of love, until he has reached out and become a man of God, a true child of the light; for then he will also be a keeper of the eternal flame, the Holy Spirit.

"I know, My child and My children, this discourse may be a mystery to you, but much cannot be understood by mankind due to the darkness and the clouding of the minds of many who have been entrusted with the vocational guidance of children, and have misused their positions to darken their souls and their intellect. However, know that no evil is ever triumphant. All evil will be turned to good. But what a great cost, My child and My children, for many will die in the great flame of the Ball of Redemption. Only a few will be saved.

"Man has the balance, man has been given in free will the balance for his own fall, or restoration of a nation to its former glory under God. Like rodents, the enemies of your God have eaten away at the foundation of the Faith. But in short time they will be destroyed, and a new House will rise, a Church stronger in faith, and sanctity and holiness. But this cannot, My children, take place until a great Chastisement is set upon mankind.

"You will all retain and wear your sacramentals for reason. Do not underestimate the power of prayer or the sacramentals. Do not be misguided or misled by the scoffers, who have committed themselves to satan with derisive vocabularies of calling sanctity, fanaticism, and holiness derangement.

"My child and My children, understand well that as I was persecuted upon earth, do not expect any less a lot. For the cross is always heavy, and unless you carry this cross you cannot reach Heaven. For the way of the cross is the true road to the Kingdom."

Veronica - Now Jesus is blessing - He's blessing the people now, like this. He's extending His hands, His two fingers together and the thumb up, like this, and making the sign of the cross: In the name of the Father, and of the Son, and of the Holy Ghost.

Now Jesus - it's very windy - He's taking His cape, because His cape was blowing. It's a beautiful burgundy cape. I can see the gold trim about His neck. And Our Lady - and He's going over now to our left side, His right side, and Our Lady is following Him. And He's looking all about. His hair is blowing. His cape is down over His shoulders, and I can see His hair. It's being caught by the wind. And He's making the sign of the cross: In the name of the Father, and of the Son, and of the Holy Ghost.

Now Jesus is turning to His left side, and He's going across the sky, He's going across the sky.

And now He's looking down, and down among the trees He's coming very close to the - our right side, that's His left side by the trees, and making the sign of the cross: In the name of the Father, and of the Son, and of the Holy Ghost.

Now Jesus is placing His hand now upon His chest, like this.

Jesus - "My child and My children, continue with your prayers of atonement. They are sorely needed. Pray for your brothers, pray for your bishops and your cardinals, and your clergy. Pray for those who have no one to pray for them. By your example can you save many from purgatory and hell."

Veronica - Now Jesus is going across the sky. He's just floating, He doesn't walk. He just floats across the sky. Oh, it's so beautiful to watch, like He's weightless. And Our Lady is right beside Him; She's at His right side.

Now Jesus is facing us. And Our Lady is standing there; She's still holding Her hands together. She comes up to Jesus' shoulder. But She has Her hands together, like this, with the beads coming through Her fingers.

Now Jesus is extending His hand out: In the name of the Father, and of the Son, and of the Holy Ghost.

"Your Vicar is not safe. There will be another attempt on his life in the city of Rome…"

Eve of the Assumption of the Blessed Virgin Mary
- August 14, 1981

Veronica - The sky all about the trees is becoming a deep pink. And high above Our Lady's statue, the sky is opening up. Jesus is coming forward, and right behind Him Our Blessed Mother is following. They're coming down now slowly. It's quite windy, and Jesus is - His robe is blowing in the wind, very softly. I see - now Jesus - He's coming down much faster now.

Our Lady is staying behind Him and She's looking from the right to the left. Oh, She - Our Blessed Mother is dressed beautifully! Oh! Now She's coming down and She's going over by Jesus' right side. Oh, She's dressed so beautifully! It's - She has on a white mantle, but the gold trim is much wider about - all about the edging of the mantle near Her gown and across Her head. Our Lady's mantle extends quite far down over Her forehead. I would say halfway between Her eyebrows and Her hairline.

And on Her head Our Lady has the beautiful Fatima crown, the one that's rounded like the world, with the cross on top of it. It's all of gold - I know it's spun gold. It is absolutely so brilliant.

Our Lady now has Her hands together, like this, in prayer, and Her beautiful Rosary is coming down, almost cascading, so gently are they folded over Her hands. And the wind is blowing. And the crucifix is now actually dangling from Our Lady's fingers. She's looking about Her, and She hasn't taken Her hands apart.

Oh, upon Our Lady's feet, She has the most beautiful sandals. They are absolutely made of gold, even the material, a metallic - type material of the strap across Our Lady's instep. It's actually across Her instep. And then in cross like formation there's another strapping from Her - the edge of Her delicate sandals up to Her ankle. I can't see that far

65

because her gown covers over almost to the edge of the instep. But perched on the sandal, on the strap that goes directly down the center, there's a small golden rosette on each foot. I say rosette, because it's a very small rose. But it's not - I don't believe it's a real rose, living. It more - it looks more like a metallic spun gold rose. It's just beautiful, but very tiny on the tip of the sandal of Our Lady, on each sandal.

Now Jesus is looking about Him, too. And I do notice, I can't help but notice that They have a very sad, restrained look upon Their faces. And now Our Lady is leaning over to Jesus. I can't hear what She's saying. He has nodded, very slowly.

Now Jesus is extending His hand out, like this, and making the sign of the cross: In the name of the Father, and of the Son, and of the Holy Ghost.

Now Jesus is turning towards Our Lady and He's nodding. Our Lady now is taking the beautiful golden crucifix from Her Rosary, Her hands are now enjoined, and She's making the sign of the cross with the crucifix: In the name of the Father, and of the Son, and of the Holy Ghost.

Our Lady is taking the crucifix, and She does have a very sad expression upon Her face. I can see Her very clearly this evening. And She's kissing the crucifix, like this, and now She's clutching it to Her breast, like this.

Now Jesus is looking away. He's gazing over everyone about here. Now Our Lady is coming closer. She had moved a bit over to the right. But She's coming closer now, and Jesus is nodding to Her. He's stepping back. And Our Lady is stepping forward, and He's nodding again. Our Lady now is placing Her first finger to Her lips, which means to listen and repeat.

Our Lady - "My child and My children, and especially My child Veronica, I have asked My Son to bring you here this evening with a disability, but it is urgent that you make known to the world that all warnings, all counsel given in the past will now take place.

"I have warned you as a Mother of sorrow. I have wan-

66

dered throughout your earth, through countless earth - years, counseling you as your Mother, begging My Son to extend unto you the time to make amends for your offenses to the Eternal Father. My children, My tears fall upon you and your nation and all of the nations of the world. Because of your blindness you failed to see what is fast coming upon mankind.

"I will not at this time give you a long discourse of reasoning for the coming Chastisement to mankind. Many minor warnings have been given in the past, to go by unnoticed or rejected.

"O My children, it truly rains teardrops from Heaven. We listen to the voices of the saints as they cry out in anguish to Us: 'How long shall You patiently wait for a generation to make atonement? How long, O Lord, must this carnage go on, as Lucifer continues to gather his armies and take many from the earth into the abode of the damned?

"My children, I cannot give you more urgent a message than to ask you, as your Mother, to go back and read all counseling, all messages given throughout the world by just seers.

"My children, I must warn you that you must test the spirits. When I gave you a message that there would be many seers throughout the world, I did not say that they would gather within one country. Understand this well, My children: it is the way of satan to delude and take from authentic visitations. You will recognize them because they cannot remain hidden. By their fruits will they be known.

I do not come... to go about in praise

"My child, you are draining your energies. As I have warned you in the past, you must not be concerned with the opinion of man. Understand, My child, were you speaking and giving to them, our sons the clergy, a message that would feed their pride and build their arrogance, you would be accepted. But I do not come to earth to go about in praise. I come to warn of an urgency upon earth, and an action of the Eternal Father to restore the earth to its former glory.

"My Son's Church has been under, and is under heavy attack by the agents of hell. But hell shall not prevail against My Son's Church.

Not to abandon your parish church

"I have asked you in the past, and I ask and continue to beg you, My children, not to abandon your Vicar in Rome, and not to abandon your parish church. You may have discord with your pastor, you may have discord with other priests in your parish, but you must remember this, My children, if it gives you any consolation in human nature, and for their human nature you must understand: you must honor them for who they are, but not judge them for what they are or have become.

Change causes confusion and error

"My Son's Church has been laid out and the course to heaven, the way to Heaven has been given by Him. Therefore, change causes confusion and error. When you have something beautiful, when you have a firm foundation, you don't start boring holes in it, or you will weaken it. However, I would suggest that you say that the walls have cracked, My child and My children. For the foundation is My Son, and in parable and symbolism, I say, the foundation is solid. My Son is the Church. Man may build another church, but he shall not have the angels assist him.

A division bordering on schism

"My heart, My Son's heart has been grieved, as We go about the world and see the carnage taking place within His Church. We can see a division bordering on schism. My children, I have asked you in the past - We cannot have this division, for it is promoted by satan. The adage of old remains forever true: United you will stand but divided you will fall.

"Do not judge My Son's House, His Church, by the man,

though he is a representative - legal, a legal representative of My Son - in His House. He is but a human in his nature. But during the time that My Son comes to you, this man will be used through the Holy Spirit, regardless of the state of his human nature, be it sin or a saint - be it a sinner or one who has led even those astray - at the time that My Son comes in the Consecration, He shall not turn aside from you, My Son. Therefore, you cannot say the Mass is invalid. This has brought great sorrow to Our hearts, for many left the fold on this matter.

"My child and My children, I say again: test the spirits. For now there is a conspiracy of evil throughout the world, going to the extreme left of invoking satan in the worship of satan, a contrary mass to My Son. Sadly, darkness of spirit pervades among mankind. How long shall the Eternal Father permit this condition to exist?

"My children, I tell you now as your Mother that My tears fall upon you, for you do not know what you are doing. You are bringing upon you a great punishment.

"Are you so blind that you do not recognize the acceleration of sin among you? Murders abound, thievery, all manner of carnage, destruction of young souls, abortion, homosexuality, condemned from the beginning of time by the Eternal Father. Yet sin has become a way of life. Sin is condoned now, even unto the highest judge of your land and your lands throughout the world. As you have sown so shall you reap. Sin is death, not only of the spirit, but of the body. Wars are a punishment for man's sin, his greed, his avarice. Pride and arrogance is bringing down into hell mitres from My Son's House.

"O My children, how long must I travel far and wide throughout your world persevering because I love you a your Mother, and I want to save you from yourselves. For I cry out as My Son, 'Father, forgive them for they know not what they do.'

Chaos in My Son's Church

"In the name of modernism, in the name of communism,

in the name of humanism you have fallen into error and discord. Chaos in My Son's Church, the falling away of souls from the Eucharist, the Bread of life. My children, without the Bread of life within you, you cannot sustain yourselves long in your world now.

"The way to Heaven is not an easy way unless you remain on the narrow road. It has restrictions. I ask you now, My children, to avoid even what may appear to be pleasures of the world that may seem to you, as you become blinded by medias, by friends, by associations, blind to the fact that they are soul - destroyers. You must limit yourselves now to seeking outside diversions from your home. For when you open your door, you go out now into a world that is now being guided through governments, and even through agents in My Son's Church, financial dynasties, national and international governments, heading fast to a collision.

"My children, do not forget in the years I have told you; you will be planet - struck. My child, you must hasten to have sent out the message of St. Benedict."

The message of St. Benedict

Veronica - Oh my!

Our Lady - "I have come to warn you: you will set loose upon earth the heavens. You will be planet - struck. Doctors must do good and cure honorably. Kingdoms, bishops, Rome must restore My Son's Church, or there will be great destruction in the eternal city.

"Do not give way, My children, to the medias that have lulled and dulled your senses in repeating to you of the safety of your Vicar. I must warn you at this time that your Vicar is not safe. There will be another attempt upon his life in the city of Rome, brought on by the red forces. My child, grieve not because all is controlled and allowed by the Eternal Father.

Medias that have labeled themselves Roman Catholic

"The second part of My last counsel with you, My child, must remain a secret. You will pray - you will all pray a constant vigilance of prayer for your Vicar, Pope John Paul II. You must beware of your medias, even those who have labeled themselves Catholic, Roman Catholic. Infiltration, My children, is everywhere now.

"You must pray for the light. Seek guidance only from Heaven. But above all console My Son at His tabernacles of the world.

"Remove your thoughts, your judgments from the man standing at the altar who represents My Son. See only in him as one who is My Son at the moment of Consecration, be he sinful or be he a saint. In time you will understand and accept this counsel.

"Be a good example to all in your parish church. Do not be deterred by the opinion of any man, whether he is of lay, or of a denomination of the religious. Remember, My children, when you come over the veil, there is no one to defend you. You will only bring with you love and prayers, and your own merits to bring to the Eternal Father for your judgment.

"So what does it benefit or gain a man if he gathers all the riches of the world and suffers the loss of his soul? Can any man who hears My counsel and My voice defy Me and tell Me that he will live forever upon earth? O My children, you seek eternal life upon earth. You seek to create life upon earth. You shall not create.

The truth is too simple for him

"The Eternal Father has been deeply offended and hurt by the man of science who is ever seeking but never finding the truth, because the truth is too simple for him. In his arrogance, in his scientific searching and knowledge, he is ever seeking but never coming to the truth. Better that man seeks a simple way of life and he shall not pass into the web of satan.

"My child and My children, you will continue to send

My counsel, My Son's counsel, throughout the world with great haste. Can you not recognize the accidents that are not accidents as they increase upon you? Think, My children, accidents that are not accidents. Satan has a great hand in dulling mankind's mind when he falls out of grace.

"My child, I had you deliver the message through Theresa for reason. Consider this, the first part of tonight's counsel, as a puzzle, another puzzle for the human race to figure out. It is not as difficult a puzzle as Jacinta was to mankind, My child. It is quite simple, if you ask and seek the answer. But I warn you now, My children, do not take the first part of this lightly."

Veronica - Our Lady is now reaching up to Her face. Oh, my! She is wiping a tear from Her eyes. I didn't realize that She had been crying.

Now Our Lady is turning to Her left, to Jesus. The light is now becoming very intense about Jesus. He's, you know - He's quite a bit taller than Our Lady. She only comes up to His shoulders. His shoulder? His right shoulder. Our Lady's standing on His right side, on our left side. But She's so beautiful. Oh, Our Blessed Mother, the light - cascading from Her as though the light is coming from within Her, outward, too. It's so brilliant, I'm certain without Heaven's grace, I would be blinded. It's a light that could never be caught in any manner upon earth. It's beyond anything but the supernatural. Jesus now is placing His first finger to His lips.

Jesus - "My child and My children, due to the urgency of your times, I allowed My Mother, who will remain with you as I will through the coming tribulation, to be here tonight. And, My child Veronica, We brought you forward under human duress and stress, to bring you here for mankind.

"The world must now listen to the counsel from Heaven. The hourglass is coming now, My child and My children, to the end of its drippings. Watch, My child...."

Three grains of sand left

Veronica - And Jesus is pointing up to the sky on the

right side, and there's forming a glass hourglass. And it's in, like a wooden base, on the top and bottom. But as I'm watching now there's pink sand in it, and it's now falling through. I would say there are only about three grains left - they're really grains. I can see three diamond like grains left. I don't know the three - why there are three.

And Jesus is smiling. Now He's pointing now to His lips, which means I must listen.

Jesus - "Yes, My child, time is running out. But do not be affrighted by the message given to you, My child. Mankind has had many warnings, many years to make restitution to the Eternal Father.

"Pray for all men of sin. Go to your brothers and your sisters, those who are in the world without counsel. For those who have received many graces, much is expected of them.

"And when you go about the world, beware that no pride or arrogance comes in upon you, or you will lose your grace. Because when you do good among man and mankind, you do it for the Eternal Father, Who watches you in secret. Therefore, you will not let the left hand know what you're doing with your right hand.

You are now in the latter days

"You understand, My children, I give this counsel to all who have joined in the Mission from Heaven to give the Message from Heaven to all mankind, as you are approaching - as you are now in - not approaching, My children, but in the latter days."

Veronica - Now Our Lady and Jesus - and now Our Lady is extending her crucifix up, the beautiful golden crucifix, like this, and Jesus at the same time is extending His hand out, like this, and making the sign of the cross: In the name of the Father, and of the Son, and of the Holy Ghost.

Now Jesus and Our Lady - oh! They, They look so beautiful! The light is so beautiful! (pause)

Jesus - "Remember, My child, I cannot promise you happiness in this world. It has always been, My child, this

73

way. You will continue now, My child and My children, with your prayers of atonement.

"My child, the strength will be given you, but you will not be able to spend full time from your bed. There is a reason for this, which you will soon understand.

"Continue now, My child, the prayers of atonement. They are sorely needed."

Message from Jesus and Our Lady to Veronica at home

November 21, 1981 - 2:45 a.m.

Jesus and Our Lady appeared in Veronica's bedroom as she lay ill in bed at 2:45 a.m. and dictated a message to her, and left at 3:30 a.m.

Jesus was dressed in a beautiful - not a red, but a deep burgundy robe, like a rich, plush velvet, trimmed in gold braid, and similar to the gold trim Our Lady has on Her cape at the vigils, but somewhat narrower. It was unlike the cape that He usually wears at the Vigils, which is tied at the neck. It was closed at the neck, and the undergarment, the gown, was not visible.

Our Lady had on a deep blue cape, a mantle, which came up over Her head, and a white gown, and She was wearing the Fatima crown on Her head.

In Her right hand She held Her large, white Rosary, the one that She has when She comes to the Vigils, that reflects the rainbow colors. In Her left hand She held a Scapular with no pictures on it, just the plain brown cloth. She was standing to Veronica's right, and Jesus was on her left.

Our Lady spoke first. Veronica was directed to write it down.

Our Lady - "You have joined the infirm, My child. Penance is humanly painful, but after all penance, there is a great joy. Accept all suffering as My Son partook of the final dregs of the chalice of suffering, to open unto all mankind the treasures to be found in the spiritual Kingdom. Your reward shall not be found on earth but in Paradise - the epitome of glory, with the angels. It is the only reward that man should strive for - all else is vanity, and passing."

Then Jesus spoke.

Jesus - "Write this for all the clergy:

"Hasten not the Chastisement by becoming involved in fruitless pursuits that are no constructive to your mission - for I am the Light of the World. PREACH My Word!

"There is much hunger in you country, and the world. Feed My sheep.

75

"I speak not of human hunger - only the starvation of the soul. Shall you stand before Me and say that your teaching has been pure in My sight!?

"The human body is the temple of the Holy Ghost. Do not spoil the flesh (by sins of the flesh) for the vapors of rot shall pollute the spirit within, and the world shall be filled with dead souls in human bodies. You shall see eyes without light, and the blind shall lead the blind."

"Beware of false prophets and those who will claim to be Christ"

Twelfth Anniversary of Our Lady's Apparitions at Bayside, NY - June 18, 1982

Veronica - With fond recollections of Our Lady's appearing on the Bayside grounds, how much I miss being able to go to the grounds, the Vatican site now, due to my illness, which has kept me in bed for so very long. But I accept all of the sufferings that Heaven allows me to have for all of the souls in purgatory, especially perhaps that one individual soul that has no one to pray for him or her. I always ask Our Lady and Jesus to allow one day's suffering - that would be the second day after the first suffering day - to allow every other day to be for a soul in purgatory. There are so many who have no one to pray for them, because others have forgotten them upon earth, or there just is no one living upon earth who knows or remembers them.

"I'm going to now take the time to place the oxygen mask, the kind that goes through your nostrils, upon my face, because the air is very humid today, the humidity very bad, and I find it very difficult to speak.

And I was told last evening - that would be 'Wednesday' evening, today is Thursday evening - that I would have to give a message to the world, and that Our Blessed Mother and Jesus will be here to guide me. In preparation, I must hold the Shrine crucifix, my Rosary, and wear about my head the usual mantilla or scarf. I do not know what to expect at this time.

This is early in the morning, exactly - I'll give you the exact time - it's 10:45 a.m. So I will have to now prepare in prayer for the arrival of Our Lady and Jesus.

Because of my intense suffering and disability, and inability to walk, I do not believe that Heaven will allow me, in any way, to be physically present tomorrow on the feast day of the Twelfth... though I long so - I really hurt in my heart, it hurts me very much to be unable to be there. But I find that even walking from the bedroom to my bathroom - for circulatory purposes, the doctor said - finds me very debilitated; and even I would attempt to go outside and go in the car for just a ten or fifteen minute ride and find that it has exhausted me. The exhaustion and the constant pain twenty four hours throughout my whole body is like living in the fires of purgatory. However, Heaven, sustains me. And I know I surely am carried forth with this suffering, this intense suffering, because I know that this is what Heaven is permitting for a reason.

I will now turn off the tape and continue the rest of the day praying until I receive the call from Our Blessed Mother or Jesus, and then I will place the tape on, and forget that it is by me, at my side, and Heaven will give the further directions to me.

Oh, how long I have waited, but now Our Lady has told me that the message will be given, not this evening, the eve, but on the feast day, which is Friday, June 18th. So I will have to wait patiently.

Our Blessed Mother has appeared to me. Oh, She is so, so beautiful. She's dressed all in white. Now there is a light about Her. The light is white. But due to the crown Our Lady is wearing, which is magnificent this evening - She has on a crown of gold, but there's a lining inside. The lining is blue, there seems to be a blue velvet in the crown that casts the light shining upon it, casts a bluish - white light all about Our Lady. The light about Our Lady is white, but tinted with blue. There's no human way I could explain it. It's not two toned in color, but it's blending white and blue.

And Our Lady - I can't see Her hair because the crown is a very large crown, like the Fatima crown we have. And the crown is placed on Our Lady's head and it covers down to the forehead. But, of course, the mantle also is down to the middle of Our Lady's forehead; I can't see Her hair. The mantle is a pure white with a gold trim all about it - oh, of about an inch wide.

And Our Lady is smiling. She has Her hands together in prayer with Her Rosary beads, the beautiful beads with the golden Our Fathers and the white Hail Marys that look like - oh, a million other colors that cascade from the Hail Marys.

And Our Blessed Mother, She is smiling, though - in fact, She is smiling much more than I have seen Her smile, even in the past - though I do notice there have been trickles of tears from the corner of Her eyes, but She's smiling now down at me.

I'm lying up at the top of my bed, my head near the bedpost, and Our Lady is standing at the foot of my bed. And now She's moving over to my right side. And oh - oh, I didn't notice through the brilliant light, Jesus is standing with Her. Now Jesus is at Our Lady's right side.

Now They're both standing, and I do wish I could see Our Lady's feet. I can't see the gown. My bed is interfering with the flooring. Oh, my goodness! They're both rising now up higher so I can see. Oh, Our Lady has on gold sandals. They're just beautiful, with tiny little gold rosettes at the tip of the middle of the toe area on the band that goes up to Our Lady's ankle - there's a tiny gold rosette. It looks metallic, it really does.

And Our Lady has on a white gown with a blue sash, and Her hands are still brought up in prayer.

And Jesus has on His red cape. The cape is a beautiful burgundy color. And His hair is flowing freely, but it's not blowing. Because I know now that they sort of adjust to the climate here, because there's very little air in my room - it's difficult for me to speak. But Jesus' hair is not blowing now.

And He has on - His gown looks like it's made, sort of a linen, the cape. I guess He feels as warm as I do in this bedroom, because His cape is very loosely tied at the neck.

And Jesus is smiling. He has - oh, such beautiful eyes. They look like gray - blue. But He's smiling, also. And now They are both nodding.

And Our Lady is now disengaging Her hands from Her beads, and She's telling me now to listen. And She's placing Her first finger of Her right hand to Her lips: that means to listen.

Oh dear! They must have - oh, oh, Our Lady is saying,

"yes", that there will be a message.

Now They're both floating downwardly, so that They remain at the foot of my bed. But all about Them now - I didn't notice it before because of the brilliant light - all about Them are the most beautiful angels. They're angels, and they have - they have like those wings that we spoke of. But they shouldn't be called wings, they're so down, soft and beautiful. They shouldn't be called wings. If only there was another name, like gossamer, or - somehow the word 'gossamer' comes to my mind, so downy and soft and beautiful.

I can't say what their faces look like. Their outlines are like human, but I just can't make out their features, like I can with Our Lady and Jesus. And they look more transparent than Our Lady and Jesus. Our Lady and Jesus look very solid, but the angels look very transparent. But they're dressed though in gowns. The gowns are very, very filmy, too, like they're transparent. Though I see nothing, they look like human gowns. There's so way to put it into human language, but they're - they're all in different shades, of the pastel shades of the rainbow: blues, and yellows, and pinks, and whites - and the white is a really brilliant white - and gold, and sort of a rose color.

Oh, their, their age, I couldn't tell you whether they were male, female, or what age, because there is no way that I could tell you. There is something about the angels, and it's so different. They're spirits, so I guess there's no way I could explain to you just exactly what they look like. But for our own enlightenment, I realize that Heaven is allowing me to tell you about their figures, because of the fact that they appear almost like to us in human, for I guess, I'd be scared to death if I saw them any other way.

Due to my illness, I never realized that I have now fallen asleep, put into a deep sleep, and so many hours have passed. My husband, Arthur, said that I had fallen now asleep. Oh, I know what it is now, and it is very, very late.

And I notice that Arthur says that he has loosened my mantilla, a babushka - or he call it a babushka - from about my neck as I slept. Finding me holding the crucifix and the

Rosary, he was very startled - and the tape recorder lying by my side.

So now I notice the day is dawning, so this must be the beautiful day of the feast day of June 18th of Our Lady. Oh, oh, how wonderful it is, because it is just about the time I can remember, back in 1970, we were to start the Vigils at 9 a.m. I knelt from 9 a.m. in the morning of June 18th until after 1 a.m. the following morning - that would be June 19th - and for three days I had to lie in bed, as I'm lying now, unable to walk, having knelt so many hours.

But at my side, at that time - I don't if it was ever known to many - that Padre Pio sustained me. An individual from a Padre Pio, promoting a group. I believe it was Joey Lomangino at Garabandal, who had given a friend a crucifix, a small brown crucifix that I'll never forget. I wore that crucifix the whole time on June 18th, 1970. And everytime I felt I was weakening (because there were times when I came out of that - oh, state of being out of myself, like in a coma or something, or - not a - I don't like to use the word 'trance', because that sounds like something in the occult or something. But actually I was in a state of being absolutely unconscious. But when I came out of it, after a few hours, after the message was given, I felt like I was slumping. But I knew that I had to remain on my knees, because it was so important. Our Blessed Mother depended on me to remain on my knees. There was so much at stake, so many souls that had to have this penance, Our Lady said.) that I would then clutch this crucifix about my neck, given to me - a small brown wooden crucifix - and I, immediately I noticed that I was renewed, and I felt vigorous and fresh, and I could go on and continue praying the Rosary until Our Lady then, or Jesus appeared, and then I had to blank out, sort of, again and repeat, as a voice box, what Our Lady and Jesus had to say.

It's very difficult for me to talk at this time, because, today, June 18th, the humidity feels just as bad as it did - and I do remember in 1970, the first lady that we had, who came from Indiana, who was writing the notes, it was so bad, the heat, that she passed out writing the notes, and someone else had to take the lapboard, one of those lapboards you write on, from her and continue writing the message that Our Lady gave.

Now, I notice here about my room - I should put down the time - I'm wholly conscious. I know I am to take up my crucifix. Arthur will be coming in, and I will have to tell him now he must remain outside the door, and lock the door. And he's wondering why I should have the scarf about my head, when it's so warm in my bedroom, but he will understand later. He trusts me when I tell him: please do not ask me any questions, that you'll understand later. And then I am to take my crucifix.

It's June 18th, 1982 - twelve years since Our Lady first started Her Vigils of penance, prior to the coming of the Ball of Redemption. June 18th, 1982, makes twelve long years of Our Lady pleading with everyone throughout the world to listen to Her Message and to try to hold off the Ball of Redemption.

I am waiting now, awaiting the call lights. I believe that they will be the same as at the Vigil because I have a ceiling here that is taking on a very blue color, though the ceiling itself is white. So I know I will await the call lights for Jesus and Our Lady to appear.

The time, it is now 12:45, that would be in the afternoon, of June 18th, 1982. And, oh, this is the room - oh, I - even though I hurt so badly, the room is being cascaded with lights, blue lights, the most beautiful blue, round - there are circlets of blue lights coming now through the ceiling of my bedroom. Oh! They're the call lights of Our Lady. Oh! I'm so happy, I'm so happy.

Oh! Our Lady and Jesus are here again, just as last evening. Our Lady is dressed in the same beautiful outfit. She has this - I would rather call it habit, as She refers to the nuns, which She - oh, the nuns whom She loves so dearly - all Her nuns and priests.

Oh, Our Lady has on the same habit - it's a - oh, She has a beautiful white gown, with a blue sash about it, and Her white mantle, with the gold trim about the outside, all around the edge - about, oh, I guess, it's an inch wide of gold metallic material.

And She has also now - oh no, it's not the same - She's covered Her own outfit, the blue, with a blue, a dark blue cape - like mantle all about on top of Her - Her white mantle. Oh! Oh! That's so beautiful. It's a beautiful deep blue velvet. It's a blue velvet. And on top of that - oh, Our Lady must be awfully warm, because it's very warm in my room; but Our Lady is smiling and shaking Her head - no, She's not warm. But She has on really heavy clothing, for my room is stifling here. I find it most difficult to breathe. I don't have an air conditioner. I do have two fans, but Our Lady has instructed, I am not to use the fans today in my room.

Oh, so - oh, Our Lady though is so beautiful that actually there's no picture that - I wish I was a painter, that I could paint for you; the description in words is insufficient to tell you how beautiful She looks. She has on the - white mantle and the white gown, but then a blue, a beautiful deep blue mantle over that. And then She has a huge crown. I call it the Fatima crown, but it also has that same deep blue velvet like material inside, that puffs out of the openings of the crown. And the crown is very bejeweled - you know, jewels all over it, all different colors. Oh, they look like diamonds. I don't know all the jewels, but they look like diamonds, and rubies, and those green stones, emeralds; and amethyst - and, oh, I don't even know the others. They're so beautiful.

And Jesus now is come - I didn't notice until I was so - the flashing lights from the jewels in the crown and the bright light about Our Lady - but I see Jesus now is at Her right side. And He also is wearing the same outfit He did last evening. And it is warm. But I notice He has His cape. It's a burgundy velvet cape. Now this cape though is trimmed also now in gold about the outside, just like Our Lady's white mantle, that goes to Her feet and around Her head.

Now Jesus has His - the headpiece that would - I believe,

like a cowl, like a hat - would be over it, He has it down, though, over His shoulders, whereas now I cannot see His hair. There's nothing blowing. There's hardly a movement in the room. And Arthur has been instructed not to come in. So that it's like a little bit of paradise here in the room, it's so beautiful.

I'm conscious of what is about me, but now Our Lady is raising Her hand now. She had Her hands up in prayer with the Rosary beads about them, but She is now touching Her lips.

They're standing, and - no, They're coming closer now around to the side of my bed. Jesus is at our right - at Our Lady's right side, but Our Lady is leaning over to me, and She's touching me on the forehead with Her beautiful Rosary. Oh! Oh! And She is handing me a rose. Oh! Thank you. (Veronica sobs)

Now - now Our Lady and Jesus - Our Lady is smiling, and Jesus now is leaning over, and with His thumb - He's making the sign of the cross on my forehead with His thumb. And now He's smiling at me, Oh, He's so beautiful.

I can see Jesus' hair now; it's a reddish - brown, a reddish - brown. And not They are both now going back a little farther toward the foot of my bed. Now Jesus is raising His hands up, like this; and now He's standing at the foot of my bed at Our Lady's right side. And Our Lady's standing there now, and She's holding the Rosary up in Her right hand, and in the left hand She has the Scapular. And Jesus is making the sign of the cross: In the name of the Father, and of the Son, and of the Holy Ghost.

Now, Our Lady is now motioning. She looks towards Jesus, and He has nodded to Her. And Our Lady is touching Her first delicate - first finger to Her lips, which means to listen.

Our Lady - "My child, you will tell My children this evening that all this is for them. I wish all to know that, as I speak with you now, I speak to you all. I am there with you, as I am here with you, Veronica, My child.

"This is a time of great urgency, or We would not have

taken these measures to come together in a manner that has never been approached before.

"My child, Veronica, you understand it is the will of the Eternal Father that you be among those who have been chosen as victims, victims for the repatriation of souls of the world.

"The world, your world, My child and My children, is steeped in deep darkness created by sin. There shall be a most terrible, heart - rending, crushing punishment, chastisement sent upon the world soon.

"I have come to you as your Mother: a Mother who loves you, a Mother who cares, a Mother who cries tears of pity for you, for you do not know what you are doing. I ask you, as your Mother, I appeal to you, as your Mother, to listen to Me. I have cried for you. I have wandered throughout your world, through countless earth - years, begging with you, begging you to listen, even to a small measure, of My Message to the world; to turn now from the ways that are offensive to your God, the Eternal Father in Heaven, for you bring upon yourself a just punishment if you do not mend your ways now and turn from your sin.

"All manner of abominations are being committed in the world, and even has entered onto the clergy. Many clergy shall stand before My Son and have to give account for what they have done, and what measure they have taken to destroy souls upon earth. Many are on the road to perdition and taking others with them.

Wars shall increase

"How long, My children, do you think that the Eternal Father will stretch His pity to excuse, or make excuses for these abominations. No longer, My children. This I bring to you as the most urgent message from Heaven. Wars shall increase, and the great world War, the greatest of all, shall befall mankind, and shall make extinct three-quarters of the world's population. Is this what you want?

"My children, awaken from your slumber! You live in a dream world. You believe that this cannot happen to you. O

85

My poor children in North America - Canada, the United States - you do not know what it is to see the blood flow in the streets, to see your loved ones torn - their arms, their legs missing, their bodies and their bowels spewing out upon the grounds. Is this what you want?

"O My children, please listen to Me. You shall not be free from this type of suffering. It is fast closing in. The enemy is all about you. You are slumbering. While the world cries peace, peace, and tranquillity... We look for prosperity and peace. But where do you look? It appears, My children and My child, that most are looking for prosperity, and not true peace. For the only true peace shall be found through My Son, Jesus in the Blessed Sacrament, the Holy Eucharist, through the Father, the Son, and the Holy Ghost.

"The peace that you seek far eludes you, My child and My children, because of the fact that you do not recognize the power of the Bear. The Bear surrounds you. Those who are with the Bear laugh at you, for they do not seek peace. And you believe in your purity of heart - of many of the leaders, I say this - for the United States, which has been always called a great Christian nation - I say this to the United States, because they do not understand the ways and means of an atheist. Behind the Bear are atheists.

"Now the Bear, the great Bear now that has clawed most of the world and nations, those behind the Bear, they know no reasoning for truth. For they believe that whatever happens in the end - their captures, their covering the world with their propaganda, and their eventual destruction of nations, to bring them, down to their knees - the means of doing this is justified by the ends. In other words, murder or lies, or anything which is in satan's realm, anything to justify their takeover.

Bear burrowed into church

"Now the United States, My children, is not free, for the enemy has burrowed from within, just as the enemy has even - the Bear has even burrowed into My Son's House, His Church. And O what a sad fact this is to Our Hearts!

86

My Mother's Heart is torn, and My Son - what can I say for My dear Son? Shall He be recrucified anew? This is the greatest hurt to Our Immaculate Hearts, because We have trusted Our children to carry forth the banner of Faithful and True through the years.

"And what has happened? The world now is in far worse a state than it was in the time of Sodom and Gomorrah, and that was destroyed. And what do We find now, My children? O My poor little ones, I repeat again, My Heart is bleeding."

Veronica - Our Lady is showing me now a heart that was implanted on the front of Her gown. Her gown is just stained with blood now. It is bleeding. Oh, my goodness! It's bleeding onto my carpeting, too.

Our Lady - "My Heart, My child, is torn and bleeding, because it is the children that I cry for now. They are being misled.

Word of God taken out of schools

"The parents who depend on the schools to teach, in the schools the word of God has been taken out; in the schools, prayer has been forbidden by many. Therefore, the major responsibility for saving the souls of your children is in your homes now.

"Mothers and fathers, where are you? You are running to and fro making money, seeking pleasures. But you are not the only ones. You turn to your pastors, you turn to My Son's representative, the priest, and other ministers in the congregations of the world, and where are they? Their heads are in the sand. Their heads are in the clouds, clouds of darkness, They, too, are running to and fro seeking riches and pleasures. How many are holy, and how many are unholy? My children, they could be sorted very easily. There are so few who are holy. We do not say this to judge My children, but We say this to bring it out as a fact. How many are holy? How many can stand before My Son and say that their teaching has been pure in His sight? What will become of these poor priests who have forgotten their mission, who have forgotten their vows? What will become of them? Many mitres shall fall into hell.

The priest - infiltrators

"And My good children, you do not pray for your priests. You do not pay - I say the word 'pay', for them - in other words, ransom them from purgatory. Ransom them even from hell. We do not wish to see our priests be cast into purgatory or hell. But there are many now in purgatory, and you must do penance for them, and pray for them, for they are misled. They do not have courage, the courage of their own convictions to stand up and fight. They have lost the realization of the existence of the immorality of the soul. And there are many now who are going about, be they true, truly ordained priests, or are they infiltrators into My Son's House? Only you, as a parent, can find out. Seek, and you will find them out. By their fruits will they be known.

Signs of false priests

"If they tell you that the words of the Bible are only stories written down by men, you will know they are false. If they tell you that it is better to believe what the theologians are saying now in 1982, in fact, saying, in so little words, that all the other theologians were stupid, know that they are not true. And that is a fact. The priest is not true.

"Now if he tells you that you do not have to worry about committing a sin, because God will not punish. He's an all - loving God, and, as an all - loving God, He will not punish you, for your sin. If that be true then, why was Lucifer cast from Heaven? If we cannot sin, and God will not punish us for our sins, why was Sodom and Gomorrah destroyed?

"My children and My child, I hesitate to speak of such things as immorality and the morals of mankind. However, it is something that makes Me even blush, My child... (Veronica - Our Lady is turning a very, very deep scarlet in Her face. I am almost embarrassed. Now Our Lady is really turning scarlet! I feel that way myself. But I will take a deep breath, as Our Lady says, because the words must be said.) ... that when a priest tells you that you do not have to speak up, out against homosexuality, because you are judging another person, and you should love your neighbor, and therefore never set him up to be judged, you are not judging. If a person is doing wrong, and you tell him in a kind manner, a charitable manner, that they are committing a sin, and that they will lose their soul and go to purgatory, or even hell, that is not judging. You are helping and loving your neighbor. What is love?

"And any priest that tells you, My child, or My children, as you have experienced - We have allowed you to experience this for the betterment of all mankind - any priest that tells you that you must love your neighbor first and God second, he is not a true man of God nor is he a true Roman Catholic priest, nor is he a true minister of any denomination. Because the first Commandment of God the Father is: 'I am the Lord Thy God, thou shall not have strange gods before Me.' 'Thou shall not take the name of the Lord Thy God in vain.'

Man not a little god

"And if a priest or a minister even has the dare to blaspheme himself and tell you that don't worry about sinning, because one day you will even be a god. And you say, 'a god?' If any of you have heard this, My children, you know it is true, that many have become so arrogant that they feel that they are mini - gods, little gods. In no way will man be a little god. There is no justification to be called a little god, no matter what place he has in his world.

"There is only one God, the Lord High God in Heaven. No man is God, even though he places himself up as God now, even trying to create life, and even trying to restore life to the dead. He shall never restore life to the dead. He shall never create a life. What he shall create is a monster, a soulless being. We will not go into this, My child, as I see you are tiring. But We must warn the parents against the immodesty of the world. My heart is torn as I have told you,

My child."

Veronica - Oh, my goodness! The blood is gushing further. Now it's all over my bed. (At this point the sound of something crashing to the floor startles Veronica .)

Oh! And it's making everything fall. The lights are falling, everything.... from the violence and the shaking that I feel. That Jesus is very angry at this. The whole light has fallen from my table. It came down with a crash. And everything is falling off my table, as Jesus is now banging the table, and He is saying:

Priests who condone homosexuality and abortion

Jesus - "I will not stand for My priests who condone homosexuality and allow it in My priesthood! I will not stand for My priests who allow the murder of the unborn with their permissiveness! I will not stand by and allow My priesthood to be destroyed!"

Veronica - Oh, I'm so frightened, Blessed Mother! You're not angry at me, are you Jesus? You're not angry at me? Everything has fallen here. The lamps have fallen down.

Jesus - "My child, I did not mean to affrighten you. I was giving vent to the hurt of My Heart. But I wish to bring across to mankind that I, too, can no longer allow these - the carnalities, the abominations that men are committing upon earth to continue. My hand is coming down and it will strike!"

Veronica - Our Blessed Mother has come over now to my side, and She's - She's rubbing my face. I am still very frightened at what happened when Jesus pounded the table. The light fell down, my light fell down. It brought me out of my unconscious state. And I can still, though, see Jesus and Our Lady - and Our Lady standing here. I am back from my unconscious state. I'm so frightened, Blessed Mother! So much is going to happen upon the world.

Our Lady - "My child, do not be affrighted. My Son is filled with anguish, and did not express Himself in a manner you expected. But it is not often that We have to come to you, My child, in this way. Were He on the grounds, there shall be thunder and lightning to emphasize His words.

"O My child, do not be affrighted, your heart is fluttering. I want you to rest now, My child. But I have a message further for My children of the earth. We shall leave you for a short while and return. But you will have your dear husband, Arthur, straighten up the room, and give you nourishment, and We will be back. Look, My child, at your wrist watch."

Veronica - I - I - I have one o'clock on my wrist watch, Blessed Mother.

Our Lady - "You have 1 p.m., My child. We will be back at 3 p.m., and conclude Our message to the world. But during these two hours I wish that you will rest and sleep.

"I know your husband is at the door listening and is trying to now get in, because he heard the commotion. You will explain it to him, My child, by playing the tape.

"But be not affrighted. My Son has no - nothing against those who are of well spirit. But you see, you, My child, will understand further when He discusses with you what is going on.

Brides for Christ needed

"My child, too, when He speaks of His ministers, His priests and the priesthood, He is also referring to the terrible abominations being committed by Our nuns. My child and My children, My heart is torn. I need so many brides for Christ, and so few are there who are willing to sacrifice their lives for Him. Oh, if they only knew the great reward."

Veronica - I will be a bride of Christ, Blessed Mother, if you want me. I will be a bride of Christ!

Our Lady - "My child, you are a bride of Christ. Did you not know that? Do you not remember when you were given the ring, many years ago?"

Veronica - Oh! The ring, the ring with R-G-P; Redemption, Grace, and Peace inside the ring. The ring when I lived in Bayside at 226 - 226th St., in Bayside, off 69th Avenue and Springfield Boulevard. Oh, yes, Blessed

Mother, I understand now. Redemption, Grace and Peace ring. I am a bride of Christ.

Our Lady - "My child, that is why Theresa had you write. 'Tomorrow My Bridegroom.' Do you remember nothing of it?"

Veronica - Oh, Blessed Mother, yes.

I walk up through the garden,
With roses in my hand,
And place my left hand out
To show you there's a band.
I've waited all these years
To see this dream come true:
I've watched and prayed,
And followed my heart
Until it came to You.

Veronica - Yes, Blessed Mother, I understand. (Veronica stammers) I don't know where the tape recorder is.

Our Lady - "Well, I, My child, will shut it off, and you will now rest until 3:00 p.m., and I will return and give you the rest of the message." (Pause)

Veronica - It is already past 3 p.m. And now the room is beginning to become lighted with that beautiful blue, translucent light that always announces Our Lady's coming. Our Lady is very prompt. It's only a few moments after 3:00. Therefore, my clock, my watch must be a little fast. I know Our Lady is very punctual.

Our Lady is coming closely. Now Jesus is with Her and the angels. Our Lady is wearing the same habit, the white gown, as She did earlier this afternoon.

And it appears that Our Lady is spacing Her time. If only I could go back to the first day of June 18, 1970. You will find that Our Lady spoke throughout the whole afternoon, even in pouring rain.

Now, Our Lady is touching Her first finger to Her lips, which means:

Our Lady - "My child, listen and repeat after Me.

"My child and My children, it is urgent that I warn you that the days are upon you, the days of wickedness and the emergence of the wicked ones upon the world.

Many false christs

"There will be many christs upon earth - those who call themselves Christ, but beware: do not listen to them. How often have I warned you in the past to beware of false prophets and those who will claim to be Christ. Only those who are ignorant and have no basic foundation of the Faith could fall prey to their beguileness.

"Because of the fact that too few are given - giving out the Message from Heaven to the peoples, My child, I wish you to open the Bible, the Book of life, and read what I point out to you."

Veronica - The signs of the Last Days - Matthew.

Oh, I don't - Blessed Mother - the chapter? Oh, Matthew 24 - The Signs of the Last Days.

Verse 23 - "Then if anyone says to you, 'Behold, here is Christ, or, "There he is, ' do not believe it. For false christs and false prophets will rise, and will show great signs and wonders, so as to lead astray, if possible, even the elect. Behold, I have told it to you beforehand. If therefore they say to you, 'Behold he is in the desert,' go not forth; 'Behold, he is in the inner chambers,' do not believe it. For as the lightning comes forth from the east and shines even to the west, so also will the coming of the Son of Man be. Wherever the body is, there the eagles will be gathered together.

"But immediately after the tribulation of those days, the sun will be darkened, and the moon will not give her light, and the stars will fall from heaven, and the powers of heaven will be shaken. And then there will appear the sign of the Son of Man in heaven; and then will all tribes of the earth mourn, and they will see the Son of Man coming upon the clouds of heaven with great power and majesty. And He will send forth His angels with a trumpet and a great sound, and they will gather His elect from the four winds, and from one end of the heavens to the other."

Veronica - And we will repeat again in verse 5 of St.

Matthew, Chapter 24.

"For many will come in My name, saying, 'I am the Christ,' and they will lead many astray. For you shall hear of wars and rumors of wars. Take care that you do not be alarmed, for these things must come to pass, but the end is not yet. For nation will rise against nation, and kingdom against kingdom; and there will be pestilences and famines and earthquakes in various places. But all these things are the beginning of the sorrows.

"And many of them, shall fall away, many will fall away and will betray one another, and will hate one another. And many false prophets will arise, and will lead many astray. And because iniquity will abound, (things will become so bad) the charity of the many will grow cold. (One will in that way be afraid to even trust your neighbor or even trust anyone out on the street. That's how bad the evil will abound.) But whoever perseveres to the end, (trusting in Jesus) shall be saved. And this gospel of the Kingdom shall be preached in the whole world, for a witness to all the nations, and then will come the end."

Veronica - Our Lady is now motioning me to close the book. I have a sensitivity of falling back to unconsciousness again, after reading the book. Although I did feel a very strange feeling of being semi conscious while reading, however, I now - oh, Our Lady now - I feel very strange, there's no way to explain the feeling when Our Lady place Her hands out - She's placing Her hands out now, and these lights are streaming from Her fingers, and I feel very warm all over.

Our Lady - "My child, I wish you also to make note in your heart and the hearts of all mankind that I am much despaired, as Theresa, Our Little Flower, is much despaired, at the lack of numbers in the nunneries. Vocations are needed for the priesthood, and also for the nunneries.

"Are there not any who care to come forward and dedicate their lives to save Our young children? Please, My children, surely among you, those who hear My voice or will read this written word, can you not give your life to win

94

your reward forever in Heaven, and perhaps also, those you love you can bring with you? So many little souls are crying. They thirst for the knowledge of Jesus and all of Heaven. Will you not solace them and comfort them in their loneliness? They are like sheep out in the wilderness, astray with no leaders. They are wandering. And what do they feast upon but weeds. No good nourishment is being given them. Will you not, My children, you who are children of the light, come forward, and become nuns, nuns with good hearts, with a good foundation of the Faith and the truth, and nourish Our sheep?

"Remember, My children, that Jesus said, 'Unless you become as little children, you cannot enter in the Kingdom of Heaven.' Just as little Theresa once wrote, My child, will you kindly repeat; it brings great joy to My heart to know of the simple things that are so lost in your world today. The road to Heaven is simple - as a narrow road that so few stay on. But if you listen to the way little Theresa places it, it is really simple. Just open your heart to Jesus as a child, come to Him and He will solace you. When you speak to Him, speak to Him thusly, as Theresa did.

Dear Jesus, all I can do is just love You,
For my riches are here in my heart;
They're not locked or chained against stealing,
They're always free to depart.
I offer this gift to You, Jesus,
Accept it with Your precious joy,
I'm Yours to hold there in Your Kingdom;
Just treat me as Your little toy!

"Yes, My child, that is how Theresa found her way into the Kingdom of Heaven. She was a gentle child and a gentle adult. Therefore, you will follow her way, which is the way of Jesus, too.

"Remember, My children, I will always be with you. My Son will always be with you. The days ahead will be great trail for you. But you will suffer much for your Faith.

"And you must always wear your sacramentals. Do not abandon them to modernism and humanism.

"No matter how learned the scholar or priest or minister, you have the basic foundation of the Faith.

"And God never changes. And neither must you change to please man. But you must change always to please God.

"And obedience: there is false obedience, if you displease God, just to please man.

"You know the truth, keep it in your heart.

"And always remember: keep the faith, My children; We depend on you, because you are Our little armies spread throughout the world - little in means, little in worldly goods, but great in faith and great in graces."

Veronica - Jesus is placing His hand forward, and making the signs of the cross.

Jesus - "I bless you all, My children: In the name of the Father, and of the Son, and of the Holy Ghost."

Veronica - Jesus and Our Lady now are smiling, and nodding. And the light is suddenly becoming dim. The room is beginning to darken. It's coming towards twilight time. So I just am sad to see Jesus and Our Lady - I'm becoming awakened now to my senses about me. And Jesus and Our Lady now are going forward. Now Our Lady is touching Her lips.

Our Lady - "My child, We are not leaving."

Message from Jesus and Our Lady to Veronica

Feast of the Visitation of Mary - July 2, 1982

Veronica - This is Friday, July 2, 1982. At approximately 1:35 a.m. on Friday morning, July 2, Our Blessed Mother left a rose, a pink rose at my typing table in my bedroom, and came forth in a very hazy, mist - like light, that grew wider and wider as She came close to the table.

As I tried to sit up, being bedfast for so long, I hesitated at the feasibility of my trying to grasp the pink rose set on the table by Our Lady, assigned for me to use the typewriter, for clarity purposes, She said. That's what Our Lady said: the typewriter would be used for clarity purposes.

Our Blessed Mother is dressed in a beautiful, luminous white mantle, bordered by a small golden trim. Her gown is also a brilliant white color, and there's a blue sash about Her waist. She is truly the shining star of Heaven. Of course, this is Jesus' designation of His wonderful Mother, Mary. Our Blessed Mother is standing at my right shoulder. She says:

Our Lady - "Write now, My child, just as I tell it to you."

Veronica - I bent forward to reach the typewriter, wondering how I was going to do any of this with my hands in the condition they are, as well as my spine. But if Heaven wants me to do it, I knew I was going to be able to do it somehow. Our Lady repeated again:

Our Lady - "Write now, My child, just as I tell you."

Veronica - Our Lady had me type:

Our Lady -

"Where do the eagles gather
To feast on decaying flesh?
For hell has opened wide
And set the demons' nest.
Why do you kill your brother,
O ye of little faith?
Have you no reason to shudder

97

When you think of your possible fate?
Have you lost your courage
To stand forth as faithful and true?
Or must you go farther forward in life,
Forgetting to wear your blue?
I am the Queen, your Mother,
On a mission so far and wide;
There's no reason to fear My Son,
But your sin you cannot hide.
Do penance, make atonement,
The time is so short;
For soon everything living
Will be treated as naught.
Give up your worldly pleasures
As well as your hoarded treasures;
For they, too, shall become as naught."

Veronica - Jesus has appeared, and startled me by standing by my chair on the right side of Our Lady. He leaned forward and said:

Jesus - "What does it benefit a man if he gains the whole world, but loses his soul? The flesh shall turn to dust, but you will retain full consciousness of your being truly alive. However, you are changed into an eternal state of being. Your spirit lives forever. And tomorrow is forever for many. Are you ready?

"Do not take My Mother's counsel lightly. You are being warned, My poor children. Awaken from the darkness that you allow to enshroud your world, or it will be the end in time. Pray, pray."

Veronica - Our Blessed Mother has been weeping, and I cannot help weeping, too. So many souls are going to hell, and many to purgatory every minute of earth's time. Pray, pray.

It is now 2:20 a.m. Jesus and Our Lady have left. It was like They passed right through the wall, going upward and outward through the wall up into the sky, until only two small lights were visible in the sky as I ran to look out the window to see where They went to. Back to Heaven, of course.

They must grow terribly sad, even a wee bit angry at the goings on down here upon earth, as St. John once said to us a short time ago. But now the Chastisement is fast approaching. Shout it from the rooftops! The Rosary, the Scapular, above all daily Mass with the Holy Eucharist. A constant vigil of prayer, I beg of you. Amen.

"He (the Pope) must not venture outside of Rome until next year…There will be another attempt upon his life"

Eve of the Feast of Saint Joseph - March 18, 1983

Veronica - All about the trees the sky is becoming filled with lights, beautiful lights, of blue and white and yellow. Oh, it's so beautiful that it's actually - the colors are cascading off the ends of the branches.

And now up in the sky these blue balls - very translucent, weightless blue balls are floating upwards from the tree to the center of the sky over the statue.

Now the sky is opening up. Previously, we found the sky was coated with dark colors, very ominous looking… hazy blue - not blue, but black, which was very foreboding, until Heaven chose to set the lights down upon the trees and, also, the good souls who are here this evening.

Now just up above the statue, about, oh, maybe ten to fifteen feet, Our Lady is coming forward. Oh, She's dressed in a beautiful white gown with a white mantle. And all along the edge of the mantle there's a small line of gold. I do believe it's metallic gold, real metal.

And Our Lady - the wind is blowing up there, too, because Our Lady's skirts are being caught upon Her feet. And I can see now Her sandals. They're beautiful. The sandals are made of spun gold, and there's a small rosette right in the middle of Her feet, on the band.

She's absolutely beautiful. Our Lady looks very delicate. And Her coloring is - there is no way I can explain Her coloring, human - wise; it's like porcelain. Our Lady's skin looks just like porcelain, but with light emanating from it. Oh, it's just absolutely beautiful.

Now Our Lady is touching Her first finger to Her lips and pointing upward over Her head.

Oh, over to Our Lady's right, that would be our left, and high in the sky, there's a pinpoint of light, but it's - no, as I'm talking it's becoming wider and fuller and opening up in a circular pattern.

And there - oh, Jesus is coming down now. He's coming through the circle of light above Our Lady's head, another, maybe, ten or fifteen feet. And now He's coming down.

Oh, He looks absolutely beautiful. Jesus has on this burgundy cape. And this evening He has the headpiece - a cowl, Our Lady called it, a cowl, C - O - W - L. And it's now blowing about His head, and it's coming down upon His shoulders.

Now Jesus has drifted down floating. They never walk, They just seem to float, Our Lady and Jesus, in the air. They've always seemed to float about as though They are weightless; yet They look as solid as you and I except for the light. The light is so brilliant that there is no human way I can explain it.

Now Jesus is going over to Our Lady's left side, that would place Our Lady's standing on His right side. Now Jesus is extending His hand out, like this, and making the sign of the cross: In the name of the Father, and of the Son, and of the Holy Ghost.

Jesus now is hesitating. He's placed His hand up near His heart. And His robe, too, is also blowing gently in the wind. Though our winds are strong upon earth, it certainly must be very temperate up in heaven.

Now Jesus is placing His first finger to His lips, which means to listen. And He's looking down now at Our Lady. Our Lady comes to just a little below His shoulder.

Now Our Lady is looking about Her, and She's taking from Her waist Her beautiful Rosary, the Rosary with the golden Our Father and the Hail Marys of white, which as Our Lady turns about now with the crucifix, the deep golden crucifix... Our Lady is now making the sign of the cross: In the name of the Father, and of the Son, and of the Holy Ghost.

Our Lady is turning now - She was turning to Her right, and She's turning now to the center. And They're moving a bit... Jesus is floating - He means to be walking, but He doesn't walk, He doesn't have to - He just floats right across the sky. And He's now moving farther over so that Our

Lady can get just above Her statue about, She's about ten to fifteen feet now above Her statue.

Now Our Lady is making the sign of the cross to Her left: In the name of the Father, and of the Son, and of the Holy Ghost. Now Our Lady is placing Her finger to Her - to Her lips, which means to listen.

Our Lady - "My child and My children, and especially My child, you Veronica, have been brought here to the sacred grounds this evening for reason. I did not mean to test you, My child, in such a manner, since you have been a victim soul for the world's sins.

"For those who receive much, much is expected of them. Therefore, My child, do not become depressed nor question any of the motives of Heaven. As you will observe, My child, having more time to rest and to meditate, the world has progressed farther back into darkness.

The Pope suffers much

"I have wandered throughout the world crying to My children, and My tears fall upon you, for as I have cried for obedience to your Eternal Father in Heaven and, also, to Our Pope, Our poor Vicar, who suffers much on the hands of the enemies of your God.

The next assassination attempt

"You must pray for your bishops, you must pray for all the clergy, and especially you must stand behind your Vicar, Pope John Paul II, because there will be another attempt upon his life. My child, that is why, principally, that I brought you here this evening, so that this message must go out to the world. Already the vermin are gathering to plan the next assassination attempt upon your holy Vicar. You must pray for him, do much penance, make many sacrifices. That is the only gauge you have to save his earthly life."

Veronica - Now the sky - Our Lady is pointing, and the sky is opening up around Her. And I feel like I am being transported to a gathering. There's a very large gathering of people. I don't know - I don't believe it's Rome, because I cannot see any building that is in Italy, that I recognize. No, this is a foreign land. And I see the Holy Father - he's riding in a car, but this car has no protection.

Our Lady - "I have asked, My child, you to get word through the Eternal Father... prayer is not enough; you must write now, My child... write and write again, and tell him, he must not venture outside of Rome until next year."

Veronica - I see a large gathering of people. And I see a man. He's dressed as a cleric, the clergy. He has in his left hand a knife. It's a long knife - no, it's like a saber... I don't know ... he's pulling it out of his pants. It seems to be in his pant leg near his belt. And it's very long. And he's pulling it out with his left hand and starting to raise it, and with his right hand he has a revolver, a small gun - not a shotgun, a small gun. And he's screaming, and everything has become silent about him with the screams, "Death to the Pope! Death to the Pope!"

And then people are frozen in shock. They don't jump on him. (Veronica raises her voice in anxiety, pleading for someone in the crowd to act in defense of the Pope): Jump on him! Get them! Stop him!

But now it's becoming black, a somber blackness upon the sky, and I can't see the people anymore.

Our Lady - "Yes, My child, you have now received a most explicit picture of the actions being planned by the enemies of God.

Bishops have not consecrated Russia to Immaculate Heart

"O My child, I have often asked your bishops and all clergy to consecrate Russia to My Immaculate Heart. And have they done this to date? No, My child, they fear more - I say they fear more the rebuttal from the clergy..."

Veronica - Now I see the same man. The sky is opening up and we're back again to the same place. And I see a man jumping forward and grabbing this man dressed as a clergy about his neck. And he turns, and he stabs this poor soul.

Our Lady now is touching Her lips.

Our Lady - "Repeat, My child, after Me:

"Unless you pray for your Vicar, Pope John Paul II, he will be removed from among you. And if this takes place, there will be far worse sacrilege committed in the city of Rome and the parishes throughout the world.

Directions from Rome cast aside

"Up to this time, My child and My children, you know full well that the wishes and the directives from Rome, from the Eternal Father in Heaven, through Pope John Paul II, they have been cast aside, each and every individual going his own way and making My Son's House a shambles."

Veronica - Now - oh, Our Lady is pointing to Her right, and high up in the sky, the sky is opening up. Oh, I recognize it now... I'm standing in the square in Rome. I can see St. Peter's. But now I see blood - blood running down St. Peter's and into the square there... and it's dividing - it's dividing the Church in half.

Our Lady - "That, My child, is symbolism of what is to be. When Pope John Paul II is removed, the Church shall be divided among itself. United it will stand, divided it will fall.

"My child, many times I have heard you calling to Me in supplication for your leaders of your country, and the leaders of all nations throughout the world. What can We say of them at this time? That very few have received the grace to turn back from their ways that have offended the Eternal Father, and We have now reached the point of history, the end days, and soon the great Chastisement will be set upon your country and every nation that has succumbed to satan.

"My child, there is much to be done before the Warning, and then the great Chastisement. In between this shall come forth the Third World War. You will see carnage, and killings, and blood running in your streets, My children.

"For a nation that has received much, this nation the United States of America, has become depraved through its medias - the newspapers, the motion pictures, the televisions - all agents of hell and of satan.

"My Son's teachings have been removed from the

schools. Only those that call themselves Catholic shall receive if but a glimmer of light of the true Faith.

"There are many nations now that promote the greatest of sacrileges. Through their medias and their permissiveness, they have brought forth satanism - the worship of satan, the adversary, to the debauchery of young children.

"O My child and My children, if I could take you step by step, you would die of fear and of horror if you could look behind the closed doors and see what is happening to your children. Many now are being trained as adults with a knowledge that cannot be absorbed into their young minds. Therefore, they become victims of their elders.

"How long shall this be permitted by the Eternal Father? My children, not very long.

"Veronica, My child, We have been forced to bring you back, though the plan was to have you join the legion of victim souls. However, it is time now to shout from the rooftops: you end is near at hand.

"I have often told you, My child, that only a few will be saved, and this has brought you great despair of heart. Do not despair, My child, the Eternal Father has a plan for all lives. You may continue to pray, for the enemy is at the door.

"O My child, My tears fall upon you when I see all of the innocent little babies being slaughtered... cast into garbage pails like nothing but dirt and scum. They are living human beings! And all murderers shall get their just recompense.

"O My children, how blind you are to think that you will live forever. My Son's clergy must return to the knowledge of the existence of a hell and purgatory.

Clergy that try to teach atheism

"Yes, My child, I know of your despair when meeting with clergy that have tried to teach you atheism. O My child, pray for them. Pray and pray more, for all that remains for your world is sacrifice and prayer and penance.

"And the United States of America shall fall to the enemy. They will not be surprised, they cannot be surprised, should this penance be placed upon you all, for they have been warned.

"O My child, how many years in earth's time have I gone about choosing from the world seers to bring forth the Message from Heaven. I am tireless, My child, as I know you will be tireless, until the return of My Son.

The worshipers of satan

"The agents of hell have gathered now. The satanism is accelerating, My child. You must all pray and act upon this knowledge that among you are those who are practicing the worship of satan. They have even become so imbued with the spirit of evilness that they murder in sacrifice another human being."

Veronica - Oh.

Our Lady - "Yes, My child, look upon the scene before you..."

Veronica - Oh, I see what looks like a cave. I don't think that this is in the United States. I get the impression it's a cave similar to the ones that I saw - the one I saw when Jesus was being crucified, and they were scourging Him at the pillar in the cave, like built out of a hill.

I see a lot of people gathered there. Now I would say about fifteen, or maybe seventeen, I'm count... no, thirteen, there are thirteen people. Now they're all standing in a circle. And in the middle of that circle is a man. He's dressed with horns on his head, like satan, and he has a black cape which is red inside. And he's turning about and he's holding a spear in his hand. It has three prongs on it. And he's dipping these prongs now into a boiling big kettle. I believe it's water boiling... he's heating up. And now he's placing - after putting water, he dips his fork, this big fork, into the water, and then places it on top of the hot coals and they sizzle. (Veronica gasps.) And now he's going over... and there's a man tied, just like Jesus was, to a post (Veronica gasps again)... and he's taking this horrible, horrible thing in his hand and he's burning the skin of the man... I can hear his screams, the man is screaming... he's burning the prongs of the pitchfork on the man's back.

Now Our Lady knows that I am getting dreadfully ill. It's a horrible sight. Now - ohh! Now one of the - there's a woman there, she - her eyes are glassy, like she's drugged or something - now she's going over to the man and she's taking a - it's a long knife, like a hunting knife, and cutting him in his back. And then - oh my... oh no! Then there's another woman - they're all dressed in black canes with red on the interior - there's another woman, she's going over... and - oh no! They - she has - oh, she has a chalice in her hands and she's placing it underneath the drops of blood that are coming out of the gash she's made in the man's back. And they're all laughing, like they're hysterically insane. They're all laughing.

And now the woman is coming over and she's passing - it's a chalice, oh, it's a chalice - but she's passing it among them all and they're drinking the man's blood. Ohh! Oh, I think I'm going to be sick, Blessed Mother! (Veronica retches and sighs.) Oh! (Pause)

Now it's growing very dark, very dark, pitch black, over the scene. I know it's a scene, but I've - I've bare... Oh, Blessed Mother, this is very, very horrible!

Our Lady - "Yes, My child, the truth is not a pretty picture, but it is the only way that I can impress upon you, My child and My children, the horrible urgency of protecting your children and your families. Because as I told you before, when you go without your doors, your children then will go out into a world that has been taken over by satan.

"My child, do not be horrified at what you see. You must understand also that the Eternal Father will have the final say in all of this horrible carnage."

Veronica - Now Our Lady is turning... it's - oh, the scene is completely vanished. (Veronica in a very relieved tone of voice): Thank God! Oh!

Now Our Lady is turning to Her right and She's making the sign of the cross with Her Rosary: In the name of the Father, and of the Son, and of the Holy Ghost.

Now Jesus is still standing above the statue. He's come

107

down closer now. I'd say He's no more than six feet away from the statue now.

Oh, He looks so, absolutely so beautiful. But His cowl now is down, you know, His covering on His head is down. And the wind is catching His skirts.

Jesus has nothing on His feet. His feet are bare. But He has on a beige - a beige gown, and, of course, His burgundy cloak about Him. And it's quite windy up there, too.

Now Jesus is looking about Him, and He's placing out His hands, like this - Jesus - and there are all lights coming out of His hands. The lights are coming out of His hands and shining all down on the people. Now as He turns, the lights go with Him. They absolutely - they - they, they seem to just emanate from His fingers. There's no way to explain it. The light is beautiful. It's a pure white, glass - like light, and it's now coming down upon the people. And He's turning slowly, and it's making an arc above our heads and going back.

And Our Lady now is raising, also, Her crucifix in blessing. And Jesus now is turning completely to His right, and His hands are extended out, and these long streams of light are coming down upon the people. Now Jesus is taking His hands back, and the lights are slowly vanishing. They're very slowly though... they're like evaporating right in the air.

Now Our Lady is - is nodding Her head, and I do notice, for the first time, that Our Lady has on the Fatima crown, the beautiful large circular type of crown that I've - I've always called it the Fatima crown.

Now Our Lady is touching Her lips, and She says:

Our Lady - "My child, it will be difficult, but you must take five photographs this evening. It will enlighten My children upon what I have showed you this evening. You must take five photographs, and I will converse with you after you do this, My child."

Veronica - You see the light ... the light up in the trees there? Jesus is standing, still standing there, and some of the light has remained from His fingers onto the trees. If you look right directly over Our Lady's statue, there are lights coming down. And I do believe that Our Lady said these lights had been placed on pictures this evening.

(Pause)

All about the trees there's a beautiful pink light. If you study the trees closely, you can see that they - the light appears to be coming from the trees. But, actually, it's a supernatural manifestation by Jesus to alert me and all those who can hear and read the message, that this is one sign that Jesus is calling. We call them the call lights, like the blue little balls in the sky, or the pink lights cascading, and also those that are in a straight line to the trees. But this is a pink that's like a vapor, and it's all coming out from around the distance of the sky over the statue.

Now Jesus is coming forward, and Our Lady is right behind Him. They seem to have been just standing - I didn't take note of it before, but They seem to have been standing over by our right side, in the highest - near the highest limb of the tree.

Now Jesus is floating back over. He just is weightless. It's so beautiful to watch Jesus and Our lady cross the sky. They're standing above the statue now, and both - They're looking about Them. And I can see that Jesus is smiling. He's very close now over the statue - I'd say no more than about seven feet directly above the statue.

Now Jesus is touching His lips with His first finger, which means that I must listen.

Jesus - "My child and My children, I shall not try at this time to enlarge upon My Mother's message to you all. I just want to add this fact, that there is little that I can say at this time but for you to all do penance, make reparation to the Eternal Father, for the sins that man has committed that will condemn him eventually to death, an eternal life in the kingdom of the damned, hell.

Restore the Bible to its natural being

"My child and My children, you must impress this upon the clergy in a kind and charitable manner: you will tell them that they must restore the good Book to its natural - to its natural being, which has given way to modernism and humanism. By this I mean, My child and My children, that the knowledge of hell and purgatory has been removed from among you. The children are growing up in a world that has been given to satan, and there is not much that you can do at this time other than pray, do penance, and guard your homes well. You will protect your children by indoctrinating them into the legion of good, purified souls who follow Jesus, My Jesus with this prayer: My Jesus, My Confidence!

"You will always remember, My child and My children, that when the struggle to remain on the narrow path has 'taken all out of you', as you say, you must remember that eventually you will all be held accountable for your soul. There is not one person who can follow you at the same time over the veil and stand up for you when you are being judged. For every man, woman, and child of conscionable age will be their own master towards their soul. In other words, My children, you must have your God - given conscience forward and placed before you always.

"Do not stifle this knowledge of your God by involving yourselves in all the pleasures of the materialistic world. You will have to return to the knowledge of the supernatural or you will fall. Your country and all the nations of the world shall undergo great test. By this, My children, you will understand in due time, because there will be earthquakes in diverse places that have never known earthquakes before. There will be floods and a great heat. Many shall die in the great flame of the Ball of Redemption.

Jesus to return when hourglass empty

"My Mother has traveled throughout your earth constantly trying to remind you that time is growing short. The hourglass is almost empty, My children, and I know that you will know what this means. For when that glass is empty, it will be time for My return.

"My child and My children, you will continue to give out the Message throughout the world.

"My Mother will always be with you, and I will be with

110

you. Even when your trials become so profuse that you feel that you cannot survive another day in your life - that you will accept as your penance.

"I could tell you the story of the true knowledge of suffering, but now, My child and My children, I ask that you pray; and another day I will come unto you with a far greater message than My Mother gave to you this evening. For there is now before you a time of trial and penance.

"We bless you all, My children: In the name of the Father, and of the Son, and of the Holy Ghost.

"Continue now with your prayers of reparation; they are sorely needed in your world today."

**"Russia plans to invade the United States with missiles"
- Jesus**

Eve of Palm Sunday - March 26, 1983

Veronica - I was startled to see the lights, the blue lights, coming out from among the trees. And there are two - you could explain them as being, like ball in shape; it is very difficult... round. And these lights - in human language I would find it very difficult to explain to you the beauty of them and where they came from. Well, strictly from Heaven because it is a miracle in itself to see these lights - which have been caught on camera, too - coming from the sky and branching outward. Now that is the usual call mark for us to know that Jesus and Our Lady are approaching.

And now just above Our Lady's statue, about fifteen feet, there are these - a round circular light is opening up within the cloudless night we have here. But, oh, Our Lady now is coming. For awhile, it was just like looking at a pinpoint; She looked very tiny in the sky, but She's hurrying forward quite fast now. Our Lady now - that's why She's called Our Lady of the Light, because the light in a - just like framing Our Lady in a circle is - seems to be following Her as She's moving forward. Our Lady is about sixteen feet, I would say sixteen feet, above Her statue.

Now, also, the trees all about us, the tips of them are now coming out with a most beautiful pink. But these pink... are not lights. There are actually cascading lines, like beams of light, coming from above Our Lady because now Jesus is coming in very fast compared to Our Lady's slow movement down, up on the base of Her statue there.

Our Lady is looking about Her. Oh, She's dressed - She has on the most beautiful gown. It's white, so brilliant. If you look at your sugar, your normal sugar bowls, you see the white - that's the only place I have found the color that describes Our Lady's gown and Her mantle. Our Lady's mantle is being caught in the wind, very slightly, but is must be a little windy up there. Our Lady's mantle has a golden border of about - oh, I would say about an inch and a half that goes all around the mantle and cascades down to Our Lady's feet. The gold looks like a real metallic gold. It doesn't look like a thread, it looks like actually spun gold.

Now Our Lady is taking Her Rosary, which has been attached to Her belting - the belting is blue - and Our Lady is taking out Her Rosary and She's going to make the sign of the cross - She's extending it forward, like this: In the name of the Father, and of the Son, and of the Holy Ghost.

Now Our Lady is moving over. She had floated, She's not walking; Jesus and Our Lady both float. It's a most wonderful think to see, because I always think that that must be what Heaven has in store for us if we deserve it. If we really make acts of reparation and do penance as Heaven has asked, we'll all, I would imagine, float, you know, float about, like that, joining Jesus and Our Lady even if it's just in Heaven. But some place between Heaven and earth, many times to other seers, I know that they have seen Them, and some of their beautifully departed souls of friends and their relatives.

Now Our Lady is moving over to Her statue and looking to Her left, that would be our right side, and She's making the sign of the cross: In the name of the Father, and of the Son, and of the Holy Ghost.

Now Our Lady is kissing Her crucifix. It's a beautiful golden crucifix. And She - Our Lady is now holding the Rosary in Her hands, like this: they're just going down through Her fingers, the beads. And Our Lady is putting on a very mournful look on Her face. It really is sad to see Our Lady feeling that bad. Now She's touching Her finger to Her lips.

Our Lady - "My child and My children, I have given you many warnings of the presence of satan upon your earth. Already he seeks to infiltrate upon the Mission from Heaven. You must pray more and not be divided by minor casual offenses, or differences of opinions, or even outright judgment - wrong judgment. I would advise you, My child, to pray on the matter that has disturbed you this week. You will understand what I am talking about. There will be no decisions made at this time."

Veronica - Now Jesus is coming down and He's standing at Our Lady's left side; Our Lady's now by His right side. And Our Lady is looking up. And Jesus now is looking all about Him. He has on His burgundy cape. And it's down from His back - I can see Jesus' hair - and the cape is extending down to His footsteps, down to His feet.

Now, Jesus is now taking His hand out, like this, and making the sign of the cross: In the name of the Father, and of the Son, and of the Holy Ghost. Now Jesus also is turning to His left, our right side, and making the sign of the cross: In the name of the Father, and of the Son, and of the Holy Ghost.

Now He's moved over. He's floated over a bit to the uppermost branch on our right side of the trees. And now He's turning and going back to standing next to Our Lady - oh, about - now They're about - I can't judge the distance through the sky, but I would say They're standing about sixteen feet above Our Lady's statue.

Now Jesus is taking His first finger and placing it to His mouth; that means to listen and repeat.

Jesus - "My child, I will not continue the discourse at this time over the matter of obedience, charity, and other virtues that have dimmed the working force within the circle. You must pray more. And do not allow yourselves to falter in bringing out the Message to the world because of slight differences of opinion and other that send you like rabbits scurrying here and there, and bringing nothing back.

"My child and My children, as I told you in My last visit among you, there was a very crucial message to be given to the world. My child, Veronica, We brought you here this evening for the facts that must be given to mankind. Perhaps, in this manner, many more will seek to hold off this terrible minor chastisement that is coming fast upon you."

Veronica - Now Jesus is pointing His hand up to the sky, like that, and He's now telling me to listen. He has placed His first finger over His mouth, like this, to His lips, and that means to listen and repeat well what you see.

Jesus - "You will listen, My child, but you will also describe what you seen now."

Veronica - The sky is opening up, and I seem to be looking at a body of water. I'm standing over on a hill and looking out, and to my shock, I see something coming out of the water. Oh, it's a submarine! it's a submarine! Now as I said that, it seemed to dive down very fast into the sea.

Now Jesus is pointing over, and I'm looking at the skyline of New York as you're coming in from Long Island. I'm looking at the skyline, and there just in front of me is that submarine. Now it's diving, and it's going about - I don't know it's - I don't know where it's heading, but it's very deep. But I noticed the submarine is off the New York Skyline, the New York side of the United States.

Now Jesus is going like this, and the scene is fading away; it's disintegrating just like it was made of smoke. And the sky has returned to its closed state of darkness.

And Jesus is now telling me to look down. I'm looking down, and it appears to be a subway station, but there's no one. I know, I recognize tracks going into a tunnel. There's no one about in this tunnel. I seem to feel that is has been discarded as a major network for the trains. Now, Our Lady and Jesus now are standing at my side. I'm standing with Them on the platform. And Jesus says:

Jesus - "Look, My child, what is coming in..."

Warhead in subway station

Veronica - And there on the tracks - it's made of wheels - there's a carting, some type of a carting - train - like board. And on this - I know I - I know it's a bomb, a very large bomb, and it has a point, like a V - shape upside down, pointed type of nozzle, or whatever you'd call it. I don't know the mechanics of bombs or anything, but I know it's a bomb.

And then Jesus touched His lips. He said: "Warhead! A Warhead!"

"It's an underground tunnel that's not being used for

115

transporting the passengers at this time. It's been abandoned. But it has made, said Jesus, an ideal parking place for a major destructive force that man has created - a missile.

Our Lady - "My child and My children, there is one fact that must be brought forward to all mankind. I know that many have tried to make up for the void that the bishops of your country and the world have created when they will not go about and consecrate the major offender in this world now, Russia - will not consecrate Russia to the - both the Immaculate Heart. My Son and I, We wish to save you from this destruction. And there is only one way that you can; that's through penance and prayer. You future which is coming to a point of what you call the end of an era, your future is upon you.

"The United States of America shall not escape this time the punishments and the desolation of the nation that has gone now throughout the world with Russia as the main force for this evil.

Major invasion of U.S. and Canada

"Man was created to live peacefully. Man was created to know his God, and in this manner to have a world that is not a paradise, but one in which man could live in peace and security. But now all of the leaders of the world run about and they say it is peace, it is security. Their words are like two prongs from the mouth; they say those words, but then they turn their backs and they are busy getting ready for a major invasion of the United States and Canada.

"Yes, My child, all who read and listen to the Message must know that there is a plan now for Russia, a plan against the United States and Canada. Your nation and Canada are surrounded!"

Cuba - one offender

Veronica - Oh, oh. Now Jesus is pointing over towards Cuba. I see a whole map of the United States, and Jesus is

116

pointing to Cuba.

Jesus - "One offender!" - He says - "one offender among many, stockpiling all manner of destruction for another, their brothers and their sisters.

"This is permitted, My child and My children, for one reason: Wars are a punishment for man's sins.

"Many warnings have been given to mankind, minor chastisements, and they go about, like their ears are deafened, their eyes are blind, and they cannot see what is fast coming upon them.

Pacifying the enemy

"You must pray for all of the heads of states. You must pray for the teachers who have been fast defiling the innocence of young children.

"This aura of modernism, pacifism - pacifying the enemy - for what? The enemy has come into your country, the United States, while you were asleep. They do not seek to take over by human methods of men. They have taken over by coming through the back door while your leaders were asleep, or their spirits had flown and they were ripe for the infiltration of satan.

"My child, the last time We spoke to you, We told you that there was a far greater message to be given to mankind. This is the message: THAT RUSSIA PLANS TO INVADE THE UNITED STATES WITH MISSILES!

"There is much that you don't know, My poor children, or perhaps some think it best that you don't know what is happening within your governments. Many of the newspapers and other means of relaying this to you have been silenced.

"But I, as your Mother, beg intercession through Jesus to the Eternal Father and the Holy Ghost to spare you these terrible punishments. If there is a need for more victim souls, let them be satisfied to know that they have been warned.

"My child, I know this has been a complete shock to you, but this message must go throughout the world. Awaken those who sleep before it is too late.

"My child, you will take now three photographs. But not one word must be said of these photographs. You may look at them, but speak not of their content."

(Pause)

Blackened bodies

Veronica - I see a road. The road looks very familiar. It's - oh, it's Long Island. And I see everyone running. I feel like I'm on the road with them, too, running. And I'm saying to a woman who passes, "What's the matter? What's the matter?" And she says, "Warheads! Warheads! Look!" And I looked back as I was running with her to see what she was looking at, and - oh, my God! I never saw blackened bodies before. (Veronica gasps and speaks haltingly) It, it - the skin is just - I can't even tell if they're girls or men or anything; the skin's been blackened, and there's a great part of this body... has melted from the heat.

Our Lady - "Terror shall grip the nation. I have tried to warn you, My children, that the United States is as like the eagle plucked bare by its enemies, plucked bare by misrepresentation, plucked bare by sin. Your country is very sick, My children.

"You ask Me, My child, why this cannot be stopped? You must now trust in My Son, Jesus. And when you become affrighted, you will say: My Jesus, My confidence!

"Yes, My child, no war has ever made a pretty picture.

"We do not stress anything that could be called political, My child and My children. By no means is this as it is meant to be. By no means! I wish to alert you all to what is coming upon you. And when it happens you will know that too few cared, too few failed... to learn a lesson from their past; too few do not give offerings of atonement to the Eternal Father.

"There is a balance now being held above you. It falls - the balance falls heavily to the left. But when that is evened out, you will know and understand this message.

"My child, continue now with your prayers of atonement. I have much to discourse with you, but that will be later.

"You will take now three photographs and read them well, but do not speak outwardly about them."

(Pause)

Veronica - All about the trees there is a deep, hazy but beautiful pink glow. Now directly up above Our Lady's statue, Jesus is coming forward. He's by Himself now; I don't know where Our Blessed Mother went to. But Jesus is coming forward, and He's standing about - oh, sixteen feet above Our Lady's statue. He has a very - it's not a serene look, but a very hurt and serious look on His countenance - as Our Lady would say, on His countenance.

Now Jesus is looking about. And He's come now quite a distance down over Our Lady's statue, and He's touching the first finger to His lips.

Jesus - "My child and My children, I realize that this has been a great shock to you all to know what is happening and what is fast coming upon you. If We could We would spare you in this emotional crisis and suffering when you hear this message. However, it is a fact that you cannot remain in the darkness and not knowing the seriousness of Our messages to you. If you had accepted the Message from Heaven, as given from My Mother to many other seers in the world, you would not have reached this point in the history of your country.

"Yes, My child and My children, the world now is being prepared by the Bear and will face a crucible of suffering. As My Mother has told you before, I will repeat again: There will be minor chastisements, and then will come the great Warning and the greatest of chastisement, a Chastisement such as has never been seen before in your nation or the nations of the world and we pray will never then be seen again. However, only a few will be left.

"You, My child, will continue to see that the Message goes out to all mankind. I ask you to put aside all your differences among you, for to unite is to stand, to divide is to fall. Therefore, you will have to not widen the wedge but close it up. You may ponder upon that, My child, and I am certain that you will understand as I speak to you what you

119

are to do. You will make your own judgment of which is most important; to pull through one soul who does not have the grace at this time to come in on his own, or to cast aside and start chasing like rabbits, as My Mother said to you, things that are immaterial and unnecessary within the circle of light.

"My child and children, there will be a great Chastisement, but this will coincide with the arrival of the Ball of Redemption and the Third World War.

Russia to use manpower of China

"Russia will also utilize the manpower of China as they make their thrust forward.

"I realize, My child, that this message has a great emotional impact upon you. Do not be afeared.

"666 - the days of suffering - are at hand: 6 is for the six who are coming: 6 is for the six days of suffering; and 6 is for those who will be sent back to hell - 666, the major of forces from hell led by satan.

"My child, you will take one more set of photographs, and this will put in print for you an additional bit of knowledge which cannot be given publicly at this time. Guard it well, My child, and do not succumb to your nature of never revealing a secret, which is soon revealed. You must be very careful, for you do not understand the danger about you now that you have received this message.

"Pray, My child and My children, often. Pray for those who do not have the light, and they also will receive the light because of the graces that you have gathered for them."

Veronica - Jesus is now extending His hand, like this, and making the sign of the cross: In the name of the Father, and of the Son, and of the Holy Ghost.

Jesus - "I bless you all, My children, and all of those known as Marian workers throughout the world. It will be through My Mother's intercession for you all that only a few will die. And only a few will be saved. But then, My child and My children, will you know and have the answer for all mankind."

Veronica - I see now the sky is becoming quite lighted. On our right side, there's a huge ball. It looks like the type of a ball that has printing on it, something that you'd use in school (Veronica chuckles). But no, Our Lady said it's a whimsical ball; however, the story it tells is not to make you glad but sad, My child.

There is a crucifix, a cross - no, not a crucifix, a cross above the ball. And now I see flames shooting out from under the ball. Oh! Flames are shooting higher and higher. It looks like a world on fire. I can hear people running. They're screaming. Something terrible has happened. The world will be aflame.

Jesus - "Continue now, My child and My children, with your prayers of atonement. They are sorely needed."

121

"He (John Paul II) must listen and act upon the message given to him or he will die" - Our Lady

Eve of Pentecost Sunday - May 21, 1983

On John Paul I - "Martyrdom by drinking from...a champagne glass given...by a now deceased member...of the secretariat of the state"

Veronica - All about the trees there are beautiful - I feel like calling them prisms - prisms - like the teardrops you find on lamps. And the - it actually looks like there's cascading tears, like teardrops... As the area above Our Lady's statue is opening up, there are lights now coming from within the circle of light high over Our Lady's head. I believe it would be about sixteen feet. Oh, Our Lady is coming down now - I hadn't noticed, I was concentrating on the prisms of light - but Our Lady is coming down now. She's floating forward; She doesn't walk but She floats. Oh, She's so beautiful.

Our Lady is standing on a ball now. That's what that big circular light - in the light I could barely see - look through it as the light kept cascading down to the grounds here. Now Our Lady is standing on a very large ball. I would say it's the world, in the shape of the world here.

And Our Lady has a long white mantle, and the gold trimming on it - there's a border about the mantle, of gold, about - I would say about three-quarters of an inch on the outer part of the mantle.

Now Our Lady has also a beautiful beige gown. I say "gown" because it's very full. And Our Lady has it belted about Her waist with a - quite a large blue sash.

Our Lady has Her Rosary, not pinned - I know it's rolled over, as Our Lady has taught me to do, about Her waist, and She's taking out Her Rosary now, the beautiful Rosary that's so tremendously big compared to an earthen Rosary that we use. It has the gold Our Father bead and also the beautiful white Hail Mary beads that... as Our Lady is turning now and raising the crucifix, the golden crucifix in Her right

122

hand, She's making the sign of the cross: In the name of the Father, and of the Son, and of the Holy Ghost.

Our Lady is looking about Her. The ball isn't moving any longer. Our Lady is standing about sixteen feet above Her statue. Now Our Lady is looking about Her, and She's pointing up to the sky, with Her crucifix still held tightly in Her hands.

And over on Our Lady's left - right side, our left side - I see a very dark cross forming; it's very somber looking. In fact, it's quite frightening, and I feel that I'm going to get goose pimples up and down my back. It's really frightening. There's something death - like about his black cross. Now it's beginning to fade away just like it was dust. It's fading away, the cross.

And Our Lady is motioning. She's placing Her first finger to Her lips, like this. And Our Lady now is kissing the golden crucifix and She's placing the Rosary into Her left hand, like this, and directing me to listen, because She is pointing now Her first finger to Her lips.

Our Lady - "O My child and My children, how sad and filled with grief is all Heaven because of what is fast coming upon mankind. In the will of the Eternal Father He has allowed man free rein on their destiny. It is only in this manner, My children and My child, that the world can be cleansed and your redemption finished.

"There are many enemies of God and those who have infiltrated into the papacy with one purpose; to set forth a plan to eliminate Our dear Vicar, Pope John Paul II. As I told you before, My children, in My discourse with you, you must pray for your Holy Father or he will be removed from among you, and then there would be more chaos in Rome.

"Yes, My child, I know of your news broadcast. I know also that this is a warning that must be noticed by your Vicar.

Death by drinking from a glass

"We will go back, My child, in history, a short history, and remember well what had happened in Rome to John, Pope John, whose reign lasted 33 days. O My child, it is history now, but it is placed in the book that lists the disasters in mankind. He received the horror and martyrdom by drinking from a glass. It was a champagne glass given to him by a now deceased member of the clergy and the secretariat of the state.

"My child and My children, these messages must be strong because they are in truth. And one cannot turn his or her back upon the truth, or they will be led into more gross errors.

"Man has become a depraved creature living not by his knowledge of his Creator, his God, but living through the pleasures of the flesh, neither caring nor wanting to know and understand what is happening at this time to all mankind.

"My child and My children, I beg you, as Your Mother and as a beacon of light to all, to pray and make atonement to the Eternal Father, or you will be chastised much more heavily, My child and children.

"As I said before in countless visits to your earth that there is a plan in Heaven for each and every life. However, man has a free will and can turn back away from the truth, becoming blinded to the truth, for man has made life most complicated.

"All Heaven is joining in a major force to try to avoid in your generation the terrible floods, the great heat, and the plague. Yes, My child and My children, the crops will rot; babies shall cry, as there will be no food to feed the hungry mouths.

The elements coming down in fury

"Disaster is coming upon mankind far greater than what has been experienced in this past year. As you will recognize, the scientists and men of knowledge all comment on this past year being a frightful one. The elements seemed to get loosened and come down in fury upon mankind. Remember, My children and My child, I have always told you that satan can control the elements.

"Man, if he falls, he falls of his own accord, because he

could not give up his riches, his life of pleasure, and seek for a far simpler way to Heaven that can be found in a spiritual childhood and a spiritual adulthood. Man in his seeking for knowledge is ever seeking but never coming to the truth.

Pope must listen or die

"My child, letters have been sent to your Vicar; and Our child, though he be a Pope, he is Our child also, and he must listen and act upon the message given to him or he will die.

U.S. surrounded with submarines

"Many warnings are being given to mankind and these will increase in nature. Horrible life - taking forces of nature shall be allowed to come upon you. All this is to take place while the enemy of God and your nation is surrounding you with submarines and planning a missile attack.

"Yes, My child, now you can understand why it was most important that you come to this Vigil of prayer this evening. We allot you the time to complete this week's work, My child, because after this week there will be much need for more prayer, more sacrifices, and more penance to make atonement to your God, the Eternal Father in Heaven, for the blasphemies and the atheistic meanderings of Our children.

"My child, My Son will be here shortly and He must speak to you. It is very urgent that you keep your attention here.

"You will take now, My child, three photographs. Much shall be given in them. You are free to distribute this knowledge."

(PAUSE)

Veronica - All about the trees there is a beautiful pink glow coming from within the trees, surrounding above Our Lady's statue and surrounding the whole circle of light here on the grounds. Now directly over Our Lady's statue, high in the sky, much more than the fifteen feet when Our Lady's came. I can see Jesus coming through this opening in the

125

sky. It's beautiful.

We're having rain here this evening, but it's stopped raining now, and and the sky is opening up, just all - like every bit of darkness being blown aside. And in a circular formation there's a tremendous beautiful blue sky with stars above us.

And Jesus is coming forward; He's floating. He also floats like Our Lady does because there's no need for Him to walk. He absolutely has control of the elements up there - and... just coming down. And nothing is impossible to God, so we can expect Our Lady and Jesus to do many things that are astounding to mankind.

Now Jesus is looking about Him. It's a little windy up there. He has on His burgundy cape. The cape looks like it may be velvet. It's a beautiful soft color, almost a plum color, but burgundy. I can't explain the colors.

Now Jesus has a pair of sandals on His feet. They're just made up like thongs almost, that we have here on earth. I would say thongs, but His is more of a slipper. And Jesus has a beige gown on. It's very long. In fact, it would cover, if it wasn't for the wind, it would cover His feet completely. And there is about His waist a belting. The belting is made of a skin - like material, sort of a light tan. But I while observing it, Jesus has come down quite a bit closer over Our Lady's statue.

And oh - and Our Lady now is coming from behind Him, coming right out, emerging from the statue. I didn't see Her before now. I guess it's because the sky is so aglow with beautiful lights that it's almost impossible to humanly explain this description so that it would be easier to understand. It's supernatural, and that would make it sometimes very difficult to understand.

But Jesus and Our Lady now are standing together. Our Lady is at Jesus' right side. And as I said before, Our Lady looks very fragile, and She comes up to about a little below Jesus' shoulder. Now Jesus, I would say, He's at least six feet tall because Our Lady just comes to His shoulder.

Now Our Lady, I noticed, has on now the Fatima crown,

126

the round one that has a ball - like formation, which we referred to as the Fatima crown. And Our Lady is standing like this, with Her hands in prayer and the Rosary wrapped around Her hands. Now Our Lady is sad, and I do see actually tears coming down from Her eyes. She's so sad. (In a childlike, compassionate manner, Veronica says) - "Well, Blessed Mother, I'm sorry You have to suffer so much."

Now Our Lady is looking up at Jesus, and He's nodding His head to Her. I can't hear the conversation that They're holding. But Jesus now is placing His first finger to His lips. That means to listen and repeat.

Jesus - "My child, you will repeat all that I say to you as clearly and perfectly as you can.

"It is urgent that mankind now take stock of what he is pursuing. I say unto you as your God, that your pursuits are making you run in circles while everyone is crying peace, peace, peace and happiness. Where is the peace? There certainly is no evidence of this upon your earth at this time.

"O My child and My children, how many disasters must come upon your country and the countries of the world before the peoples will become awakened to the reality of a very angry God?

"Yes, My child, I know at one time that you did meet up with one of Our priests who tried to disclaim the evidence about you of sin, and mankind's sinning and abandoning himself to all the pleasures of the world, leading to all measures of degraded life.

"My child and My children, I say unto you again, that man must make a complete reversal from his present way of life. While the body lives, the soul is dying within. That, My child and My children, explicitly explains to you the condition of mankind in this generation, which cries out to Heaven for the stopping of this generation, the cleansing. Is this what you want? Have you no fear of your God? If you cannot express a love to your God, better that you at least know fear and that many of you will be taken from this earth in the next year. Are you ready to go? Have you forgotten the reality of the places you can go to when you leave your body?

"There is a Heaven - yes, you know that. But there is also a hell and a purgatory. And at this moment, this very moment throughout your world, there are many souls that are being taken now into hell, the abode of the damned, forever lost.

"O My children, I have asked you to pray for your pastors, pray for Our priests. Pray for your bishops and, especially, for the life of your Vicar, Pope John Paul II.

"Yes, My child, it is not the first time that murder has been and will be committed around the city of Rome in Italy.

Prayer can save Pope

I can only assure you, My child and My children, that prayers can move mountains, and, therefore, prayer can stay the execution of your Vicar. Pray a constant vigil of prayer. Keep these prayers going as link to link, bead to bead, throughout the world for your Vicar.

"I shall not at this time tire you, My child, by repeating part of the message of February 1971. Now that message was addressed to all the priests of the earth about their pride and their arrogance in these times when all men and clergy are being tested.

"Pride is a sin, and a more formidable barrier against sanctity and holiness. And that title, My children and My child, has been accepted by many of your bishops, not just in the United States, not just in Canada, but throughout the whole world.

"Man will fall from pride and arrogance, and fall into the clutches of satan. Is this what you want? Please, My children, have pity on your brothers and pray for them.

"All Heaven is alerted to the days ahead. 666 is among you in full force, so you must wear your sacramentals and protect your children from the forces of evil when they leave your homes. You must teach them at home the truth of your Bible and the prayers that are being lost to mankind.

"Graces shall be given in abundance if you ask for them.

Have a true heart, a pure heart, My children, and trust - just trust even the littlest bit if you cannot accept the truth, but trust in the Immaculate Heart of My Mother and My sorrowing Heart for you all.

"Continue now with your prayers of atonement.

"My child, I would advise you to be sure that you have locked the doors at your home because the enemy is about you. Do not be afeared, My child. I did not wish to give you a message that was frightful, but I can impress you in this manner enough to protect your life, My child."

Veronica - Now Jesus is putting His hand out, like this, and making the sign of the cross: In the name of the Father, and of the Son, and of the Holy Ghost. the name of the Father, and of the Son, and of the Holy Ghost.

Now Our Lady and Jesus are floating upward. And Jesus is now placing His hand out, like this: In the name of the Father, and of the Son, and of the Holy Ghost.

Jesus - "I bless you all, My children, through the Eternal Father and the Spirit of life. Continue now with your prayers of atonement."

"The third World War will leave...no human beings but a grouping... taken up into Heaven... to await the terrible devastation... upon mankind"

In Honor of the Queenship of Our Lady and Eve of Trinity Sunday - May 28, 1983

Veronica - All about the trees there are cascading shafts of light, beautiful pale, pale blue lights coming from the edge of the trees over Our Lady's statue. The area all about the trees is now become quite lighted up because it's - it's going centrally to the area above Our Lady's statue. But it's so beautiful. And these rays now are coming out of Our Lady's hands as She places them in front of Her, like this.

Our Lady has come down suddenly, and I do sense - have a sense of urgency because of the way Our Lady is descending so fast. I could see Her ... while I made the description of the trees, Our Lady was slowly coming forward, and I could not cast my eyes further upward in order to see Our Lady - the lights were so brilliant and beautiful that my full attention was on the lights. But Our Lady now has come down. As I told you before, She doesn't walk like we do; She has a beautiful way of floating, though Her gown now is - is blowing about Her feet. It's very long, Her gown.

Our Lady's gown is a pure, pure white, and Her mantle is also white but with a border of approximately one and a half inches about the mantle. Our Lady is wearing very delicate - looking golden sandals. They consist of one part of the material across Her instep and a more shoe-like affair at the tip of Her feet. But each sandal has a rosette, a small rose centrally located right on the instep of Our Lady's shoes. They're really more of a shoe - like - I can't explain it - but I believe the first explanation was better, that it's a sandal, because the only closed part of the shoe is at Our Lady's toes. So you can see the - you concentrate more on the goldness of the band about Our Lady's leg because I never saw the rose placed at that level.

Now Our Lady is taking Her Rosary from about Her sash - She had it tied to Her sash – and… the beautiful Rosary with the golden Our Fathers and the translucent Hair Marys that are white, but as we pray upon them they turn, Our Lady had said, they turn, and all colors of the rainbow come from the beads themselves.

Now Our Lady is floating upward a bit to move out of the range of the trees so that all can see Her if They are willing to - if Heaven permits it. Anyone who is given the grace to see Our Lady will certainly be surprised to see how human She looks this evening. I can fully see Our Lady's face now. She's just as She was on earth. And She says now, Our Lady is saying:

Our Lady - "Just a little more tired, My child… just a little more tired."

Veronica - Now Our Lady is taking the crucifix, the beautiful golden crucifix, and She's going - moving over, floating over, to our left side, which is Her right side, and Our Lady is making the sign of the cross: In the name of the Father, and of the Son, and of the Holy Ghost.

Our Lady is looking about Her. It's a little windy up there because Our Lady is trying to control Her mantle, as it went a little askew, as Our Lady would say, from the wind this evening. Now Our Lady is floating back over Her statue and extending the beautiful crucifix again and making the sign of the cross: In the name of the Father, and of the Son, and of the Holy Ghost.

Now Our Lady is still looking about Her. She looks sad this evening, very sad, and I can see a tricklet of a tear coming down Her face. It's very sad. But Our Lady is nodding "yes", affirming that it's true. She is sad. But Our Lady now is turning to Her left, our right, and She's moving slowly, floating up to the top of the second tree from the right. Our Lady is standing just above the branches, and She's looking down now and making the sign of the cross: In the name of the Father, and of the Son, and of the Holy Ghost.

Now Our Lady is cutting across the sky - She's floating, and returning back to Her place above Her statue. Now Our

Lady is looking all about Her. And now She's placing the Rosary about Her waist with Her blue sash. And now She's placing Her hands up, like this, and taking the Rosary back from the sash into Her hands, like this. Now Our Lady is placing the first finger of Her right hand to Her lips, which means to listen well and repeat.

Our Lady - "My child and My children, the urgency of prayer and reparation needs immediate fruits, good fruits that will have seeds that can go throughout the world to promote peace.

"O My children, I have often cautioned you about the sins that you commit willingly or unwillingly, which is for the Father to judge.

However, man is fast going to his own devastating future now. Man has become so corrupt and so evil. This evil extends not among many, but the source of the evil has been placed, the responsibility for this evil has been placed upon the shoulders of your government, both federal and immediate governing bodies.

Syria holds key to peace

"Wars are a punishment for man's sins. Syria holds the key to peace at this time. However, I place in front of you, My children, a graphic picture for you to understand. It will be a parable for some, and some will turn away not willing to hear what Heaven has to say in these desperate times."

Veronica - Our Lady is pointing up with Her finger, like this, to Her right side, and high above Her the sky is opening up - all the clouds are floating away and the sky is opening up and I see a map of the Mideast. And then Our Lady is pointing up farther and that's another map of China and Russia. Our Lady is turning back now: She was looking upward also.

Our Lady - "My child and My children, there are scoffers who will say there shall not be a Third World War. They do not know and cannot conceive of the plan of the Eternal Father. Be it known now that the Father has great heart for all His children, but when the sin reaches a peak

132

only known to the Father the amount of sin among mankind, then the Father will take action. He will allow you to go upon your reprobate way until there will be few souls to save upon earth, for the others will have died in battle and also at the hands of a corrupt generation of the young.

Death at hands of young

"Fathers will be attacked by their sons; mothers shall find death at the hands of their children. This has been told to you many years ago, but too few listen until the evil comes into their homes. Then it is too late. Protect your children from the evil that is fast accelerating throughout the world. Your country, the United States of America, and Canada shall not be free from invasion. That is why you must pray a constant vigil of prayer going throughout the whole world, and you must turn back from your sin or you will die!

"My child and My children, I wish in My heart that I could bring to you a more bright and cheerful message, but that would not be true, for there is at this time too many souls falling into hell - souls that listened, but, somehow, turned back onto the wide roads, the road to perdition.

Our Lady weeps for Hierarchy

"O My children, speak to your pastors, speak to the bishops, the Hierarchy, and let them know that their Mother is weeping for them. They do not know what they are doing, or they do not care of the consequences because they have lost their faith and no longer have they received graces to keep them from the abyss. I repeat again: man shall be left to himself, because the Spirit will not remain within him if he becomes a purveyor of such evil and sin as the corruption of the children. Pornography and other all vile natures of mankind this hits, My children, to the very core of children on earth, their being. We place upon the parents a far greater measure and responsibility toward their children than We can place on the schools or the government. No, parents must now guard their children or they will weep when it is too late.

Your sons being sent to Mideast

"Wars are a punishment for man's sins. Already your sons are being sent to be there with the invasion in the Mideast. Is this what you want, My children? Can you not give your prayers and acts of reparation for those who have no one to pray for them? They are all Our sheep and We wish that they would be gathered into a holy land. The word 'holy' strikes a chord of misery, My child; I have no way to explain but to tell you, misery.

"Yes, My child, you have never seen but on the screen of your box, war. You have never felt the loss of one in war, though, My child, forgive Me if I brought a bit of sadness to your heart. Your son was removed for his own salvation. Other parents will have to face a similar occurrence in their homes. But should they have the knowledge and the truth in the supernatural they will understand that Heaven has chosen them to leave this vale of tears and return to Heaven from whence they first came.

There will be a Third World War

"My child, you will see that the Message goes throughout the world. Do not be slowed down in your endeavors by scoffers, those who say there will not be a Third World War. Are they God? Oh, no, they will know what it is to see blackened bodies along the roadside, their children, stomachs distended with starvation. 'This cannot happen here in the United States.' I hear voices saying. O My children, it will! Your crops will rot. Your children will be barred from their own homes because they have become a source of murder.

"Please, My children, listen to your Mother. It is urgent that you pray and protect your children. You must see that they wear the brown Scapular, and also any medals that will keep satan from their door.

Give out St. Benedict Medal

"My child, you will continue to give out the medals of St. Benedict. Yes, My child, I know you are doing this, but we must accelerate also the dispersal of the medals.

"I tell you now, My child, because the road has been filled with thorns, that Heaven, all Heaven, is greatly of heart for you and those who came with you from Heaven's direction to build up an apostleship that shall be forever written in the annals of the Church. This surprises you, My child; I understand you are quite shocked, but, pleasantly so, I hope.

"Now, My child, you will take three photographs and continue with the prayers of reparation; they are sorely needed. Remember, My child and My children, the Third World War is approaching."

Veronica - Now Our Lady is taking Her Rosary in Her hands, like this, holding up the crucifix and making the sign of the cross: In the name of the Father, and of the Son, and of the Holy Ghost.

Now Our Lady is placing the crucifix about Her hands, like this.

Abortion never condoned

Our Lady - "You will remember, My children and My child, to guard the young. Your clergy have fallen into darkness. Abortion will never be condoned. But We must have others who fervently will go forward and bring out to the minds of those who have actually seduced the country and the children - bring them the knowledge of Heaven, hell and purgatory. Then they will not have free license to sin."
(Pause)

Veronica - There are lights coming out from the trees, the upward part of the trees; the light is fanning out upwards. It's pink in color, a very pale translucent pink, almost smoky - looking in appearance. Now as I'm watching, just above the trees you can see these lights, these fabulous colored lights coming down from the sky. Now I can't perceive whether they're coming from the trees upward or downward to the trees because the lights now are fully up in the top part of the sky.

Now as I'm trying to describe what Jesus is doing there... see, He's coming forward now in the light. It's a beautiful pink translucent lights. And I would say it's made of glass, but I have a feeling it's not glass. It's supernatural - the light is supernatural that comes out from within Their bodies. Now Jesus is floating downward. It has become now a cir- clet of light. And Jesus is moving over to His right side, our left side.

He has a mantle now on, but He has now taken it and put it down on His shoulders because it was windy. The mantle is beautiful - more like a robe really, not a mantle. Our Lady - I reserve that, for Our Lady it's a mantle, but Jesus has a robe. It's - the color is like burgundy. It's not a pink and it's not a red, but it's a very beautiful - let's see, the material looks like it may be sateen because it has brilliance and light to it, and color. But it also could be like a velvet, a velveteen - type of pale burgundy and - a mixture of burgundy, the col- oring, and, oh, maybe a plum shade. I can't describe it, the robe that Jesus has. It is burgundy, but with sort of a - with a background of another color that makes it very translucent - the robe Jesus has on.

Now He's looking about. And He's just tied His - He has a cord like belting about His waist, which He has now tight- ened because of the wind. And Jesus has on a very long gown. Now His does not look like white, like Our Lady's, it's more like a beige color. Now Jesus in the light - His hair looks like a beautiful auburn, light auburn and brown mixed.

And I know many people will ask, 'How old does He look?', or... And I will tell you, I would say He looks like in His early thirties, and Jesus does. And He's smiling now, and He's shaking His head, "yes". Now He's touching His first finger to His lips, and that means to watch and wait and listen.

Now Jesus is taking out a Rosary, which He has also tied about His waist, like Our Lady does - He's taking it out. And the Rosary is similar to Our Lady's in the respect of the golden Our Father, but the Hail Mary beads are all bright red. Oh! Yes - yes, see there's a golden Our Father and the Hail Mary beads are a brilliant red. They're just beautiful.

Now Jesus is turning to His left side, that would be our right side, and He's coming across now, swiftly, across the sky. And He's now standing above Our Lady's statue, I would say about fifteen feet or so; I'm not good at trying to describe the length of something without a ruler, but I would judge to say it's about fifteen feet.

Now Jesus it taking His hand, like this - the Rosary, I don't know what He did with it... it's about His waist, I see - and He's taking His hand, like this, and making the sign of the cross: In the name of the Father, and of the Son, and of the Holy Ghost.

Now Jesus is tightening the Rosary about His belting. Jesus has His belt on that looks like it's calf - skin or something, animal skin; it's not like a rope. It's an absolute, very thin type of - I - it looks like - I saw that before, and I believe I've seen it in handbags, too. It's like a hide of some kind of an animal, but very thinly cut so it could go about as a waistband.

And Jesus is now - as He's coming above Our Lady, I do notice that He has sandals on. They look like leather sandals, I don't know exactly, but they do look like leather sandals.

And now Jesus is taking His finger, like this, and placing it upon His lips, which means to listen and repeat.

Jesus - "My child and My children, My Mother has given you a synopsis of all that is taking place upon your earth. The voices of the young and dying and the voices of the saints in Heaven, are gathering to cry in supplication to the Eternal Father to forewarn the earth and the earth's peoples, their sisters and brothers in the eyes of God - to forewarn them that they now are on the edge of a terrible catastrophic occurrence which will lead, without your prayers and acts of atonement for your sins, it will lead you straight into the devastating knowledge that you, the United States of America, and Canada, will be invaded. You ask, My child, in shock, 'What can be done?' I repeat again, My child, that wars are always a punishment for man's sins. When they reach the point of having to be judged as reprobate, then it is too late for that grouping.

"My child and My children, already those who are involved in conflict - and many souls coming out of this conflict cast into hell and purgatory - it is then time for Us to say: The hour approaches and you will be too late.

I do not wish to drain your meager energies, My child, but it is necessary at this time to warn My sheep that they are on now the pinnacle of self destruction. I will not, this evening, continue or converse on the sins that offend the Eternal Father and the Spirit of life, the sins of a nation that cry out to Heaven for punishment.

"My Mother begs for a stay of execution within the world. How well My children will follow the course of Heaven to Heaven given through the many visits of My Mother to you - how well you will find this course, and others will not find this course - so, My children, as you have received the grace, and many graces, much now is expected of you and all who have heard the messages from Heaven. I beg you... as your Mother... to keep a constant vigilance of prayer going throughout your country and the world. Have pity on your brothers and sisters. O My children of the light, have pity on them and pray for them: many have no others to help them to come back from the abyss.

"Yes, My child, as I explained to you in numerous years and apparitions that the world may not accept and cannot understand, I have told you that many souls are falling into hell as fast as the snow falls upon your earth, as fast as the drops fall from the rain. That, My child, is symbolical indeed of the state of your country and the world.

"We are not bargaining now to save the human skin, My child and My children, the bodies, We are here to reclaim the souls. Life goes on beyond the veil, and all of you - who among you can say that one day or night you will not be here on earth, but must be taken from the world? And taken does not mean the body, it means the spirit, the soul - the everlasting miracle of life that the Eternal Father extended to

138

you all after the tumultuous time when Adam and Eve were created. As they walked over the garden given to them, often called, the Garden of Eden, sin then became a way of life. It matters not whether you have committed one sin or many, your punishment shall be meted accordingly.

"My child and My children, My Mother has cried endlessly, hoping that Her children would only offer Her a small measure of satisfaction that Her work is being with good fruits - producing good fruits, My child.

The sin of Adam and Eve

"Yes, My child and My children, My Mother has meant to preserve you upon earth without hurt, without suffering, but his cannot be. The sin of Adam and Eve was so great that it has placed man upon the earth to suffer. But once you have learned, My child and My children, the true value of suffering you will understand that through this suffering, accepted in good spirit and with firm meaning as reparation for the souls in purgatory, the Eternal Father shall bless anew those who have given themselves as victims, victims offered to the Immaculate Heart of My Mother.

"Now, My child and My children, you will firmly now go forward without any hesitation. You must get the Message from Heaven out as fast as humanly possible, for your time is growing short. Remember, without prayers and atonement, the world will become devastated. The Third World War will leave no earth upon the land. There will be no earth, there will be no human beings; but a grouping would have been taken up into Heaven, My child and My children, to await the terrible devastation that falls upon mankind.

"Yes, My child, numerous earth - years ago I told you that some will be removed before the great cataclyst. All who are of well spirit need not give their lives to the Father in fear, but all who are of good spirit will receive many graces to save their families and themselves.

"Continue now, My child and My children, with your prayers of atonement. They are sorely needed.

"My child, Veronica, there is a very urgent message that I must give you, but you will not repeat it at this time. Do you understand Me, My child?"

Veronica - Yes, I understand...

(Pause)

Jesus - "Continue, My child, with your prayers of atonement; they are sorely needed.

"Remember also, My children, to pray for your Vicar, Pope John Paul II. And I repeat again: unless this plan has been pursued and all has been done to alert the Eternal Father's message, to alert the Pope, My child, the Eternal Father will make this less complicated and more evilly..."

Veronica - (In an astonished voice) It does? It does?

Jesus - "... The message must go throughout the world because satan evilly will set out to halt the message. You will understand in time, My child. You must not mention that I have told you; remember that now, My child. (Pause)

"I'm going to repeat it, My child, once more so that you will have every detail, but you will not give this as a public message. I repeat again..."

(Pause)

Veronica - It's very upsetting....

(Pause)

Veronica - It's awful!...

"I...warn you of the vast danger... approaching. The enemies now are gathered from within"

13th Anniversary of Our Lady's Apparitions at Bayside - June 18, 1983

Veronica - There are the most beautiful white and blue lights coming from within the trees. They are going upwards high over Our Lady's statue's head; I would say that the lights range at least twenty feet above Our Lady, coming from the tips of the trees. Now directly over Our Lady's statue the sky is opening up, and it's a most beautiful color of blue. And directly in the center of the blue circular light, I can see Our Lady coming down. She's hurrying, She's coming fast - most swiftly.

Our Lady is looking all about Her. She is so beautiful tonight! She's always beautiful, but Our Lady is really something to explain - in human language it would be almost impossible.

But She has on a pure white gown. And it's a little breezy up there because the gown is rustling back and forth with the wind. Our Lady has on sandals. They're golden sandals. And on each foot I can see a small gold rose - a rosette, a tiny rose. And Our Lady has on a mantle, pure white, with gold trim around the outside edging about - the trim is about a good three quarters of a - not a yard, three quarters of one ounce gold, Our Lady is trying to tell me now. I often wondered if Her trimming was really gold or just something sewed on to simulate gold.

No, Our Lady says.

Our Lady - "My child, this is pure gold. I say this not with pride but to allow you to know the secrets of Heaven."

Veronica - Now Our Lady is looking all about Her. She's taking from Her waist - when She came down Our Lady had Her hands folded, like this, together - and now She's taking from about Her waist - there's a sash, a deep blue, a beautiful blue - and Our Lady's taking Her Rosary from about Her waist. Now the Rosary has the golden Our

Fathers and the most beautiful white Hail Marys that, as Our Lady turns back and forth, all the colors of Heaven most beautiful that even an artist couldn't paint on earth, the colorings and the colors that Our Lady is setting forth by taking Her Rosary and holding it out, like this.

Now Our Lady is taking the golden crucifix - a most beautiful gold - and Our Lady is turning to Her right, our left, and making the sign of the cross: In the name of the Father, and of the Son, and of the Holy Ghost.

Our Lady is looking all about Her with a smile. She has a very soft, sweet smile. Oh, it's so beautiful. And Our Lady is floating over. As I told you They don't walk; They're just carried like on the wind. They just float. They're weightless. That must explain it. It's one of the mysteries of Heaven. They're weightless.

And as Our Lady's going across now, She stops directly above Her statue - oh, about fifteen feet, and She's now looking about Her and raising the crucifix again, and making the sign of the cross: In the name of the Father, and of the Son, and of the Holy Ghost.

Now Our Lady is looking over completely to Her left. But now She's moving. Our Lady has gone now above Her statue, far above our statue, and cutting across until She's standing just on the tips of the trees to the right side where the dense trees are, and just above the Vatican flag. Now Our Lady is looking all about Her. And the wind is catching Her mantle. Now She's coming over again back to Her place above Her statue.

Now Our Lady is putting the Rosary back into Her sash. I'll always remember how to tie it. Our Lady is putting it back onto Her sash. And now Our Lady has placed Her hands together in prayer, like this, and She's now motioning with Her finger. She has a very dainty finger, and just every piece of Our Lady, every bit of Her, is perfection. Heaven has created a most beautiful mystical perfection. That is what Jesus called it one time; a beautiful mystical perfection of Our Lady. Now Our Lady is placing Her first finger to Her lips.

Our Lady - "My child and My children, Our hearts are lifted to a great degree by the show of love and humanity here this evening.

A plan this evening on Pope's life

"My child, We have started on a little late on your calendar to start giving out all messages that pertain to the future of Rome. I know you are all wondering of the safety of John Paul II while he travels about to gather the sheep. I assure you, My children, We are gathering all the prayers for your Vicar, and there is a balance above him. This will be in your hands, My children, to keep this balance even, that it does not completely go over to the left side and you will lose your Vicar, Our child, John Paul II. He has many enemies, as you, My child, know full well that in any mission from Heaven there will be enemies of God. I ask you, My children, to pray for your Vicar. Pray for him, and in your acts of charity, give all to your Vicar that he may remain upon this earth. There is a plan, a terrible plan, My child, being developed this evening to remove the Pope, Our child, Pope John Paul II, from among you. Pray, My children, a constant vigilance of prayer. Have these prayers going from end - to one part of your country to the other. Have these prayers lift to Heaven. All acts of mercy for the Eternal Father shall be gathered also for His reparation.

"O My children, if only you could understand My grieving heart. I have heard words of 'Immaculate Heart' as it is passed among My children. I accept all that the Father would give Me in suffering for the repatriation of souls upon earth.

Danger ahead for invasion

"I have come this evening, My children and My child, specifically to warn you of the vast danger that the United States of America and Canada are approaching. The enemies now are gathered from within. I say also, My children, that this also will caution those who live near the waters of

143

the great seas. There is danger ahead for invasion. O My children, pray - pray a constant vigil of prayer. Wars are a punishment for man's sin."

Veronica - Oh, I see Our Lady is pointing to the sky on Her right, our left, and there is forming a cross, a crucifix. It's iron - an iron cross. Oh, I don't know - it has a very dominating, serious aspect to that cross. I never saw one like it before. But now the cross is fading away, and then there is a chalice. This is at - the statue of Our Lady ... if you look up perhaps you can see it. Over to the left, beyond the first tree, there's a chalice. It looks like it's made of pure gold. And this chalice now is dripping. Oh my, oh! What's coming forth from the chalice is blood. Our Lady knows that this has given me a terrible inner shock. Our Lady places now Her fingers, first finger to Her lips.

Our Lady - "My child, you will understand it is the blood of the victims, the victim souls who will give for their Pope, John Paul II.

Most men removed from devastated earth

"I repeat for the third time this evening that you must pray a constant vigilance of prayer that the enemy does not cause your country and the other nations of the world destruction such as has never been seen from the beginning of creation and never will come forth and be practiced again, when most men are removed from an earth that has been devastated from the hands of mankind. Mankind goes about now gathering all measures for warfare, gathering all instruments of war, for warfare.

"O My child and My children, do you not understand why I have come here for countless years upon earth trying to counsel and warn you that the end is near at hand?

"My child, I gave you at Our last meeting the second secret. Now the third I will give unto you. You will listen well but not speak of it. You will obtain six photographs. Read them well, but you must not speak one word of what you see.

"O My child, there is so much that I want to tell you to

pass on to Our children of the world, but there will be a great message given to you all from My Son, Jesus, and the Eternal Father in the Spirit of light - the Holy Ghost, My child.

"You will now sit back, My child, and contemplate on the mysteries within the photographs, and I will be back again with My Son."

Veronica - There are blue lights tinged in a - they're like, almost like a chandelier is made, these lights this evening; they're almost like the prisms I spoke of the last time Our Lady came to us. And actually they're cascading upward. It's beautiful. It's a whole sky of light, but the light is beyond anything that I could put into words. The light is crystal clear, beautiful, bright - brilliant, that if you looked into it too long, without Heaven's grace given to you, I'm certain it would burn your eyes. It's so intense.

But now the trees are starting to burst forth with a color of pink. It's a pink color, the most gorgeous pink. There's no way - I don't think anyone has been able to put down in color the beautiful colors that Jesus has assumed to let us know when He's coming.

Now just above the trees, I see the sky is opening up now. It's a beautiful color blue. And oh! Jesus is coming down now. He's floating quite fast. He doesn't walk, He floats. And He's standing now just above the statue, about - oh, I think about sixteen or twenty feet. And He's looking all about Him.

Now Our Lady is coming down also from the same circle of light, and She's coming over to Jesus' right side. Now Our Lady looks very petite, and I do notice now - when She first came this evening, She didn't have on the crown, but now Our Lady has on the beautiful Fatima crown. It comes over Her mantle. The mantle is blowing in the wind now. And Our Lady is looking all about Her with a smile; She seems to be pleased. And yet in Our Lady's face there is a picture of - I could only explain it, of sadness, a sadness that She has absorbed, and a beauty that She is trying to give out to mankind even though She knows from Jesus all that is

145

transpiring upon earth.

Now Jesus is motioning - He's nodding to Our Blessed Mother, and She's just standing there now with Her hands together, like this; and the prayer beads, Her beautiful Rosary, is strung in Her fingers. And Our Lady is standing there. She almost looks like a statue now. And She is motioned - nodded with Her head to Jesus, and He's looking all about Him. Now Jesus and Our Lady are moving over to our left side above the trees, that would be Their right side, and Jesus is extending His hand out, like this, and making the sign of the cross: In the name of the Father, and of the Son, and of the Holy Ghost.

Now Jesus is turning to His left and He's floating above the statue and over to our right side, His left side. Our Lady is right behind Him. They don't walk. There's no way I can explain it. They're weightless up there. It's really something that makes you think, you know, how we're all going to assume a similar type of spirit, as Our Lady and Jesus, when we're taken from the earth. Of course, we'll never be in the - I'd say the stage of beauty that Our Lady has and also that Jesus has; it flows from Them, the love and feeling of such warmth when you see Them that actually there's no fear or dread of going over the veil. It's something that is a part of life of all of us human beings, Our Lady has said. We will all go over the veil and feel just as Our Lady feels at this moment, She said, when we see the Beatific Father, and/or if we're not that fortunate, perhaps we will actually meet Jesus, the Second Person of the Blessed Trinity.

Now Jesus is touching His first finger to His lips; that means to be quiet and wait now for His instructions. Now Jesus is nodding, because He said:

Jesus - "You accept this well, My child."

Veronica - And He now is turning to His left side and floating over by the trees, and He's extending His hand out, like this, and making the sign of the cross: In the name of the Father, and of the Son, and of the Holy Ghost.

Now Jesus is coming back slowly across the sky. He's looking all about Him. He looks very tranquil. You know, like Our Lady and I, we both get very excited, but Jesus has a tranquillity about Him. And, also, I think you would like to know, when Our Lady speaks through me Her lips are moving, but when Jesus speaks it seems to come from within Him with no need to move His lips. It just comes from within and comes inside of you. I can't explain it any other way.

Now Jesus is stopping again, just over the statue, about fifteen feet above, with Our Lady at His right side, and He's extending His hand out, and making the sign of the cross: In the name of the Father, and of the Son, and of the Holy Ghost.

Now He's touching His lips.

Jesus - "My child and My children, many have accepted the Message from Heaven at this time, but there are many more of My sheep who have not received the knowledge of Our coming here to the sacred grounds. You will all be sure to keep the Message going out as fast as is humanly possible and within your means from prayer and dedication.

"My child and My children, your country is now in a terrible state. As I gave you the photograph with the plucked eagle, you can well imagine that the eagle, representing the United States, looks like it has drawn its last breath.

"O My child and My children, how often I have had to use symbolism to approach you, but I give you the reason now. Much was to remain in secret until told to come forth. At the present time? No, My child, those pictures I gave you they are to be deciphered and not make known until My Mother or I tell you to. You understand that, My child."

Veronica - Yes.

Jesus - "If you do release what is in those photographs, My child, you will bring much unnecessary torment to yourself.

Great heat to come soon

"My Mother has directed you well through this stage of man's progressing towards sanctity. However, you must remember this: words were given, and actions have taken

147

place. Our Lady told you several years ago that there would be great floods, and there were great floods; that there would be a great heat, and that will come soon; and after that there will be a great plague. You had a plague now, My children - two diseases unknown in cure for mankind. Did not My Mother, pass along to you that knowledge that there would be diseases that your scientists will not be able to explain nor stop? They will find not cure for it.

"Now, My children, I tell you this: I do not wish to come to you as a visitor with dire warnings, but the object of My coming is to warn you that you may do something and correct the evil that has been perpetrated by the few.

Devastating plague within six months

"There will be one more most devastating plague upon you. That will come within the next six months, My children. You ask, My child, why is this allowed? My child, you have forgotten the real reason for all this: man will benefit from it in the end. For I once said to you many years ago that penance is difficult, but after penance there is a great joy.

"There are many things that cannot be understood because of a man's human nature, but that you must trust in God the Father, and listen to the words My Mother brings to you and the dire warnings of what is to come upon mankind. Do not accept it lightly, or with derision. For the answer will be given to you, and you will still not know that this has come to you from the Eternal Father as a measure of penance.

"All mankind will be tested before the great day of My return. There will be floods taking many lives; there will be famine and many will die; and there will be the great heat and many will die. My child, I know you are affrighted at My words, but Our purpose is to save you.

One grain in hourglass

"Many are not listening, and others have not received the Message from Heaven. Therefore, we will be living, My

148

children and My child, by a time clock, and there is only one grain remaining to go through the hourglass.

"My child and My children, I beg of you, through the Trinity - the Father, the Son, and the Holy Ghost; and I am in God, I was in God, and I always will be in God - even those children who cast aside My warnings and laugh in derision, they will learn too late to save their souls.

"All who have come to the sacred grounds have come with reason. The Eternal Father has a plan, and everyone who comes to the sacred grounds has been called there by the Father.

Slight plague of rats

"I, also, must tell you, My child, to tell the world of the coming second part of the plague: the first you must remain secret with for awhile, My child. I will tell you there will be a slight plague of rats. Do not be affrighted, My child, this plague will be kept within only the eastern area.

"O My child and My children, the response this evening is greatly appreciated and loved by Heaven. As long as there is one man who will come forth and tell the world of the Mission from Heaven, the world can be saved from complete extinction.

"Armaments are being made to destroy mankind. The more armaments that are made, the less chance there will be for salvation; not the salvation of the soul, but the salvation - the keeping of the bodies. For bodies will be burned upon earth, burned to a crisp. Many shall see death as they have never seen it before. Is this what you want, My children? Your brothers and sisters of good, will hold forth their hearts to you; do not slam the door in their faces, for you will cry bitter tears if you lost this chance to be among those who call themselves Faithful and True.

"My child and My children, continue your prayers of atonement. There is much more that must be said soon, My child, but the three photographs will remain hidden, the meanings, just for this time being, My child. You will speak of it to no one."

149

Veronica - Now Jesus is placing His hand out, like this: In the name of the Father, and of the Son, and of the Holy Ghost.

Oh, Jesus is touching His cape. I don't believe that I described His cape, and Jesus does wish that everything be made open to mankind - the knowledge of Heaven. Jesus has on a beige gown; it's a very long and very loose. And He has, like a leather type of band about His waist.

And Jesus has on brown - they look like leather sandals. I don't know what they used in Jesus' time, but they look like they were made from some kind of a skin. They're like a thong type of shoe. They're brown.

And now Jesus has on a - not a mantle, it's a cape - it's not like Our Lady's mantle. It's a cape tied at the neck with a golden piece of cording He has. And then there's also a headpiece like the monks wear, but Jesus has that down now. It's just falling on His back and held there by the gold pieces of cording. And Jesus is nodding, 'Yes.'

I've often heard - people have asked, "What does Jesus look like?" Well, there's no words I could use to explain what Jesus looks like. He's got the most beautiful face. That's what joins me with Him in the knowledge that Our Lady has given to me, that through - I mean through Our Lady, with Jesus' knowing - that He has on a very silky type of cape this evening. And it's blowing in the wind, so it's much lighter than the burgundy cape He had been wearing in the past months. I would think it would be to assume the seasons, in His clothing.

That makes me feel also, the human nature of Jesus is so like our own that it really makes it easier for you to approach and talk with Him, because He is human as can be. Whereas, St. Theresa and Padre Pio and all others who came to us in the past years, they had a fragile look about them where you could almost see they were transparent. But Jesus and Our Lady have never been transparent; They're as solid as you and I, and nothing but true humans. That's the only way I can explain it. And, of course, that makes you feel very good in your heart, because you know you can speak to Them, because They're not beyond your reach. All you have to do, Our Lady says, is to lift your eyes to Heaven and ask and you shall receive; pray and you're heard. You are heard. If you ever wonder why your wish was not granted you must understand that Heaven, Our Lady says, knows just what is in store for your future. And if you don't get what you want, you'll find at the end of a certain period in your life that it would have been the worst thing that could have happened to you. For Jesus and Our Lady are guiding you, every one of you, as long as you stay within the light.

Our Lady now is pointing to Her lips.

Our Lady - "I have one thing to say, My child. I grieve in My Mother's heart for My Son, for they are defiling the Eucharist. My child, make this known to mankind, that there are so many offenses to My Son's Immaculate Heart, that I, as a Mother, grieve, too, for Him.

"Now, My child and My children, you will continue with your prayers of atonement; they are most sorely needed."

"Your country...will lose a great statesman"

In Honor of St. Theresa of the Child Jesus - October 1, 1983

Veronica - All about the trees there are the translucent blue lights that always announce the coming of Our Lady, and that means to get ready. There is a beautiful white light now opening up in a circular pattern high above the trees in the sky. And directly in the center of the light, I can see Our Lady, Our Blessed Mother. She's coming forward very fast. And right behind Her I notice there has been a cast of pink also, pink lights all about the trees. And right behind Her I can see Jesus coming forward. They are coming forward very fast.

Now Our Lady is moving over to the right. She has on a beautiful white gown. And the light about Our Lady brings out the vividness of Her gown, so that it looks absolutely brilliant. Our Lady has on a white long gown. And also Her mantle, which reaches from Her head to Her feet, is also white but trimmed with a border of gold all around the edging of Her mantle.

Our Lady has on Her head the most beautiful crown. It's Her Fatima crown. Our Lady has worn it on several occasions before. And it's an absolutely gorgeous crown.

Our Lady has Her hands together, like this. And about Her fingers She has the beautiful Rosary, the Rosary with the golden Our Fathers and the white Hail Marys.

Our Lady is looking upward, and She's motioning now with Her hand. Oh, and Jesus is coming forward. He's dressed also in a very brilliant cape. Now it's burgundy color, but the light all about Jesus makes Him very translucent and brilliant.

And Jesus' hair is blowing very softly about His shoulders. It must be quite windy up there this evening. Now Jesus has nothing on His feet. He has no sandals.

And Our Lady has on Her golden sandals that have at the tips of the toes - across one bracket of Her sandal, She has the little gold rosettes on each foot.

Now Our Lady is looking up and smiling towards Jesus, and He's nodding. Our Lady now is looking all about Her, and She's taking Her beautiful Rosary with the large golden crucifix and placing it out, like this, and making the sign of the cross: In the name of the Father, and of the Son, and of the Holy Ghost. She's blessing the people.

Now Our Lady is looking up towards Jesus, and He now is extending His hand out, like this, and making the sign of the cross: In the name of the Father, and of the Son, and of the Holy Ghost.

Now Jesus is pointing up to the sky on our right side, His left side, and high up in the sky there is forming a ball with a cross on the top, but the ball is all black. And underneath it - there are flames forming under the ball.

It's very awful - horrible - looking. It's frightening that these flames are now reaching up to the ball.

Now Our Lady is motioning to me, when She's placing Her first finger to Her lips, which means to listen and repeat.

Our Lady - "My child and My children, and My child, Veronica, We hasten to bring you here this evening in your ill state because of the urgency of what is to take place within your world.

To hold back the flames

"There is only one recourse to hold back the flames. My child, that you have viewed; that is an outpouring to Heaven of penance and prayer, and sacrifice. Your world is heading towards a cataclysm of massive proportion. Many parents shall lose their sons and shall cry to Heaven, 'Why, oh why, has this come upon our world?'

"O My children, how often have I appealed to you to listen to My words of caution and warning. I have tried through countless earth - years to guide you away from this cataclysm; but no, so many have chosen to ignore My warnings. These warnings came from all Heaven - the Eternal Father Who watches and knows all that has taken place, that will take place, and that has been taking place.

"O My children, so much is in store for you in Heaven,

153

and yet so many shall not see these pearls.

"My child, you must hasten to get all of the messages out as quickly as possible.

"Your country, My child and My children, will lose a great statesman. You must pray for all of the leaders of the nations of the world, and pray for your country, the United States, and Canada.

"You understand, My child, that there are instruments of destruction now created from the mind of satan, using the fallen nature of mankind to prey upon the weak, and to use them to bring forward missiles of destruction.

"O My child, I realize your debilitated state this evening, but you must understand, My child, that for the great graces extended to you, much is expected of you, and you will suffer much, My child, even in the future.

"You will now take three photographs, but they must be kept secret. I must caution you again, My child, for I realize that it is difficult for you to keep a secret, but not one word must be spoken of these photographs, My child. We trust you."

(Pause)

Veronica - The sky is turning pink all about the bushes, and high up in the sky there is an opening which is starting about the size of a dime - that's the only way I can explain it - and it's opening up now, and it's a brilliant white light coming from like a pinpoint in the center of the circle. It's circular. And now it's opening up and covering just about all of the sky up above Our Lady's statue.

Now coming through the center of the circle is Jesus. He's alone now, I don't see Our Lady. And He's coming forward. He has on His burgundy cape and His gown which He had on before. But I don't believe I did mention that His gown is a beige color. It's not a white like Our Lady's but a beige color, and like, almost like - I saw material similar to it before, but it's like - oh, I don't know - I just can't explain it.

Well, anyway - oh, Jesus is now - He's hastening like this with His hand - oh, He's now taking His hand out, like this, and making the sign of the cross: In the name of the Father, and of the Son, and of the Holy Ghost.

Now Jesus is looking over to the right and to the left, and He's smiling. He seems to be very pleased. Oh, He's smiling. Now Jesus is coming forward, He's floating forward. He's just above Our Lady's statue, and He's placing now His first finger to His lips.

World in danger of giant destruction

Jesus - "My child, I will not enlarge upon My Mother's counsel to you this evening. However, I must repeat this: that you country and the nations of the world are in dire distress and in danger of a giant, terrible crisis - a giant destruction upon you and all mankind. I say this in comparison to size. I use the word 'giant' for one reason: that others who have heard My counsel and did not listen - perhaps could not understand My wording - therefore, I say, like a giant walking among mankind, there shall be this conflagration.

"Many parents shall weep tears of great sorrow at the loss of their sons. I have warned you that you were fast approaching a war of giant proportions, My children. And I warn you again that unless there is restitution made for the sins of mankind to the Eternal Father, We will not - We will not turn Our backs - but We will not stop the advance of country upon country and nation upon nation, until the whole world shall be engrossed in a major world war.

"O My children, you have deafened your ears, deadened your hearts. You are like bodies, living bodies in dead souls. O My children, how many words must be out to you from seers throughout countless nations in the world before you will listen?

Statesman to be removed

"I repeat what My Mother has said to you: a statesman will be removed from among you. And then what will happen?

"My child, you will continue to hasten the sending out, the dispersal of the Message throughout the world. Do not slacken in your pace, because there is little time left.

"The world must now give itself over to penance, great penance. But this penance shall go much farther that We would have wished to see upon Our children. That is why, My child, you were called here this evening. I know of your weakened condition, but it was necessary that you warn the world now that there is little time left.

"My children, We have in Heaven beauties beyond all human knowledge. We have in Heaven the ultimate joy and the ultimate expectation of anything man could conceive in his human mind. Are you going to cast this all aside for a few short years upon earth? Is this worth casting aside for? Think, My children, before it is too late. Many of you who hear My words will not be ready. I say, not be ready! Unless you protect yourselves by a constant vigilance of prayer, you will not be ready when you are called unexpectedly. Many shall be removed from the earth very soon, and many will not be ready.

"My child and My children, you cannot, and I shall not burden your minds, with the manner in which Heaven deems it necessary to allow the world to continue.

"You understand, My child and My children, that no one, no one will fall into hell, unless it is of his own free will. I assure you, also, that no one will go to hell unless they lead themselves there, and have preferred the pleasures of this world, your earth, and not counting their blessings on the road to Heaven, but following all the pleasures that lead to damnation in this world, your earth.

"Remember, My children, love is the outstanding word being used in your world today, but so few know the true meaning of love. So few have practiced the true meaning of love, for much of this in your world, My children, is based on self-love.

Very little time left

"You will all continue a constant vigilance of prayer: bead to bead, Rosary to Rosary going throughout the world, nation to nation. And with the cooperation of all good souls, there is still time - although very little time is left - there is still time to hold back the destruction.

"My child and My children, because We love you, and My Mother loves you, We do not wish to see you destroyed. We do not wish to see you lose your chance to enter Heaven. Heaven was made for all mankind, but only if they follow the road, the simple road, the narrow road. It's only when you become engrossed in the world's pleasures, and seeking treasures that are not the type or the kind that will take you to Heaven but take you onto the road to damnation, then you have lost the way.

"Come, My children, follow Me, for I love you, My Father loves you, and I am your God, in the Father, the Son, and the Holy Ghost. I always was, I am, and I always will be.

"My child and My children, continue now with your vigil of prayer. You cannot know the value you have for the salvation of your brothers and sisters."

Veronica - Now Jesus is taking His hand - He's moving over now to the left side of the trees, and He's looking over - and He's making the sign of the cross: In the name of the Father, and of the Son, and of the Holy Ghost.

Now - oh, Our Lady is coming down now. Oh, Our Lady is coming down from high in the sky. I didn't see Her; She was beyond the treetops. And She has still on that beautiful gold Fatima crown. And Our Lady has Her hands together, like this, with the Rosary draped on Her fingers. And She's coming now and moving around to Jesus' right side. And - oh, Jesus is giving Her such a warm, beautiful smile, and Our Lady is looking up at Him.

Now Our Lady is taking Her Rosary, Her specially graced Rosary, and with the golden crucifix, She's making the sign of the cross: In the name of the Father, and of the Son, and of the Holy Ghost.

Now Jesus is moving to His left side, which is our right side, and He's just over Our Lady's statue now, and He's extending His hand out, like this, with - and Our Lady now is joining Him at the same time - I never saw Our Lady do that before - now She's extending Her crucifix out, as Jesus extends His hands, and They're making the sign of the cross, and going high above Their heads with Their fingers, too: In the name of the Father, and of the Son, and of the Holy Ghost - like They're marking the very place here. The crucifix that Our Lady used has left an impression in the sky, of a cross in the sky, right over Our Lady's statue.

Now Jesus is going far over to our right side, which is His left side, and He's now extending His hand out, like this, and making the sign of the cross: In the name of the Father, and of the Son, and of the Holy Ghost.

Now Our Lady is following Him. She's right behind Him. Now She's caught up with Him there, and She's extending Her Rosary out with the golden crucifix - it's a very large crucifix - and Our Lady is making the sign of the cross: In the name of the Father, and of the Son, and of the Holy Ghost.

Now Jesus is turning... and it's quite windy because the wind is catching His skirts, and also Our Lady's. And They're coming across the sky, like, you know - They don't walk, They float; They're carried like They're weightless across the sky. Yet Jesus and Our Lady look just as solid as you and I. But yet They seem to be weightless when They go across the sky.

Now They are both above Our Lady's statue. Oh, They look so beautiful. The light is very brilliant, and I can see Their faces very clearly now, though I don't see any hair. I've never seen Our Lady's hair. Oh - h.

Now Jesus is touching His lips.

Jesus - "My child, you will listen to what My Mother has to say, but you must not repeat it."

(Pause)

Veronica - Now Jesus and Our Lady are moving back into the sky, but They're not moving out of the range, so we can see Them. Our Lady is touching Her lips.

Our Lady - "My child, I am not leaving; I will be here the rest of the evening, and I will be here always."

Veronica - And Jesus is also standing off to the right.

They've taken now - Our Lady is on the left side by the trees and Jesus is over on the right. Oh, and They're looking about them.

Now the pink glow that's coming out of the trees and the blue signal lights seem to be fading back into the sky, like this. And I notice now Jesus is moving up and Our Lady is moving up. Now They are just above the trees on either side. Now They're coming together across the sky, and They're standing together looking down.

Our Lady - "My child, you will take three more photographs and repair home."

Veronica - Yes.

"Do not take lightly the reports of ships out on the sea and submarines.... It is all part of the master plan for the takeover

Eve of Palm Sunday - April 14, 1984

Veronica - All about the trees there's a beautiful blue light. The light is running in streams of lighting up to the center of the sky, directly above Our Lady's statue. It is so beautiful and warm that - there is no feeling of coldness or rain - that I know that it is something beyond all human words to describe - the light. It is warming many times. The light has come upon us while we are in different positions about the Shrine. And it is a warming light, directly supernatural. But it's so beautiful now. The light is cascading about, which means that I must be ready.

And now, directly over Our Lady's statue, high into the sky, there is a beautiful circular white light. It's almost glass - like because of the way it takes like a diamond - shape, a diamond - shaped glass - like partition. I say 'partition' because the sky is being now lighted in a most unusual way.

Our Lady now is coming down in the center of the diamond - like light. It's as though She was a statue transferred onto a medal. It's just beautiful.

Our Lady is dressed in a white gown that reaches down to Her feet. But I can see that Our Lady has on the most beautiful sandals. They're made, I would think, of pure gold. They are absolutely beautiful. In the center of Our Lady's instep, by the strap - the strap goes in a T - formation on both Her feet - there is a little rosette. Oh, it's so beautiful.

Our Lady has on Her white mantle, and all about the mantle there is a trim of about, I would say, a half an inch of pure spun gold. It is all about the outside of the mantle and down by Our Lady's feet. The cape of the mantle has the gold trimming on its outer edge. It's absolutely beautiful.

Our Lady is pointing up now to the sky, and over on our left side above the statue, there is a large globe forming. But it is a globe of the world. I can see that immediately because of the outlines of the various parts of the world and the hemispheres.

Our Lady now is taking Her Rosary from Her waist and She's extending out the beautiful large golden crucifix on the edge of Our Lady's Rosary that has the gold Our Fathers and the white Hail Marys, that take all the colors about us and make them into one. There's no way of explaining the colors that cascade from Our Lady's Rosary, the Hail Mary beads, as She turns to and fro. She's looking in both directions now, right and left, but She's extending out now Her Rosary, like this, and making the sign of the cross: In the name of the Father, and of the Son, and of the Holy Ghost.

Our Lady is smiling very softly. But I notice now Our Lady is taking the time to wipe the tears from Her eyes. Her tears are just flowing down Her face.

Now Our Lady is taking Her Rosary and placing it back onto Her belting where She had it originally and then took it off in order to bless us. Now Our Lady is placing the Rosary down about Her waist, like this. And now She's taking Her right hand, the index finger, and placing it upon Her lips; that means to listen and repeat.

Our Lady - "My child and My children, My dear, dear children of the world, My tears fall upon you. I send My heart and My love to all who have taken up My Son's cross as a way of life to follow Him.

"There is so much confusion now, My children, in your world that, Veronica, My child, We brought you here this evening because of the crisis that is fast heading to your country.

"Do not take lightly the reports of ships out on the sea and submarines. They are there, My child and My children, and they are not out for a joy ride. It is all part of the master plan for the takeover of the United States and Canada.

Not long to exist as free nation

"I know, I heard the voice also, My child, that said that the United States shall be taken over without a shot to ring out.

161

That is not true, My children. Should they advance upon you as they plan, there will be bloodshed in the streets, blood flowing and mothers' hearts breaking in sorrow. Oh, how they will gnash their teeth and cry bitter tears of regret that they did not foresee or listen to the voices from Heaven crying out: Prepare now, for you do not have much longer to exist as a free nation.

"My child and My children, I could go back through the years and remember how many times I came upon earth to try to warn you. Those nations that listened were free from harm. But they had to pray the Rosary - the Rosary and Scapular.

"I hastened to and from the corners of your earth, begging you as your Mother to listen now, for the time is growing short.

Maneuvers not a joy ride

"The maneuvers about your country are not a joy ride. They are there with precise decisions in their mind.

"O My child, how My heart aches, for I have been with you here for so many years, and how many have We gathered? There are thousands of souls who have heard the Message from Heaven and they have turned their backs, so hardened are their hearts, and have deafened their ears to the call from Heaven. They will come down upon their knees and beg in repentance, but it will be too late for them. Is this what you want, My children? Must you be punished to be brought back to the fold?

Consecrate Russia or die

"O Our wandering sheep are going without true leaders. My priests of the world, I say to you now: you must listen to My voice from Heaven. You must consecrate Russia to My Immaculate Heart or you will die.

"O My children, I hear the pleas of mothers with children that have vanished, it seems, from the face of your earth. So big and so numerous are the catastrophes to a home that you

would think, My child and children, that they would understand and accept the truth that satan is loosed upon your
earth, satan and his whole legion of devils. Satan and his
legion are known to you as 666.

Illnesses without cure

"Do not cast the knowledge I give to you, My chose few,
the knowledge that 666 is satan and his legion of demons.
Do not fall victim to those who are going about the earth dis-
crediting the actual knowledge of the supernatural. They, in
their theology and their new mode of living for mankind,
what do they expect to happen when there comes upon them
illnesses without cure. Illnesses without the knowledge of
how it developed and where it came from. All this and
much more shall be sent upon your nation and the world as a
last resort to bring you back to the fold.

"My child and My children, the Eternal Father does not
wish to lose one of His children. And what can He do with
all of the murders of the unborn taking place. For that one
reason among many, the United States will suffer unless
there is placed into your government a group that fears the
Lord if they cannot love the Lord. They will fear Him and
find measures to stop the slaughter of the unborn. You are
taking these babies, these children, from the world before
their mission has been performed. Each and every unborn
child has been sent upon the earth with a mission to fight
satan. Remove them without the knowledge of God,
remove them and it is truly said with great sorrow that satan
now rules your governments and the world.

A most terrible cataclysm

"Who but you, My children, that hear My voice and My
pleas, only you will be saved. Those that are saved shall be
counted in the few. There will be a most terrible cataclysm
and destruction."

Veronica - Now Our Lady is pointing to our right side,
Her left side, and there's a ball now glowing in the sky,

directly over on the statue's left side, our right side. And the globe now is one of the world, but there are flames on one side. I am almost looking now into the area. There are flames, and there's a big hole; oh, it covers half of the globe, the hole. It's like burned out, as though it's been hit by a tremendous, big ball of fire. Oh, it's terrible. I can feel the heat.

Now I notice that there is a tremendous ball now setting out in the sky by the sun. It's like two giant suns in the sky. But the ball on the right has a tail, and it's starting to move now around the sun. And as it goes it's bouncing crazily, as though it's going off course in some manner, this ball. And it's heading now over towards the earth again. It's hit it once, and something happened. And now it's heading for another part of the globe. And now it's heading for another part of the globe. It's turned its course completely around and is striking the globe. I can see now the whole underside of the globe in flames.

Our Lady now is placing Her first finger to Her lip and She's placing Her hand out, like this, and the sky now seems to be, the - the balls and the picture seem to be evaporating because they're blowing away like a mist.

And Our Lady is crying now. Our Lady has moved over to the left side of the sky. And, oh, She's sitting down now on a huge rock; Our Lady is sitting down on a huge rock. And She has now upon Her head... Before when She first appeared, Our Lady had on the Fatima crown, but now I notice She has changed into a different gown. I don't see the gold about the trim of Her gown. But She's sitting there very dejectedly. But She has - Our Lady has on Her head a crown that's made of, like spokes, spires of gold. The crown is all gold, but it seems to be all circled about with spires on it.

And Our Lady is crying. Now She's looking up, and She's saying:

My visit at LaSalette

Our Lady - "See, My child, how I sorrowed in the days

gone by. Do you not recognize My crown, My child? I heard you mention that in the discourse. It is, My child, the crown of LaSalette. I mention this to you, My child and My children because there was a lesson to be learned. Those who listened did not lose their crops or be subjected to the other means chosen by the Father to bring them to the fold. You, My child, will obtain more knowledge if you will find a copy of some instrument that will tell you of My visit at LaSalette."

Veronica - Now Our Lady - She's going back into the sky a bit on the left-hand side. And the sky - now She's pointing upward. Now the sky is turning very pink, a beautiful pink color. It feels very warm. In fact, it's - the breeze is blowing, and I can smell flowers, beautiful flowers. It's like a bright, sunny May day. Ohh!

Now there, high over the statue in the sky, I see a circular opening now. It's as though this beautiful light is enlarging upon itself as it's coming forward. The light is coming forward, and I can see Jesus now. He's in the center of the light. And it's like a ball of light. It's much different than what I saw Him come through before. This is a round circular ball of light, and it's just as though He's riding within that ball of light, and it's carrying Him down, down, down to.... He's now standing over Our Lady's statue. He's looking all about.

Our Lady now has returned wearing Her white gown with the mantle with the gold trim on it. And, oh, She has now on Her Fatima crown.

Now Our Lady is joining Jesus. He's come just above the tree beyond the statue, and He's standing there now looking all about Him.

Jesus has on a linen - like - it looks like linen, the gown. And He has on brown skin - like - made, they look like they're made from some kind of skin - sandals on His feet. And Jesus is wearing this linen - like looking gown with a belting about it of the same material as in His slippers, like an animal skin.

And Jesus has this cape about His neck. It's a burgundy

color. It's a beautiful cape with a golden attachment, a roping at His neck to hold the cape closed.

Now Our Lady is standing on Jesus' right now. And Jesus is whispering to Our Lady. I'm not able to hear what - oh, Our Lady is now touching Her lips, which means I must listen.

And Jesus is now making the sign of the cross, like this: In the name of the Father, and of the Son, and of the Holy Ghost.

Jesus is looking about Him. His cowl, that hat - piece He wears, has fallen down so that His hair now is blowing in the wind. And He's looking all about. Now He's going over with Our Lady - Our Lady is remaining on His right - but They are floating over to our left side, but Their right side, just beyond the trees, and Jesus is making the sign of the cross: In the name of the Father, and of the Son, and of the Holy Ghost.

Now as Jesus looks around, He's motioning to Our Lady, and They are going across the sky now. Our Lady now has gone ahead of Jesus. He motioned, and I would believe He told Her to go ahead first. And She's going across the sky and standing directly over the trees on our right side. Now Jesus is coming over, and now He's touching His lips, like this.

Jesus - "My child and My children, I send to all who come to this sacred ground the grace of perseverance in the days ahead. I want you to remember, My children, always, that when the thorns come among the roses you will say, My Jesus, my confidence!"

Veronica - Now Jesus is turning to His right side and He's starting to float. That's the only way you can explain it. He floats across the sky like He's weightless. Yet Jesus and Our Lady look as real as you and I. Others have come to the Shrine with Our Lady and Jesus, but they look different. They were sort of transparent, like St. Theresa, and Pope John, and all of them. They looked transparent, but Jesus and Our Lady are just as solid and human like as you and I.

Now Jesus is motioning to Our Lady and They're going

across the sky now, and They're coming up just over the statue, high in the sky. They're moving up, a little farther up over, so They're a little higher in the sky now, almost equal, I would say, to the last limb of the tree that's on our right side, the pine tree.

Now Our Lady is looking up, and Jesus whispered something to Her; I couldn't hear it. Now He's placing His first finger to His mouth.

Jesus - "My child and My children, it is most urgent that you read and live the messages given by My Mother from the Eternal Father in the Holy Ghost, and from Me, Her Son.

"She gave to you Her heart for all the past years of earth's time. I want you now, My children to understand and listen to My words, for soon they will be few, and actions will start.

"There will be much gnashing of teeth and woe set upon your country and the nations of the world by satan. Some say, My children, that he controls the world now. From looking in as a bystander, others may say there is time, there is much time. But no, My children, that is a delusion. You do not have much time. One grain remains now in the hour-glass. Your time is growing short.

"I must say to you now from the Eternal Father and the Holy Ghost, that We will not accept excuses coming from the human mentality of Our priests, Our bishops, and Our cardinals. They look about askance at the Message from Heaven. Would they have accepted it better if We patted them on the backs and just went about lackadaisical, figuring that perhaps they will figure out what this Message means in time? But they do not have this time! That is why, My child, We brought you tonight from your home and your bed, because the time is growing very short.

Children ensnared with evil In schools

"I could repeat over and over the Message from Heaven of the past years. But I say to you: murders abound, immorality abounds... all the immunisms of humanism, lesbianism... homosexuals roaming. Children! The dear chil-

167

dren, what will become of them? What kind of an example is being set in their homes? Parents who lack the light, how can they guide their children? Send them to schools? That will be no escape, for the children will be ensnared with evil.

"Oh, My Mother told you many years ago you were to bar your doors, for when your children left their homes they would enter into a world that is now being guided by satan to destroy your children. The only reason that this is taking place is because you could not understand, as a human being, the ways of Heaven. They are not the earth's ways or human ways.

"The Eternal Father has a plan for each life; however, in His merciful heart and His goodness, He gave you a free will to make your choice. When He placed satan, the fallen angel, upon earth, and the others who fought with him to dethrone the Eternal Father, they left him upon earth. And with good heart and love, the Eternal Father created man and all his descendants upon earth to fight this evil one who sought to dethrone the Eternal Father.

"But what has happened now? Many have turned against Me."

Veronica - Our Lady is crying. Our Lady is crying very hard now. It's - it's almost too heartbreaking to watch it.

Now Jesus is touching His lips.

Jesus - "My child, I know how this touches the hearts of Our loyal children, but I must warn the world, My child and My children, because only a few will be saved. But those few have just about been chosen, My children. I want you to know that no one - no man, woman or child of con- scionable age - will be lost unless he follows the path of satan, willingly, with his eyes wide open but blind; his ears, well and healthy, but deafened in a spiritual way.

"My child and My children, there are all manners of per- versions now going on throughout your land and all the nations of the world. And why? Because too few pray enough, too few are willing to make amends to the Eternal Father as victim souls. Too few care enough, thinking that life will go on eternal upon earth. Just remember, My children: each and every one of you has already had your name placed with all the members of Heaven. We know what your fate will be and We try to caution you.

"My child, suffering will be great upon the earth. Many shall be removed before the cataclysm.

Save the clergy

"You must all pray for your bishops, your cardinals and your pastors. It is like an illness among them now going from one to the other. They will have to accept their fate... not to take themselves away from the Church, My Church, My children. We do not want satan to close the doors. You must remain in your parish and stand there as an example as you speak with the priests and the cardinals and the bishops. You must keep your courage up and bring forth as witnesses, disciples of the latter days - you must go forward and try to save your brothers, those in the clergy. So few do pray for the clergy. The general idea, My child, is that they have a special passport to Heaven. But that is not true. Their temptations are far greater then yours. Therefore, they are to be pitied. For hell opened up would show unto you the numbers of mitres that have fallen in the past earth - years.

"Pray, My children, a constant vigilance of prayer. Pray that the murders cease - the murder of the unborn. Pray that Heaven will accept all of your prayers and your penances done with great heart for your priests, the clergy. Pray a constant vigilance of prayer, like a worldwide chain of prayers. You will take your Rosary and make it the leading point of your life. He who does not pray the Rosary once, at least once, in their homes, he who refuses to accept penance when given it to them by the Eternal Father, not knowing perhaps the value of penance, he you must pray for. There are so many prayers to be given, but We do not have enough, My children, to pray.

"The peoples, many are lukewarm. They come with great heart. They've heard the messages from Heaven, but what do they do? They get carried away with earth's pleasures and the pleasures of the flesh. I want you to know now

169

that that is what satan relies on. They watch and they wait while you fall to sin, and sin is the pleasure of the flesh. And man has this battle to win. It is a stomping ground now for satan, My children.

"You must always be on your guard. Let them call you fanatics. Let them try to break you down. There's only one thing to say to them: I have my eyes on Heaven. Where do you cast yours?

At last one Rosary a day

"Now, My children, you will continue with your prayers of atonement. Remember: one Rosary a day at least, at least I say, must be prayed in the home that is to be spared."

Veronica - Now Jesus is making the sign of the cross, like this: In the name of the Father, and of the Son, and of the Holy Ghost.

Now Jesus is nodding.

Jesus - "Continue, My children, with your prayers of atonement; they are sorely needed."

"You are surrounded now by reconnaissance planes and also by missiles"

14th Anniversary of Our Lady's Apparitions At Bayside - June 18, 1984

Veronica - Beyond Our Lady's statue there are lights emanating from the branches of the trees. The lights are blue and pink. I never saw this combination before at one time, blue and pink. That means that Our Lady and Jesus will be appearing. Now high over Our Lady's statue, there is a circular light, a light that seems to be growing closer and also wider in appearance.

Oh! Oh, directly over Our Lady's statue, I can see now the light has dimmed a bit and I can see Our Blessed Mother coming forward. She has on a most beautiful white gown; it's pure white, like sugar. And all about Her, there is a cape that's swirling in the massive winds tonight. The cape that Our Lady is wearing has gold trimming about three-quarters of an inch around the outside of the mantle. Our Lady has on very dainty slippers. They are closed, but on each foot of the slipper there is a small golden rosette. Our Lady looks absolutely beautiful.

Now I hadn't noticed since my full concentration was on Our Blessed Mother ... I looked up and there's Jesus now coming through the clouds. There are white clouds all surrounding Him. And He's coming forward now... He's very - He's not walking. He's floating. Our Blessed Mother and Jesus don't walk like we do, They float, like They're weightless; yet Jesus and Our Lady both look as solid as you and I.

Our Lady is looking now over Her left shoulder and She sees Jesus coming down... now getting closer to Her over the statue, and She's smiling; Our Lady is smiling. Now They're standing both together: Our Lady is on Jesus' right side, and now They're standing in perfect unity above the statue, I would say at least, maybe fifteen or twenty feet now above the statue. Now Our Lady is looking around, and She's taking from about Her waist Her Rosary, the Rosary with the golden Our Fathers and what appear to be the rainbow colors of the Hail Marys on Our Lady's beads. I do believe that the beads change color as Our Lady turns in each direction.

Now Our Lady is looking up to Jesus ... He's standing there. Jesus has nothing on His head now - no cowl. He has on a cape, a beautiful red velvet cape, which is held together - fastened by a bow made of like, gold silk cord, about His neck. Jesus' hair is blowing slightly in the wind. Now He's looking over to His Mother and nodding with a smile.

Our Lady now is taking out Her Rosary from about Her waist and She's blessing the people on Her right, like this: In the name of the Father, and of the Son, and of the Holy Ghost.

Now as Jesus is watching and He's nodding, Our Lady now returns over above the statue; and Jesus is over Her now - He's not standing beside Her but He seems to be higher in the sky. Our Lady is nodding with a smile and taking Her crucifix, Her golden crucifix on Her beautiful Rosary, and holding it up, like this, and blessing the people: In the name of the Father, and of the Son, and of the Holy Ghost.

Now Our Lady is turning to Her left, that would be our right, and starting to move towards the right side of the field here above the trees. Now Jesus is following... And Our Lady now is for the third time extending Her crucifix from Her Rosary out, like this, and making the sign of the cross: In the name of the Father, and of the Son, and of the Holy Ghost.

Now Our Lady is turning to Her right and She's now floating across the sky to join Jesus, Who's standing about fifteen to twenty feet above Our Lady's statue. Now They are both together: Our Lady is at Jesus' right side. Now Jesus is looking at Our Lady and nodding His head, and the Blessed Mother has touched now Her lips with Her first forefinger, which indicates directly that one must listen now and repeat.

Our Lady - "My child and My children, Our hearts are surely gladdened by all who have come here to the sacred grounds to be with Me and My Son on this wonderful occasion.

"It was many years ago that I came unto you, My child, Veronica, for a reason - and this reason has been accomplished by the mere fact that the words from Heaven have reached every major nation in the world, and the United States and Canada. The European market for the Message has been plentiful and fruitful.

"Know, My children, that nothing has been wasted - no act of charity has been wasted, and none shall say that they didn't try; because that is also the secret of success into the Kingdom of God, is that you will try to follow in My Son's steps."

Veronica - Now Our Lady is turning over and looking at Jesus, and motioning. Now Jesus - He's not moving His lips the way Our Lady does; He is actually - the only human way I could say is that He transfers His Being, the Holy Spirit, within you, to kind of, like take you over so that you could be a voice - box for Heaven. Now Jesus is nodding, and He's now touching His first fingers to His lips, like this.

Jesus - "My child and My children, We come with a joyful heart for all who have come to these sacred grounds. But Our hearts are heavily laden with grief because so many are still on the road to perdition. Ignorance may give them a short reprieve.

"In Portugal, My children - there's something I must tell you - in Portugal, I have made an appearance there, and I was among those who did not know Me because of the states' appointments - states, S - T - A - T - E - S appointment.

Floods shall increase

"My child and My children, you do not recognize the floods that have been set upon you. These floods shall increase, and many will die; and these floods shall be in diverse places, places not known before to have had such an occurrence. Many mother's hearts will be saddened.

"Also, My children, I have tried to warn you through My

173

Mother and countless other personages from Heaven to prepare, for you are fast heading for a war - the Third World War - the War that shall make mankind extinct but for the few who are chosen to keep up the Faithful and True banner before mankind - the Faithful and True banner that states. 'This is my Jesus.'"

Veronica - Now Jesus is going over slowly towards the top of the statue. He's standing there now and looking all about Him. There seems to be something very serious happening because He can barely talk. Jesus' voice is choked with emotion.

Jesus - "My child and My children, you must keep the Message from Heaven going throughout the world with haste, great haste, for no one knows the day or the hour. But We have recognized the signs and have given these to you, My children.

"The Eternal Father knows all and sees all, and knows every heart that has been placed upon earth. However, the Eternal Father has said there will be a great destruction upon mankind very soon, because of their lack of listening to the cautions of My Mother and Our appearances throughout the world. War is a punishment for man's sins. There will be wars and more wars, and yet their hearts are hardened, and their ears have deafened to the fact that this can happen in the United States, Canada, and any part of the world that the enemy has infiltrated to.

"My child, this is not a lesson in politics. This is but a lesson of reality, what will happen if you do not accept the messages from Heaven and pray, do penance; do much to help My Mother in Her Mission, for so many are needed, so many prayers are needed for those poor souls who have no one to pray for them.

"You ask, My child, countless times, in the power of God, why do you not just take them from the earth and cure them of their illness, the illness of ignorance and the illness of avarice. My child, there is one thing you must understand: man has a free will and shall not be forced through the gates of Heaven. He must come of his own free will.

"Many prayers and penance's that have taken place throughout the world, given to those souls who need them most, have saved many from purgatory. The day will come when all of you will understand fully the Message from Heaven, and the existence of hell, purgatory, and Heaven.

Plot afoot against Vicar

"Do not let those who preach heresy change your hearts and take you away from My Church. Your Vicar is in great danger. Once more, there is a plot now afoot against him. He has many enemies. Though he has a loving heart, he has many enemies, as so did I upon the cross.

15 decades a day

"My children, you will all pray your Rosary daily, even if it means to stop the work you are doing. You will excuse yourself and retire to a quiet place in your office threshold. The Rosary must be said at least once a day, the fifteen decades. All who pray the Rosary and wear My Scapular shall be saved. All who place the crucifix upon their front doors shall be saved like the passing of the lamb.

"My child and My children, I do not have to stress to you the numbers of young souls that are being destroyed in wars that are going on now throughout your world. Do not become complacent, My children; do not think that this cannot happen here and there is no danger. The greatest danger for the United States and Canada comes from infiltration into every manner of business, and even the Holy Church of God.

"Satan has entered upon the world sometime ago, as My Mother expressed to you, and he roams now like a ravenous wolf; and if you do not keep your sacramentals about your neck, the chances are 99%, My children, that you will fall. If you understand the necessity of the brown Scapular, you will understand also the necessity of keeping yourselves in the world, but not of the world. You must work for Heaven with a fervor that comes from the heart. And do not go about with lip service; there must be acts of charity among your people.

"My child, I request that all will relearn the acts of Faith, Hope, and Charity. Now, My child, you will repeat:

'I believe in God, the Father Almighty, Creator of Heaven and earth; and in Jesus Christ, His only Son, Our Lord; Who was conceived by the Holy Ghost, born of the Virgin Mary, suffered under Pontius Pilate, was crucified, died and was buried. He descended into hell; the third day He arose again from the dead; He ascended into Heaven, sitteth at the right hand of God, the Father Almighty; from thence He shall come to judge the living and the dead. I believe in the Holy Ghost, the Holy Catholic Church, the communion of saints, the forgiveness of sins, the resurrection of the life, and life everlasting. Amen.'"

Veronica - Jesus is now going over to His Mother... He has placed His hand protectively upon Her shoulder, and Our Lady is smiling, but there are tears coming down Her face; I can see the tears. Our Lady is crying. Now Our Lady is trying to compose Herself, and She's leaning over now and looking at everyone. And then She nods to Jesus, and Jesus is standing over Our Lady's area now; He's not above the statue, He's slightly to the right of the trees.

Now He's extending His hand out, like this, and making the sign of the cross: In the name of the Father, and of the Son, and of the Holy Ghost.

Now Jesus is turning... Our Lady had remained above Her statue silently with Her hands crossed, like this, across Her chest, with Her Rosary dangling in Her right hand; She has Her hands crossed about Her chest. And Jesus is coming over now... And Our Lady is taking Her Rosary, which was about Her waist, and holding it in Her hand; and the golden crucifix that Our Lady has on Her beads, it's shimmering so brilliantly that it's very difficult to look into Our Lady's facial area, because of the way the Rosary is shining all about Her.

Now Jesus has come over, and He's touched His fingers to His lips as Our Lady does. Our Lady has a very sad smile; She's trying desperately to smile, but the tears are just pouring down Her face. Now Jesus is extending His hand out, like this, again, and making the sign of the cross: In the name of the Father, and of the Son, and of the Holy Ghost.

Now Jesus is starting to float with Our Lady. They don't walk; They're - it looks like They're weightless. It's very difficult to put into human language the way They are able to maneuver in the air - on the air.

Now Jesus and Our Lady are both moving over to our left side, beyond the statue between the trees. And Jesus is looking down now, and He's making the sign of the cross: In the name of the Father, and of the Son, and of the Holy Ghost.

Now Our Lady is nodding. And She has on now, on Her head - I did not notice it before, but Our Lady has the Fatima crown, the large Fatima crown, upon Her head. And now She's got Her hands together, like this... and Our Lady looks so regal - every, every inch a queen. Her beauty is perfection. There is no human way to describe this, and the light that emanates from Them, there is no human words to describe this either. It's a phenomenon that's beyond human understanding, but not beyond the power of God.

Now Our Lady is taking out Her crucifix and extending it for everyone to be blessed again with the Rosary: In the name of the Father, and of the Son, and of the Holy Ghost.

Now Our Lady is kissing the crucifix of Her Rosary, and She's placing it back now in Her belting.

Now Jesus is - He looks a little stern. Now Jesus is touching His fingers to His lips, which means to listen carefully and repeat.

On brink of World War III

Jesus - "My child and My children, you do not understand how close you are on the brink to the Third World War, which could break out any day now. All who are ready will not suffer the great cataclysm brought on by evil minds.

177

You must all work and pray and do penance for peace among all nations; for We love Our children and We do not want to see them die, for many are unprepared and they come without Baptism.

"My child and My children, there must be many missionaries throughout the world that must help these lost souls, these ignorant souls. It is your duty as a Catholic, a Roman Catholic, to spread the Message of God and save some of these poor souls, for each one is a blossom upon the rose-bush, and we cannot let them be trampled on. Love your neighbors as you would love your children, your family. Love them also as part of your family of Christian souls upon earth."

Veronica - Now Jesus is floating over towards the left side of the exedra. And He's extending His hand out, like this, again: In the name of the Father, and of the Son, and of the Holy Ghost.

Now Jesus is touching His first finger to His lips, which means to listen.

Jesus - "My child and My children, and especially My children of the United States of America, you are surrounded now by reconnaissance planes and, also, you are surrounded by missiles. Know that your world is not safe any longer. This must be told to you, My children, to try to waken you up to the fact that now is the time to pray, that now is the time to do penance. Do not put it off for another day, for many of you shall not see the dawn of that day.

St. Michael Exorcism

"I admonish you all, My children, as the Father in Heaven admonishes you in the Holy Spirit, to do what you can, with your heart and your love of charity, to help others and help them back onto the narrow road. So many have lost their way and are traveling the wide road that leads to hell. Lucifer is upon earth; you understand that his powers are great. That is why you must always test the spirits and say the St. Michael Exorcism when it is possible. When it is not possible, you will say:

178

'St. Michael the Archangel, defend us in battle. Be our protection against the wickedness and snares of the devil. May God rebuke him, we humbly pray. And do thou, O prince of the heavenly host, by the power of God, cast into hell satan and all evil spirits who roam now throughout the world seeking the ruin of souls.'

"You will remain seated, My child, and receive further instructions. But We wish now, through our media of the camera, that you take three photographs and read them carefully."

Veronica - Now the light is growing very dim above Our Lady's statue. And there's a quietness that is so difficult to explain, as though They've gone beyond - the only way I can explain it is like going through a looking-glass without shattering it. They - Our Lady and Jesus are now rising above Our Lady's statue, and Our Lady is smiling and She's placing Her finger now to Her lips.

Our Lady - "Do not be affrighted, My children and My child, We are not leaving. We will be here with you until the end of this struggle for the power of God to replace the heresy of the world."

[Pause]

Rosary beads shall turn color

Our Lady - "With the extension of the Rosary, many shall now receive the power through the Holy Spirit, the Holy Ghost, to bring health of body and health of spirit to each soul. You will find that your Rosary beads shall turn color again. The stems will become pure gold. So do not cast aside your Rosary, thinking falsely, as satan would whisper into your ear that they're not good anymore and must be thrown away. That you will understand, that every Rosary that has been blessed by the presence of the Mother of God, Jesus, and the Eternal Father in the Holy Ghost, know that these Rosaries are very powerful. So you will keep them with you always for they will have the power for cure and for conversion - cure of the ailing body and conversion of the sickened soul.

"My child and My children, you will continue to spread the Message throughout the world in great haste. And you, My child, shall not count the cost of keeping the Mission going, for all will be supplied with your needs."

[Pause]

Veronica - Now there will be three - three photographs taken, Our Lady said.

"Communion in the hand is a sacrilege"

In Honor of the Visitation of Mary - June 30, 1984

Veronica - All about the trees now there are beautiful cascading lights, pink and blue. This always summons us to the knowledge, and gives us the knowledge that Our Lady and Jesus are approaching within range of our seeing.

Now all about the trees there's a beautiful light forming, and it's cascading, the light, upwards, high into the sky over Our Lady's statue. Oh, it's just so beautiful, the light. I can't explain it in human words; there are no words that can fit the beauty of the light that is emanating all about the trees and high now into the heavens. Now directly over Our Lady's statue, the sky is opening up in a circular pattern of light. It appears that we are having the most beautiful evening. The stars are shining, the sky is clear.

And Our Lady and Jesus now - I can see Them - They are coming from quite a distance, but They're both coming down together. Our Lady now... I can notice the shining crown upon Her head... And Jesus now has tapped Her on the shoulder and He is pointing all about Him, bringing attention to Our Lady of all of the wonderful peoples who are here to greet Them this evening. Now Jesus and Our Lady are coming now slowly through the sky downward. I would say now that Jesus and Our Lady are about fifteen feet above the statue.

Our Lady has on the most beautiful white gown. It has a border of gold of about - oh, about an inch all about the mantle, the cape. And on Her head She has the most beautiful crown. I've always referred to it as the Fatima crown, because that's exactly what it looks like.

Now Our Lady is looking about... And it's a little windy up there because even Jesus' cape is being caught in the wind. Jesus has on a burgundy colored cape, and His gown is an off - white, like a beige. And Jesus has a tie about His neck. It's made of gold. It's a cord - like tie, and that's holding the mantle, Jesus' robe, on His shoulders.

He has on a pair of slippers that are sandals. I believe they're made of some type of animal - skin because the sandals are open, and Jesus would be barefooted but for the sandals.

Looking over to Our Lady, I notice Our Lady has on very dainty slippers. They're white, but in the center of each instep there is a little rosette, a beautiful little golden rosette.

Now Our Lady and Jesus are coming closer to us now. Jesus is raising His hand, like this, and making the sign of the cross: In the name of the Father, and of the Son, and of the Holy Ghost.

Our Lady now has taken the Rosary from about Her waist - Our Lady has Her Rosary wrapped about the cording around Her waist - and She's taking it out now and She's making the sign of the cross, like this: In the name of the Father, and of the Son, and of the Holy Ghost.

Now Our Lady and Jesus are standing there... Our Lady has placed Her hands together, like this, in a prayerful stance, and I notice that Her Rosary. Our Lady's Rosary, is dangling from her fingers. She has the crucifix in the palms of Her hands, and the rest of the Rosary is dangling. And as it is going to-and-fro from the motion of Our Lady's hands coming upward, all the colors of the rainbow appear to be cascading from the Hail Marys of Her Rosary.

Now Jesus has tapped Our Lady on the shoulder, and He's motioning with His finger to His lips; that means that Our Lady would like to converse with me privately.

[Pause]

Veronica - Yes.

Now Our Lady is touching Her lips again with Her two fingers, which, means that I will listen and repeat.

Our Lady - "My child and My children, Our hearts are heavy this evening because the evils that We have warned you of have accelerated throughout the world.

Mass celebrated without honor or sacrifice

"My Son's heart is bleeding because of the manner in which His Mass is being celebrated, with neither honor nor sacrifice. My Son is not pleased with the manner in which His Body and Blood is being given to all of the humans upon earth. Communion in the hand has not been, and will not be, accepted by Heaven. This is a sacrilege in the eyes of the Eternal Father, and must not be continued, for you only add to your punishment when you continue on in the ways that have been found to be unpleasing to the Eternal Father.

Gross cult taking children

"Your children have become innocent victims of their elders. Many parents are crying because their children have been taken from them, never to be seen again. I want you to know at this time, My child and My children, that there is a gross cult, a cult in your country now, that is taking children from their homes to be grown up in an atmosphere of debauchery. O My children, whatever shall become of you?

"I have traveled throughout your world through countless earth - years warning you that you are approaching a most terrible punishment. And how can we stop this now? It has progressed and is too late to be stopped.

"O My children, I know there are many that cry with Me. I go about the world now with tears constantly flowing upon My children. My tears shall not stop, for I know now that all of the cataclysms, and all of the floods, and all of the droughts shall continue. Mankind must be awakened from their slumbers, for they shall be punished in a way far worse than the human mind could comprehend.

"I tried to warn you, My children, that there is great talk, talk, and action going on now throughout your country, but the talks will get you nowhere, for they do not talk of the Eternal Father. They talk of peace, peace, upon earth where there is no peace. There shall never be peace without your God. No man is a god, and as such he shall not make himself a god in the eyes of others.

"O My children, I beg you, as your Mother, to listen to Me. My voice grows weak. I have raised up other voice - boxes throughout the world now to try to reach those who have not deafened their ears to Our pleas. We ask you all to keep a constant vigilance of prayer going throughout your country and the world.

Plan In motion for invasion

"Your country, the United States of America, is in great danger for invasion. Already the plan is in motion. I warn you again: The United States of America is in great danger of invasion. You are surrounded now by the enemy.

"Do not be misled by your news medias. They are not telling you the full truth. There is much going on that is kept hidden from you. Your country, the United States of America, and also Canada, has been invaded from within. The enemy has worked their way in well. It has taken years - years in which I came to you, as your Mother, and begged you to listen while there was time. But who cared enough to listen? Only those few who We now depend on to go forth and bring the Message to the world.

A mysterious disease

"The children, the innocent children, are victims of debauchery. The children - many of them shall die. We shall set upon your nation, and other nations of the world, a mysterious disease. But be it known now: It will not be a mysterious disease but the hand of the Eternal Father placed down to remove these innocent souls before they are sent into debauchery. O My children, the missing children in your countries are not just missing because they want to be adopted, or others wished to take them into their homes as children to be loved. They are being taken to be used in all foul manners.

"O My children, I beg you, as your Mother, listen to Me. I shall never give up hope that you will listen to Me as My tears flow upon you."

Veronica - Our Lady now is crying. The tears are just - it's like raining from Heaven; the tears are falling down now upon us. I can feel them washing my face.

"But, Blessed Mother, I wish that I could help you in some manner of more sacrifice..."

Now Jesus is looking down at His Mother; She's turned Her head away to wipe the tears from Her face. And Jesus now is turning towards me, and He's placing His first finger to His lips.

Blood In New York streets

Jesus - "My child and My children, My Mother - My Mother, My dear Mother - Her tears are falling upon the nations, for She knows as I do what has befallen mankind and what the future holds. I warn you all now; You are approaching a terrible crisis, a crisis that will involve death. Blood shall flow from the streets of New York soon.

"My children, that does not mean that you will flee, for you will find it will be of no use to flee the carnage, for you will not be safe anywhere but under the mantle of My Mother. And all who wear their scapulars and the Rosary will be saved. But all those who cast them aside as superstition shall be lost.

"My children, you must wear your armor and protect your homes. I have asked you many times to bar your homes to all but your immediate family and close Shrine workers, for those who knock upon your doors will be evil, and will be sent there to invade you.

"O My children, what a world We are looking upon! Never has sin been so sophisticated and accepted as normal. No sin shall go unpunished. I want you to know now: there is a Heaven, there is a hell, and there is purgatory. And you, My children, of your own free will, will choose where you will go. No man shall go to hell unless he wants this and accepts it, and has turned to satan as his leader.

Many satanic cults

"There are many satanic cults, My child, in your country, in Canada, and in all the nations of the world. Satan has done his work well, but he knows that his time is limited.

185

Therefore, he will now gather more disciples to be among you. You will be given the knowledge, My children, when you wear your scapular and keep your Rosary with you - you would be given the knowledge to recognize the face of evil. Though they wear the bodies of men, they are demons in human form.

"I warn you now: All of those - what they call flying saucers, My children - they are not flying saucers. They are vehicles from hell transporting demons from place to place. Though they be spirits, there is a mystery of the living dead that you do not know. They must be transported; they cannot go upon their own. This is a mystery that I shall, perhaps in the future, give you the knowledge of.

"My child and My children, you must pray constantly. The sound of prayer is like cymbals clanging through their ears, and they must run and flee from you. So you must keep a constant vigilance of prayer going throughout your life. Your station in life means nothing. You must pray, for you will lose everything - your station, your home, your children, your lives.

"O My child, if only I could come with words of cheer. But can I deceive you? I am not the deceiver, I must tell you the truth. And the only way you can protect yourselves and your family is by knowing the truth.

Grain starting to go through

"Keep a constant vigilance of prayer going throughout your world, your country, your home, and you will be saved. There is still time to turn back. How much time is given to you? The one grain is beginning to now go through the hourglass. That will tell you, My child and My children, how serious a situation now is upon us.

"Look up into the sky, My child-"

Veronica - Directly over Our Lady's statue there's a large glove, but it's very black - looking and dark. But I know it's a globe of the world with a huge cross on it. But now flames - flames are leaping out from each side of the ball. It looks like the world's afire. It's a frightening thing, the most

186

frightening thing! Oh, God have mercy upon us all! Mercy!

Now Our Lady is coming forward, and the burning world is now evaporating, and Our Lady is touching Her first finger to Her lips. She's still crying; the tears are coming down from Her eyes onto us. And I know these tears are falling on many, because I can feel them now on my face.

Our Lady - "I cry, My tears fall upon you, My children. O how blind many are! I love each and every child that has been placed upon earth, but My heart is burdened by those who have been aborted. The Eternal Father sent the little ones upon your earth for a reason, and they were murdered! This shall not be allowed. They were murdered! Any country that allows the murders of the young and the unborn shall be destroyed. Any country that allows homosexuals to roam and to seduce the young shall be destroyed. Any country that has defamed My Son in the Holy Sacrifice of the Mass will be destroyed.

"My child and My children, I know how concerned you are with the sternness of the message, but you must understand the truth must be told. It is only by truth that you can be saved."

Veronica - Our Lady is pointing over now to Her left side, that would be our right side, and over... I can see a map, and I know it's a map of Europe, Western Europe. There's something going on there.

War in western part of Germany

Our Lady - "It has not started, My child, but there will be great confusion, and war shall break out in the western part of Germany."

Veronica - Now Our Lady is pointing over to Her right side, our left side, and there's another map. And I see Israel, and countries about it; they're all aflame. And the way it's circular, it looks like part of the flames that I saw coming out from within the ball before.

Our Lady - "Wars, My children, are a punishment for man's sins. The wars shall increase, and the carnage shall increase, and those who are living will often envy the dead, so great will be the suffering of mankind. All of this suffering, My children, mankind has brought upon himself. When he left the Eternal Father he turned to satan, and this is his reward.

Masses and sacrifices to save Pope

"O My children, pray, pray! Pray for your Vicar. There will be another attempt upon his life. Pray for your Vicar. Do not judge him by the medias, for he is a good man, with a heart that is soft, and often he can be misled. However, he is a good man, and he is one who I keep now under My mantle for his protection. But We need your prayers, My children, your Masses and your sacrifices, if you want him to remain among you. As I say, I will repeat again: There will be another attempt upon his life, and this one, My child, shall be serious."

Veronica - Now Our Lady is going over to our right side, that would be Her left side, and She's lifting Her Rosary - the beautiful golden crucifix, with the beads of all colors - and She's making the sign of the cross: In the name of the Father, and of the Son, and of the Holy Ghost.

Our Lady now is kissing Her crucifix, and She is also touching Her first finger to Her lips.

Our Lady - "My child, you must make it known to all that all of the Rosaries blessed this evening, and all of the sacramentals, shall be used in the future for cures and conversions: cures of the body and the spirit; conversions of the soul, conversions of unbelievers."

Jesus - "This We give to you from Our hearts that are filled with love for Our children, even those who have turned away from Us. We love you all, My children, and We want to save you. That is why My Mother has constantly appeared upon earth: because We don't want satan to have one of Our children. Pray for your brothers and sisters; do not judge them, but pray for them that they have the strength to come from within and out of satan's grasp."

Veronica - Now Our Lady is making the sign of the cross again: In the name of the Father, and of the Son, and of the Holy Ghost.

Now Jesus is coming... Jesus was standing by the tree over on our right side, and He's coming over to Our Lady, and He's placing His arm about Her shoulders. Our Lady is crying. It's been many years since I have seen Our Lady cry so much and so hard.

And now Our Lady is holding up in Her hand a heart. It is actually a pulsating heart, but it's got all knives in it - wounds.

Our Lady - "See My heart, My child, torn with grief due to the abuses to My Son. I love My Son, and I want you all to love My Son, as He loves you all, in the Father, the Son, and the Holy Ghost. We bring these words to you and these words of caution from the Eternal Father. For satan is loosed upon your earth, and many have already been taken captive by him.

Crucifix on front and back door

Jesus - "Pray and wear your sacramentals. And, also, My children, I ask you again to place a crucifix upon your door. Both front and back doors must have a crucifix. I say this to you because there will be carnage within your areas, and this will pass you by if you keep your crucifix upon your doors.

"My child, Veronica, you will not become duly concerned about finances. As I told you once before, I will see that the needs for My Mother's Shrine are filled."

[Pause]

Veronica - Now Our Lady and Jesus and rising high into the sky; They're not leaving. They're going to stand there. Our Lady is saying something to Jesus; I can't hear from here. Oh! Oh, Our Lady said They are not leaving; They will be here. And you must continue with your prayers of atonement.

Hail Mary, full of grace, the Lord is with thee. Blessed are thou among woman and blessed is the fruit of Thy womb, Jesus. Holy Mary, Mother of God, pray for us, sinners, now and at the hour of our death. Amen.

"That treaty must be rescinded"

Eve of the Feast of the Visitation of Mary - July 1, 1985

Veronica - There are blue lights cascading all about the outside of the trees, directly over Our Lady's statue. Now high overhead - I can't actually figure in lengths of miles - I see Our Lady's beautiful white light. It's coming through like a ball. Oh! It is, it's a ball. And Our Lady is standing on top of it, but She's so luminous it's very difficult for me to look through the light until She comes down farther from the sky.

Now Our Lady is riding this ball very fast, and She's now directly above, on the ball, above the tree that's above Our Lady's statue here. Now Our Lady is stepping off. The ball is suspended in mid - air. It looks like a ball, yet I can't make out the figures on it. Yes, Oh, it isn't a ball, it's actually a globe of the world, because the figures I can't make out are in all directions, and some of them are blackened, some of them are in red, and some in white.

Now Our Lady is motioning to me. She's holding Her Rosary, like this, while the ball is suspended, our earth, at Her left side. Our Lady is going over to our left side, just beyond the first large tree towards the statue, and She's extending Her beautiful crucifix on Her Rosary, the Rosary with the golden Our Fathers and the white Hail Marys, that cascade all colors as She's turning. Our Lady is blessing everyone: In the name of the Father, and of the Son, and of the Holy Ghost.

Now Our Lady is looking about. Her beautiful white gown - She has on the beautiful white gown, and also a mantle. The mantle is pure white. Now I can see above Our Lady's waist, just a little above the narrow part of the waist. She has on a gold chain - like, corded belt like, to hold Her gown. Now Our Lady has Her mantle completely about Her head and Her shoulders, I cannot see Her hair. The mantle is a pure white, that's actually luminous and glistening. And about Our Lady's mantle there's a small border of

190

about a half an inch of gold, all about Our Lady's mantle.

Now Our Lady is taking the crucifix of Her Rosary and kissing it, like this.

And now She's going over. And the globe is remaining stationary, though it had moved while I was watching Our Lady on the left side. The globe has obviously moved farther over to our right side now. And Our Lady now is approaching the first tree, the very tall tree over Her statue.

Now Our Lady is taking Her finger, like this, and motioning to Her lips, which means to listen, My child, and repeat. Our Lady is bowing Her head, yes. She's holding Her Rosary, as though to give Her strength for some very urgent Message to the world.

Our Lady - "My child and My children of the world, I come to you with great news, not one, though, of joy, but of pity and sorrow. I say sorrow, because for many earth - years I have wandered among you, from place to place, and country to country, trying to warn you to avert this coming Chastisement, which is fast approaching mankind. Many shall die in the great flame of the Ball of Redemption.

"All scoffers will learn too late that the Mission from Heaven was urgent and sorely needed, for the numbers of sin, those children in sin, are counted now not in the few but in the multitudes, falling fast into hell."

Veronica - Now Our Lady is looking up and pointing towards the heavens. And as I watch Her, She's going over and She's now, though directly by the ball, and She's showing sections of the ball to me with Her finger.

Our Lady - "There it will burst in flames, My child."

Veronica - Now that's - I can see from the ball that it's an actual globe of the world, like we have on our desk in school. And the first place to burst into flames is Africa. Now Our Lady is pointing farther up on the globes, and She's saying now.

Our Lady - "Listen, My child, and repeat this well. "The United States of America is fast approaching on the start of the Third World War. My children, your newspapers and your medias give no account of these secret missions.

There are men going from the State's Department, back and forth, hinder and yon, looking for peace, peace, where there is no peace; and peace where there shall be no peace, unless they follow the directions of the Eternal Father and the Messages given from Heaven in the past years; not alone on these grounds, My children, of Bayside and Flushing Meadows, but also to various seers, young and old, about the world. The world is crying, peace, peace, and there will be no peace, unless the world will recognize My warnings of caution from years ago in earth's time, and they do something about it.

"I have promised you peace, My children, if you will go forth with your Rosary in one hand and the Brown Scapular about your neck. How many have cast aside their armor because they fear or they are afraid of the mockery of those who have already hardened their hearts to the truth. And their eyes and hearts are eternally blinded, for many of them shall fall into hell, and many of them shall be wearing their red birettas.

Clerics planning death of Pope

"My child, I say this, for satan has entered into the highest realms of the Hierarchy now. And this I say unto you, stop them now while there is time. Approach your priests, for they are planning the extermination of Pope John Paul II before the Synod.

"What can I do, My child, you say to yourself, as this goes through your head with fear. There is nothing to fear, My child; I have given you the course. You will pray the Rosary daily. My children, link to link, bead to bead, going throughout the whole world. For I repeat, your time is about up; any day, any hour, you will face the major part of the Chastisement.

"My children, I caution you now, and I wish that you remember these instructions from several years ago in earth's time that I gave to you, to keep in your homes a good supply of canned good. They have shelf value, My children, they will not spoil. But better that you keep them and they spoil than to have come upon you the great Chastisement. It will be a ball of fire which will ignite many of the chemicals that are being stored up for the destruction of the nations.

"My children, I repeat anew: Why has Rome and Our Vicar given up the course that the Eternal Father give to Me to pass on to you children? Why are they opening the doors for another attempt at assassination to your Pope, Our son, John Paul II?

Store canned goods, water and blankets

"My children, not only with the canned foods will you store just food, but you must also make known to your families and your friends that they had best keep blankets and water in tight containers; for there will be on the onset of the Chastisement, there will be nothing that you can buy due to contamination.

"Your homes are protected by a supernatural being, with St. Michael, the head of the armies from Heaven. Just as in the days of old, so will it be, My children, that there will be sent to you an angel of death, but in human form.

"While the world cries, peace, peace and salvation, they do not look in the right direction. They are depending on the scientists of the world, who are ever seeking but never coming to the truth. These scientists have created now arsenals of ammunition, and warheads and missiles, in which they seek to gain control of the world.

Nations to disappear in 3 to 5 minutes

"And, My children, it does not take much knowledge or a learned being to understand that Heaven alerts you now to the dangers of the onslaught of Communism. Satan, being at the controls, will soon have one who is possessed, and of, also, a major rank in the world today, to press that one little technical, technological wizard, not in human form but in mechanical form. Like a robot, this will go forth among the nations, and nations shall disappear from the earth in the short time of three to five minutes."

Veronica - Oh! Oh! (Veronica sighs heavily.)

Our Lady - "My child, I cry tears of great pity for you. Do not be afeared, My child; I have made a promise to you that if you do My Mission, using every ounce of the energy that you can in a broken down body, you will save many souls, My child. For a reward, I say unto you: your children will be saved.

"The world may call it the onslaught of holocaust, but not many will have the opportunity to try to figure what has happened about them, as they run back and forth and try to flee before the Chastisement. Don't look back, My children, as you find the bodies, black - dead bodies - lying among your roads. Do not touch them or you will die, also.

Russia has not been converted

"This will tell you, My child and My children, that the major Chastisement shall be a Third World War, which is in the planning now. Russia has not been converted. And why? Because the Message I gave many years ago to the little children, and to those who had the heart to seek for the truth, I told them that unless they prayed the Rosary and wore their Brown Scapulars, death shall be a place among the living: death, such as no man could perceive in his human mind, to see the destruction of missiles and other contemptible, technological implements, made strictly from the knowledge of satan.

"In the Church, My child, cry with Me. My tears fall upon you and your children, and all of the children of the world, because of the fact that many shall die in the great flames of the Ball of Redemption; and, also, the technological weapons of the enemy, Russia. All of these munitions are being sent throughout the world. They are building up armaments beyond what man could conceive. This you must know, because only you, My children, who hear My words and act upon them, shall be saved.

"Your children, I cry for you, poor mothers. Know that My Mother's heart is solaced only by the knowledge that these children shall not be lost to Heaven. But your young children have been disappearing from your homes. And where are they, as you go to and fro, looking for your children, and My Mother's tears fall upon you? Many shall be found dead, but others shall never be found, for they are disposed of in a most despicable way by a group known as the satanist.

Twelve major covens on Long Island

"These groups, My child and My children, are increasing, even on your island of Long Island. There are at least twelve major covens, and they are using human sacrifice. These bodies, My children, cannot be found by the police, or other authorities who seek to help and to solace the hearts of the family members of the lost child.

"But I tell you this now, why we have the abomination of murders of children, for they are possessed by satan, those who will set into motion laws, laws that are against God. Your country, My child, the United States, shall feel war as never have they conceived in their minds, that this could enter upon the glorious nation of the United States and Canada. No, My children, you cannot escape this. Your time is running out.

Boil water for home use

"My child, I wish that you boil the water in your home. I will tell you now, My children, if you are receiving waters for your use in your homes, it must be boiled, because the contamination of chemicals and waste matter - nuclear waste matter - is driving down into the soils of the nation and polluting these waters, which will bring imminent death to many.

"My child, you are affrighted at much I have to say, but that is the reason, My child, We took you out of your sickbed and brought you, through the grace of the Father, to these grounds tonight.

"It was imminent that on the 18th you listen and follow My directions, My child, and you did well, for you have saved a soul from hell. Yes, My child, I know you are shivering when you think of hell. And when I took you down to see hell and purgatory, My children and My child - My child, especially you Veronica - you know that My words cannot be taken lightly, for you lived them. You lived the consequences of such evil when you could not attend on the 18th. Pray, My children, a constant vigilance of prayer.

"And also, at this time, I wish to extend My Mother's heart of comfort to Father S. It was the Eternal Father's will that he come unto you. But, naturally, as he joined the flock from Heaven, the wolves were after him and dispersed him from among the flock. His heart is known to Me, My children, so do not seek to find reasons for his present conduct. He will come back, but he will have a heavy cross to carry when he returns. We are proud of Our son that he did much to spread the Message from Heaven.

"My child and My children, pray for those poor mothers who had the missing children. There will be great punishments before this major Chastisement, My child. There will be many punishments; many tears shall flow from the mothers eyes, and their hearts shall be opened for mercy, begging for mercy.

"My child, I wish at this time that you will take three pictures. They are very important, because as I have made known to you before, and you will repeat again: satan has entered into the highest realms of the Hierarchy. A Church in darkness wears a band of death about it. Better that there be a few with quality than nothingness. For without the light of God truly shining within My Son's churches on earth, they will become darkened, as they take with them onto the road to perdition many souls. Do not judge them, My children, when you come upon these lost souls, but pray for their salvation, for many have been misled.

"As I said before, My Son's Church is in great crisis. The enemies of God, with Russia as the head, now seek to destroy the knowledge of the Eternal Father in the Trinity. My Son, they seek to take My Son from history and try to defame Him for their own gains.

"And, My children, warn others throughout the world that they must not use My Son's name in profanity and anger. My Son's name is being abused to the point now where the Eternal Father has His heavy hand near the Ball that sets at the foot of His throne."

Veronica - Our Lady, Our Lady is pointing over now - She's standing directly over the statue in the center of the Pavilion. Our Lady is pointing over and She says to listen, My child.

Our Lady - "See that picture, My child. There is silver, much silver being placed upon a table, and hungry eyes look at it until like the magic of satanism their minds are clouded. And I see among them many clerics; they are Roman Catholic clerics. They are among those..."

Veronica - Oh! (Veronica sighs with much distress.)

Our Lady - "... who are plotting the assassination of Pope John Paul II. May God, My children, have mercy on their souls, and stop them before it is too late. They cannot hide their guilt from the Eternal Father. And as they mislead the flock, and even stoop to murder to get their way, the are nothing but agents of hell.

"My child, take three photographs, and then I will speak again."

Veronica - Our Lady is pointing up to the sky, and high up in the sky, I see St. Peter's in Rome. Our Lady is now over the dome of St. Peter's and She is taking Her mantle, and it opens very wide, Our Lady is spreading it over St. Peter's Basilica.

Now Our Lady is touching Her lips, which means to listen well.

Our Lady - "My child, I shall send many agents from Heaven, angels to protect the Holy Father. But you who are on earth must do your part, for in no way must you have a measure, in the end, of responsibility for your lack of cooperation with the instructions from Heaven to save your Holy Father, the Vicar on earth, John Paul II.

"My child, immediately take the three pictures, and remain within yourself until I speak to you again."

[Pause]

Veronica - I can repeat?

Our Lady - "Yes, My child, you may repeat. The pictures will bear this out. Do not be affrighted of retaliation; never be affrighted, My child, for you are following the directions from Heaven well, and must continue to do so."

Veronica - Our Lady is holding up a parchment of paper.

Our Lady - "Look, My child, what has been written down. From where and whence did this parchment of reconciliation with Russia originate, signed by many Cardinals? O, My child, My heart is bleeding."

Veronica - Oh! (Veronica sighs.) Our Lady's mantle has set apart a bit, and I see a heart, Her heart, and there are knives and thorns, a whole cluster of thorns, just like they put on Jesus' head before He died. Oh!

(Veronica sighs heavily.)

Our Lady - "Take the pictures now, My child, and I shall ponder whence to give you the last of the Message."

[Pause]

Our Lady - "Among those who went forth to harm the Church of Rome, there was Cardinal Jean Villot. He has received his just penance.

Rescind Vatican - Russia treaty

"The parchment of paper contains the words that made a treaty between the Vatican and Russia. That treaty must be rescinded. There are, My child, still living ... three living upon earth, who were members of the drafting of this treaty.

"Now, My child, you will read the photographs."

Veronica - All about the trees and back of Our Lady's statue, there are pink lights coming down in streamers from the heavens. And directly over Our Lady's statue, high in the sky, there's a circlet of light. I always feel since seeing that with St. Theresa and other personages that are in Heaven, that it had something very, very special about that circlet of light, that someday Our Lady may reveal to us; it's something supernatural.

But! Jesus is coming forward now. He's hearing me.

He's smiling and He - the light is dimming quite a bit as He's coming down now. He's standing directly over Our Lady's statue. I can't count in feet, but I would say He's at least seven feet over the statue. Now Jesus is looking all about Him, and it's quite windy because His cape is blowing out from Him as He's looking back and forth with a smile.

Now His hair is down... He has no cowl on the back of His robe. Now the robe is a burgundy color. And this evening - I don't know if I saw it with gold on it - it has gold all about the outside, about a half an inch of gold trimming all throughout the cape.

Now Jesus, His gown underneath is not that long, that I can see His feet. He's wearing sandals, but they look like they were made from some kind of brown skin, skin - like material, animal skin.

Now Jesus is looking about Him. Now He's moving over to our left side, that would be - people on the other direction, their right side - but from where we are, He's moving over to His right side, our left side.

And now He's raising His hand, like this, and making the sign of the cross: In the name of the Father, and of the Son, and of the Holy Ghost.

Now Jesus is looking over to our right side, and He's moving very slowly. He's looking all about Him. And He's now directly over again Our Lady's statue. He had wandered over, and then seemed to hesitate for some reason, and come back to the center.

Now He's extending His hands and His arms, like this: In the name of the Father, and of the Son, and of the Holy Ghost.

Now He's making a fast turn to His left, our right, and He's going across the sky, and He's standing now about two feet above the bushes, the trees, about two feet above.

Now Jesus is looking about, and He's raising His hands very high: In the name of the Father, and of the Son, and of the Holy Ghost.

Now He's doing something very, very strange. He's extending His hands out, like this, in front of Him, and there are all rays coming from His arms and His hands. The rays are extending high over our heads. They go beyond to a place back here (Veronica points to her right.) I believe there is someone, Jesus says, that is very ill, but he will be cured this evening, right over, in this section, over there.

Now Jesus is looking. He shook His head - yes, I understood well.

Now He's going. He's turning fast to His right, and He's coming above Our Lady's statue now, again. He's looking about Him, and now he does this, like Our Lady does, which means to listen and repeat.

Jesus - "My children of the earth, how happy I am to know that there are those among you who are willing to dedicate and sacrifice their lives, for the entrance into Heaven through the salvation of many souls upon earth.

"You must all make it known to mankind that there is a hell, there is a purgatory, and, of course, the Kingdom of Heaven. The road to hell is swift and wide. The road to Heaven is narrow, and too few are not finding it.

"My child and My children, you must do your utmost to bring back into My House, My Church upon earth, the Faith. I often cried through My Mother's tears. Her tears and Mine abounded over the earth, because through the Eternal Father, man was given a conscience and a free will, to either accept Heaven by sacrifice and penance, and having to face the rebuke of a darkened world.

"I want everyone upon earth to know that the great Chastisement and the punishments of droughts, earthquakes, hurricanes, tornadoes, are but minor compared to the number of lives that will be lost with the great Chastisement.

The abomination of homosexuality

"I hold your country, My child, at fault because too few who are in power in the government and the teachers from My Church on earth, too few are willing to fight against the abomination of the homosexuality that is raging throughout the United States, Canada, and the world. In no way will homosexuality be accepted, for it means damnation and destruction. And I say this to you, once fair maidens in the convents of the world, who have chosen to cast aside your profession and your oaths of allegiance to your God to seek a more pleasurable life upon earth without your habits, without your convents, and living the life of a lay person.

"All who have received Holy Orders, legally, shall be held accountable for their casting aside their profession, for they are weakening the structure of My House.

"Many because of the mistakes made issuing forth from the good hearts of John XXIII, Pope Paul VI; many have taken the messages and the directions given at the Vatican Council and twisted them to suit themselves, reading in the Bible words of their own, or finding excuses for their sinning, through the Bible.

"My child and My children, the murders of the unborn will bring great Chastisement upon the United States, Canada, and the nations of the world, that are now contributing not only to the delinquency of your children and the world's children, but are condoning murder and euthanasia. Euthanasia, My child and My children, is murder!

"We have been very patient. The Eternal Father has voiced His decision within My hearing, and I tell you, My children, your Chastisement is just at hand.

"We expect all of you to read and re - read My Mother's directives, for they are My directives in the Eternal Father and the Holy Ghost.

"No man shall fall into hell unless he wishes it. For his heart and his eyes are blinded; his heart is hardened, and the pleasures of the world, and the popularity of a generation that has gone insane with sin - for these he will give up his eternal soul.

"And especially, My children, I repeat anew the words of My Mother when She said to you some time ago, that anyone who has even a small measure, responsibility for the deaths of the unborn, shall be judged as a murderer. No nation that has become so corrupt that their legal rules and regulations are changed for those who are in sin, shall not stand. They will burn in the embers, as the bodies will burn upon the roads and the streets.

"My children, I have great compassion for all of My children of the earth. But I say unto you, you have a free will. My Mother has accepted Her role as a Mediatrix between God and man. If you listen to My Mother's counsel you will be saved, and you will also share in the struggle to right the wrong that has been done against the Eternal Father and all the personages of Heaven.

"Theresa wished to be with Us this evening, but due to the time and the condition of your physical body, My child, I send you her words, though she chose at first to appear herself. I send you her words: 'My sisters, what have you done to yourselves? I can see through the Eternal Father what has happened within the convents. I can only beg you to open your eyes and ask the Holy Spirit to guide you. Accept not the counsel of man, for satan now and all hell has opened up and the demons are upon earth. This is the final struggle for souls.'

"My Mother told you some time ago that soon Her words will be few, and this soon has now covered a year's time. But you must know that as a voice - box We had to seek and bring you, My child, back to the grounds so that We can go forth, and together try - I say try - to save the world from its own destruction.

"Satan has poisoned their minds and your great scientists now seek only one thing - to please the Bear. For money. And what is money? You cannot take it beyond the veil. You will go out as you came in, but you will be judged when you go out.

"My child and My children, I stress anew for My Mother that you keep a vigil of prayer going throughout your countries and the world. It will be through My Mother's Brown Scapular and the beads of prayer that many souls can be saved, and there will be a lessening of the Judgment against mankind, where he will lose his body as he becomes an ember, so great will be the flames.

"My child, do not be affrighted. I will show you a picture now. Now you hold onto your crucifix and do not be affrighted."

[Pause]

Veronica - It's horrible! Who are they?

Jesus - "The good and the bad shall die together, My child. Yes, you may describe if you wish, My child, what I have just shown you."

Veronica - I see a road. I see people fleeing, their clothes are ragged. It seems as though they had been hit by some kind of shrapnel, or something that's tearing the clothes off their bodies. But the worst part of all is that beyond the roads I see bodies, dead bodies strewn all over, in the streets, through the houses, in the lots. And I see the waters aflame. And I see waters churning and churning, and rising higher and higher, as they wash onto the shores that border the seas.

Jesus - "Yes, My child, in the great Chastisement a ball of fire shall fall into the waters killing all that is living in the seas. And, also, unfortunately, because they could not listen and change their ways, many will die also from the flames and also from the waters. Those living along the coastlines, We caution them to keep a sacramental and a crucifix upon their doors, for the angel of death shall not enter your home.

"Now, My child, because of the long term of rest and illness, you will take three more photographs. They will stress what I have just given you in words, that sometimes, My child, one photograph can convert many, because seeing to some is believing. Blessed are they who do not have to see to believe. But if they must believe by some physical sign, We send all of this to you, My children: conversions, cures, photographs. Surely you cannot turn away from the pleas of My Mother.

"Now, My child, you will take the photographs, and I will put explicitly in them what I have told you. Sit back, My child, and rest."

[Pause]

Old Mass must be returned

Veronica - Jesus is not pleased with the manner in which His clergy are carrying out their vocations, and, also, the

Mass. Jesus wishes that the Old Mass be returned to wipe out many of the errors that have crept in since the New Mass has started.

Jesus - "And I must repeat again, My child, for the consolation of mothers. They must watch over their children carefully, for there will be thousands upon thousands that will vanish without a trace. The satanist cults are turning into armies, My child. They have already tried to attack you through the powers that they retain from satan. Do not be affrighted, but you must be more careful, My child, whom you let into your house. For the souls of those who knock upon your door are knowingly, or unknowingly to themselves, sinful and on the road to destruction, and trying to take others with them.

"It will take courage, My children, to carry this Mission forth. But you will be guided by Our Blessed Mother. My Mother has accepted Her role and She promises you, as I do, also, that We will be with you until the end of time, and the beginning of a giant, great renewal. That, My child, shall be given in time to all mankind.

"You will take the photographs now, My child; it is most important."

U.S. headed for race war
"Your time has been shortened"

Eve Of The Feast Of Saint Anne And Saint Joachim
- July 25, 1985

Veronica - All about the trees - it's beautiful - there are blue lights; they're the calling lights for Our Lady. And just up above the statue, high in the sky, I can't judge by feet or distance, Our Lady is coming down very fast. Oh, She must be very agitated about something. I notice Our Lady is not coming down slowly, but She's descending very, very fast.

And oh, Our Lady looks so... absolutely so beautiful. The white light that seems to come from within Her and shine our makes it very difficult at this time to see Our Lady's clothing.

But now She's coming down, and She's going a little to the right. Now She's just over Our Lady's statue, right about I would say - about maybe four feet from Our Lady's statue, upward.

Now, I can see Our Lady very clearly now; She's smiling. She has on the most beautiful white gown. The white gown has a border of gold, I would say about a half inch of gold all about the inner rim and down by Our Lady's feet. Our Lady has on sandals; they're very beautiful. They have a strap, a gold strap, that may be material - it looks like material. But at Our Lady's tongue section She has the most delicate rose, but the rose is gilded, like in gold. And Our Lady is nodding and saying yes. And now also I notice that Our Lady has changed Her color, and She has about Her waist - instead of the gold buckling, She has a blue scarf. I would say it's a scarf because the ends are now coming forward in the wind from Our Lady's cape.

Now Our Lady is coming down closer, and She's motioning, like this, to listen and repeat after Her.

Our Lady - "My child and My children, especially My child Veronica, I knew of your suffering, and I knew that you would not turn your back on My pleas to come to the grounds this evening. I will not tax you, My child, with too long a Message for the world this evening. But most of all, I come to say, My children, that your time has been shortened. The cataclysm, the day of sorrow, and the dark, long days are coming upon you.

Heaven searched years for a Veronica

"I have gone throughout the world for many earth - years, searching and seeking out those who would give their lives to Heaven for the salvation of their brothers and sisters. The calling, My child and My children, did not go as you would expect. By the time We had reached you in Bayside, in your home, My child, We had looked with Theresa a long time for a Veronica. I know this does boggle your mind, My child, but what I mean to say to you is that, yes, even though the highest - the hierarchy of Heaven you would call it - the highest in Heaven approach many souls to be messengers, voice - boxes, for the Eternal Father, through My Son, and the Holy Ghost, but sorrowfully, My child, they turned Him down. I know this shocks you, My child, but you understand in a man's human nature he is given the choice to go on the long road or to search and work for entrance to Heaven by the narrow road.

"My child and My children, I have cried great tears, My child, since I last saw you, for the fathers and mothers - the poor mothers - they do not know what lies ahead for their children, their children of all ages. Satan and his legion of demons and devils are loosed now upon earth in full force. They are doing very well, My children.

"And I sorrow and cry bitter tears because many of you who have heard My voice through the years have taken on a firm, undisciplined attitude of, 'Oh well, nothing's happened now; it shall not happen soon, for everything remains as it was when the Father started it.' My child and My children, that is not an attitude that should be taken by anyone. The Eternal Father, with My Son, and the Holy Ghost, are all - merciful, but you do not even recognize the Eternal Father, My children. You cast Him aside as a myth or a story, but there is definite proof, My children, in the Book of life and love, the Bible. But how many have taken the time to even check through the Bible?

Indulgences for reading Bible

"I say now, My children, that you must understand there are great graces given for reading the Bible, even a short time of fifteen minutes; you will be graced by indulgences. Have you forgotten, My children, in the modernization of My Son's Church, have you forgotten the meaning of indulgences? They are applicable to the time you may have to put in purgatory, My children.

"I cannot lie to you or try to fashion My words to suit the widened area of the world that through their seeking of riches and positions of high nature and powers beyond what is needed for their soul, they seek to discard all of the knowledge of sacramentals, penance, and all other means that Heaven has given you through the Book, the Bible. My children, I say again: If you will just read for fifteen minutes, first giving yourselves over to the Holy Ghost, and employing the Holy Ghost to help you open your hearts and clear your eyes that are clouded by the world's goods... I say goods because, My children, many have sold their souls to get to the head. They place more value on their coins. No coins shall jiggle on their person when they come for judgment. One day there will be a great General Judgment, and all mankind then will be forced to accept what he has sown. Many are throwing away the time allotted to them to right the wrong, to restore My Son's Church to it former glory, to bring your children out of the darkness and into the light.

"Oh, My child, I am crying tears; My heart is torn when I think of the children of earth. The parents - they look away as they are in pursuit of riches and material things of the world. None of this can be brought into Heaven to buy your salvation. No, My children, My Son has often said that it will be easier for a camel to go through a needle's eye than a rich man to enter Heaven."

Veronica - Our Lady is looking about Her now, and

She's wiping the tears from Her eyes.

Don't cry Blessed Mother. (Veronica speaks with heartfelt compassion.)

Now Our Lady is going over to our left side. She's just above the high tree, the highest on the left side, the right side of Our Lady's statue.

Our Lady now is taking Her Rosary which She had about Her waist, like this, and She's holding it up now and making the sign of the cross: In the name of the Father, and of the Son, and of the Holy Ghost.

Now Our Lady is looking all about Her. She's moving now towards our right side, that would be between - She's just about between the tree and the statue now. And Our Lady is coming quite a bit lower now. I would say as She goes to the right, She'll soon be standing on Her statue's head; Our Lady smiled. And She's rising higher. And now Our Lady is directly above the statue, and She's holding Her crucifix, the beautiful golden crucifix on Her Rosary out, like this, and making the sign of the cross: In the name of the Father, and of the Son, and of the Holy Ghost.

Now Our Lady is motioning, "Come with Me, My child, Watch now."

And Our Lady is going over to the right side of the statue, that's our left side, not right side; but to the others on the other side it might be confusing, but Our Lady always follows the same type of pattern of going from left to right.

Now Our Lady is extending Her crucifix out quite a bit in front of Her, like this, and making the sign of the cross: In the name of the Father, and of the Son, and of the Holy Ghost.

Now Our Lady is doing something different. She is placing Her Rosary, the beautiful Rosary with the golden Our Fathers and the white Hail Marys that cascade like the colors of the rainbow as She turns ... And Our Lady now is holding Her Rosary just on Her arm, and She's extending Her hands out, like this, and out from the fingers, down over the crowds - they go beyond, but I can see - Our Lady has radiating lights coming from Her fingers, going directly over in

that direction (Veronica points behind herself to the right),
that would be our right side. The lights are tremendous;
they're piercing. Our Lady now is motioning now to me...
Her head; She had not taken her hands away because the
lights are still there.

Man In wheelchair cured

Our Lady - "You will see, My child, and know soon,
why the light of Heaven has fallen upon two individuals
who, as of this moment upon earth, are now cured. Get up
and walk, My son."

Veronica - Now the lights are, like, vanishing; they're
like smoke. I cannot explain it in human language. They
weren't drawn back, but the light is like, dissimulating into a
smoky pattern and gradually fading away.

Now Our Lady is going backwards. She came down
quite far to get to the individuals who are somewhere over
here on the right. (Veronica again points behind herself to
the right.) And the lights were so far - I would say that they
are beyond the point of half of the crowd, out to the street
and beyond that point. The man - Our Lady said the man is
sitting in a wheelchair. The man is sitting in a wheelchair,
Our Lady said. And the other, a lady, is now rubbing her
arms.

Now Our Lady is turning; She's looking over to the right
side now, and gradually She's going over above Her statue.
Our Lady does not have to walk, She floats. There's no
human way to describe it; it's beautiful to see. It's as though
She has no weight at all. She is floating over; it's so beautiful. And Her cape is catching with the wind and going out
behind Her. And I tried to look to see if I can see Our
Lady's hair, but somehow She always has Her hair covered,
to me.

Now Our Lady is smiling, and She's standing over the
statue. Now She's taking Her Rosary again, like this, and
kissing the crucifix, like this. Now Our Lady is placing Her
Rosary about Her waist, like this, and She's touching Her
lips now; that means to be silent and listen.

Our Lady - "My child, it lifted My heavy heart to be able to bring from the Father these gifts of conversion and cure for the crowd."

Veronica - Oh - h!

Our Lady - "There will be two others on Our left side; they have not been forgotten. One will be conversion, the other will be cures.

"My child, I have much to say to you this evening, but it is best at this time if you sit back and take three photographs, and I will be talking with you as soon as you are able to regain your strength, My child; I feel it ebbing."

Veronica - Now Our Lady is standing very patiently; She's just about four feet over Her statue's head there. Our Lady is looking about Her. And it's quite windy because Her mantle is being blown to and fro - not too badly, the wind isn't too strong. And Our Lady is smiling. Now She's touching Her finger to Her lips, like this, which means to listen and repeat.

Remain away from other apparition sites

Our Lady - "My child, since others wish to know how I personally feel for the episode that went on here on the sacred grounds only a short time ago, it made Me much unhappy for two major reasons, My child. As I told you in countless earth - years of visitations with you, that you must always test the spirits, and also to remain away from other so - called apparition sites or other seers. I say this to you, My children, because in your anxiety or your anxiousness to find the supernatural, you run to and fro, seeking something that you would never find; for there is much evil upon earth now, and even the good will be deceived by satan and his legion of demons. Yes, My child, I tell you that it was beautifully done to remove a sad situation from the sacred grounds. I want you to remember, as I tell you tonight, that soon you will be confronted with two children. They are young, but they are true seers of Chile. They live, My child, since you ask, outside, in the meadows beyond the city of..."

Veronica - Saint Angelo?

Our Lady - "No, Santiago, My child, Santiago."

Veronica - Now Our Lady is rising higher, and She's pointing up now with Her Rosary, like this, to the sky; and directly over Our Lady's head, the sky is opening up. Oh it's beautiful. It's a round circle of light. Like I'd say, it shines like the prisms. I think you call them prisms - Our Lady is bowing Her head yes - on your lamps or that you have in your chandeliers... the glass - like prisms of the light shining from over Our Lady's head. And directly in the center of the light that's opening very wide, encompassing Our Lady now, too, Jesus is coming forward.

Oh-h, He's wearing His burgundy cape. And He has a head - attachment for it, a cowl, I believe Our Lady said, a cowl. And He has on sandals; they're made of a skin - like material, they're brown. And Jesus has no socks on. Our Lady thinks that's funny, She's smiling, but He has no socks on.

Now Our Lady is moving over to our left side beyond the statue. She's coming down quite close to the trees.

And Jesus is coming forward. Oh, He looks absolutely beautiful in the light. His hair looks sort - many people would like to know what Jesus' hair looks like. It's so beautiful. It has a tint of, sort of, not red, oh, I can't - rust color... but no way to explain it, I cannot explain it. It must be His hair is containing the light that was opening the sky, and that makes it difficult to explain the coloring. But He wears it quite long, it would come to about His shoulder now.

Jesus is looking over to the right side, and He's smiling. Oh, oh yes. Now Our Lady is moving up, and Jesus is coming back. He was taking a good look over on the right side. I think He's looking for the man in the wheelchair. Oh, now Jesus is smiling. Now He's coming over to Our Lady. Our Lady is at Jesus' right side now. And Jesus is standing about two feet over the statue, just about two feet. It's very low compared to where Our Lady usually stands.

Now Our Lady is nodding Her head, and Jesus is looking about Him. Now He's touching Our Lady on the shoulder and pointing over to the left-hand side. Now Our Lady nods yes, and Jesus is now going up higher. He floats too; it's just beautiful to see. He's going up higher and coming down now, straight down, and He's touching just the tip of that tree over there. And Our Lady is following Him now. She'll be at Jesus' left side. Now He's taking His hand, like this, and making the sign of the cross: In the name of the Father, and of the Son, and of the Holy Ghost.

Now He's turned a little bit to the right, and He's extending His arm out, like this: In the name of the Father, and of the Son, and of the Holy Ghost.

Now He is whispering to Our Lady, I can't hear it; but They're both turning now, and They're going over to the center of the statue. And now Jesus - Our Lady is now holding up Her crucifix, like this, the crucifix on Her long Rosary, the beautiful Rosary. She's holding the crucifix while Jesus now is extending His hand out, like this, directly in front He is now, over Our Lady's statue directly in the middle, and He's making the sign of the cross: In the name of the Father, and of the Son, and of the Holy Ghost.

Now He's moving, He's motioning to Our Lady to follow, and He's going over to our right side directly about the middle. Now Jesus is extending His hand out, like this, and making the sign of the cross: In the name of the Father, and of the Son, and of the Holy Ghost.

Now Our Lady is turning, and They're both going over; Jesus is a slight ways behind Our Lady. And They're both floating over; They don't walk, They just float. It's beautiful to see.

Our Lady - "My child,...."

Veronica - Our Lady is saying.

Our Lady - "... you ask will everyone float like that when they come to Heaven? I assure you, My child, they will."

Veronica - Now Our Lady and Jesus have reached back, They're back over Our Lady's statue. Our Lady is standing at Jesus' right side. She's quite a bit shorter than Jesus; He's quite tall. I would say Jesus is about at least six feet tall, six foot one or two even, because Our Lady only comes to His

212

shoulder, here.

Now Jesus is making the sign of the cross again. Now He's placed His hands, like this, and He's touching His lips.

Jesus - "My child, Veronica, and My children of the world... I say My children, because you are Our children; and Our tears and Our smiles are for you all. My children, I could wish to say at this time that I bring you great news of joyousness, but I cannot. I must tell you now that My Mother has gone throughout the world, through time and time again, to turn you back from your course of destruction.

"My child, I wish you to view one scene. You will hold your crucifix and you will not, My child, pass out."

Veronica - Over on the left side, I see... I know it's Africa. It's all in flames. I've seen the flames before, but this is horrible. They're going wild; they all look dark - skinned, yet they're killing each other.

Jesus - "My child, you see war, the beginning of a war. It will be father against son, mother against daughter, and satan will be in their midst. Those who have the power are exercising it now in the wrong direction, My children. Better that they take the monies coming to them from out of the world, better that they try to construct a country with joy and happiness and peace among the brothers.

The true meaning of love

"Thou shalt not kill, and yet you kill. Thou shalt not bear witness, and you condemn others to death with your testimony. Where is your love that you call out for? Love, My children, how many of you know the true meaning of love? Love is in giving, love is kindness; love is not murder, love is not selling your soul to the devil for power. Many of the rulers throughout the world are doing this now.

"Nuclear warheads, missiles, all manner of contraptions: what dignified name can I give to them, My children? They are destruction to all mankind. I repeat again: If you commit this to come upon you, there will soon be no flesh left. My child and My children, and those who hear Our pleadings, Our hearts are extended to you to help Us to save mankind

213

from his own course of destruction. You have very little time to do this in, My children. I assure you, your time is running out.

"My Mother, for many earth - years, has acted with Her heart to protect you. How many times the heavy hand of the Eternal Father reached down to start out the calamities with the Ball, and how many times did Our Lady rush forward. How many times did My Mother rush forward to save you? The world knows My Mother, but they cast Her aside. And those who are agents of hell now, demons in human form, they cannot be retrieved; their abode will be hell. But sad to say, it hurts My heart to know that I cannot be rid of these thorns that I am forced to accept for your salvation."

Veronica - Now Jesus is taking His right hand, and He's pointing it upward, like this.

Jesus - "See, My child, what mankind shall suffer."

U.S., Canada coastlines washed away

Veronica - I see the United States, I see Canada, but I see part of the coastlines being worn away. There are waves, high waves, washing over the land. People are running, but they waited too late; they didn't listen, and they're being carried out to sea ... dead bodies.

Race war covers U.S.

Now in the United States I see people running, but this is a race war. I see a whole group - it looked like the whole continent - running, but they're dark - skinned, they're black - skinned. And they have all types of instruments. I think one is a machine gun that shoots many bullets, and he's tat - tat - tat - tat - tat - tat - tat - tat - tat - tat. Oh - h. (Veronica sighs heavily.) And they're lying on the ground, dead. Ugh, oh, and it's terrible. (Veronica sighs heavily again.)

Now I see Jesus is pointing upward.

Jesus - "Look high into the sky, My child, look high. Raise you head."

Veronica - I see a ball of fire; it's coming fast through the sky, and it has a long red tail. It's red, it's fire! And now it's coming down to what looks like a ball, but no, it's the earth. And oh - h, oh, it has hit through the water, it's brushed through the water. And there are waves rising higher, higher than anything possible I could have seen. The waves are terrible. They're washing half of the continent out to sea.

Now the sky is growing very dark. Jesus is pointing to Our Lady, and They're coming down from the sky. They had moved up so I could see. Our Lady is touching Her lips.

Our Lady - "Do not be affrighted, My child. It is best that you bring forth what is to be. Perhaps, with your prayers and your penances, you can reach some of these souls in darkness before their time runs out.

"My child, this is only one part of the world. There are many now. You will see nations rise up against nations, obliterating one or the other within the time of three to five minutes. There shall be a world war, the Third World War, more grievous in suffering, more debauched."

Russia will use ray guns

Veronica - Oh, and I see that - Our Lady is showing me now - there are some kind of implements they're using that... it doesn't look like a gun, it looks like a flashlight, but I know it's not a flashlight; it's some object of some kind of a ray they've got. And then - now he's lifting - I see a man in a very odd looking uniform; I don't recognize the uniform. But he's raising high, like this, this ray gun. That's what it is, it's a ray gun. And he's now pushing the trigger, and I see... it looks like long streams of light, but everything it hits just disintegrates and melts. (Veronica groans.)

Our Lady - "Russia, My children, has this implement of destruction. While the United States and Canada, and most of the world, go about crying for peace, tranquillity, love, they are not aware of the fact that Russia has every mind to take them over, be it good or bad. And if they have to annihilate the whole land of it people, they want that land, and they will use any means to get it.

215

"You understand, My child and My children, when a man is not with his God, his god then becomes Lucifer. He is then taken over to be an agent of hell. And he has many helpers, for all hell now is opened wide in these last days. All the demons of hell are loosed.

"And do not become smug, My children, and think that you will be saved. Do not take this lightly. They are very powerful and cajoling. Yes, My child, you have every reason to be affrighted.

"I do not say, My children and My child, that the situation is a hundred percent hopeless. I say that each and every child upon earth is wanted back, as the man whose sheep has scattered, and he will await that one lost sheep to return. And much joy should be had over that one lost sheep than if the whole fold had returned.

"My child and My children..."

Veronica - Now Jesus is turning about. He's whispering to Our Lady; She's nodding. And They're going across now in the center of the trees above Our Lady's statue about, oh, three feet, I think three feet. Jesus nods.

Jesus - "Now, My child, I must tell you, since much of your penance for the priesthood has been accepted, My child, I at first chose not to mention the sorrow We have because of the manner in which My House upon earth is being continued - a House - because of modernism, satanism, and seeking the profound, not in the history of My House, but in the new modern way of doing things. This new modern way has been promoted by satan.

Satan took over Vatican II

"Yes, My child, even with Vatican II, it started out with the best resolves, but then satan took over the scene. And with his agents he reached into the highest professions, the highest league of the Hierarchy, until, it saddens Me to say that many priests now are on the road to perdition and taking many others with them."

Veronica - Our Lady is starting to cry. Jesus has taken His hand, and He's patting Her on the shoulder.

Jesus - "My child and My children, My Mother is crushed, because you know that She has given Herself over to being your protectorate, and now She sees an almost hopeless road ahead for the world. The time is very short, My children.

Discuss actions with your angels

"I gave you photographs, photographs not only of what My Mother has brought to you this evening in words, in figures, in actions... but My Mother has sought now to console those in Heaven, who stand by, the angels. Oh, My children, the world would not be in such a sorry state if man hadn't forgotten the angels in Heaven. Each and every soul upon earth has an angel guardian. If there is any question or any doubt in your actions, your earthly actions, that you need to discuss, discuss this, My children, with your angels; they are always there. I know, My children, in My House upon earth they have thrown out the angels, the statues, calling them irreverent, calling them objects of worship. We know that is not true. But they have adopted that attitude, and that is why I say that even many wearing the highest rank in the Hierarchy are like rats burrowing into the foundation of My Church. They, too, shall be judged.

"My child, there will be very many victims upon earth; those who are willing to sacrifice their own pleasures, their own human pursuits, to give them over to the salvation of souls, their brothers and sisters, who are marked with the mark of satan and are seeking to take it away. There is only one way: conversion, and then cure of the sick soul.

St. Benedict medal - highest indulgenced

"My children, now that the time has grown shorter, the attacks shall be greater upon mankind. There will be accidents that are not accidents. Satan has a plan to eliminate the good. Do not be affrighted, My child or My children. You will wear your sacramentals. Specifically, We have asked you, and My Mother has asked you, to wear the Brown

217

Scapular, and also a crucifix, and with that the highest indulgenced medal in the Church."

Veronica - And now Jesus is pointing up to the sky. And out in the sky, there's a huge St. Benedict medal, a huge one. Oh - h, it's so plain. Oh - h.

Jesus - "My child..."

Veronica - Yes.

Jesus - "... remember the St. Benedict medal. Many years ago, We gave unto you through long searching the second hidden meaning of the St. Benedict medal. You will bring that out again, My child, in publication for the salvation of souls."

Veronica - Now Jesus is turning to Our Lady, and They're both going over to the left side of the statue, our left side, and Jesus is looking down. He's talking to Our Lady about something; I can't hear it all. But Our Lady and Jesus are discussing someone upon the grounds.

Our Lady - "My child..."

Veronica - It's Our Lady.

Our Lady - "... We cannot give you the name at this time, but you will know when you read the pictures."

Veronica - Now Jesus and Our Lady are going over. They're just above the statue now, and They're rising above the branch of the tree out of our right side. They look very beautiful. Now Jesus is making the sign of the cross again: In the name of the Father, and of the Son, and of the Holy Ghost.

Now Our Lady has taken Her Rosary from about Her belting, and She's making the sign of the cross: In the name of the Father, and of the Son, and of the Holy Ghost.

Our Lady - "Continue, My children, now with your prayers of atonement. Many are needed, for there are still souls to save before the catastrophe."

Veronica - Three. Three pictures?

Our Lady - "No, My child, you cannot discuss this at this time. You will please keep it confidential for the time being."

AIDS - Plague from God "I shall not allow a cure"

Eve of the Feast Of The Immaculate Heart Of Mary
- August 21, 1985

Veronica - There are the call lights of Our Lady... blue round balls, very dark in color. I would say that they are, like a - not a baby blue, a beautiful blue coloring, similar to, bordering on the purple; which must indicate the suffering that the world is now going through, and also what Our Lady is trying to stop, in Her pursuits all over the world.

Now high above the statue - oh, a distance - more than a mile I would say in distance, there is a beautiful stream of light. They're coming down and they're ricocheting off the trees now, the lights; they're very brilliant, they're like clear water. I have no human words that could describe the lights; they're clear as crystal. They're beautiful.

Now, as the circle of light above us is opening up, I see Our Lady now coming through the circlet of light. Oh, She is absolutely beautiful. She has on a white gown, a very brilliant white gown, that catches all of the movements of the trees, and all about Her. I feel that this is Her glorious attachment in Her earthen life, when She was on earth, to everything about us, which She's very familiar with.

Now Our Lady is coming down slowly. It's quite windy, and Her gown is blowing about Her - Her ankles. The gown is very long; it goes be - , also past Her shoe instep. Now, as the air has now appeased a little, Our Lady is looking about Her. She has on a mantle, a beautiful white mantle; but all about the mantle there is about a half inch - it would be, yes, about a half inch of gold, all around Her mantle. I cannot see Her hair; Our Lady has never allowed me to see Her without Her covering on Her head.

Now Our Lady is looking about Her and smiling. She's just now about a foot above the statue, just a foot, directly in the center.

Now Our Lady is taking Her beads from about Her waist. She has on a gold - type of braided waist piece. It doesn't seem to be like a belt; it seems to be sewed into the waist of the gown. And Our Lady now is taking Her Rosary, the beautiful Rosary with the golden Our Fathers, and the Hail Marys in white, but that actually are gathering all the colors of the rainbow... And they're very, very difficult to explain, the effect on your eyes, because you're looking through clear diamonds... the most gorgeous sight I have ever seen in my life. It's absolutely beautiful.

And Our Lady is coming a little closer now. She's looking about Herself. And She's looking back and pointing up to the sky. And there above Our Lady, I can see the sky opening up again. The clouds have drifted apart, and Jesus is coming through the clouds now. They're drifting apart from Him so that He is almost in the oval circlet of light. Now Jesus is coming down and He's now approaching Our Blessed Mother. She's looked back now and smiled. And he's nodding - I know he's telling Her to go ahead.

Now Jesus is moving slowly, to be on Our Lady's right side. But Our Lady now is going over to our left side, just above the large tree, and She's extending the crucifix of Her Rosary and making the sign of the cross: In the name of the Father, and of the Son, and of the Holy Ghost.

Now Our Lady is looking and smiling. And She's drifting now. She just floats; She doesn't walk the way we do. She just floats so beautifully. Now She's above Her statue. And Jesus now has followed Her over; He's standing still now at Her right side. And Our Lady is looking over to Her left side, which would be our right, and She's holding the crucifix up, like this, very high, and making the sign of the cross: In the name of the Father, and of the Son, and of the Holy Ghost.

Now Our Lady is coming over, with Jesus following Her, and They're standing just above Our Lady's statue. Now Jesus has touched His first finger to His lips. Now Our Lady is also nodding, and She is touching with Her crucifix, She's kissing the crucifix on Her Rosary, like that. And Our Lady now is touching Her finger to Her lips.

Our Lady - "My child, will you not succor Our son in

Rome, Pope John Paul II, My child, by repeating to all the world one of the prayers so close to My Son, the Eternal Father, and the Spirit of life. You will repeat this, My child:

> O my God! I am heartily sorry for having offended Thee, and I confess to all my sins, because I dread the loss of Heaven and the pains of hell; but most of all because I love Thee, my God, who are all good, and deserving of all my love. I firmly resolve, with the help of Thy grace, to confess my sins, to do penance, and to amend my life. Amen.

"My child, you must know in your own area and throughout the world about Catholic nations: they have forfeited another key to Heaven when they discard the prayers that Heaven has given to them to guard their souls and the souls of their families and their children. These are all parts of the armor of Heaven in the fight with the antichrist forces. My child and My children, I must constantly warn you and repeat over and over the necessity for wearing the Brown Scapular and also praying My beads of prayer, the Rosary. You must keep the Rosary going link to link, prayer to prayer, throughout your country, Canada, and the world, My child.

"There is one grain left only in the hourglass. I know this bereaves you, My child, for Me to have to bring such dire tidings, but My heart is also heavy; for there are many who are coming to Us over the veil, and what can We do with them, as Our tears fall with their pleadings? However, as has been ordained by the Eternal Father, where there has been no repentance upon earth, that soul must be rejected. Or will there be mercy for that soul, My child and My children, through you prayers for the dead, that they be given a short or long term in purgatory?

"My child and My children I do not have to tell you that the knowledge of hell and purgatory has been slowly corrupted, cut apart, and cut asunder from the Church. My child and My children, you are all My children. I judge you

221

not by color or race, and I do not judge you by your creed; however, should the knowledge of the One True Church be given to you, and the way to Heaven along the narrow road be given to you, you will follow it or you will be rejected. There are, My children, so many poor souls now that are languishing in purgatory; some will be there till the end of time. Will you not succor them, My children; will you not pray for them and shorten their time in this place of dark suffering?

"You ask, My child, for those who are in hell. Remember, My children and My child, that if they are in hell it is because they willed it so, preferring to have the materials and power of the world, even power over mankind, which they did not exercise for the glory of God, but for their own selfish, human gains.

Lost Children - captives of satanists

"My child and My children, there is an evil plan now in your country, the United States of America, and, also, the boughs are reaching like an evil tree into the land of Canada. Children are disappearing from the earth. My child and My children, I feel it necessary that I repeat to you again, that you do not be bored at the repetition of the Message, for it is urgent. Will your child be next? Many mother's hearts are torn asunder, but they have found not the whereabouts of their children; but many have found the possibility of the whereabouts of their children, held as captives, for the whim and humor of the satanist. They are increasing in your country, My child, and all of the countries of the world. It is satan and his armies now, knowing the time is short to battle with the children of God.

"You, My child, must accept your suffering for the priesthood. It is a great gift of grace, though you cannot escape the torments of the body, My child; you cannot escape the suffering, for the suffering is the balm, b - a - l - m, My child, the balm of those who are waiting to enter over the veil.

"Day by day, man is killing now. Many countries shall be embroiled in wars, until we have the greatest war ever seen, nor shall ever be seen again, the Third World War, which shall engulf the nations. And many nations shall disappear from the force of the armaments being gathered now throughout Russia.

"Yes, My child, no matter how the world reacts to the truth, you will shout it from the rooftops that Russia has not accepted any overtures from Rome. Unless Russia can be dedicated to the Immaculate Heart of Jesus and Mary, unless they will recognize the truth, they will continue to go throughout the world sowing seeds of discord, discontentment, and war. You know, My children, that war is a punishment for man's sins, but also, war is an indication of the loss of the knowledge of God.

"My children, I cannot enforce Myself upon you. I can only plead with you as a Mother of mercy to turn back now while there is still a little time. Your time is growing short. I repeat again: there is only one grain left in the hourglass.

"My child and My children, do not be affrighted. Were it to be that I can come to you as a Mother of glad tidings, I should be the first to come to you and throw My arms about you, and solace you with the great knowledge that you have received a time permitted only by the Eternal Father to settle your estates, and your way of life to change it, to be on the narrow road to Heaven. Do not forfeit your life, your eternal life, by wishing or coveting material gains of this world, for none shall follow you over the veil to plead your cause.

"The enemies of God are all about you. Russia has planned these days, My child and My children. And how I have begged for years of earth's time that Russia be consecrated to My Immaculate Heart. When she is consecrated she will be converted, My children, and then you shall see the world of joy again. Tears shall be banished, and mothers shall not sorrow until they die of grief for the loss of their children and their sons.

"My child and My children, I want you to understand

that We have been patient with only the patience that God the Eternal Father in the Holy Ghost could manifest to you. No human being can understand the suffering that We have resolved Ourselves to for your salvation and the salvation of all of the souls upon earth.

"My children, you are all My children; do not allow Me any longer to see the great evil that you are developing upon earth. You are giving yourselves over to seeking armaments to kill. And for what, My children? The Eternal Father shouts from the rooftops: Thou shalt not kill thy brother!

"My child and My children, I wish now that there be taken three photographs; I say three, because within these photographs, My child, you, and you alone, will find the date of the Third World War. Sit back, My child, now; awaken, and take three pictures. You understand what I said to you, My child."

Veronica - Three pictures.

[Pause]

Veronica - side. She is atop, on the top of the tallest tree limb, on the right side of the statue, but our left side. Now Our Lady is pointing up with Her finger, like this, to Her left side, and - oh, over by the tall limb, above Our Lady's statue on the right side, Jesus is coming slowly down now. He has been standing just above - I'm fascinated at the way He's coming down, because He doesn't walk the way we do; He absolutely floats, as though He's weightless. It's so beautiful to see.

Jesus is smiling now. He has on a burgundy cape. And there is a trim of gold, also, about His cape on - around the outside edge, I would say about - oh, about an inch. And Jesus is now - He is tugging at the top of His clothing, like this, and I notice that He's loosening the gold tassel like fringe that He has about His - top of His cloak. And in the back of Jesus' cloak there's a cowl - Our Lady calls is a cowl - also the same color; it looks like a burgundy plush color, almost like a velvet.

Now Jesus is smiling. I can see His hair. Everyone asks what does Jesus' hair look like? Well, I believe His hair is sort of a light brown, but with the coloring of His cape, His cloak, there is a resolence and a feeling of light coming from about Him outside the cloak, which seems to give you the impression that He's all aglow in light.

Now Jesus is taking His finger and placing it to His lips, like this.

Jesus - "That means to listen, My child, and repeat.

Jesus - "We have wandered throughout the earth, My child and My children - for many earth - years have I accompanied My Mother, through the will of the Eternal Father and the Holy Ghost, to reach you, My children, before the dire catastrophes are upon you.

Legionnaires', Herpes and Aids

"Little did the world recognize the three plagues which originated from the mind of the Eternal Father. These plagues were called The Legionnaires' Disease, Herpes, and AIDS. But, My children, as I told you in the past, many years ago, My child and My children, the bad shall be glorified and the good shall suffer. However, these diseases that came upon mankind originated through the merciful heart of the Eternal Father. Sufferings were brought upon those who must cleanse their souls to avoid hell.

"You ask, My child and My children, why must also the good suffer? As it was in the beginning of time, so it will be now, that no one shall be above the crucifixion or beyond it. In order to reach the eternal life of Heaven, you must take up your cross and follow My path.

Aids - punishment for homosexuality

"My children, I shall not allow the scientific world to find a cure for AIDS, because of the horrible nature of what brings in this disease called AIDS. It is being flaunted now as though the good were to be stomped upon, and the bad shall receive the glory.

"My child, I know to speak again upon this subject of homosexuality shall bring much mail of a dire nature to you, again. But man must know that the Eternal Father perseveres to the end of His nature, for there is a point in everything in the creation of the Eternal Father that must come to an end when it is become the means for satan taking souls fast into hell.

"Homosexuality shall never be accepted. In the writings of the good Fathers, My child and My children, you were made fully aware in the Old and the New Testament of the Book of life and love, the Bible - you had been made full aware of the dastardly acts of mankind, as men consort with men. This shall not be accepted nor condoned by the Eternal Father even if He has to send another plague upon you. No, My children, they shall not, NOT be given the cure.

"I see and understand, My child, your feelings in this matter. I know you have pity for all. Many are fast on the road to perdition. Many are to be pitied as they follow this road; especially, My children, by advancing farther into the mores of satan in practicing illegal, immoral acts.

"One of the Fathers of the Church, St. Paul, made it known to you quite licitly, that men shall not consort with men; and neither shall men dress as women. These are all abomination in the eyes of the Eternal Father, Whose Hand steadily rocks back and forth the comet; Whose Hand steadily seeks to raise and throw upon you, so that you will be planet - struck with the comet.

"My child and My children, pray constantly a vigil of prayer going throughout your world and the earth, for the little time that is being allotted to mankind.

"If I told you, My children, now, in clear sound when your end is coming, you would hasten forth, running here and there, to and fro, trying to warn mankind. However, only a few will be saved. I say this, My child and My children, as you count the millions of souls upon earth, only a few will be saved.

"I, also, must give to you at this time another fact of your lives upon earth. You as parents - mothers, fathers - must guard your doors well and rule; take discipline in the lives of

226

your children, for they will bring much sorrow to your hearts as they grow - they grow in a world that has been given to satan. When your child opens his home, the door, he will face the agents of hell loosed upon earth to reclaim his soul. Protect your children, My children; be sure that as a parent you do not fall down in your duties to teach your children, for many are now receiving schooling that is based on atheism. Their books and manuals you do not read, My children. You must as parents be a safeguard, a home of holiness for your children, or they will perish; and your parent's tears shall flow upon the world, crying, too late, too late.

"My child and My children, you will also pray for John Paul II, for his time is growing short. There will be an attack upon him - I say 'will be.' The outcome I cannot give you now, for only you, and you alone, My children of the earth, can save your Vicar, John Paul II.

Three close to Pope planning his fate

"Yes, My child, it is sad to have to report to you that those who are close to him - three figures in your photographs, My children - three figures with great power, who are planning the fate of your Vicar. You must warn him to be clear of those about him. When he reads their writings he will understand. However, We also ask that he spend less time in going to and fro across the nations, for he makes it doubly difficult for Us to protect him.

"Pray a constant vigilance of prayer. You have a good and holy Father now in Rome, but should he be removed there will come disaster.

Veronica - victim for Pope and Church

"My child, I want to tell you at this time that We are not unaware of your physical suffering. It has been given to you, My child, because those who have received great graces, much is expected of them. And We accept you, My child, as a victim soul with other victim souls to save your Vicar and My Son's Church upon earth."

Veronica - Our Lady has placed Her hand upon the shoulder of Jesus; there are tears in Her eyes. She spoke up and wishes you to know that Her Heart is truly bleeding. She suffers many thorns because of what is going on now in Her Son's churches upon earth.

Our Lady is now going around Jesus. Jesus is standing right over Our Lady's statue. And Our Lady is going just around - Jesus is going just about Our Lady. They're both moving over towards our right side, Their left side. Jesus now is taking His hands, like this, and He's making the sign of the cross: In the name of the Father, and of the Son, and of the Holy Ghost.

Now Our Lady is murmuring to Jesus; I cannot hear what She is saying, just a murmur. But They are pointing. They're going over further to Their left side. Now Jesus is extending His hands out, like this, and making the sign of the cross: In the name of the Father, and of the Son, and of the Holy Ghost.

Now Our Lady is motioning, like this. Oh, They're going - They're coming across the sky. Oh, They look so beautiful, because They're - They're weightless. I see now Our Lady's slippers. She has on very delicate golden slippers, with... I call them rosettes; they're little golden roses on the instep of Her sandal, like a slipper.

Now Our Lady is going over, and She's pulling Her cloak about Her. And Jesus is following. And He's looking about Him now, and He's placing His first finger to His mouth. He's standing now over the blue banner. And Our Lady is still proceeding to get closer to Her statue, above Her statue. Our Lady is standing about six feet above Her statue. And Jesus is now right next to Her, but He's over the blue flag, about six feet. Jesus is much taller than Our Lady; She only comes up to about His shoulder. But now Jesus is looking, and He's extending His hand now in the center: In the name of the Father, and of the Son, and of the Holy Ghost.

Our Lady is turning to Her right now, and They're floating over to the left side, our left side, just above the statue.

And now They're following across the trees: They're going as far as They can to the trees there, and now Jesus is leaning over and making the sign of the cross: In the name of the Father, and of the Son, and of the Holy Ghost.

Our Lady, too, is extending Her Rosary with the beautiful crucifix, golden, and she's making the sign of the cross: In the name of the Father, and of the Son, and of the Holy Ghost.

Now Jesus is looking all about. He seems to be very pleased. He's smiling very softly. And Our Lady now - Jesus is turning to His left, and He's now floating back across the sky over Our Lady's statue, and He's standing now just above the blue banner. And Our Lady has followed Him. She's coming straight across very slowly, but She's carried on the wind as though She's weightless - just beautiful! And the light is still cascading all about Her. She seems to be, like Ray (Veronica's son who died in 1974) once said, all lit up. There's no way to explain it; She looks beautiful. Now Our Lady is looking over, and Jesus is touching His lips.

Restore statues, main altar, and railings

Jesus - "My child and My children, be it known now that We have looked into the churches about the world, and We are much confused and perhaps cannot understand the nature of humans who can in such little time do so much to destroy My Church; My House upon earth. You must restore My houses to their original condition. We ask that you return the statues to My churches, that you restore the main altar, that you re - place the gating so that others may kneel in adoration to their God. This is only the beginning; there is much else that you, My pastors, can do, and those who wear the mitres shall do, or they shall find themselves quickly in hell.

"My child, you will see and continue with the work for Heaven. It will become more difficult, as the end is coming near and satan will gather and concert his enemies all about the world. He will send forth demons in human form. That startles you, My child, but you cannot fully understand in your human nature the power of satan. It will be as though dead bodies had come to life, but they shall be demons within the bodies for but a short time.

"I cannot accept the world's reasoning for all of those changes that We hear of and We reach in prayers for. My child and My children, make it known to the world that there is not much time left for those upon earth to re - adjust their lives, and turn back and restore their souls to a pleasing manner for God your Father, the Eternal Father in Heaven, and the Son, and the Holy Ghost. I speak to you as for Myself, My children, for as I am one, so am I in the Father and the Holy Ghost; as the Father is in Me, and the Holy Ghost. This is not complicated, My child, if you will remember the Trinity."

Veronica - Now Jesus is extending Himself - He's got now, He's brought forth, Jesus has brought forth from His cape a Rosary. Oh! And He's now taking the crucifix of the Rosary ... Jesus is holding a beautiful Rosary. It's not the same color as Our Lady's; it's all red, like suffering. I get the feeling of tremendous suffering, as I look at this Rosary that Jesus is now holding up and making the sign of the cross: In the name of the Father, and of the Son, and of the Holy Ghost.

Jesus - "This, My child, is a prayerful means of suffering. We wish that the blood of Christ be upon mankind, and not the blood of his brothers.

"You will now, My child, sit forward, and take three photographs. Only one will you make known at this time."
[Pause]

Veronica - The sky is filled, it's just filled with the most beautiful angels. Oh! All about the trees and all above our heads, I can't count them all. They're just absolutely beautiful! They look, sort of like young children. They don't have faces, so you don't feel that their faces are missing. They're so beautiful that I would say, in my human language, that some of them are young. They look like children; or, perhaps, it's their spirit of being so child - like that they look like children when they appear to us. They are wearing gowns of pastel shades, the most beautiful.

Now one of the angels has gathered - by placing his hands out, like this, he's gathered a whole handful of roses, roses from a bush. I don't know where they gathered the roses, but he now has a whole handful of roses, and he's taking them over to Our Lady. Our Lady is smiling. And now as he gives Her the roses they seem to multiply, and Our Lady is holding now, it looks like dozens of roses. And they're all red, bright red roses in Her hands. Now Our Lady is taking them - oh - h, She's going to throw them the way we do! Our Lady is taking the roses now and She's throwing them, like that! But they're going way beyond us, because Our Lady is heaving them this way - one, two, three, four. And Our Lady is turning - I'm counting the roses as they go by; they're going completely over our heads. Look at that! One, two, three, four, five, six, seven. Now it looks like Our Lady has given much more than I counted - seven - many more, because She has only about three now roses left in Her hands. Now She's going over very fast, She's floating over to Her statue now, and Our Lady is placing the three roses on the statue, right at Our Lady's cape. She's placing them, She's putting the ends of the roses into the cape of Our Lady, and two on the statue's right side, and one is on Her left side. They're just beautiful roses. And Our Lady said, now you shall take a picture of the statue.

World monetary crash
One massive depression

Eve of the Feast of the Nativity Of Our Lady - September 7, 1985

Veronica - All about the trees there are columns of light; I say columns because they're like long streamers coming from high in the sky. Now directly over Our Lady's statue, many feet in the air, I can barely see the coloration of the light that is slowly coming through the clouds, the sky. Now the light is becoming round, circular, not cascading down as originally, onto the trees below.

And I can see Our Lady; Our Lady is smiling. She is coming fast down to the trees. Now Our Lady is looking all about Herself; She's looking to and fro. And, also, She is going over slightly to our left side, which would be Her right side. And Our Lady is now taking our Her Rosary; it was about Her waist. And Our Lady is wiping tears from Her eyes. I don't know why, at this time, Our Lady is crying.

But for the first time I see a wisp of hair on Her mantle. Never in all the apparitions of Our Lady have I ever seen even a wisp of hair. But I can only tell you - in the light it's difficult to describe - but Her hair is not black; Her hair is a dark brown. Now Our Lady is smiling, and She is taking the Rosary which She had about Her belt, out, like this; and She is taking the crucifix, the beautiful large crucifix, which cascades its golden contents onto the Our Fathers and the Hail Mary beads of Her Rosary - Our Lady is taking the crucifix now and blessing all at Her right side, which would be our left side: In the name of the Father, and of the Son, and of the Holy Ghost.

Our Lady is looking about Her, and She's slowly turning to the left. Now as I watch, I can see coming down from Heaven, two angels. I know they're angels because of the way they float, and the angelic goodness that seems to stem into your very emotions. There is no human way to explain the approach of these two angels. They are carrying between them a pillow, a beautiful blue velvet pillow. And setting on the pillow is a crown, a beautiful golden crown, set with all of the colors of the rainbow stones. I know they are precious stones.

And they are going to Our Lady now. Our Lady is coming over, directly above Her statue. Now each angel is holding - and before Our Lady, they have now come over in front of Her - and they're holding up this pillow. And I see an invisible force - there are no hands lifting it - but the crown upon the pillow is rising slowly now, and it's rising and coming right onto Our Lady's head. It is a fantastic view; I wish that everyone could see this. The crown is just beautiful. But the crown is similar to what we have come to know as the Fatima crown.

Now Our Lady is smiling. Her Rosary beads have been placed about Her waist again, and Our Lady is standing like this.

Our Lady - "My child, I wish for prayers of atonement, especially for the protection of the Holy Father in Rome. As I warned you, the time is growing short, and the enemies of My Son's Church are accelerating in their plan to do away with your Vicar - your Vicar who has been sent to you by God the Father to save the whole institution of religion in the world, and not have it fall into the hands of the egomaniacs that reside in the land called Russia.

"My child and My children, I speak to you and I come to you as your Mother, a Mother of love; if only you could be as one with Me and My Son. How grateful We are for those who have chosen to dedicate their lives and give up all of the attachments that bore into the human spirit and destroy it. Material things, My children, shall not be judged as making you worthy to enter the kingdom of Heaven. The kingdom of Heaven, I repeat, is a narrow road and so few today are finding it, because they have hardened their hearts and closed their ears to all that We say to them, that We cry for them in Heaven.

"My child, I wash that you would exercise more caution in going out of your home. You must not venture alone. I

233

have sent to you your daughter, and another, to help you in this trying time.

"My child and My children, I speak to you all as one voice from Heaven, one among many, telling you that the time is short. The grain in the hourglass is beginning to filter through. Look, My child, and see what is ahead for mankind."

Veronica - Our Lady now is standing directly above Her statue, and She's pointing high into the sky. And I see a whole globe of the world; I know it's a globe, but it's frightening because all points that are pinpointed with a black dot are now in flames. Our Lady is touching Her lips now, as She stands with Her face - and tears streaking down Her face onto us all. Our Lady is looking about Her, and She is touching Her lips. I must listen carefully and repeat.

Save the Pope

Our Lady - "My child and My children, this could be an occasion of great joy, My coming to you. But the fate of humanity and the world lies in the hands and the hearts of the faithful. Without your prayers and your acts of penance, you cannot save your Pope, and Our son, your Vicar. I will say, in My Mother's heart, from My Mother's heart to you, that your Vicar will soon meet with an enemy, who comes as an angel of light to him, but is an enemy of My Son's Church, and all of My Son's churches throughout the world. We choose, My child, to call them the House of God, because it is a home, a refuge, for all of Our children who suffer and are brought to naught by modern science. In this way We hope that modern science will accept the supernatural, but they rather would cast it aside, My child and My children.

"I have warned you all to protect your children. I come to you as a Mother. So few can understand My role throughout life on earth. I, too, know, My children, all of your hardships, your sorrows, and the temptations from satan. For I, too, was upon your earth, My children; this you have forgotten. I am not unapproachable, as some think,

234

because I was as one of you, until the Eternal Father lifted Me up into Heaven.

"My child and My children, I shall continue to beg the Eternal Father to hold His heavy hand from coming upon you. Your peace and joy - that words are spoken of peace and joy when there is no peace and no joy. How can there be joy when others have assumed a power, which they expect to transcend to Heaven with by bringing back the dead? No, My children. I know of your modern science and how they are trying to now resurrect the dead. This shall never be.

Aids sent because of sin

"And I repeat to you, My children, listen well. The disease you call a modern disease, I call it a disease of satan. That disease, known as AIDS, shall have no cure. It has been sent upon mankind because of their sin.

"Wars are a punishment for sins, and the wars will accelerate, until all of the world is engulfed in one fire. Only My Son can ask the Father for a reprieve from what is coming upon you. However, there is a balance carried by Michael. Look, My child, and see..."

Veronica - High up in the sky, over on the right side, I can see Michael. Oh, he's absolutely beautiful. He's not wearing a short skirt like they depict here upon earth; he has on a long white gown. But he's magnificent. His size is, in human language, five times larger than any of the angels I have seen. He is a magnificent warrior of Heaven. But he's carrying in his right hand a scale, and I see it loaded, actually loaded - it's the only way I can explain this - with what appears to be ingots, or blocks of gold. And on the other side, I see miniature figures of people, and it seems that the gold is winning out, and forcing these people to slide from the scale, the balance.

St. Michael - "The world, my children..."

Veronica - That is St. Michael; his voice is booming.

St. Michael - "... the world, my children, I repeat, is sorrily on the path to its own destruction. The balance is far to the left."

Russian plan of attack finalized

Our Lady - "My child and My children, and especially, you, My child, Veronica, We have brought you to the site this evening to give a dire Message of warning to all mankind. At this very hour, on this very day, a plan has been built now in Russia to attack the United States and Canada.

"My child, I understand that your government has been greatly deluded by their visitors. They come to see and remember what they have seen, to advance their unspiritual and diabolical coercion with satan.

"My child and My children, I wish you to know at this time that We want to protect you, and We warn you constantly. How many times can you count on your fingers the warnings from Heaven given through various seers upon earth?

Massive world monetary depression

"My child and My children, the days will grow darker, and there will be hunger in your land. Yes, My child, what I brought you here for this evening is to tell the world that there will be a crash in the monetary doings of your government - an absolute crash that will affect every man, woman, and child in the United States and Canada, and then, like a serpent, creep all over Europe, until the world sees one big, massive depression. I can illustrate to you, My children, what I mean by this monetary depression.

"Should you go and wish to buy a small instrument, even a guitar, that We hear plucking away at the dervishly, and devilry, of what is called the musical Mass, strung by guitars, and other creations of satan. My child, I go on to tell you, you will say that the guitar is not a costly item, but in order to buy this guitar you will carry an actual satchel, an overnight bag - size, My child - let Us put it that way clearly - of notes, your currency. It will take a whole suitcase of paper - paper money that no longer has a value. You will soon be reduced to bartering for your food.

Subs offshore In contact with KGB

"My child, how can you stop this? Are you going to sit back and allow them to ravage your land, as they go about in the outer waters, sailing and diving, and watching, and coming into your land, keeping with them contact with an organization called the KGB.

"My child, I know you are affrighted at this knowledge, for I have given you others - other means of avoiding this in your country by spreading the words from the Eternal Father throughout the world. Yes, My child, the whole world must listen now, or they will be engulfed in a total world war. This war will be like no other war that man has ever suffering or seen. It will be the end of the world.

"My child, I know you are affrighted at this word 'war'; 'death', 'turmoil', 'depression', but what can I do but tell you the truth. I cannot smooth over it, for I would be accepted like those upon earth who like ostriches, they walk about, proud in their scientific knowledge. However, they are fooled by satan, for satan has made it known - and We here, My children, as defenders of the Faith, defenders of My Son's House upon earth, We, also, know the truth - that satan is loosed upon earth. All hell is opened up wide. Every major and minor demon - called the devils by others - only they remain upon earth now. Those who perish now in the name of their Faith shall be held in abeyance to meet with My Son, in His second descent onto the earth.

"Yes, My children and My child, you cannot look back and say, 'Well, this may be happening to my neighbors in Africa, in Europe, but why should we care? For we can go on marrying, and singing, and being materialistic in our modes.' But where is your soul, My children and My child? I ask you this because if one parent refuses, and has conscionable knowledge of his refusal being offensive to his God - if one parent cast aside his child, no matter what age that child is, and even into womanhood and manhood...

237

That parent has a responsibility to the children, his and her children, to see that they learn fast of the knowledge of God and what is coming upon them.

"Fear shall be struck into the hearts of most; but as you know, My child and My children, I, as your Mother, will be with you throughout all of the conflagrations of the world, to see that those who have lived in justice, those who have shed their blood for the salvation of souls, and those who have accepted their roles - as a person would on your earth, before all of Heaven ... There are many who have accepted the role as victim souls.

"My child, I wish that you at this time take three photographs; it is urgent. The one you will explore and not read out. The second you may read, but the major message you must leave out. And the third you can explain, but the third part must be a remaining secret, until We find it best for the world to know.

"You see, My child, the enemy is very cagey. He has it all planned that man shall capitulate to save his body, to save his material goods, to save his money; as money has become the god for many. Money and power - this, My child and My children, is what brings upon the wars, and the killings, and the murders.

Russia lining up major strikes

"Your country, the Unites States, and Canada, and most of the nations of the world now, are being lined up by Russia for major strikes.

"I tell you this because I cry tears of pity upon you all. How many years, My children - count back - how many years have I come to you as your Mother, and made known to you plans of the enemy? And what have you done to help out your brothers and your sisters? Do you sit there smugly, confidential in your own arrogance, and say that this shall not happen to me, this is for someone else. I assure you, My children, this will happen to you, and it will not be the 'someone else', for it will be you. For as two men are working at the till, one will be taken and one will remain; as two women are working at the fields, one will be taken, one will remain.

"My child, it will remain a mystery for you but for the second photograph. You will read these photographs, My children, and await My Son, for His Message is far more dire than that which I have given to you this evening. Sit back, My child, and read the photographs, and be very, very careful that you do not forget My directions to you."

Veronica - All about the trees there are cascading long lights. I call them 'lights', because I can't know of any way that I could judge them, be it physical or supernatural. The lights are like slivers of glass - sharp, and coming from a point directly over Our Lady's statue, in the center of the sky. All about us there are graces being given, they're coming down as slivers of light, all about our heads, and they're shining down onto the trees. And they're falling like ... the only way I can explain it is that they're falling like slivers of material type of - I don't know what you would call them.

Our Lady - "Instruments from God, My child, instruments."

Veronica - Yes, instruments from God, Our Lady said. Now Jesus is coming forward. He's dressed in a beige smock, I believe you call it - a gown. And He has on His burgundy cape, the one I am so used to seeing Him in. I love that burgundy cape. And Jesus knows it, and He wears it. And He has about a half inch trimming of gold upon His cape. And I do believe that there's a cowl, a headpiece, but it's now down. Jesus' hair is blowing in the wind slightly. It's not too windy tonight because I can see Jesus' feet. He has on sandals. They're made of a leather like material, and they have a band about His ankle.

And now Jesus is looking all about Him, and He's placing His finger, His first finger, to His lips, that means to listen and repeat. Now Jesus is taking a Rosary, which He had in His hand, I didn't notice that, but He's taken out of His left hand, a rosary, in particular, and He's raising the Rosary, the crucifix on it, high above our heads, and making the sign of the cross: In the name of the Father, and of the Son, an of the Holy Ghost.

Jesus is speaking now.

Jesus - "My child and My children, I use My Mother's Rosary in order to enlighten you upon this day of, I should say, the formation this day of an interlude in your life. I say 'interlude' because no words will be able to contain the exact knowledge that We give you this evening, whether by parable, or symbolicness, or anything that you may call scientific. This, My child and My children, is a direct Message from Heaven.

"And I come allowing My Mother first to precede Me, because it is Her day of birth upon earth, and I have great love for My Mother. But I waited with My heart aching for you all, for if you could only see with the eyes, your human eyes - which, of course, My children, is not possible at this time - you will see what is going to happen to all of your relatives and neighbors, and friends, and others throughout the world, as the plans continue in Russia to destroy the world. They shall never take over the world completely, but they will use the power of money and instruments of war to make the nations rise up against each other. This is happening slowly, but due to the state of man's souls upon earth it will now accelerate very fast, My child and My children.

"I wish to have this evening with you a time of great rejoicement for My Mother, but She wills that We not rejoice on Her day of birth, for there are far greater things to rejoice for."

Our Lady - "My Son..."

Veronica - Our Lady is speaking now. She's been crying. I don't know how I could actually sit here and hear Our Lady cry, the way She has been crying. (Veronica speaks with emotion.)

Now Jesus is going over to Our Lady. All this time He was talking. Our Lady has been standing over on our left side. She has both of Her hands together, with the Rosary between Her fingers. But Her eyes are cast down, and the tears, they're glistening in the light of all of the transcending back and forth - these rays that are coming from Jesus onto the trees and down among us. There are glitters of graces all about Our Lady. But Our Lady stands motionless, and watching Jesus, nodding Her head.

Now Jesus is looking all about Him. Now He's going over to Our Lady, and going on to Her right side - that would be our left side - and He's making the sign of the cross, like this: In the name of the Father, and of the Son, and of the Holy Ghost.

Now Jesus is turning to His left side - that would be our right side - and He's coming just above the statue. He's standing there and looking about. He has - Jesus, I can see Him so closely now that I feel as though He's standing right before me. He's very tall, you know, so it's difficult to see in the sky how magnificently Heaven has structured Him, that He must be at least six foot two tall, if not a little taller.

But now He's smiling, but His smile, too, is of sadness; there's no way to explain it. It sort of wrenches at your heart, and you feel that there must be something that can be done to have everyone in Heaven happy. But Jesus and Our Lady say together.

Jesus and Our Lady - "There cannot be happiness where there is sin and destruction."

Veronica - It was like in one voice, Our Lady and Jesus are repeating it again.

Jesus and Our Lady - "There can be no happiness upon earth..."

Jesus - "... and I shall enlarge upon it, My children, at this time."

Veronica - Jesus is placing His hand up and making the sign of the cross. Now Jesus is looking down at me, and He's putting His first finger to His lips.

Jesus - "My child and My children, how long do you think We will be able to go across the nations and warn them that war is in preparation. How long can We wait for those who do not wish to be saved, because they have lost the Faith. They have accepted all the beguilement of satan and given themselves over to lives of eating, and drinking, and marrying, and making all manner of aversions, which are nothing but insults into the heart of My Mother.

"Do not think, My children, that I am not aware of what is going on upon earth. For I have counted every hair on the head of every single living creature upon earth, human - wise. We see you all, My children, and I could only say to you at this time that I find you lacking, and in dire need of something to straighten you out fast.

"Since the world has given itself over to murders, murders of the unborn, father against son, daughters against mothers, all manner of carnage; also, being perpetrated in My House, My Church upon earth. How long do you think I shall stand by and watch the destruction of the young, because of parents who should not accept the role or the name of parents, for they are destroying their children's souls by their example.

Sacred Heart in all homes

"Too few now even carry in their homes a visage of Mine, My children. I ask that that visage of the Sacred Heart be placed in all homes as protection against satan. Already, they are being discarded and thrown in the waste-baskets, My children, so little is the Faith.

"I could go on and on, My child and My children, stating to you and writing out a great discourse on what is to happen to the world, and shall come upon you suddenly.

"Do not follow the scoffers who continue to say, 'His promise has not and will not come true, to return in the Second Coming.' I assure you I shall come to you all as a thief in the night. Little will you be prepared unless you listen to My Mother's counsel and keep your heart open for the truth. The more you seek riches in this life, the less you will have in Heaven, for they do not coincide, My child and My children. You cannot have a god, symbolized by money, before you, for you will love one and hate the other. And whom will you hate, My children, but Me?"

Veronica - Jesus is looking all about Him now, and He's turning very fast, but He's motioning Our Lady to come with Him. They're crossing over until They're about at the

242

top of the first bough on our right side, the very thick tree, on the first bough. Now Jesus and Our Lady are looking about everyone, and Jesus now is extending His hand out, like this, and making the sign of the cross: In the name of the Father, and of the Son, and of the Holy Ghost.

Now Jesus is looking and He's placing His hands out, like this, in front of Him, and all from His fingers there are rays of beautiful light. Oh, there's no way I can humanly tell you what this light is like! It's beautiful! I feel if it came my way now, I should perish with joy. The light is so beautiful. But it is falling now upon others on our right side - in the infirm and the ill, and those who are sick of mind or body - these lights are now cascading down. I almost touched one of them, but there was something so supernatural that I knew I had to withdraw my hand, or I would die. I knew it.

Now the lights are beginning to dim. They were straight lights. They were similar to the lights that were in one of the photographs taken on the site here, all cascading down onto the exedra; only they are the lights over by the trees, cascading down onto the sick and the infirm.

Now Jesus is moving fast. The wind is catching His gown and His robe. And Our Lady looks - I can't explain how Our Lady looks... She looks crushed. The only thing I can say, I did not expect Her to be so sorrowful. We wish to make this a happy birthday for Our Lady, but Her heart is too torn. She says this:

Our Lady - "The best present, My child, that man could give to Me is to turn back from his ways, which are unpleasing to My Son, and the Father, and the Holy Spirit - the Spirit of life, the Holy Ghost, My child."

Veronica - So now Our Lady is - She's ahead of Jesus now; while He talked, Our Lady went ahead. I could see Her skirt blowing in the wind. Oh, Our Lady has on a beautiful pair of slippers. They're gold. I know they must be real gold. They're beautiful, the slippers. And on the tips of the slipper there is a single - on each, one, the right and the left foot - a single little gold rosette. Our Lady calls it a rosette; it's very small, but it's a beautiful golden rose.

Now Our Lady is wiping Her eyes with Her hands. And I know She's bravely trying to stand upright, but She's now standing at our left side with Her head down. I know She's crying; I can hear Her softly crying. Now Jesus is going over there by Our Lady, He's come from our right side and is going over to the left, and He's placed His arm about Our Lady, and He's patting Her back. He feels very bad that this Message had to be given on Her birthday, but Our Lady says this.

Our Lady - "Do not be sorrowful, My child and My children; there will be times of great joy for all of us. This will not be a permanent state upon earth; earth that is covered with sin and defilement, children against their parents, murders in every street, killing of the unborn, and much more; much more that, My child, that I would wish you to know, but I cannot, for the purity of heart, instruct you on the vile deeds of the satanist."

Veronica - Now Our Lady is rising high over into the sky, and She's pointing now out towards Her left side; She's standing on our right side, over the statue, and She's pointing out over to our right side, and She's now touching Her lips fast.

Our Lady - "Look, My child, and see man scurrying to and fro, and where is he going but to damnation! Man has given himself over to satan, as satan roams the world. And if you had only listened to Me many years ago; I warned you that satan would be loosed upon earth with every demon out of the abyss. What chance do you have, My children, if you are so proud and arrogant that you think that you can consort with satan and come out the winner. No, My child, his powers are too great. I cannot explain to you at this time why this is allowed. It is a mystical feat against satan."

Jesus - "My child and My children, My Mother wishes that you know that regardless of the state of your souls, that are so darkened by the manner in which you are constructing, but destructing your lives - My Mother has promised you, and She shall not fail in this promise, that She shall remain with you until the end of time."

Our Lady - "My children..."

Veronica - Jesus is looking about...

Our Lady - "... and I say, My poor children, remember My words: When you become ill, be it physical, mental, or sorrowfully in your heart, you will say, my Jesus, my confidence! And I will truly succor you. I use that word, My child, 'succor', because it was a favorite word of one of Our sons of My Son's House. Yes, you know, and all know who this was, though he met an untimely death, as did the other who came after him."

Jesus - "My child and My children, I must also warn you that My Mother was not light, or can be taken lightly, in what She has just given to you as knowledge of the KGB. They are now holding the major stations in your government. They come as angels of light to your leader; and though he has a good heart, he has not the knowledge to understand, nor look for, the very evil that is about him, that can lead this country directly into a confrontation with Russia.

Russia planning takeover without a shot

"It is true, My child, that one of the KGB agents who rose to power was allowed to appear in the Senate and slam his shoe upon the table and say, 'We will take the United States without firing a shot!' Do not take this lightly, My children, for that is exactly what they are doing."

Our Lady - "Do not be affrighted, My child. You will meet with much controversy over this Message, but the truth must be made known. And also, My child, I prepare you well now; you listen to Me and remember, your life will not be easy, for these agents will seek to destroy you. Do not be affrighted, My child; I have promised to protect your family. Do not ever feel that I would turn My back from you, no matter how grave the times.

"You will be very careful, My child, to keep your doors barred to all but your immediate family and the close Shrine workers. None others must enter your house. You must instruct your husband to seek only those from the Shrine to help him in any major repairs in your home, for he will enter, and you will die!

"Yes, My child, I brought you here this evening so that you will understand that your time has come. Before it was a war of nerves upon you, but now there shall be physical war, My child, and you must prepare for it. The world will not take this Message lightly. Those in the know will understand; the others will seek to hate you.

"I say unto you, all who wish to be saved must at this time be apart from the world. They can live in the world, but they cannot be a part of it. That you will ponder over, My children, and you will understand. Sometimes, I understand that you have difficulty in understanding the symbolism, and the manner in which My Son brings His Message to you. But just remember, nothing is hidden from you. All you will do when you become befuddled, My children, all you will do is pray to the Holy Spirit, the Holy Ghost; or pray directly to the Eternal Father, and ask Him to enlighten you as to the day's woes that come upon you.

"You are not abandoned, for you all have been given an angel of protection. Yours, My child, is Tomdarius. No, not Tomdarius, My child; that was Ben, who has chosen to remain away from the graces given him. They cannot be continued unless he returns to the Shrine. He cannot enter into the circle, but he must still remember his role as a pilgrim for Christ in the world. He is giving himself over to worldly pursuits, and this takes him farther from the road to Heaven.

"My child and My children, every Message that is given is as from Me a personal Message to each and every one of you, to prepare you for what lies ahead. It will not be easy to accept the judgment of mankind against you, for only a few will be saved, My children; and I am sure, as your Mother, that you will wish to be among those who are saved.

"Remember, keep a constant vigilance of prayer going about your country and the world. Wear your Scapular. Wear any crucifix that you can find; it does not have to be big or small, but an image of My Son."

Veronica - Now Our Lady and Jesus are both - Our Lady is raising the crucifix, the beautiful golden crucifix on Her Rosary, like this...

[Pause]

Oh, Oh. Our Lady said:

Our Lady - "Up high."

Veronica - In the name of the Father, and of the Son, and of the Holy Ghost.

Our Lady - "I bless you with the shield of the Immaculate Conception: In the name of the Father, and of the Son, and of the Holy Ghost. May you be protected by the shield of the Immaculate Conception."

Veronica - Now Our Lady is touching Her lips.

Jesus - "My child, We will be here for the rest of the evening prayers. My Mother must then go on to Lourdes.

"Yes, My child, you cannot understand the humanism that lies even in Our hearts, though everything has become a spirit for the Father. In our human nature upon earth, We have not forgotten. Yes, My Mother is traveling on to Lourdes. But She returns as soon as possible. She has the world now to try to awaken them before it is too late. My Mother does not rest, but has gone endlessly, timelessly, on to all the nations of the world, appearing personally, to implore everyone to stop the carnage that is fast coming upon the world. She does not want to see the world destroyed.

"Now My children, remember; wear your armor, the Scapular, the Rosary. I say the Rosary; I do not mean that you will wear it as a decoration. You will wear it about your neck, though hidden from the view of others, just in case you are one of the many who will flee with what is on their backs. You will have no time to turn back, you will have no time to ride; all will depend upon your own years of preparement, through learning the only true way to save your souls is by following the Message from Heaven.

247

Not to be involved with other apparitions

"There are false prophets throughout the world; many who are also coming as angels of light to deceive you in the end. Remember, My child, I ask you not to become involved with any other apparitions in the world, because sorrowfully, My children, I must tell you, many of them are not true. So you see, My child, were it not so, I would tell you; but many of them have come forward for gratification in their human natures.

"Now, My child, remember that I warn you to bar your doors, and do not venture without your house unless there is someone with you. Yes, My child, I sent Grace back. I sent her back to make sure that you do not forget Our warnings to you.

"Now, My child, you will sit back and continue with the prayers of atonement. Keep the Rosary about you, My child, too. I say - what I say to you I say to the world. But do not cut yourself out, My child, in your reasoning. Many of the messages are for you and the world."

Veronica - Now Our Lady is motioning to Jesus, and He's raising His hand. They're both directly over Her statue now, and He's raising His hand, like this: In the name of the Father, and of the Son, and of the Holy Ghost.

Now Jesus is looking towards Our Lady; Our Lady is on our left side. And He's motioning, like this, and She's saying, yes.

Now Jesus is motioning, like this, to me.

Jesus - "Continue now, My children, with your prayers of atonement."

Veronica - Our Lady is still very sad, it's not a very happy birthday to her tonight. The news is too grave, Our Lady said; the news is much too grave.

Save the Pope! John Paul II begs for prayers

The Triumph of The Cross & Eve of Our Lady of Sorrows - September 14, 1985

Veronica - All about the trees, there are golden and yellow - symbolizing the papacy - and next to these golden and yellow cascading lights, that are coming from high in the sky, downward, like banners - I know that the yellow and the gold does refer to the papacy - and next to it, I see the Pope, John Paul II, standing there. He's looking all about. And he's stretching out his arms, like this, and saying:

Pope John Paul II - "My children of the world, pray for me."

Veronica - Now as he looks over to his left, our right, I can see a figure, high in the sky, but he's like a picture of death. He's got the face of a masked man. I cannot understand why I cannot see his full face, this masked man. But he's dressed, though, with a cassock, and also, the clothing of a priest, the collar and all. However, from his neck up, he looks like something so horrible that... I know I'm getting a horrible reaction from looking at him. Now he carries with him a scythe for cutting down fast, people. I know he's not out to cut grass, but he's out to cut down our Holy Father.

Now it's growing very dark, and that figure is now disintegrating into a huge black cross. And forming under the cross is a large globe of the world. And then I see a darkness, starting from the blackened cross, moving downward slowly over the whole world, until there isn't a light on the earth.

Now the sky is beginning to grow a little more brighter. And I can see now that the figure is disappearing as in a mist. And high above Our Lady's statue, about, maybe twelve to sixteen feet, I see Our Lady. I didn't notice Her approach; I was so startled at the figure of death, standing right before us, that I did not look forward, upward.

Our Lady is coming down very slowly. The sky has opened up about Her, and the evening is one of tranquillity and joy, because I can hear the voices of angels singing. I cannot make out what they're singing, but the humming and the droning of the song sound like a Gregorian Chant.

Now Our Lady is coming slowly forward. I can see now Her tiny sandals. Our Lady has on golden sandals with the little gold rosettes at the tippytoe. Our Lady always refers to that section as the tippytoe.

Now Our Lady is looking all about Her. She is now descending, and I would say She's around nine feet above Her statue.

Now Our lady has on Her mantle, which is blowing in the wind. Her mantle is a beautiful white color - so beautiful, I often wonder what the material is that could be so shining, and translucent, and beautiful. And all about the mantle Our Lady has a fine - about a half an inch of gold thread going all about the outer parts of Her mantle.

Now Our Lady has on a white gown, a pure white, translucent gown. I say translucent - you cannot see through it, but it gives you the feeling of, as though you could almost walk right up, and walk through Our Lady. I know that this is a feeling, experienced once when I was in a locution with Our Lady, and She took me by the hand, and I moved forward. I felt like I moved forward through something impenetrable normally, but it was light as a feather, and I walked through a mist, not knowing that Our Lady was taking me down to see purgatory.

Now Our Lady is looking all about Her, and She's now taking Her Rosary from about Her waist. Our Lady has a golden sash about Her waist this evening. She looks so beautiful. And the shining of the gold, upward, seems to be so mystical that I have no words to explain it. It's so beautiful that it actually takes every bit of feeling and emotion to explain the beauty of Our Lady standing there.

Now Our Lady has Her Rosary in Her hands, the beautiful Rosary with the golden Our Fathers and the white Hail Marys, that as Our Lady is turning, they're cascading in all colors of the rainbow. Now Our Lady is moving to our left, Her right, and She's extending Her Rosary out, like this, and making the sign of the cross: In the name of the Father, and of the Son, and of the Holy Ghost.

Now Our Lady is looking over to Her left, our right, and She's slowly moving upward, and going to the left, Her left, until She's directly over Her statue. Now, Our Lady is now raising the golden crucifix on Her Rosary and making the sign of the cross: In the name of the Father, and of the Son, and of the Holy Ghost.

Our Lady now is looking all about Her. I notice now that She has in Her hand a Scapular, which She must have taken from about Her waist to give to mankind the message of the Scapular. Now Our Lady is walking over, though, first - She's walking, but She's really floating. I use the words on earth here of walking, but Our Lady never walks; She absolutely - floats so beautifully.

Now Our Lady is moving over to our right side, Her left, and She's extending the crucifix on Her Rosary, high, like this, and making the sign of the cross: In the name of the Father, and of the Son, and of the Holy Ghost.

Now Our Lady is looking all about Her, and She's pointing upward, with Her hand to the sky. And coming through the sky - I didn't notice that the sky has opened up into a crystal - like atmosphere, round in circumference, but crystal - like. And directly in the center of this crystalline ball - that's what it appears to be a crystalline - ball and Our Lady is still pointing upward, She hasn't moved Her hand; and Jesus now is emerging from the light. He's coming down very slowly. His hair is blowing in the wind. It must be quite windy above us. Jesus' hair is quite long. It goes down to His back - I don't know how far, because I've had few chances to look in back of Him, since He's always facing us, and floats that way.

Now Jesus has come down, until He's only about four feet above Our Lady's statue. Now Our Lady is coming across the sky slowly. She's floating. And She's joining Jesus over the statue Now Jesus is looking all about Him, and He's placing His hands, like this, before Him, and making the sign of the cross: In the name of the Father, and of the Son, and of the Holy Ghost.

Jesus is smiling. He has a smile that is a composite of heartache and joy, gladness and sorrow; I don't know where the balance is, so heavy are the trials of the world upon Jesus. These trials, though, are produced from sin, sin of mankind.

Now Jesus is nodding. And He's going with Our Lady. Our Lady is following Him. She's on Jesus' left side, that would be our right side. And Jesus is going over to the left side, almost to the top tree, the one - yes, right directly to the left of the banners. Now Jesus is extending His hand out, like this, and making the sign of the cross: In the name of the Father, and of the Son, and of the Holy Ghost.

Now He's looking about Him, and He's now floating over - Our Lady knows where He's heading, because She is going on, and He's floating behind Her. And Our Lady is floating over to our right side - She's not stopping over the statue, but going over between the banner, and the banner of the papacy. Now Our Lady is looking down at the papacy flag, and She's nodding. She's nodding.

Now Our Lady is touching Her lips with Her finger: that means to listen and repeat. Jesus now has become very quiet. He's nodding, which means that I am to listen to His Mother, and repeat.

Our Lady - "My child and My children, and you, My child, Veronica, I caution you again to be extremely wary when you go outside your home. I have told you before, My child, that you must not venture forth alone, or you will disappear from the face of the earth.

"Do not be affrighted, My child, I speak to you not to place fear in your heart, but to protect you and your family from any harm."

Veronica - Now Our Lady is looking towards Jesus, and He's nodding. And now She's turning - Our Lady is turning, as She plans to go back over Her statue. I can see Her heading for Her statue. And Jesus is standing just above the statue. While Our Lady spoke with me, He moved over, just above the statue. Now He's making room for Our Lady to stand above the statue. Now Our Lady is touching Her finger to Her lips.

Scapular - rules and regulations

Our Lady - "My child and My children, I speak with you this evening to caution you, and not - to not fall into despair because there is a conflict over My Brown Scapular.

"You will know, My children, that there are always rules and regulations for everything that man holds sacred. Therefore, because so few priests in My Son's Church are willing to intercede with the Scapular, and enthrone those who wish it, it has become necessary to give a Scapular to every child upon earth; and he or she of reasonable age shall go forth and find a kind - hearted and true, holy priest to enroll them. It will take, My children, much doing to find these priests; there are not many left.

"O My children, how difficult you are making it for Me, especially the priests in My Son's House upon earth, His Church. I cry tears endlessly when I know that every day My Son is confronted by numerous souls who have lost their way, and refused the redemption that will come to him through wearing the Brown Scapular.

"My child, do not be stopped in your efforts to give out these Scapulars. I directed you well, My children, in several instances throughout your lifetime. Think back, My child and My children, think back to the days when you were enrolled in the Brown Scapular.

"I tell you now that should you wish to be enrolled, I can only suggest - though the outcomes may not be as you wish - I could only suggest that you approach a Franciscan priest, a Carmelite priest, or a Dominican priest. The others have fallen away to a certainty, and your chances of meeting up with success would be very little. My child, among the others.

Never see the fires of hell

"I promise you all, when you wear My Brown Scapular,

you shall not be condemned to hell. I repeat: if you pass on over the veil and are wearing the Brown Scapular, you shall not see the fires of hell.

"My child and My children, it will take great courage for you to fight, for the others in your parish, and those who are your friends, who do not have the courage of their convictions - courage to go forth and promote the Brown Scapular... I do not go back on My words to mankind: I have often said to the world, that if you wear My Scapular, you will be saved.

"To understand this better, My child, I will converse further with you. Now this be it known: that the Scapular cannot keep you from purgatory. I purposely gave this knowledge to St. Simon Stock, the knowledge of the existence of a sacramental so powerful that a man who would fall fast into hell shall escape, through the mercy of his God, and the existence of a shadow of faith that he may have.

"My child, you will watch the Scapulars carefully as they come in. To be of perfection you cannot make a substitution, or you lose the graces, My children. It is a simple cloth, and can be obtained in many nations. And those that do not have the means to make these cloths shall use the only passage known to man - to approach another, who can help him or her to obtain this perfection in cloth.

"My child and My children, I have wandered for years throughout your land, with tears streaming from My broken heart, warning you that the hourglass is almost empty. Like a thief in the night, the Chastisement shall come upon you. Are you ready, My children? Have you read, and reread the messages from Heaven given from the years that go back to 1970? Those prior to 1970 are, also, most urgent to be given to the world.

"My child, I notice that you have completed one side of the book. Yes, the messages were taken from the tapes. As soon as Heaven deems you ready, you will receive the lost book of messages, and you will, also, place them on tape. Conversations with Jesus must now go out at a fast pace; there is little time left.

"Look up, My child, to the sky; look high into the sky."

Veronica - I see a ball. It's a horrible ball. It's red and white, and it's traveling very fast through the atmosphere. I have such a feeling of fright that I think I shall fall over. (Veronica speaks with trepidation.) It's frightening, It has a long tail. And this is huge, this ball is huge. It's starting to cover the whole sky. It's orange and it's white, and there is something - Our Lady is pointing, She's letting me know that She's there by the trees - not to be affrighted at what I see. But there are streams of molten lava coming out of this ball and sending what appears to be meteors down into the waters and the seas. And I see the seas and the waters burning - burning!... the actual burning! Water burning, this is almost impossible, Our Lady!

Our Lady - "No, My child, you do not know the force of these meteors. They shall burn until they hit the land."

Veronica - Now it's growing very dark, very dark. And I see, high in the sky, a building becoming evident. It is in Rome. I see a large basilica, St. Peter's Basilica. And I see a black flag draped over the doors and the windows. Oh, it's so frightening.

And I see Our Lady now. She has moved from beyond the trees, where She was talking with me, and She's going forward, and fast, up high into the sky. She has emerged now out of the sky, and is standing directly above the Basilica. Our Lady now is desperately trying to take Her mantle from both sides and stand on the Basilica. All about Her, I see faces - hundreds of faces, shocked faces ... tears crying and falling upon the multitudes. What is this, Blessed Mother?

Pope Paul VI: smoke of satan In Vatican

"My child, you are looking into Rome on that horrendous day when the Holy Father shall leave you. I say 'shall' because the Message is being rejected in Rome. The previous messages about this carnage to the Holy See and the Holy Father has been taken with a manner of laughter. Too late will they laugh and refer to My visitation in New York as being absurd. My child and My children, that is satan. And as a holy Pope once told you before he died, he knew that the smoke of satan had entered into Rome and the Vatican. Well did he understand My visit to him, My child. The world has never known how close I was to your Vicar at that time, Pope Paul VI. Yes, My child, he was removed from the earth, also, with his impostor."

Veronica - Now Our Lady is passing Her hand over Her eyes, like this. Her tears have now come down upon Her face, and the light that is shining so brightly has almost obliterated Her face from my view, so much is Her sorrow.

Now Jesus is touching His lips.

Jesus - "My child, you cannot see My Mother's face at this time, because Her sorrow would bring you to Our door; for this sorrow of My Mother's cannot be accepted in the human heart, so powerful is Her grief."

Our Lady - "You, My child, must continue to see that the messages from Heaven are going throughout the world.

"The Rosary must be recited daily, and twice a day, if possible. All others we leave to you to say for added graces. In your world of corruption and evil, My children, you cannot gather enough graces. For those that you will not need when you come over the veil to eternity will be given to those whom you love, or those who you have fought to save, and yet, you felt unsuccessful. All the children of the world shall be counted in those who will see the ultimate Chastisement. Many will die in the great flame of the Ball of Redemption.

"My child and My children, there are many sins among mankind, but none have been more vile than the abortions, the taking of human life before birth.

"My child and My children, We cannot accept the political and the rational views - I say 'rational', because they do not use the supernatural, but they curry, c - u - r - r - y, My children - they curry on those who do not have the Faith, to understand their so - called 'enlightened' messages to the world. This I speak of, My children, for I know the influence of the clerics over the laity.

"You cannot judge your brothers and sisters, for you do not know their hearts. However, should you see them going on the wrong path and fast falling from the narrow road to Heaven, you will do your utmost to convince them of their folly. For in the end, it is they who will suffer, because no man knows the day or the hour in which he will depart from the earth. No man can say he is a master of his own life, and therefore, will not die.

"In the Book of love and life, My children, every name has been counted, and every name has a date. Yes, My child and My children, the Eternal Father has looked far into the future, and the book is already made up - those who are to be saved, the sheep; those who are to be lost, the goats.

"My child and My children, I wish that you all keep a constant vigilance of prayer going throughout the world, your country, the United States, and Canada. I warn you again that Russia plans an attack upon the United States.

Russia secretly supplying firearms and missiles

"You must remember, My children, when you accept the talkings and the words of an atheist: there is no honor in the atheist. There is no truth in the atheist. They will cajole you, and buy you, until you no longer are what is called a 'free nation', but you will be enslaved - if they do not kill the multitudes before, My child. I say 'if', because it is their plan to destroy your nation and rebuild it by themselves. The cost of life means nothing to them, as you can recognize in all of the countries around your world that have been invaded by Russia, or Russia is the secret agent giving over the firearms and the destructive missiles to destroy the United States and Canada.

"My child and My children, you cry for peace. I come to you as a Mother of peace. My messages to you are not to frighten you, but they are to reveal to you what will happen if you do not act now upon My counsel, My Mother's counsel to you. I expect you to think of this, and consider what is more important to you: to have a life filled with glory, and money, and materialistic things? Do you think, My children, that you will take them with you? You will come from your world, the earth, with nothing, just as you arrived in it.

Communists' one goal: world domination

"My child and My children, since the world no longer considers the tiny, little babies as being important to life, they no longer will consider the necessity to have the elderly and infirm among us. That is communism, My children! They will destroy the elderly; they will destroy the newborn, and they will destroy anyone who gets in their way. They have one object: that is to conquer the United States and all of the nations, until, like a fan, it will open up and will border upon all the nations of the world.

"I asked you many years ago, My children, I asked you, with a Mother's heart, to follow My rules. I appeared in Fatima. My child, how many actually know the story of My visitations to Fatima, to Lourdes, to Bayside; and others, which I will not name at this time, because others, My child, have fallen into serious errors.

"Now, My children, I wish you to continue your prayers of atonement. Only a few - I count you, My children, upon these grounds this evening, as counted in the few - through the millions of peoples on the earth now, only a few are staying on the narrow road.

"Remember, My children, you know not the day nor the hour; therefore, you must be prepared to leave this earth at any time. There is so much, My children."

Veronica - Now Jesus looked over, and He looked at His Mother, and Our Lady has been crying. Our Lady is crying very hard. Our Lady now is just extending Her arms out, like this, very pitifully, and saying:

Our Lady - "My child and My children, I have come to you under many names in the past, but I want you to acknowledge Me as the Mother of Grace. Because that is why I come to you now. My children: to give you the graces necessary to remain upon earth in a state of purity and perseverance, and knowledgeable to the truth, that will lead you and keep you on the narrow road to Heaven.

"My child and My children, many miraculous photographs have been given to you to try to make you understand how futile it is to go about seeking to buy happiness in a world that is materialistic. You cannot buy happiness, for that is one thing I instilled in mankind: the knowledge that the spirit within him is to be guarded and nourished with the fruits of true life - the knowledge of the Bible, past and present and future.

"My child and My children, you may ask your priests for knowledge of the stories coming from the old, elderly fathers of My Son's Church, but can they tell you the truth now that their seminaries have become polluted with errors? Mothers cry to Me; I hear all of their prayers, prayers to Heaven to save their children. And where can they find the knowledge of the truth to teach them? That will depend now upon an earnest mother and father, and discipline. Children are like soft flowers that must be nourished so that their stalks will grow; and their faces, the purity of their faces, shall rise toward Heaven and be nourished with the fruits of life.

"My child and My children, there must not be any allowances made for the sacrilegious acts of those who call themselves humanists, and, also, those who promote homosexuality in the name of freedom - freedom of religion, freedom of what you want to do: do anything you want, as long as it offends your God. That is what We hear coming up to Us from Heaven. That is what We hear coming up to Us. High into the heavens, I hear - I hear the saints crying, 'How long, O Lord, will you accept this carnage upon earth? When shall we restore it to its former beauty and purity?'"

Veronica - And Jesus has replied now...to - I see the sky opening... I see hundreds, maybe thousands of people. They have, though, one thing in common; they all look like clerics, and they have on their habits. Some are brown, some look black, and others are all pure white. The ladies - they're nuns - are dressed in the all-pure whites, and the others are men.

Our Lady - "My children, you see before you the saints

259

who have gone by, having sacrificed their lives upon earth for the courage that they needed to go forth and bring to the world the truth of the living God.

"My child and My children, I wish that you continue now your prayers of atonement. And you, My child, Veronica, will take three pictures. One you can acknowledge, and two you must keep a secret at this time."

[Pause]

Our Lady - "My child, do not be affrighted. I took you on this journey once before. But I understand, My child: the unknown is often questionable and often disregarded. But you, My child, have been given this knowledge to perpetuate the truth throughout the world.

"Now take the three pictures, My child. Remember: one you may reveal, but the other two must be kept secret at this time."

[Pause]

"... and the other two must remain a secret for this time."

[Pause]

Veronica - Our Lady looks very sad. It actually breaks your heart to see how sad She is. And there's no way other than sacrificing our lives and ourselves to succor Her. Always Jesus and Our Lady want to use the word 'succor', because They know of the visit of Padre Pio to my home many years ago, and often he mentioned Pope Paul VI: he's crying now, "Succor, my children! Succor!" And, also, Padre Pio repeated, "Succor, my little children! Help, help!"

[Pause]

Veronica - ... They're standing by the trees, but I didn't expect for Them to come forward. They have been standing by the trees all this time. Now Jesus is moving away from Our Lady, because Our Lady is standing over the trees on our left side. Now She's looking over at Jesus, and motioning Him, yes. They've been conversing, but I couldn't hear what They were saying.

Now Jesus is coming forward. He's on Our Lady's statue, almost - almost standing above Her head, on the point. And now He's looking about Himself. He's looking to the right and left, and I don't understand the look on His face; it's one of puzzlement and not happiness. There's no words to describe it. Now Jesus is going to touch His finger to His lips.

Jesus - "My child, this evening there is one more subject that must be resolved and dismissed quickly. All over your country and the world, there are groups forming that have alienated themselves from their hierarchy. I have asked you many times to not form another church. I have asked you to remain and suffer for all of the souls upon earth - suffer, even though you know that the Eternal Father watches what is going on. We do not want a schism. We do not wish that new churches be formed. Though the meaning is well, they can lead to nothing but destruction and schism.

Traditionalists being led astray

"We hear all names coming forward to Our ears of churches being born anew, called the Traditional Roman Catholic Church. My child and My children, We need no more Traditionalists running around and creating new churches. We have to remain steadfast and firm in our convictions that with enough prayer, and, also, the firm example of holiness among many, this will not happen.

"We do not condemn those who make these side churches, the Traditional Roman Catholic churches; they mean well, but they are being led astray. There will be eventually an American Catholic church if this continues. This is not approved by Heaven. Man's judgment can always err, especially when he discounts the knowledge of the supernatural.

Breaking away must stop

"Remember, My children, I have asked you to remain steadfast in your parish churches, even though it will be a crucifixion to you. We cannot have schism in the United States and Canada. For those who are united shall stand, and those who divide themselves shall fall. My child and My children, do not discount this part of the Message from

261

Heaven. It is most urgent that this breaking away stop now before it evolves into a major schism.

"My child, you will continue with the prayers of atonement. There is much that We wish to discourse with you at this time, but I understand, My child, the weakness of your human body. We do not expect you to give in to all of your wishes to do as much as you can in short a time. You must also exercise good common sense, My child, and not wear yourself thin. For you will not be able to do your mission well. Take each day as it comes, My child, for tomorrow is another day. I also want you to remember this, My child: to allow yourself to go without sleep gains nothing. There are seven days of the week. There are six days in which to do your work, a seventh shall be a day of rest and prayer. Remember, My children, that the moon has come and the sun has gone, it is time for all children, good or evil, to rest. For the moon has come and the sun has gone, I repeat: it is time for all children to rest. That, My child, will now end the discourse with you this evening.

"But I assure you, We shall not put you through the strain again that forces you to miss My Mother's Vigils here at the Vatican site. Yes, My child, you will not be free from suffering, for you have accepted once those sufferings sent upon you, and in this manner will you keep yourself in the state of grace so necessary for the deliverance of Our Message to the world."

Veronica - Now I can see the sky closing up. Our Lady and Jesus are moving slowly, up, up, up. Now They've stopped. They're going over to our right side, and They're standing there now, and looking down. And Jesus is extending His hand again, and making the sign of the cross: In the name of the Father, and of the Son, and of the Holy Ghost.

Now Our Lady has turned, and She seems to be scurrying... I've seen movement now. She is very anxious to get above Her statue, with Jesus following Her. And Our Lady now has taken Her Rosary, the beautiful Rosary with the golden Our Fathers and the Hail Mary beads, that are just like each bead is a rainbow - it's just beautiful - and Our

Lady is blessing everyone: In the name of the Father, and of the Son, and of the Holy Ghost.

Now Jesus is just behind Our Lady. And She's moving farther over to our left now. And now Jesus has approached Her, and He's standing there. Our Lady is looking up to Him. Like I told you once before, Jesus must be a least six - foot - two tall or more, because Our Lady just comes up barely below His shoulder.

Now Jesus is smiling, and He places His hand out, like this, and makes the sign of the cross: In the name of the Father, and of the Son, and of the Holy Ghost.

Jesus - "Now, My children, We are not leaving. We wish to hear the prayers of atonement, for it is like music to Our hearts. The Rosary has always been music to Our hearts."

[Pause]

"There will be three more photographs. These can be interpreted, My child, but they must be kept. You'll understand why at a future date."

263

Earthquake!
New York, California to be struck

In Honor of the Feast of Our Lady of the Rosary
- October 5, 1985

Veronica - High in the sky, directly over Our Lady's statue, there is the most beautiful shadings of blue and pink
intermingled. And now these colorings, which only bordered - when I first noticed them, the hue of them, they were
only bordering the outside of the trees that lead from the left
to the right side of the exedra. But high up in the sky, I see
beautiful cascading of banners: they are beautiful banners of
blue and yellow, a golden yellow color, and, also, pink. I
know that the blue and pink coloring will signify the arrival
of Jesus and Our Lady.

Yes, now, did you look high into the sky? There will be
several others who will see. High in the sky, oh, about a
good twenty feet over Our Lady's statue, the sky is opening
up. It's absolutely beautiful! And I see, as it grows wider in
circumference, the light is like looking through a pane of
glass that has diamonds set in somewhere within the glass to
radiate outwards. And these radiating star - like diamonds
are beginning to now disintegrate from the circle and are
coming out in a million pieces each, it looks like. That's the
only way I can explain the explosion of these beautiful star-
like diamonds, coming from the circle. It seems as though
Heaven is saying, now this is an occasion of great joy.

Our Lady now is coming forward first. Jesus has
stopped; He was coming down, as I was directed to tell you
what there is about us this evening. Now Jesus is coming
down in back of Our Lady. Our Lady has descended first.
And She's looking up now and pointing toward the sky.
And Jesus, also, has taken His right hand and is pointing up
to the sky on the left side.

High up in the sky, I see a very large globe. It's a globe
of the world. It's becoming very illuminated. And as Our
lady turns, frantically She is waving to a side of the globe.

And She's going over, with approval from Jesus - She had asked him - I couldn't hear what She was saying, but I could hear the drone - like of Her voice. And Jesus is nodding, yes, to go over. Our Lady is approaching the globe of the earth. It is an actual globe, as though taken from space, that only Heaven could present to us this evening. Our Lady is pointing to Africa. I see Africa with a blackness, starting in the southern part, and going up and up.

Africa - war, famine and droughts

Jesus - "And there will be, also, great warfare in Africa - famine and warfare, droughts. O My children, all of these, with wars included, are allowed to come upon you so that you may understand and learn the hard way that there is a God - One who could stop the massacres; One who could stop all the suffering upon earth. However, it is a test for all mankind; for by this test, many shall be cleansed. O My children, My desperate children, I hear your voices coming up to Us, and My Mother sheds tears of pity for you.

"Look, My children, beyond where My Mother is standing; look carefully, and you will see the globe of the world, as it starts to turn."

Russia on the march

Veronica - And now it stops on a massive nation. I see men in uniform, doing what appears to be a goose step - that is the only way I can explain it. And now I see them marching, six abreast, row after row, across nations and countries.

Now Our Lady is motioning to me, and touching Her lips. Our Lady is saying:

Our Lady - "This, My child, is reason for a dirge. For this nation of Russia shall bring much sorrow to the world. In many years past, I begged of you to convert Russia, but, instead, there is a fear of Russia that should not be. There is only one individual to fear in your world, and that could be, My child and My children, the fear of an angry God.

"My children, understand Us: We do not come with messages to upset you or to make you afeared of Us; that is not necessary. All you have to do is think, and use your hearts, not just your head; I say, not just your head, for the scientist and those who are in charge of the souls of your children are implanting in these souls dark seeds of hate, and envy, and the need for materialism. O My children, I could repeat over and over again the sins that make it a world of destruction for those who are trying to stay on the narrow road to Heaven, while all obstacles are placed in his way."

Veronica - Now Our Lady is looking up, and I can see - I can see missiles, I know they're missiles. They're frightening! I see part of the world now beginning to light up again. Our Lady is motioning, and the ball is floating closer to Her, as She points; and She is pointing at the United States and Canada.

Our Lady - "My child, I point for this reason: though, My child, it is a most difficult message to bring to the world, you must not be afeared; but you must shout it from the rooftops: Russia has the upper hand now at this time in world peace or world destruction. You must understand, the heart of the atheist is closed to mercy and goodness; a darkened soul has shut out the light. And they seek nothing but the destruction of any man, woman, or child who stands in their way, to assume and gain through hatred and deception among families, and also, the ruination of the lives of the children of all families.

"My child and My children, I ask you as a Mother of grace, to please, in your darkest hours which are descending upon you - please turn to Me, My children, and I will help you. Your hearts have hardened against My Son and the Eternal Father in the Spirit of light. Do not seek your knowledge from a mortal being at this time, but find yourself a place where you may be even a recluse, a place where you can open your heart to Us, and We will speak to you.

"Yes, My child and My children, as a Mother of grace I have been given many powers, through My Son, in the Eternal Father, and the Holy Spirit - many powers to recover souls that are on the way to their destruction and ultimate death in hell. I day 'death', My children - I do not wish that you misunderstand Me: you yourself know that your soul is immortal; there is no death as you know it - only to the body, which in time the good Lord, the Father in Heaven, in His mercy, will return that body and soul and make it one again at the end of time. That will be the resurrection of the body and the soul.

"My child, you must comfort those who cry and weep for their lost children. There will be many other mothers who shall suffer the horrible crimes against their children. All is coming to pass because of the sins of the older generation. Those who should know better are so enshrined in their own love of the material that they cannot even visualize what they are doing to their children. In order for your children to be saved, My parents, you must keep a constant vigilance of prayer going throughout your home, and those homes of your immediate families. One good example can save a dozen, My children.

"Today, and this evening, I am happy at heart because there are so many enlightened souls who have come to do honor to the gift from Heaven of the Rosary.

"My children, I know if you will only place your confidence in Me, that with the Rosary and the Brown Scapular, we can turn this all about. But it must take the efforts in grace of all mankind. And there, My children, is little time for you to turn about.

Blasphemous movie "Hail, Mary"

"O My children, My Mother's heart is now torn asunder. I hear those words that are making a mockery of Myself, My children. Yes, My child Veronica, I am referring to the pornographic movie called, 'The Hail Mary.'

"My Son has wanted and wished that direct action be taken against those who have had even a small measure in partnership with those who have sought to blaspheme My name, and, also, to cut My heart asunder.

267

Another plague to come

"My Son has asked that I report to you that there shall be another plague upon mankind. Yes, My child and My children, another plague. For AIDS is a plague, and other illnesses that have gone by without any scientific recognition, are plagues from Heaven. They are allowed for the individual to retain a measure of love for his God. As long as he knows, as his time grows near to death, that is was because of his misconduct that he died a most unhurried and unscrupulously recognized a death. Yes, My children, there is much now in the world that you must protect yourselves against."

Coming tribulation in Australia

Veronica - Our Lady now is pointing upwards, and I see now the world is stopping now, the ball of the world is stopping at Australia. Our Lady now is nodding and She's placing Her first finger to Her lips.

Our Lady - "My child, this you can make known to mankind, that there shall be now a next tribulation in Australia. There will be many deaths, My children. That is why We do hope that the world will recognize two seers in Australia. The one who has presently come forth must be placed aside. There are two legitimate seers which shall come forward from Australia.

"Now, My child, I wish that you take now the time to have three photographs made. The first you may discuss to others, and the next two must be kept hidden for a time at least, My child."

Veronica - Three pictures, three pictures, please.
[Pause]
Veronica - The lights that had dimmed and then like a smoky atmosphere had suddenly cleared away, the lights are returning. Now I didn't realize, as I examined the photographs, that Jesus had moved from His original position over Our Lady's statue. Now Our Lady and Jesus - Our Lady is following Jesus. He's turned towards His left, that would be

our right, and He's moving over, over beyond the flags, and He's standing just above the high tree to our right. And Our Lady has come up, and She's standing next to Him. Now Jesus is nodding to Our Lady.

And Our lady is taking Her Rosary, which She had in Her hands - the beautiful Rosary with the golden Our Father and the white Hail Marys that cascade with beautiful illumination of lights all about Her - Our Lady is taking the crucifix on Her Rosary and making the sign of the cross: In the name of the Father, and of the Son, and of the Holy Ghost.

Our Lady is turning to Her right now and making the sign of the cross: In the name of the Father, and of the Son, and of the Holy Ghost.

Now Our Lady is moving over, and She's nodding to Jesus: and He's now turned. It's quite windy up there. I can see that the cape on Jesus' back is blowing. He has on, I notice now, it looks like a weave that I'm not familiar with, but like linen - linen - like cloth, gown, that's very long and it's covering His feet this evening. Jesus has on a belting at His waist. It's made of a skin - like material, like brown in color, but I know it's a skin, an animal skin - like material. And, also, His sandals seem to be made from the same material because they're brown in color and open. Now Jesus is nodding.

And Our Lady is floating over, over to our left side. She's just above the statue now. And, oh, Our Lady looks absolutely beautiful. She has on a white gown that goes all the way past Her ankles. And I can see that She's wearing golden sandals. They're made with three straps, and one about the ankle; and at the center, near the tip of the toes, I can see a beautiful little rose, made of gold. I don't know it it's gold metal, or material, but it is absolutely beautiful. And Our Lady, also, is wearing Her mantle, Her white mantle, with the trimming of gold about the outside. The gold trimming is about a half an inch in size, and it goes all about Our Lady's cape.

Now Our Lady, as She asked me to describe what is going on, She was standing still. But now Our Lady is going to Her right side, that's our left side. She's floating over. And Jesus is also - He is behind Her now. And Our Lady has turned, and Jesus had nodded, yes, to Her. Now They are just beyond the tree. They've gone over quite a bit to Their left side, and They're leaning down now. Our Lady - Jesus looked over to Our Lady, and He spoke to Her.

And Our Lady now is taking out Her Rosary again. I didn't notice it, but She had placed it about Her waist, and kept Her hands together, like this. Now Our Lady is taking the Rosary out from Her belting and She's making the sign of the cross: In the name of the Father, and of the Son, and of the Holy Ghost.

Now Our lady is looking up to Jesus, and He's coming forward now, and He's making the sign of the cross: In the name of the Father, and of the Son, and of the Holy Ghost.

Now Jesus is whispering to Our Lady, and Our Lady smiled; She was saying, yes. I couldn't hear what Jesus was saying to Our Lady, but They are both turning now, and Our Lady is following Jesus, as He slowly goes across the sky. He's floating. It's so beautiful to watch. They're like weightless yet They're as solid as you and I. The other saints that appeared seemed to be different. They're always, sort of translucent, but Jesus and Our Lady are solid, just like you and I. It's so wonderful to see Them floating across the sky. Now They've reached the top of the tree on our right side. And Jesus now is bending over, like this, with His hand, and making the sign of the cross: In the name of the Father, and of the Son, and of the Holy Ghost.

Now Jesus is motioning for Our Lady to return back towards the statue area. Now Our Lady is moving quite fast; She's floating quite fast. I don't see any action of Her slippers; She's just being carried over. And Our Lady is now standing up above Her statue, about maybe twelve feet; She's quite close to the statue at twelve feet. And Jesus now is joining Her. He's standing now - He's moving about, and He's coming over into the center of the statue. And Our Lady is moving over. And Jesus is standing there now close to Our Blessed Mother, and He's making the sign of the cross: In the name of the Father, and of the Son, and of the Holy Ghost.

Now Our Lady is looking up to Jesus. He just conversed with Her, but I could only hear - I could only hear, like the rustle of trees, and, also, the murmur of His voice, but no words. Our Lady is smiling. Now Jesus is placing His first finger to His lips, which means to listen and repeat.

Jesus - "My child and My children, it has come to Us in Heaven that so few are reading their Bible. How, My children, if you do not seek the truth, shall you find it? From others? No, this cannot be. We have left with you all a testimony of truth, the Bible of life and love. Mankind must read his Bible, or he shall be lost in the world. He shall go to and fro, hinder and yon, seeking peace and tranquillity, but never finding it.

"I could bring to you a truth, My children, a truth that goes by unnoticed. That you cannot have Heaven on earth, or you could not share in Heaven - in Heaven, My child. I offer you a key to the Kingdom, My child and My children. All you have to do is seek and you shall find the truth. I ask that all who hear My voice will take their Bibles, and if they do not have one, search, but find the right Bible, those printed not after 1965, My children. There is reason for that, which I shall not go into this evening.

"Our hearts are torn asunder here in Heaven. The saints cry out, 'When will justice be meted to mankind? How long, O Lord of Lords, must we wait for the return of the good souls to Heaven? Seeing them crucified on earth makes our hearts grow heavy. How long, O Lord,' the saints cry, 'shall this carnage be permitted?' My child and My children, by now if you have only read a portion of My Mother's travels and Her words to the world, you will have an idea how much time is left.

"My child and My children, I bring you sad news, but it is the news that can cleanse many of their present sins if they listen and learn by it. Death now is becoming prevalent with wars, with droughts, with personal murders; murders of the unborn, father against son, mother against daughter; all man-

271

ner of carnage being treated in the homes, and being conducted in the homes of children - children who cannot
longer be children because by their viewing of the diabolical
box, they are learning to act as adults with the hearts but not
with their heads.

"I hold all parents responsible for the fall of their children's souls. Remember, My child and My children, I have
warned you often that once you open your door and you go
out into the world, you will enter into the kingdom of satan.
You ask, My child and My children, why is this allowed?
That you must trust to the goodness and in the goodness of
the heart of the Eternal Father. You cannot, as a human
being, understand His ways. But know this, My children,
that no evil can come upon mankind if he watches and
waits. And We offer you three sacramentals in your wait for
the future.

"I promise you, My children, one day you will see Me, as
you Veronica, see Me now. All will see Me, but many have
fled already, in fear of what is to come upon mankind. But
think, My child and My children, how disastrous it will be
when many flee at the thought of My coming, but they will
have no place to hide. Though they flee to the mountains,
they will be found out. Yes, My child and My children. I
know, My child, it frightens you. I do not seek to put fear in
your heart, but as a voice - box, you have no recourse but to
speak what is given to you, known as the truth in your God,
and from the Eternal Father.

Hurricane Gloria

"My child, We specifically brought you here this evening
after the last trial of the past week. This was allowed to
come upon you with no destruction to your home.
However, you knew the fear of fleeing to the mountains.
We directed you, My child, and you did well. And you
escaped having to suffer the hours of darkness, and the
sound of the howling of the winds, and the rise of the waters.
But, My child and My children, it will happen again, but this
time it will claim lives.

"Do not be affrighted, My child; I did not say that this will happen to your home on Long Island again. You suffered not the moments of terror. We did not wish for you to succumb from sorrow at that time, My child, so We sent you to the mountains; and you returned once the winds had died down to find a home still intact.

Crucifix to guard entrances to home

"I must reveal, My children, to the world again, that you are to keep a crucifix on your front door and your back door. All entrances to your home must be guarded by the crucifix. There has not been one home on Long Island that had a crucifix on its door that did fall to any evil. I do not speak of the trees, My child; I speak of mankind. You did not know a major disaster as has happened, My children, in Mexico. You see, My child, I set you down in that area to bring the word to mankind, and it was through these words that many listened and they passed through the horrible experience of a hurricane.

Earthquake in New York and California

"My child, the earthquakes will increase now. There will be one in New York. Now, My child, I tell you this to prepare. You are allowed, My child, to experience all that mankind can suffer. How well you listened to Us when We told you to place on your shelves cans of food, jars of water, blankets. You found it very cold, My child, without heat and without light, and without any form of recreation other then to pray. And that was God's way of letting the world know that they will be on their knees; and one of these days they will be praying, for many the first time in many years. But why, My children, must We allow all these disasters to happen to you, and have to bring you to your knees in prayer? Can you not listen, and can you not seek for the truth, all who call themselves atheists, and those who have half - hearted interest in religion at all? They call it a thing of the past. It is not a thing of the past, but it is a means for your salvation: accept it and you will be saved; reject it and you will be lost.

"I repeat again, the earthquakes will increase in volume. California shall be struck. New York shall be struck. As I told you once before, there will be earthquakes in places that have never known a quake. It will startle them and frighten them, but will they come to their knees? Few will, My child, because I can tell you this: they will not have the time to make amends; that is the sad part, My child and My children.

"I tell you as Messenger from Heaven, I, too, My child, was just an innocent child growing up in a family enlightened by God. I knew My position upon earth, and I went forth to try to save you, My children; and in My sacrifice there was salvation. I am asking you all now, for the little time left to your country and the world, to pray a constant vigilance of prayer going throughout your world, link to link, Father to Father. And the Hail Marys shall be one to glory to My Mother, and not will Her name be disturbed again, as though it were a tombstone laid to rest.

"My child, all those who promote that moving picture shall be destroyed.

"I know there are many who shall parade against this horror, My child, but let them know that by example others may come to their senses and seek the blessings of a God Who has given them more than enough time to make amends.

"My child and My children, I ask you all to come forth as citizens of Heaven... (That makes you happy, My child, does it not? Well, My child, you shall be citizens of Heaven one day). I ask you now to do whatever is within your human nature, and directed by the Holy Spirit, to oust these interlopers with their blasphemous movie.

Great action against theaters showing "Hail, Mary"

"I shall not stand by and allow My Mother to be debauched and defamed. I will take action, great action, against the theater where this picture shall be shown.

274

"My child, I brought you here this evening, for I know, regardless of your physical illness, you would be here if We ask. And you waited and waited, My child, for hopefully, in your heart, you knew that by the time you were to come, you would be stable enough on your legs to get there. Yes, My child, We called you because We needed you, My child, as We need all the seers of the world to gather now and stop the coming Chastisement. The Eternal Father now has taken into His hand a most luminous ball; it is a red ball of fire. It is growing very heavy in His hand. It no longer sets at the base of His throne, and He shall poise now to throw this. It will be thrown, My child, at the world - a ball of fire.

Sudden great cold to come

"Do not be afeared, My child; retain your crucifix on your doors. And keep your supply of earthly goods, though they are needed for your human body; the canned food, the candles, the water, and the blankets. A sudden cold shall come upon mankind and many shall die from the cold.

"Now, My child, you will continue with three more photographs. These are taken for great reason. One day they will be given to the Bishop to examine.

"Yes, My child, I am speaking to you now, but I seal your lips, for I do not wish that you repeat what I tell you."
[Pause]

Prayers to return to schools

"I have but one more discourse with you, My child - that is that you must go forward and demand that the prayers be returned to the schools. In that manner, We can approach the children, and return them to their rightful place in the reign of God.

"Now, My child, you will sit back and receive three photographs. The first you may repeat, and the other two must be kept secret for the time being. The time being, My child, means until We allow you by contacting you, whether it be at your home or in the circle, to make known what is in

275

these pictures."

[Pause]

Veronica - Our Lady is putter Her finger to her lips, like this.

Our Lady - "My child, I did not wish to tax you with a long discourse this evening. However, as the time grows so short, We have no choice but for you to help Us, My child.

Aids received through inhuman relationships

"You will tell mankind that the sins of the flesh shall send many souls to hell. My child, the need for materialism is wrong. And the need for modernizing the world and My Son's Church is wrong. And passing over the grievous sin of immorality and, also, pornography, and all the other evils, are placed under the heading of humanism - even accepting without a frown, or proper attention to a sin, in accepting the aftermath of AIDS, received through inhuman relationships. I say 'inhuman' because those relationships are not from God, My children, but they are from satan. Homosexuality shall always be condemned, because it is against the nature of man; and it is a violation of all human morality, and shall not be tolerated by the Eternal Father in the Trinity.

"My child, I want you to do all you can to foster the return of mortality and morality to the medias; and, also, to those you love - your neighbors, your children. And do not be affrighted or flee from the sinner, for he, too, can be saved by your efforts and your prayers. As this child was born, so he must return; a simple child, to the Eternal Father. If you remember, My child, the lessons from Theresa - yes, St. Theresa, you will remember that it is a simple way to Heaven: if you accept the Eternal Father into your heart, you will always be His children of love.

"My child, We will strengthen you in time, so that you will be able to conduct your mission without missing the Vigils. However, the last one was for reason. Know, My children, that whenever you find yourself being taken from a Vigil, and you see the worldly reason or the godly reason; you must judge which is most important for your salvation.

Arthur Lueken talking with Father Gene Alvesteffer from Grand Rapids, Michigan after a Bayside prayer vigil.

Veronica's Crucifix, which was kissed by Our Lady, is on display at the first anniversary of her death in 1996.

The Statue of Our Lady of the Roses, Mary Help of Mothers, used at the Bayside prayer vigils.

Our Lady - "I shall stand upon the head of a serpent. My heel will crush him; but not until man and the world has been cleansed." (3/18/73)

These Last Days radio program host Gary Wohlscheid
and Mrs. Ann Ferguson at Veronica's gravesite.

Pilgrims from Michigan on June 18, 1989.

One of the most outstanding miraculous photographs ever - taken a few hours before the Vigil on Nov. 25, 1978. Tom Bachor of Little Neck, N. Y., was taking a picture of John Miles (foreground), approximately 70 yards from the Vatican Pavilion site (situated at the bottom of Our Lady's mantle). Supernaturally, the Virgin Mary, the Mother of God, appears out of nowhere dominating the sky above Her apparition site. The fingers of Our Lord (top left) are pointing toward Her, as if to say: "Behold thy Mother! Come and journey to this Her sacred site, chosen from the beginning of time."

Veronica at the wake of Ted Cach on June 4, 1991.

Veronica at a Bayside prayer vigil.

Above: August 5, 1974: Veronica attends a prayer vigil at the Vatican Pavilion Site in Bayside. Veronica was suffering from back pain when this picture was taken. She was often on crutches as seen here or in a wheelchair.

Right Page: Father Gene Alvesteffer of Grand Rapids, Michigan Diocese. This photo was taken after he blessed the gravesite of Veronica Lueken.

An incredible Kodak photo taken at the Vigil of Feb. 1st, 1979, by Ray Welch of Hartford, Connecticut. St. Francis miraculously appears above the Vigil statue of Our Lady. There wasn't even a statue of St. Francis on the grounds.

Veronica kneeling at a cold winter prayer vigil.

This is a photo of the sacred vigil grounds looking out over the crowd from the Vatican Pavilion site. It was taken with a Pentax 35-mm camera by Yvonne Hanratty of Brooklyn, N.Y., on August 14, 1993, the Vigil of the Assumption. But what miraculously appears on the right is a translucent image of ST. MICHAEL (facing toward the reader), all aglow in a grayish tint.

Note the long, white gown, the wings on the upper left and right, and the form of an arm on the right side, as he is seated (on something invisible, as it were) just to the right of Veronica's empty chair. Also, note the brilliant radiance from his being that emanates onto Veronica's secretary and close personal friend, Ann Ferguson, and the pilgrims in general.

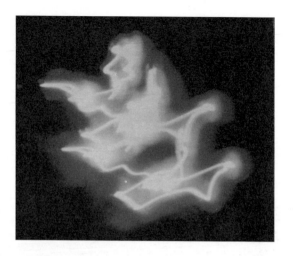

This particular photograph is a startling visual that bears out Our Lady's prophecy this evening. Note on the top, a woman with a head-covering (man dressed as a woman?) pointing a gun, her arm extended and her finger on the trigger (see illustration above). When you turn the photo slightly to the left, you will note 2 large "Ps," an "8" (in between the "Ps"), and a "Y" (formed by the top of the left "P" the "8," and the full "P" on the right, see illustration below).

The 2 "Ps" stand for the Pope and prayer. The "8" represents the priesthood or the Holy Eucharist. Our Lady symbolically uses the last letters of the alphabet, "X, Y, Z. " to denote the end times. The meaning now is quite evident. Unless we pray (P) - and pray hard - for the life and safety of John Paul II (P, 8), the satanic plans which are in the final stages of development (Y) will achieve its cursed objective: the brutal and violent end to the life of the beloved Vicar of Christ.

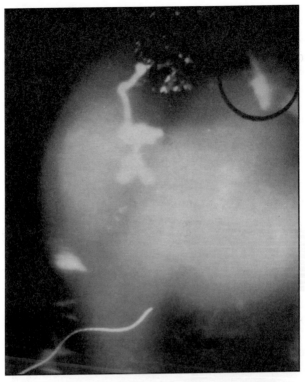

Above shows a side profile of Susan Hayward's face (circled), the famous Hollywood actress. The central part in the picture represents the brain tumor which miraculously disappeared after receiving a Bayside rose petal. On the upper part of the tumor one can see an ostrich, a symbol of stiff-necked pride, as she kept her head buried in the sand rather than acknowledge the true source of her cure - Our Lady at Bayside. Her tumor mysteriously reappeared a year later, and she died shortly thereafter.

Veronica surrounded with guards in front of Statue.

Thousands of pilgrims come from all over
the world to pray at the prayer vigils..

There is a Holy Hour every Sunday morning from
10:30am till noon for priests. Here are some priests
leading the Rosary and the prayers.

Pictures of May Crownings, Rosary Processions,
and Holy Hours for Priests at Flushing Meadows Park.

Veronica's grave site.

I wish, My children, that you learn a little by example when We take those from among you to be seers for Heaven. They are voice - boxes and suffer much for this reason: the fact that the supernatural is always working with the natural, mortal human being. I say this to you, My child: you may not understand as I talk to you, but as you repeat it, and you will hear it again, you will understand.

"Remember, My children, you cannot condone immorality.

"I ask that the world continues to make Rosaries, and send the prayers, link to link, throughout the world. For I still promise, that if you will listen to My directions, given through My Son, in the Father and the Holy Spirit - I promise to do all that I can, My children, to save your lives upon earth; and, also, if you must come across the veil, to save you from eternal damnation through the Scapular and the Rosary. Pray, My children, all a constant vigilance of prayer: that is all you have now, for the enemy has been allowed to come into your homes.

"You ask Me, My child, why We don't just put the heavy hand down on mankind, and that would be the end of the sinning. No, My child, the Eternal Father knew that once satan came into the world and was released from hell with all his demons, he expected many to fall to his cajolery's. However, though they fall, they must pick themselves up and walk a rough road, the road of the cross, back to Heaven. It will be a road of sacrifice and deprivation; however, in this way, My children, can you be purified for an entrance into Heaven."

Veronica - Now Our Lady is taking Her Rosary, like this, and making the sign of the cross: In the name of the Father, and of the Son, and of the Holy Ghost.

Now Our Lady is touching Her lips.

Our Lady - "I bless you all, My children: In the name of the Father, and of the Son, and of the Holy Ghost.

"I bless you, My Son blesses you and the Eternal Father seeks your love in the Holy Spirit.

"My child, you will now sit back and continue the

prayers of atonement. Then you will repair home. And be most careful because you will be followed this evening.

"My child, listen now, My Son has been waiting for us to finish this discourse; however, you will look straight ahead - there He is."

Veronica - Oh, Jesus is standing over the statue. He's quite high in the sky. Now He's giving me a direction.

Jesus - "When we leave, you will be followed by your normal escorts, who will then when they are given a sign, will turn off. You will proceed then, My child, to go to"

Veronica - I cannot repeat it.

Jesus - "And you will be most careful now in the next week to have someone with you at all times."

Veronica - Now Jesus is taking His hand out. He's standing just directly above the statue, and making the sign of the cross: In the name of the Father, and of the Son, and of the Holy Ghost.

Jesus - "I bless you all, My children: In the name of the Father, and the Holy Ghost, and in My Spirit of one with God."

[Pause]

Children to be taught The Trinity

Veronica - Oh, Our Lady is mentioning here, and I think I will repeat it, that the children must be explained in a simple manner as possible, to the children, the meaning of the Trinity, because, Our Lady says, it is most misunderstood. However, if a parent will take the time they can make it known to their children. They shall not be taught the truth in the schools.

Our Lady - "That is all, My child."

278

Stop homosexuality
Enact just laws to prevent its spread

All Saints' Day and Eve of All Souls' Day - November 1, 1985

Veronica - All about the trees - I happened to glance up and see beautiful blue lights cascading from high in the heavens, down onto the boughs of the trees. The blue is a most beautiful blue color. I don't know exactly what earthly name to give the coloring, whether it should be a satellite blue, or sky blue - no, that's too light - or... they have different colors, stardust blue and royal blue. I believe that the coloring is more similar to a royal blue - between a royal and an aquamarine, because there are tinges; if I look closely, I can see there are tinges, of, also, light green all about the blue.

Now, high in the heavens, I can see a light now. The lights are dimming on the trees; however, they're going - pointing upward. They're becoming very long, elongated and lighted, in a color now that is hard to explain. It's a mixture of a blue, a green, and a pink. They are all the colors of - Jesus is pink, blue is Our Lady, and the green is St. Michael.

Now over on our right side the sky is opening up, and [Veronica gasps.] - oh, my goodness! - I haven't seen St. Michael for a long time; I've forgotten how huge he is! He is tremendous! He's covering the whole sky. His head is a size - I couldn't put a human size to his head. But he looks so beautiful. He's dressed in a long gown, a white gown, with a gold belting about it. Now I notice that - I can't see his feet because he's now coming across the sky. Although, by his crossing the sky - he's almost on top of the bushes on our left side, that's how big he is. He covers the whole sky now. I have to go backwards in order to see his hair. His hair is a golden color. I know from many years, Our Lady has referred to him as "Our Golden Boy."

Now Michael is holding in his right hand a balance. It's

made of pure spun gold. I know because it's glistening; and every time Michael just turns a bit, the glistening actually would damage your eyes it's so powerful. But I notice that Michael is placing ingots, or something, on the balance because it's becoming very uneven now.

And now Michael is doing what Our Lady and Jesus do - He is placing his first finger to his mouth, and saying:

St. Michael - "Veronica, my child, announce to the world that the end approaches for your most illustrious President of the United States, and, also, your Pope, John Paul II.

"I know, my child Veronica, that this has affrighted you, but it is most frightening to know that We cannot get enough peoples upon earth to pray and assist the Holy Father in his day of suffering. Yes, my child, and my children, tell the world immediately that the Holy Father suffers greatly, for he, too, has been given insights in visions to know what lies ahead for him. But he is willing to suffer all for the salvation of souls and the good of the Holy Church.

Warn the president

"Your President must be warned to stay out of his gardens. He must not go there without due guardians.

"My child and My children, your world is heading for a great catastrophe. Earthquakes will increase. Floods will increase. There will be much weeping and gnashing of teeth throughout the world as calamity upon calamity befalls mankind. And why? Because you do not listen to the Queen of Heaven, Who has come to you as a Queen of Peace to bring the world back from the cataclysm it is facing.

"I give you now, my children, the Queen of Peace; for I shall back away and open the heavens and bring forth to you your Mother, Who has been awaiting this moment with you.

"Look up, my child, and tell what you see."

Veronica - Now Michael is pointing up high into the sky, and I see what appears to be a comet. There's a large comet. It has colorings of red and white and yellow; and the tail behind it is streaming red, and yellow, and white, and smoke. Now I see a huge hand, a human - like looking hand, being raised now; and as it is raised like that, it holds back the comet. Now, Michael has now placed his face over and obliterated the sky. And he is now touching his first finger to his lips.

St. Michael - "My child, listen and repeat after me.

"The Queen of Heaven shall give you a history that must be written down and recorded for all mankind."

Veronica - Now Michael is beginning to - I can't explain it - he seems to be fading out, like he - like, almost like a smoky figure fading out. And he's touching his lips.

St. Michael - "No, my child, I am not fading out; I am only going to place myself so the glory of all, and the attention of all, shall be given to the Queen of Heaven and earth."

Veronica - Now he's pointing up - he still has the balance in his left hand - and he's pointing up high into the sky. Now the sky is opening up, and it's beautiful. It is like a clear day in spring, or the clearest day of fall, neither hot nor cold. I feel that it's one of the most beautiful days I have ever seen. Now coming through this great light, this great light that has no human words to explain.... It's like going through a tunnel and then looking at a light that is so bright that is comes over you like an emotion, an emotion of peace and joy so great that were I just a mere mortal, without Heaven guiding me, I am certain I should pass on from the glory of that beautiful light.

Now through the light, Our Lady is coming forward. She is dressed beautifully in Her whole Fatima habit. I've always called it Her Fatima habit when She wears the Fatima crown upon Her head. Our Lady has the Fatima crown, and She also has under it Her mantle, the beautiful white mantle with the golden edging. The edging is so fantastically golden that I'm sure it must be spun gold, pure spun gold. Our Lady has on Her a beautiful gown that comes high up upon Her neck, and is also lined with a border of I would say, about a half an inch of gold about Her neck; and Our Lady's gown is white, pure white. Now Our

Lady has a belting, a gold - corded belting now which cinches in, sort of, Her gown.

And Our Lady is taking from Her gown Her Rosary, the beautiful Rosary with the golden Our Fathers and the white Hail Marys that are cascading in the light and assuming all the colors of the rainbow. Our Lady now is extending out Her Rosary, like this, and making the sign of the cross: In the name of the Father, and of the Son, and of the Holy Ghost.

Our Lady now has turned to Her right, which is our left, and She's going slowly over across the sky. She has a very slight smile on Her face. It's a smile that covers so much to explain. It has neither full gaiety nor full sorrow. It's a smile of tenderness, of love, of compassion, but, also, of great sorrow, as Her eyes and Her heart knows the future of mankind. Our Lady is extending out now Her Rosary, the golden crucifix, and making the sign of the cross: In the name of the Father, and of the Son, and of the Holy Ghost.

Now Our Lady is smiling quite sadly, and She's looking all about Her. Now She's turning to the left and She's floating over: Our Lady doesn't walk, She always floats, which is so beautiful. Our Lady is floating over now to our right side, Her left side. Now She's just above the first tall tree, and She's holding out Her Rosary, like this, and making the sign of the cross: In the name of the Father, and of the Son, and of the Holy Ghost.

Now Our Lady is making a farther trip over; I have to follow Her beyond the trees, She said, because She does not want anyone to be forgotten. Now Our Lady is quite far over on our right side. I can only see Her back now as She's extending the Rosary and making the sign of the cross: In the name of the Father, and of the Son, and of the Holy Ghost.

Now St. Michael has appeared. The whole sky is all lighted up now. And he's placing his hand out, like this. And Our Lady has been floating over. I think I've told it many times that in Heaven and on earth, when Our Lady and Jesus appear, They float; they don't walk like you or I. It's the most beautiful thing to see. It's like They're weightless, yet They look as solid as you and I. And Our Lady is coming across now. Michael has extended his hand. Our Lady has taken his hand, and he's guiding Her over to the statue. Now Our Lady is standing above the statue. She's looking about Her and placing Her first finger to Her lips, like this.

Our Lady - "My child and My children, especially, My child, Veronica, We had to bring you this evening from your sickbed, knowing that what We asked of you would not be denied. It was urgent, My child, for you to be here this evening, though satan sent his cohorts to try to stop you and thwart you at every step and turn.

"My child, you must shout it from the rooftops: The enemies of your God have now held a meeting, and they have listed on parchment, a paper, which I will show you, My child... The first two names you will reveal, and the other three must be held for another time."

Veronica - Our Lady is pointing up now to the sky, and I see a large parchment of paper. I call it parchment because it doesn't look like the paper we use; it looks like something that has had, like oil on it. And it's heavy, and the writing is very heavy. And I see numbered up to the number five - I see number one: it says RONALD REGAN. I see number two: JOHN PAUL II. I see number three: VERONICA LUEKEN.

Our Lady - "My child, do not be affrighted. You must understand that nothing will come to you and harm you unless it is in the plan of the Father for the good of all mankind. Your heart is pounding, My child; I repeat again: Do not be affrighted but pray for your President, and pray for you Holy Father, Pope John Paul II.

"My child, you have had much discord this week in your household because of the prayers to satan of those on your island who belong to the church of satan. They know where you live, My child, and they pass many times in vehicles before your home.

"You ask Me, My child, what can they do. They can do nothing, My child, while there is a crucifix upon your doors.

I would suggest also, My child, that you go back to your previous habit and plan to keep a St. Benedict medal on each windowsill of your home. A St. Benedict medal, My child; then you will not be tormented at night by their weird chantings, that have kept you awake many nights.

"Yes, My child, there were twelve groups of satan in your community. I say 'community,' because the island of Long Island, within a sixty-mile radius, has thirteen covens now.

Innocent babies sacrificed

"Yes, My child, they are the worst of the worst, for they sacrifice the innocent babies, and they, also, are using animals again. Many dead carcasses shall be found on the beaches and in the woods.

"I know that this knowledge make you very ill, My child. That would, also, affect anyone with a heart, a human heart of goodness. For how can man be so cruel to his fellow man, to slay him, to give him over to satan in rituals.

"Yes, My child, you had to know that they are very close. They walk at daylight through the streets as common citizens, unknown to others for what their true nature is. They are agents of hell.

No vehicles from other planets

"While We speak of agents of hell, My child, I also wish that you make it known that there are no vehicles coming from other planets - extraterrestrial vehicles. No, My child and My children; they are agents of hell in transport. Now you may ask, why must they be transported if they are spirits? Ahh, My child, this you may not understand. These are not ordinary spirits; these are the demons from hell: satan's cohorts, and satan himself. He is also on one of the transports.

"There is a reason they must use the transports. I will not go into it at this time, for I am sure it would befog the mind of any scientist should I give this knowledge to them before they are ready for it. They must find out something for

284

themselves, My child, before We will help them to the end-ing of this great sorrow upon earth. Anything that results in murder and death is sorrow upon earth, My child, just as the great wars that are prevailing.

"Look over, My child, to your left. Yes, that is true: you are looking at Africa now, My child, another map. And what do you see, My child?"

Veronica - I see all flames. And I see many people who are hungry. I see babies with their stomachs all swelled up; and babies with their bones sticking out of their skins. And to think...

Our Blessed Mother is crying. She's touching Her lips now.

Our Lady - "My child, and to think how much food is being wasted in your country and the affluent countries of the world. One little morsel could keep a child from starv-ing to death.

"If you think that this could not happen in your country, you are mistaken, My child. If you think this cannot happen, I must tell you now that there are still many who are hungry in your country this evening. You see, My child, man is always self - seeking, and cannot see what lies ahead of him.

Destruction of world monetary systems

"You will understand and broadcast the message to the world that there will be a great destruction in the monetary systems of the world. It will affect both the United States and Canada, and all the great powers of the world. And I repeat again: You will go to your stores to do your shopping carrying papers which may as well be newspapers, for the value they will have to purchase even food will be nil.

"How can a great country like the United States fall, you say, My child? You ask Me in your heart. I read your heart. I will tell you why. Because they have given themselves over to satan. When a country has lost its morality and seeks the pleasures of the flesh, giving over, themselves over, to all manner of abominations, like homosexuality, and condoning this up the highest courts of the land, then that

285

country shall fall.

"It is the will of the Father that all men be saved. But you must understand this, My child and My children: You have all been given a free will. I repeat: The road to Heaven is narrow, and so few are finding it. The road to hell is wide, and thousands are falling into hell every day. The road to purgatory is also narrow, and there are many who have been there since the beginning of creation, because they have no one to pray for them.

"You must remember, My children, the souls in purgatory. I also tell you this, My children: On one Saturday of the month, I shall take out of purgatory many souls, if you will save them.

"I see, My child, that that gives you a great lifting to your heart, which has been bowed with sorrow from the beginning of this day.

"Yes, My child, there is a hell, there is a Heaven, and there is purgatory. Most, lately, My child, have been going to purgatory and hell. It is not impossible to immediately go to Heaven, My child, but it will be some time before the Beatific Vision can be met. It is reserved for the few.

"I want you, My children, to wear the Brown Scapular. You must wear the Brown Scapular. The time of times is approaching. The great Chastisement is approaching. The hours upon earth should be counted in the few. These are truly, My children, your latter days. You cannot escape the oncoming fury.

"Now, I want it known to you that the very ones who plan the extinction of Ronald REAGAN and Pope John Paul II are sitting at this time at a table in Russia. They do not do their own murdering, My child; they have others do it for money.

"I know this makes you affrighted. My child, that there is so little value for life, but did not I tell you many years ago that if they started to murder the unborn, they will murder the living, even the adults. They may murder the children, but then they will also murder the elderly.

Common law marriages not tolerated

"O, My child and My children, never have We seen from the beginning of time a world in such chaos. And, also, I shall not speak with words that affright your heart, My child, but I wish it known that this new modern role of what they call 'marriage without marriage' - which means living as 'common - law,' I understand, My children - shall not be tolerated in Heaven. It was never the plan of the Eternal Father that man and woman shall live as animals.

"Fornication shall never be accepted. There is no excuse for fornication. If you cannot remain celibate, better then that you must then be married. It is better, My child and My children, to be married than to burn in hell.

The Ten Commandments

"I also ask that all of My children of the world review the Ten Commandments.

"In your tabloid, My child, I wish that the Ten Commandments be printed in large letters for everyone to see. I wish that they be printed in a manner that is like the tablets given to Moses. Remember, My child, the tabloid must have the Ten Commandments.

"And also, remember, My children, when you break one commandment, you break them all. So better that you follow them through, and when you are ready to pass over the veil you will not have to be gripped with fear if you cannot have a priest on hand in your last moments upon earth. You see, My child and My children, not everyone is taken from the earth with the final blessing from the priesthood. That is a special grace.

"Now, My child and My children, you will continue to pray the Rosary, and remember to wear your Scapular about your neck; and keep Our Lady of the Roses, Mary Help of Mothers - that medal must also be about your neck with the St. Benedict medal."

Veronica - Now Our Lady is taking the crucifix from Her Rosary, like this, and making the sign of the cross: In the name of the Father, and of the Son, and of the Holy Ghost.

287

Our Lady is turning to Her right, our left side, and making the sign of the cross with Her crucifix: In the name of the Father, and of the Son, and of the Holy Ghost.

Now Our Lady is turning to Her left, our right, as She's moving slowly across the sky now. Now She's bending over and making the sign of the cross: In the name of the Father, and of the Son, and of the Holy Ghost.

Our Lady - "I bless you all, My children, as the Eternal Father blesses you in the Son and the Holy Ghost. Remember, My children, the Trinity. Always try to understand the power of God in the Trinity.

"Now, My child, you will take three photographs: one you may speak of, but two you cannot at this time.

"I will remain here because My Son will soon be down to speak with you, My child and My children."

Veronica - All about the trees now there is a beautiful color of pink. It's a very pale pink, and it's cascading also upward, high into the sky. They're like ribbons, almost around - they remind me of when I was a child and I went to a Maypole, one time, dance, with all streamers coming from the top and leading down. Well, this is what it reminds me of, though it's not paper; it's a supernatural light, a beautiful pink light. And there must be at least fifty to sixty of these lights going up high into the sky. Now as the points of the lights gather together, I see a host - like opening in the sky. I say host - like, because it's not the clear glass gleaming light that I'm used to seeing as the sky opens, but it is a milky white, almost like the color that you see in the milk glasses on flowers, and flower pots.

Now over on our right side, I see letters forming in the sky; and they're in black, and they say 'war' W - A - R, on the right side. Then over on the left side, my attention is drawn to the left side, where there are letters in white, block letters, that say 'peace' P - E - A - C - E.

Now directly in the center over Our Lady's statue, of maybe about forty or fifty feet into the air, Jesus is coming forward. I can see His burgundy cape. And He's coming forward very fast. Our Lady has been standing over by our right side by the trees, and She's coming, also, over across the sky to stand by Her statue. But She's looking upward, as Jesus is coming down.

He has on His burgundy cape. It's a beautiful burgundy color. And I notice that this evening it's also trimmed in gold around the outside of the cape; I would say it is about a half-inch of gold. It's very beautiful. And Jesus' cape is made of a velvet-like material. I can't explain it, because I never saw this kind of material on earth. It's sort of a cross between a sateen and, oh, velvet.

Now Jesus has on sandals. I can tell because the wind is blowing heavily now above the statue, and the trees are bending a little; and I can see that Jesus has on a pair of sandals. They're made of some type of animal skin, because they're not - they don't look like a material, like of cloth; they look of, actually of animal skin. They're made like a sandal with two pieces going up towards the ankle, and held in place by - that was from the toes - and held in place by a band across His ankle.

Now Jesus has His cowl of His cape down across His shoulders. His hair is quite long. And, like, I repeat, as in the past, His hair is very difficult to describe because of the light; but from here is looks like a reddish blond. It's a very beautiful color, and very shining. And the illumination from Jesus that seems to emanate from within Him, going outward, makes everything so gorgeously beautiful that I'm sure, without a supernatural help, I would certainly pass out in sheer shock. It's so beautiful.

Now Jesus has been coming down slowly. He's increasing His pace now. And now He's standing right next to Our Lady. Our Lady is smiling at Him, but tonight, I repeat, Our Lady has on a very sad, sad smile. Now Jesus is looking about Him, and He's now going over to our left side, His right side, of the trees, and He's extending His hand, like this, and making the sign of the cross: In the name of the Father, and of the Son, and of the Holy Ghost.

Now Our Lady has turned to Her left side and She's floating over to the center of the statue, and Jesus is following Her. He is also floating too; He's right behind Our Lady. Now They are both turning our way, and Jesus is extending His hand out and making the sign of the cross: In the name of the Father, and of the Son, and of the Holy Ghost.

Now Our Lady has been watching Jesus, and He's nodded to Her, yes. And now She is leading over to our right side; She's leading to the very tall tree over on our right side. And Our Lady now is looking down and smiling very sadly, but Jesus is extending His hand out now and making the sign of the cross: In the name of the Father, and of the Son, and of the Holy Ghost.

Now, Our Lady is now facing towards Her right side and Her way slowly across the sky, as She looks about Her. Our Lady is being followed by Jesus now, and They will both be soon over the statue. Yes, Our Lady has reached the statue now, and Jesus is standing right next to Her. Our Lady is looking up at Jesus; She is saying something. I can hear Her voice, like the rustling of the leaves, there's no way I can explain it. I can't hear in my intellect what She is saying to Jesus, but I can hear Her voice. It's soft like the rustling of trees, a beautiful, whispering softness. Now Jesus has said, yes; I can say that because I've noticed He's nodded, yes, to Our Lady.

Now Jesus is turning and facing us. Now Jesus is placing His first finger to His lips, like this, which means to listen and repeat.

Jesus - "My child and My children, I shall not give a long, dissentive discord with you this evening because My heart has been torn at the necessity of having My Mother repeat over and over the warnings from Heaven. However, this She has chosen to do; for as a loving Mother, a Mother of great heart, She wishes that no one be lost to Heaven. Her heart is torn everytime a soul descends into hell and purgatory. My Mother is truly the Mother of the world. And at this time, only She can save the world, for She has come to you as a Mediatrix between God and man. And as such unto the time that no flesh shall seem to remain upon earth, My Mother will be with you, and I, also.

Cannibalism

"My child and My children, need I repeat to you all of the abominations being committed upon the earth now? I can also repeat to you that in some of these horrible, excruciatingly painful cults that are growing up fast in your country and other countries about the world, they have even gone so far as to dab now in cannibalism, the eating of human flesh as a sacrifice to satan. That is why, My children, so many cannot be found who are missing - mostly, My children, young children. Mothers have cried; their hearts torn with anguish when their children disappear from the streets. Your police do not investigate fully. Sending out photographs of the missing children, this is of little help when they fall into the clutches of the satanists, for they do not remain about long. Their bodies are often cremated on pyres to satan.

"I know, My child, this gives you a great twinge of heart when I tell you of these satanists, for you have not lost your fear of them yet. I understand, My child, how you feel. You must not let this affect your work in any manner, for that is what they plan to do: to fill you with such fear that you will not move from without your house.

"I tell you, My child, if you follow Our directions to the full, you will have no problems with the satanists.

Sacramentals as protection against satanists

"There are many armors worn by My children that will protect them from these satanists. I know that those who are satirists - I call them satirists, My child - they will laugh and scorn you when you wear, altogether, your Scapular, your Rosary, your medals, and your crucifix. Let them call you what they may, for one day they will call upon their God to have mercy, and He will find them lacking, with no seal of armor, and they cannot be accepted; they will be rejected from Heaven. All of this armor was given to you throughout the years of mankind. And it was given for reason, for this very day now that is approaching.

"You are living in the times of the coming of the great Tribulation. And were it not I to return - I will tell you also,

My children - were not I to return, there would be no flesh left.

"But I wish to, also, caution you, there are many christs now appearing upon earth. Do not listen to them, or their discourse. For as I ascended into Heaven, that is the way I will return; with the angels of Heaven and the saints behind Me. Do not go out if they say: 'He is in the barn', for I shall not be there. Do not go out to the woods when they say: 'He is teaching and walking through the woods,' for I will not be there.

"I repeat again: when I return to earth, I shall return the way I left. I ascended, and I shall then descend, with the armies of Heaven. You will see a banner that shall be raised at that time called 'Faithful and True,' and in that way you will know Me. My Mother will, also, descend during the time of tribulation. Now do not become confused; that does not mean that My Mother has left you, or is leaving you. My Mother has promised that She shall be with you until the end of time; and She will.

"Now I speak to the parents. Parents of all young children, are you earnestly making an effort to protect your children from a world that has been given over to satan? What do you do when the teachers in your schools teach your children sexual conduct, taking from your young children the purity of heart and the innocence of the youth? What do you do? Just let them take over? Parents, you say it will not affect your child? Look what is happening to the children of the world, young of age, three years old and upward, even younger than three. I cannot upon these holy grounds use the words given in print for all of these abominations being committed to the young child. But, My children, I tell you: it is happening to those who do have good heart and a right mind. They feel as though the world has gone - shall I use the word, My child, 'crazy'? Yes, I will use the word 'crazy' My child - insanity, too. My Mother has always told you that sin is insanity.

Homosexuality must be stopped

"And the great issue now of homosexuality in your country, that shall be on the balance that Michael holds. Unless this balance is evened by removing this evil from your country and bringing in just laws to prevent the spread of homosexuality, you cannot be saved; your country cannot be saved. Because I repeat again, as I have repeated in the past: When a country has given itself over to immorality and all pleasures of the flesh, and abominations of the flesh, then that country will fall! If you do not believe Me, My children, I say: You will read your history books, and you will find out that there was a Sodom and Gomorrah. And what did We do to that abominable city, Sodom? We destroyed it! And what did We do to Gomorrah? We destroyed it! And We destroyed all who did not follow the plan for their redemption.

"My child and My children, do not become as Lot's wife, who had to look back and be turned to a pillar of stone - salt it was, My child, not stone; it was salt. But I tell you this, that this will happen again many times.

"You will see all things come to pass that We have warned you of for years. My Mother has been speaking to you for now fifteen earth - years; over and over, repeating what you must know to save your family and your own soul, and your children's souls. And what do you know? Modernism! That's what stymies mankind, modernism! Nothing was ever good enough; God the Father was not good enough. They're seeking other beings on other planets. For what?

"There are no beings on other planets. We've explained to you about the vehicles from hell. So if you keep on wasting your country's money by looking for life on other planets, you will have more starving in your nation. And your country shall go down the drain, so to speak - economically, morally, and actually, factually destroyed.

"I realize, My children, that your country, the United States, has always been under the protection of My Mother. But now many have cast Her aside.

293

"I wish at this time to extend to one among you, Vincent, Our greatest heart of approval, and We wish to say to you: We in Heaven thank you for the fact that you went forward with others to right the wrong to My Mother when they produced that abominable motion picture called, 'Hail Mary.'

'Hail, Mary' promoted for money

"Even though the Pope, himself, wished this movie to be stopped, yet for the sake of money they sold out the Eternal Father. They sold Him out like they did to Me, many years ago, for pieces of silver. Yes, My children, that is all it amounts to - money! That is the reason for the showing of that picture. But how many could stay there without vomiting for what came forward from that screen.

Get film out of U.S. and Canada

"I say again: I extend Our hearts to all who made such a great effort of show to stop the abomination from being committed in the theaters of New York. Surely, My children, if they could get it out of Italy, you can get it out of the United State, and Canada, which it is approaching.

"My child and My children, and especially, you, My child, Veronica, I do not wish to tax you with a long discourse because I know how difficult it was for you to remove yourself from your bed this morning. But know this, My child, you will be here with Us as We need you, for I know that you will come if you have to come by hand and by cart.

"You will all keep a constant vigilance of prayer going throughout your world and all the nations of the earth. Because if you do not, all the nations of the world shall cry. You have been given minor warnings with hurricanes, and all kinds of earth disturbances, with droughts: with everything, My child, that should have alerted mankind, but did not. What are they waiting for? The Ball of Redemption?

Do not be caught short of provisions

"The Eternal Father has the Ball poised in His hand; your end can come by day. It will come upon you quickly, and how many shall be prepared? Do you have your candles? Do you have your water, your canned food, and your blankets? It will become an extremely cold day with the start of the Tribulation, and you will welcome having these on hand, My children. Do not take this lightly, but abide by Our direction and you shall not be caught short of provisions.

"I bless you now, My children, as the Father blesses you: In the name of the Father, and the Son, and the Holy Ghost.

"You will continue now with your prayers of atonement; they are sorely needed.

"And remember, My children, no sin shall ever be condoned or rationalized upon, for sin means hell, or purgatory. No matter how much man has cast aside his knowledge of the existence of hell, and purgatory, remember, My children, one day, in your heart, you will meet one - it is inevitable in every life, that you meet one who is approaching his end, and he will scream for mercy. In pity, will you pray for his soul because you do not wish to see him in hell, as Our Lady does not wish to seem him in hell.

"Keep a constant vigilance of prayer going throughout your world and, also, your immediate nations. I say this in particular because there is another trial approaching mankind in the United States, and this can also extend up to Canada.

Tribulation of an earth force

"You will pray constantly, My children. The prayers can reach Heaven in short time, and perhaps can stop the next tribulation. This is called a tribulation what will come upon you next. It will be of an earth force again. However, with your prayers, and your guarding of your homes, as We have always told you to, with the crucifixes, you can escape with little damage, or none at all. It will be as though the angel of death has passed by your home. To some it will seem like a miracle, but to others it's just an accepted part of life. For they will repeat: We are doing as the Eternal Father has told us, and we are following the directions of Our Blessed Mother, as She stood before us so many times, and said, 'I am Mary, Help of Mothers. I love all My children, and as such I will stand beside them, not wishing that one shall fall into hell.'

"Pray for your clergy, for the bishops are misguided. Pray for your cardinals, for some will fall into hell. Pray for all mankind, for prayers are never wasted. If you have any prayers left, My children, in your full day of praying, give some to those in purgatory. There is such dire need for prayers for those in purgatory who have no one on earth to pray for them.

"Now I will bless you, My children."

Veronica - And Our Lady is also extending Her Rosary, the crucifix on Her Rosary.

Jesus - "I bless you: In the name of the Father, and of the Son, and of the Holy Ghost.

"May you be protected by the shield of the Immaculate Conception: In the name of the Father, and of the Son, and of the Holy Ghost.

"Continue now, My child and My children, with your prayers of atonement.

Consecrate Russia!
Contact and beg the Pope

Eve of Pentecost - May 17, 1986

Veronica - All about the trees Our Lady's blue lights are beginning to cascade back and forth. And they are traveling at a very high speed, which makes it urgent that Our Lady appear this evening; because She has something to tell the world that is so urgent that I know satan did everything to keep me from coming this evening. I don't feel very well, but I know as soon as I see Our Lady, She will give me the strength to carry on.

The lights are growing brighter now. Now high up in the sky, over our heads, I see now a circlet of light, but it's bordered by a golden circlet. It's small now, but it's opening up and growing larger. Oh, how beautiful!

Through the circle of light I see Our Lady; Our Lady is coming down. Oh, I feel better already. Oh, Our Lady looks absolutely beautiful. Oh, She has on a white gown, pure white gown, and a white mantle. And all about the mantle there is a narrow border of gold. The gold is brilliant, it's flashing now as Our Lady looks to the right and left.

Now behind Our Lady there is a large golden globe. And I see that it's turning into a white globe - no, it's not a globe now. I know it represents a host . Our lady has now, right behind Her, a huge host.

Now. Our Lady is pointing up for me to look over to the right side. Her left side. Oh! Oh, I know who it is; it's Michael coming though the clouds. There are clouds there, all about the trees. But Michael is coming forward. And he doesn't have the balance this evening. He has something golden in his hands. As soon as he gets a little closer.... I can see what it is. It's become enlarged for my sight. Oh, St. Michael is carrying a chalice. It's a very large golden, beautiful chalice. And Michael is now nodding, yes.

He's looking over to Our Lady. Our Lady is standing at

Michael's right side. Now Michael is very difficult to describe. He is so huge! A real warrior of Heaven. But I cannot see his features; there's something about Michael that his features are unexplainable, like the spirit. But he does look gorgeous. His hair I do see. His hair is a golden color. That is why Our Lady names him, `Golden Boy'.

Now Our Lady is whispering something to Michael; Michael has come over to Her. And She's pointing now down to me, and Michael is nodding his head. Now Our Lady is turning to me, and She says:

Our Lady - "Pause one moment, My child; I have a very important mission for you. That is why I brought you here this evening. But first I must bless these multitudes of wonderful souls, that have come this evening to honor My Son in the Pentecost, in the Father, and the Holy Ghost."

Veronica - Now Our Lady is moving over to Her right, that's our left side, and She's taking Her Rosary from about Her waist; Our Lady had it on Her belting about Her waist, and She's taking the Rosary now and She's holding the crucifix up, like this. She's over, directly over on our left side, and She's, making the sign of the cross: In the name of the Father, and of the Son, and of the Holy Ghost.

Now Our Lady is looking over to Her left side, and She's moving very daintily. I just noticed Our Lady has on beautiful slippers; they look like golden threads, but on the edges of each toe, by Her toes, Her dainty feet, there are rosettes, golden rosettes.

Now Our Lady is moving over to above Her statue, and She's raising the crucifix on Her Rosary and making the sign of the cross: In the name of the Father, and of the Son, and of the Holy Ghost.

Michael is standing there. He looks like quite stern. I don't know just what is passing between them, but he is waiting for Our Lady's signal. Our Lady said to Michael - I heard Her say,

Our Lady - "In one moment. Your anxiety, Michael, I can well understand."

Veronica - Now Our lady is going over to our right side, which would be Her left side, by the trees, and She's looking down and She's smiling beautifully. Oh, I can see Our Lady very clearly now. And I don't hurt anymore the way I did when I first came and arrived here. I feel well again. Our Lady is making me feel much stronger. Thank you, Blessed Mother. In the name of the Father, and of the Son, and of the Holy Ghost.

Now Our Lady is nodding to Michael. But She's crossing across the sky now, until She's directly over Her statue. Now She is placing Her first finger to Her lips.

Our Lady - "My child, I know you are in wonderment of why Michael is holding the chalice with anxiety. I must tell You: within the chalice in Michael's hands are the Hosts collected from throughout the world that had been discarded by the faithless. I have asked that My Son's Body be protected upon earth. But many clergy now have cast aside My warnings from Heaven, and His Body has been placed and thrown on the floors, and into the water fonts of many of My Son's churches throughout the world.

Veronica receives Holy Communion

"My child, I ask this of you this evening - that is why I requested that you do not eat - I ask that you accept My Son. You will do heavy penance for the world in the coming months, My child. But you will accept My Son for the world. I want you, My child, to raise your heart to Heaven now, and beg forgiveness to mankind from the Eternal Father. My child, you will now receive one of the Hosts taken from the water fonts."

[Veronica is helped from her chair, drops to her knees, extends her tongue and receives Holy Communion invisibly from St. Michael; then she recites the following Act of Contrition.]

O my God, I'm heartily sorry for having offended Thee; and I confess with all my sins, because I dread the loss of Heaven and the pains of hell; but most of all because I love Thee, My God, Who are all good and deserving of all my love. I firmly resolve, with the help of Thy grace,

299

to confess my sins, to do penance, and to amend my life. Amen.

I beg pardon for all those priests within Jesus' Church who have cast aside their major roles as saver of souls. I ask God to forgive them, and give them another chance through the messages given by His Mother, Jesus' Mother, Mary, going throughout the world at this time. I beg that Her pleadings with mankind can actually, factually, turn them back to the Eternal Father, and use His plan, His method for salvation. Amen.

In the name of the Father, and of the Son, and of the Holy Ghost.

Our Lady - "You will be seated now, My child. I wish that you would take now three photographs."

[After a short pause, Veronica responds to specific instructions.]

Veronica - Yes. Yes.

Our Lady - "Three photographs, My child. You will read them, but do not give the meaning to a soul; not one soul must know. It is most urgent."

[Pause]

Our Lady - "My child, now we must continue, even in your debilitated state, we must continue with an urgent message to the world.

A nuclear disaster

"In the past few months My child and children, much has happened within your country and other countries of the world. There have been earthquakes, floods, and, also, a nuclear disaster. Know now, My children and My child, that this is not the end of suffering for mankind. Because of the fact that My Message has reached many but not all at this time, there is evil now brewing within the world that is heading for the Third World War. In my desperation, My child, I have even entered upon other countries to try to stop the evil among man - the evil of murder: murder whether planned or accidental, in accidents that are not accidents.

Our Lady appears again in Egypt

"Now, My child, you have been much concerned about My appearance in another country, Egypt. Yes, My child, you do not understand all. Saint Demyana is a Coptic Orthodox Church, My child, and I must say: though My heart grieves because they are not with Rome at this time, they will join in the future. But at this time the only thing that eases My heart is the knowledge that they have kept the Faith as they know it. In that Church, My child, the Coptics - which are few in Egypt - they are devout. They do not rush through the service of the Holy Sacrifice of the Mass, where My Son, daily, gives Himself to you. They are few in number but devout.

"I must tell you, My child and My children, that they have suffered persecution throughout the years. I came there this time, My child, to try to draw together those about them who seek to persecute them: the Moslems, and others, the Arabs. This is going on throughout the world.

"You see, My children, satan always says: to divide is to conquer. But I do not want to see the world in chaos, and a Third World War. That is why, My child, I brought you here this evening, though I knew that your strength was waning by this afternoon. There is only one recourse for mankind now to avoid a Third World War - that is more prayer, more penance, and more sacrifice for sinners. Those who are keeping the laws of the Eternal Father must remember that they have been given a special grace from the Father, and have an obligation to seek out the souls who have not received this grace. Bring them the light; show them the way. For they are wandering, and they can be seduced in nature by others who are not in the light. Your example, My children, is very important.

State of marriage becoming nullified

"This I can tell you - because We are much grieved as We look into the hearts of the mothers and fathers throughout the world - not many are in the light. Families are disintegrating; the state of marriage is becoming nullified. Now it is fashionable in the United States, and many nations of the world, to discard the Sacrament of Marriage and to live together in sin. This, My child and My children, cannot be tolerated. Man must come back to the laws of His God, or he will be destroyed.

"There will be in your country, the United States of America, a similar disaster as in Russia. Know that this can be avoided if you pray more for your leaders. For in their haste to build up armaments, they deceive the world in saying that these armaments are being really cut down or discarded. No, My children, they are being stored, and added to day by day.

"You see, My child and My children, We allowed the disaster in Russia. It was to try to awaken Russia into coming back to the fold. They are creating much chaos throughout the world, and for this reason we must bring them to their knees.

"You must pray for your Holy Father, the Pope. There will be another attempt upon his life.

"Yes, My child, though he means well, it would be best if he discards his habit of going to and fro. For it is upon one of these journeys that he will be destroyed.

"You will keep a constant vigilance of prayer going throughout your nation and the world. So few now are reading Our messages from Heaven. They think that they have found the solution, but they must remember this, that satan is loosed upon earth now with all the demons of hell, and they will do anything within their power to fight the plan of Heaven for the redemption of mankind. Redemption, grace, and peace will only come to man when he returns to his God.

Abortion: the foulest of sacrileges

"My child and My children, children, I wish that you make it known to your countrymen in the United States, and Canada, and all the nations of the world, that We cannot tolerate the murders of the unborn. This is a sacrilege of the most foulest manner in the eyes of the Eternal Father, and shall be punishable by death.

"My children, more young souls sent upon earth by the Eternal Father have been destroyed in the past years - since the passing of lax laws by your government, more young souls have been destroyed than in many World Wars. Therefore, We say unto you now, and I plead with you, as your Mother, to turn back from your life of sin. Sin has truly, My children, become a way of life in your nation and the world. And the Eternal Father says He shall not allow this to continue much longer. The hourglass now is beginning to run."

Veronica - I see now a huge hourglass. And there's only one grain of sand, but it's beginning to pass through. I see Michael now with his chalice, and his hand raised over the hourglass. And it seems to be suspended in midair.

Our Lady now is motioning with Her hand to Her lips, to listen.

Restore St. Michael as guardian of Church

Our Lady - "My child, I want the world to know that Michael is the guardian of the highest Heaven. You must also tell the priests within My Son's Church that they must return Michael to his rightful place as guardian of the Church, or they will be subjected to terrible trials. What has happened to nations throughout the world, through Russia, shall happen to the United States and Canada. Russia, My children, is not entering where you can see them. They are infiltrating now into every side of your nation: north, south, east, and west - on the outer fringes and the inner fringes.

"My children, much of the evil now that is spreading in the United States and Canada was promoted by these men and women of satan, known as Communists, who have been allowed to enter not only into your country and the countries of the world, but also into My Son's Church upon earth.

Seminaries infiltrated

"Yes, My child, I want you to let the world know that

303

Our seminaries were not pure. Many had entered for this very day to try to destroy the Faith and the Church of My Son. You must know that the Eternal Father will not permit this.

"The world is fast hurtling to a baptism of fire. My child and My children, can you not go back and read, and reread, the Messages from Heaven given to you throughout the years. I, as your Mother, have traveled to and fro, hinder and yon, seeking to bring My children back to the fold. For every soul that is lost I pine, and I sigh and I cry, and My tears fall upon you, My children; My tears fall upon you."

Veronica - Our Lady now is crying, and Her tears are falling upon us.

Now Our Lady is pointing up, and high in the sky over Her head, there's a large ball with a black cross on it. That means suffering; I know that means suffering for the world. We are in for additional chastisement. Our Lady is now nodding Her head, yes.

Our Lady - "My child and My children, if you could receive the knowledge from the Eternal Father of what is fast coming upon you, you would spend your days, and your nights, on your knees. All who have been given the grace to be a part of the legions of Heaven must go forward in these latter days, and do everything they can to bring the world back to the Eternal Father.

Our Lady to appear over St. Robert's

"Yes, My child, I am going about the world appearing in various places, and I have reason for all. One day, My child, the waters will come up at Bayside, and I will appear over the old church building. Your Bishop then cannot deny My Appearances.

"I realize, My child, that it is almost sixteen years since you accepted Our request to go forth as a beacon of light in the darkness. Now I know that your heart is lightened that the Eternal Father has sent through the years many other beacons of light. It has made your road easier. I know, My child, you thank Him every day for this blessing; but it is the plan of the Eternal Father. Many graces shall be given and increased in the days ahead. The world shall know the power of the Eternal Father.

"Satan is loosed upon earth, but he knows that his time is growing short. Therefore, he will make a concerted effort to destroy those who are not in the state of grace, so that he can take them into hell. That is why, My children, you must always wear a medal, your armor about your neck. And the best armor of all is the Scapular, the Rosary, the St. Benedict medal; and, also your newest armor: Our Lady of the Roses, Mary Help of Mothers. My child and My children, I tell you this because you cannot do without any of them. At this time, all armor is needed for the fight ahead.

"As I told you before, My child, you cannot understand the ways of the Eternal Father. So many deaths in the Mexican earthquakes, so many in the floods; starvation, sorrow, murders - all this was known and burdened the heart of the Eternal Father for years. He knows what lies ahead; but we also know through His words, through the Holy Ghost, and Jesus, His Son, that one day He will return and restore this earth. However, many saints shall come out from this conflagration, saints who have washed their robes in the blood of the Lamb. Many shall die in the great flame of the Ball of Redemption.

"I cannot, My child, give you your request of last week of the date. But you will keep those photographs that I gave you, and you will know the date. But you must promise me now that you will not reveal this either by mouth or by writing."

Veronica - I promise, Blessed Mother, I won't reveal it.

Our Lady - "You see, My child, if you give dates, others will run to come back to the fold, but as soon as the danger passes they will go back to their old ways. We must have a complete redemption, not just a temporary state of goodness. For it is a selfish reason that does not reach out and give to the Eternal Father what He asks: your love, your compassion, and your willingness to help Him in this crisis.

"I will continue, My children, to go throughout the world.

The Eternal Father is much pleased with the manner in which you have given out the messages to the world. Know that We do not expect you, because of this compliment, My children, to slacken your pace; for it must increase, because the time is growing short.

"Pray for all sinners. Pray for those who run the governments of the world. And above all remember to pray for the Holy Father, Pope John Paul II, in Rome, for his time is growing short.

"Now, My child, you will take more photographs, and My Son shall join Me. He has a most urgent plea to the world."

Veronica - There is pink coloring all about the trees just above Our Lady's statue. Oh, the color is beautiful. I call it 'pink', but no human words could describe the colors from Heaven; even a paintbrush could never pick them out.

But just in the center of the sky, I see a round circular ball, and it's coming towards us. It's turning bright red. I know it's a globe of the world, and it looks like it's all on fire. It's a - it's a horrible thing. (Veronica gasps!) I can feel the heat, and I can taste the smoke. It's a horrible thing to see coming through the sky. It's a large ball. Oh! Oh, I think - I can't stand the heat. Oh, it's scorching. (Veronica gasps heavily again.) Oh, now it's going back into the sky. Oh, it was most frightening!

Oh, now there over by the trees on the right side, Jesus has been standing. The ball was so luminous and so frightening. I didn't see Him coming through the clouds. There are many clouds above us; it's like dense smoke, still the smoke from that large ball. That must be the Ball of Redemption that Our Lady always speaks of, even at home She tells me of the Ball of Redemption coming closer.

Now Jesus is looking all about Him. He's coming over now, He was standing by the trees. The pink lights are now glowing again. They give a beautiful cast to His face, and also His garments. Now Jesus is moving across from our right side, and He's coming directly across above the statue. He's looking all about Him, and nodding.

Jesus has on a burgundy cape. And His tunic, His gown, looks like it's mad of some kind of hemp; I can't explain the material. But it's something - I don't think I saw that type of material before. But it's a beige color. Kind of rough - looking type of material. And Jesus has about His waist a belting made from some kind of skin - like material - like leather, almost like leather. I don't know if it's leather, but it looks like some type of animal - skin belting.

And now as the wind is blowing. I can see that Jesus is wearing sandals, brown sandals. They're open at the toes. They're two straps across the foot, the bottom of the foot, and one strap by the ankle. Jesus is raising His foot a bit. He's smiling. He's very amused at the way I'm describing His clothes.

Now Jesus is looking all about Him. He's moving over now to His right side, high across the sky - no, He's coming down now. Jesus is coming down near the trees. Now He's raising His hand, like this, and making the sign of the cross: In the name of the Father, and of the Son, and of the Holy Ghost.

Now Jesus is turning towards His left, and He's slowly floating. He doesn't walk like we do. He just seems weightless, and He's carried like on the wind. He's going slowly across the sky, and looking about Him. Now He's turning, He's just above the statue, and He's turning towards the people. And He's raising His hand out, like this, and making the sign of the cross: In the name of the Father, and of the Son, and of the Holy Ghost.

Now Jesus is looking over to our right side, which is His left side, and He's moving over slowly. He's looking all about the grounds, and over the heads of the people. Now He's raising His hand out very much in front of Him, as though to reach over the whole crowd, and making the sign of the cross: In the name of the Father, and of the Son, and of the Holy Ghost.

The four Evangelists

Now I notice Jesus is starting to move back towards the

center of the sky here, the opening in the sky. I say 'opening', because as Jesus was blessing the multitudes here, the sky started to open, and coming through are people. I think they're angels; I'm not sure yet. They're dressed in white gowns. No, they're human beings: Mark, Luke, John, and Matthew. Oh yes, Jesus said they are, Saint Mark, Saint Luke, Saint John, and Saint Matthew. And Jesus is nodding, yes. Now He's coming across the sky, and He's standing; He's nodded to them. They're coming down closer. I do notice they have a similarity; they all have beards, and they have long gowns on. And Jesus is now touching His first finger to His lips. which means to listen and repeat.

Jesus - "My child and My children: yes, they are some of the few who have washed their robes clean in the blood of the Lamb, through, suffering upon earth. You know, of course, My children, that to follow the road to Heaven, they had to be martyred. But they left upon the earth a legacy for all, the Book of life and love, the Bible.

"I wish that all homes have a Bible within their doors. I say within their doors, because these children that they are raising must go out into a world that has been given over to satan. The Bible must be ever before them, for it is their true guide to redemption.

"My child and My children, many punishments have gone by unnoticed, and many more shall be given. I say this with a heave heart, because daily the prayers of the multitudes reach us, asking forgiveness for those who have sinned. My child and My children, I must tell you that they have a free will and conscience.

"I know that all who hear My voice now and read this Message are doing all they can to restore the earth to what the Eternal Father calls a bit of normalcy. For the world has gone crazy with sin. Is that not true, My child? Sin has become a way of life among many. Now I ask you, as children of God, all who hear My voice, to continue a constant vigilance of prayer, penance, and sacrifice. Many more disasters are heading for your country, the United States, and the world.

Russia seeks to capture whole world

"Russia, being an atheistic country, My children - Russia, you cannot believe what they tell you, nor what they print in their tabloids. Russia has but one plan: to capture the whole world. They will do this without heart or conscience. Therefore, know that I ask you again, as your God in the Trinity, I ask you to contact the Holy Father - through pen or prose, or the written script - to contact the Holy Father and beg him to consecrate Russia to the Immaculate Heart of My Mother. This has not been done, My children. That is why as time goes on, until that grain goes through the hourglass forever, that is why you will undergo great suffering.

"My child, you have to understand that the human body is frail; but you will suffer no more, no less that the Father expects of you. We have asked for very many victim souls in the world. They are necessary in the plan for man's redemption. I would not question, My child, the reasoning of the Eternal Father, for He is your God, and knows all, sees all, and will do what is best for you and mankind."

Veronica - Now Jesus is looking all about Him. He's looking over to Saint Mark, Saint Luke, and Saint Matthew, and Saint John, there. And He's whispering something to them, but I can't hear it. I guess I'm not supposed to hear it; I can't hear it. It sounds like the rustling of the wind, but He's talking to them. Oh, I see now. They're holding up what looks like pens. They're very strange - looking pens; they look like a feather with just a point on the end. And they're writing - each one of them has a book, and they're writing in the books. Now Jesus is nodding.

The Bible - cornerstone of Church

Jesus - "You have taken that correctly, My child. That is the manner in which the Book of life and love was written for you. I say for you, because it was to be established as the cornerstone of My Church - let us say that, My child, the cornerstone of My Church is the Book of life and love, that you call the Bible.

"You will now, My child and My children, continue with

your prayers of atonement. And you, My child, shall take more photographs, because there is much that cannot be revealed at this time. And I will call upon you again to return to these grounds.

"You will be given the stamina, My child. And I assure you, once you reach the grounds, you will be able to continue your mission from Heaven."

Veronica - Now Jesus is raising His hand, like this again, and He's making the sign of the cross: In the name of the Father, and of the Son, and of the Holy Ghost.

Jesus - "Continue, My children, now."

Veronica - Now it's growing dark in the sky. It was so lighted before. It's difficult to explain the brilliance of the light, even coming out of the saints - the glow, the light. Without Heaven's intervention, I'm certain that my natural, human eyes would be destroyed from the light. But this is something that's beyond words to explain... that the light is more brilliant than a hundred suns. And yet, the beauty of it holds you transfixed, where you don't actually feel it. I'm certain, without Heaven's intervention, I would have no eyes, because it was like looking into another world. But so beautiful. And I notice now, and I wish to be known to all, that this light also emanates from Jesus and Our Lady whenever They appear here. And I'm sure that should we all be graced to enter Heaven without much suffering, even if we have to go to purgatory perhaps awhile - God forbid that we should go elsewhere! - but should we go to purgatory, we could always think of the day when we, too, shall enter beyond the veil into the beautiful light.

Now it's growing dark. And do you know, the circle of light is closing up, just as though it's becoming smaller and smaller. And I can't see now the saints anymore; they are behind now the curtain, like a curtain that has been drawn over them.

And now Our Lady - oh! Our Lady is coming forward again. She's touching Her lips.

Some will see Jesus and Our Lady

Our Lady - "My child, We are not leaving. We remain here all evening. Until the last soul has left the grounds, My Son and I are here. Some will see Us, and some will not. The day will come when all will see Us.

"Continue, My child, now with the prayers of atonement; you must join them."

The Third Secret of Fatima

Satan in Church; plead with Pope to have Lucy tell…

16th Anniversary of Our Lady's Apparitions at Bayside -
June 18, 1986

Veronica - All about the trees there are immense lights.
Now there are not the round blue balls that normally cascade
across the sky at Our Lady's arrival. They are like long
sheets of light coming from the tips of the trees, and going
upward, high up into the heavens. Oh, it's a beautiful light.
It's lighting up the whole sky. And directly over Our Lady's
statue, if you go up about perhaps, I would say around sixteen feet, you can see Our Lady now coming through the
clouds. There is a cloud - like formation, as though Our
Lady has just passed through some type of an ordeal, some
type of a catastrophe. Because the clouds don't look like the
clouds of our sky, but the clouds are coming up smoke - like
from some type of a chasm, a deep well or something.

Now Our Lady is coming down closer to the top of Her
statue. She's come down quite fast. Now Our lady is wearing the most beautiful gown. She has on a white gown with
a blue sash about Her waist. And Her Rosary beads are dangling from this sash, the Rosary with the golden Our Fathers
and the white Hail Marys, that actually become all the colors
of the rainbow, as Our Lady turns. Now I can see - I can
never see Our Lady's hair; Her head is well covered by Her
mantle this evening. Her mantle is a beautiful white, a beautiful white! And it has a trim of about - oh, a half an inch of
gold all about the outside.

Our Lady is smiling. It's a sad smile, but Our Lady does
look like She is happy. Now Our Lady is nodding, and
She's placing Her first finger to Her lips, which means to listen and repeat.

Our Lady - "My child and My children, My heart is so
lightened with joy at the numbers of wonderful souls who
have come here this evening to honor the Eternal Father
when He sent Me sixteen earth - years ago, down upon

earth, to try to stop the crisis in the Church, and the chaos that is going throughout all the countries of the world.

Explosion about to take place

"My child and My children, I came to you many years ago, at Fatima, with a plan for the salvation of mankind. And I must say to you this evening, as your Mother, that none of My words must be kept hidden any longer, for it is urgent that the world make this final atonement. The hourglass now is almost empty; days can be counted by hours. For at this very moment We see a most terrible explosion, with the loss of many lives about to take place.

"O My children, you do not understand what I have given to other seers upon earth to bring to you. Not only words of consolation but words of truth. The truth sometimes does hurt, My children; but I, as your Mother, must treat you at this time as adults, being able to reason with the God - given reasoning that Heaven gave unto you when you were conceived by the Holy Ghost. I say this for this reason: The Eternal Father is much disturbed at the numbers of abortions being committed throughout your country and the world. These numbers go upwards to fifty to sixty million in one year throughout the world. And this is too much for the Eternal Father; and also, for the souls who are now victim souls - victims to try to save their brothers and sisters who have gone astray from gaining their rightful deserts of destruction and death. These victim souls, that have become victims of their own accord and their own placement, they are the ones who have kept the just punishment from coming upon you and mankind.

The Third Secret word for word

"I wish at this time, My children, to repeat again the need to write, to speak, to meet with the Holy Father in Rome, and plead with him to have Lucy come forward and tell the Third Secret word for word, as I give to you each evening on My appearances upon the grounds of Bayside, and

313

Flushing Meadows.

"O My children, if you knew what was in store for you in the near future - and that means, My child and My children, this year - you would understand why I feel, and why I cry tears that fall upon you. If I could, I would as your Mother, make all atonement for you, but it is the will of the Eternal Father that you come forward now and stand up to protect your own souls, and, also, the souls of your children and your families.

"Mothers, and fathers too, have gone astray in these dark days. Materialism has replaced spiritualism, and that is why the many catastrophes are being allowed upon your earth. There will be more floods with death; more volcano eruptions with death; more accidents that are not accidents; until you will surely come to your senses and realize that there is a higher power working at this time to bring you to your knees.

Atonement on first Saturdays

"My child and My children, I have asked in the past for certain days of atonement: the First Saturdays, the First Saturday of each month. Can you not give this to Me, My children, in order to place it before the Eternal Father? For you must pray for sinners. I beg you, My children, as your Mother, your loving Mother, who cries tears of sorrow upon you all, please remember this: The time is growing short. I have wandered throughout earth trying to warn you, My children, depending on a small handful of loyal souls to bring these messages to you upon these grounds, My child. We chose you to come forth, in illness and in health, in order to save your brothers and sisters.

"As a victim soul, My child, We cannot promise you happiness upon this earth. But We will give you - if you remain steadfast and true, My child, in your own free will - We will give you a reward that far surpasses all of your imagination, your inclinations; and anything that is beyond the human mind to understand now, you will be given in return for yourself. Do you understand this, My child?

"You will continue, My child, to send the messages throughout the world with great haste. Satan has come with his agents to try to stop you. They are now planning a measure of retaliation. Be prepared, My child; when it happens you will know that it is straight from satan.

"I ask you now to give the warning in poetical form, given to the world some years ago. It must be applied now.

The end is not as far as you can see;
Already there is apostasy.
Man cast his lot and gathered the coals
To stoke the fires that burn the souls.
The days are numbered, the hours are few;
So work and pray, and try to do
The work that's given in the light,
Until that sad time when all is night.

"My child, you said that well. it is a riddle, as the Father gives many riddles: but those who have the grace will understand and act upon it.

"Now, My child, for reasons that you are not to give out, I wish at this time that you take three photographs. They are very, very important, My child. They will contain a date for the next catastrophe. You must know for reason because you must move from your house at that time. You will take the pictures now, My child, and I will be with you again."

[Pause]

Veronica - Oh, the trees now are turning pink at the tips. It's a beautiful colored pink, it's nothing frightening, though I had a great fear in my heart that the trees were going to go on fire for a moment, because it's a startling pink. Now there are long rivulets of light, going from the tips of the trees, high up into the sky. And there, directly over Our Lady's statue, about maybe - oh, I would say about forty or fifty feet, Jesus is coming down through the sky. The sky was dark, but it's becoming now a very bright white, translucent type of light all about Jesus. And it makes Him shine very clearly, and stand forth very clearly.

Jesus has on a burgundy cape, and it has a headpiece, but He's not wearing it this evening. I can see it over His shoulders because there is a belting - like, tied at His neck. It's made of a gold - like material, the tie. And Jesus has on a gown. It's made of a hemp - like material. It doesn't look like a soft material; it looks very stiff. And I can see Jesus' feet now as He's coming down closer. He has on sandals. They're made of some kind of animal skin. They're a brown color, but they just have two straps; one across near the toes, and one across the ankle area - two straps. I don't know how they stay on.

But Jesus now is floating down. He doesn't walk; He does what Our Lady does - She floats, also, downward. And now Jesus is looking all about Him. It's a little windy up there because His hair is blowing. His hair comes down by His shoulders, where His cape comes to the end near His neck.

And Jesus now is looking, and He's smiling - over to the right, and over the left. Now I can see over on the right side, there was a light by the trees; and I notice that Our Lady is standing there. Our Lady has moved over to the right. I didn't know where She had gone to, after I saw Her and took the photographs. But Our Lady is standing over by our right side. And Jesus is directly now over Her statue. He's looking about Him. Now He's taking His hands, like this - Jesus - and making the sign of the cross: In the name of the Father, and of the Son, and of the Holy Ghost.

Now Jesus is looking over to His right side, that would be our left side, and He's moving over now. He's going over slowly, as He looks about Him. Now He's turning straight to face us, and He's directly over, near the tall tree; and He's making the sign of the cross: In the name of the Father, and of the Son, and of the Holy Ghost.

Now Jesus is looking over towards Our Lady, and Our Lady has a slight smile on Her face. She's so brightly lighted this evening that I can see Her face very clearly now. Our Lady is smiling. She has delicate features. Our Lady, I would say - I never asked Them about Their heights or anything like that; that would be embarrassing to do - but I would say Our Lady must be around - oh, five foot five tall. And Jesus, I know, is about six foot one. That's why She always seems to come over to His shoulder, when They come together. Now Our Lady is smiling and shaking Her head, yes.

Now Jesus has moved over in the meantime. He's come over above Our Lady's statue, and He's leaning down again and making the sign of the cross: In the name of the Father, and of the Son, and of the Holy Ghost.

Now Jesus has a look on His face; I can't explain it. It is both of great sorrow and of joy. I know that He's very happy this evening for all the numbers of peoples and souls that have come here to honor His Mother, and Her appearances here with Him.

Now Jesus is placing His hand out, like this, and He's calling to His Mother. Oh, Our Lady is coming over to Him; Our Lady is coming across the sky quite fast. Now She's come over and She's standing by Jesus' left side, and He's motioning for Her to come about on His right side. Now Our Lady is standing at the right side of Jesus, and He's whispering to Her. I can't hear what He's saying, but it's just like the murmuring of a tree. I can't explain it. It's the only sound I can hear. I can't make out the words, but Jesus is smiling assuringly. And now He's turning towards His left side, and He's said something to His Mother, and She nodded. I think She's going to remain there; yes, He's moving.

Jesus is going now over to our right side; He's moving quite slowly. He's just floating. He doesn't walk the way we do; He seems to float as though He's weightless, yet He looks as solid as you and I. And Jesus is now looking down, and making the sign of the cross: In the name of the Father, and of the Son, and of the Holy Ghost.

Now Jesus is doing something very strange. He's going up higher and higher, and He's going to the top, the tippy-top of the highest tree here in the park; and He's bending over now and making the sign of the cross: In the name of the Father, and of the Son, and of the Holy Ghost.

Now Jesus is placing both of His hands out in front of Him, like this, and there are long rays of light going from His fingers, out towards - way behind us in the back. I feel that He's trying to reach people way back behind us. We're quite up front, but Jesus is now purposely motioning to His Mother, and She's coming over. Our Lady is now crossing the sky to Jesus, and She's taking Her Rosary, the Rosary with the golden Our Fathers and the white Hail Marys, that are luminous in color when She's turning about Her ... She's doing now. And Jesus has mentioned something to Her about blessing - that I heard ... it was blessing. And oh, Our Lady is now raising the crucifix on Her Rosary and making the sign of the cross: In the name of the Father, and of the Son, and of the Holy Ghost.

Now They are both turning towards Their right - our left side - and They're coming across the sky, very slowly, as They're looking about. Now They're approaching the statue area. They're very high in the sky. Now Jesus is murmuring to Our Lady, and Our Lady is nodding. She's standing there. And now Jesus has placed His first finger to His lips.

Jesus - "My child and My children, I do not wish to elaborate nor add to My Mother's statements to you this evening of facts and what is to be. But there is one incident that has appalled us all in Heaven that must be made known to mankind, because I feel in My heart for My Mother, Her great hurt and sorrow that Her Message at Fatima was not completely given to mankind. This evening I speak to you, My child Veronica, for you to tell the world that to hide a fact is often destructive. And this fact will be make known now - with or without Lucy - or others who cannot speak out because they are under obedience to their elders. You will repeat this, My child, though it may shock you.

Satan sat in on Vatican II

"I say this evening, as your God, that on that date, as promised at Fatima, satan entered My Church upon earth. He brought with him his agents - and satan himself, the deceiver of all mankind - sat in on Vatican II and maneuvered all the outsiders to come in and distort My doctrines and distort the truth.

"At Fatima, My Mother tried to warn of this coming event, but who cared to listen? Who was interested in listening? Not those who were years - earth - years away. All Heaven was crying in that time, for the Eternal Father had made it known how His message would be received. To this day, to your earth - year of 1986, you have not been given, My children, the full secrets as given to the children at Fatima.

"Therefore, I must make it known at this time to you. If you are perceiving and interested in My Church upon earth, I do not have to explain Myself too fully; for you will already know of the chaos that satan has wrought when he entered My Church. And why did he enter, you say? This I want it made known, My child - and you will not be affrighted as you are now - you will speak out for Me and My Mother, and the Eternal Father in the Holy Spirit; you will speak out and say that satan is in the Church, My Church upon earth. He knows his time is growing short.

"And if you think you have seen carnage now already in the Church, the worst is yet to come, unless you follow the rules, given by My Mother many years ago, of prayer, atonement, and sacrifice. By your example you may be able to save others. For soon there will come upon you the great Chastisement. It comes in two parts, My child and My children: the Third World War and, also, the Ball of Redemption. These can no longer be delayed. For the good seem to go about their way, perhaps pridefully. We do not seek to accuse or place a stigma on any, but some may pridefully sit back and let others go forth and make these sacrifices and prayers and penance. Because they have become smug, or because they have not the grace to understand, that once you receive this grace much is expected of you. You must even work harder to save your brothers and sisters.

319

Lucy has been silenced

"My child and My children, this message will not be greeted gleefully by your clergy. But since Lucy has been silenced, it is necessary that the world knows the truth. I will also send this message out through one more seer in the world, and if it is not abided by I have nothing to do but to allow the Chastisement to fall upon mankind.

"Your world has become steeped in debauchery. The killings of the unborn shall not go by without reprisals. And anyone who has any measure of incidence in the killing of the unborn shall be destroyed.

"My child and My children, do not take My words lightly. I do not speak to frighten you but to try to jar you from your complacency. There will be many minor warnings given to the world: more floods, accidents that are not accidents. There will be more murders upon earth; father against son, mother against daughter, homes torn asunder, for satan is loosed upon the earth. He has been given a time, a short time now for him to gather his souls.

"But I assure you, My children, We, in Heaven, have great faith that you, Our children, who hear Our words, will act upon them and help to recover as many of your brothers and sisters as you can throughout the world. You will keep the Rosary, the beads of prayer, going throughout the world, bead for bead. For every bead, there shall be a soul. That is how important the Rosary is to the world today.

"My child and My children, you will now go on with your prayers of atonement. They are sorely needed. We need more who are willing to become victim souls. They are not easy to find, My child. The choice is always given.

"You, My child, now will take three more photographs, but these you must be most silent on. I understand how you like to show them, My child, but I know that these are some that it's best that you keep to yourself for the time being.

"I will be speaking to you, My child, a little later on a very, very important matter. Now you will take the three photographs."

[Pause]

Veronica - Just about the trees those beautiful lights, those pink lights are glowing again. But now they are not cascading upwards, like streams of light, but they're just stationary. And coming down, I can see Jesus. Oh, He's in a brilliant white light. It's almost like looking through a pane of glass, pure, clear crystalline type of glass.

Now Jesus is coming forward - oh, very fast; He seems to be in quite a hurry. Our Lady now - I can't see Our Lady, but I know that She's standing somewhere near the bushes there; but there's a cloud, there's a large cloud up there that seems to be covering Our Lady. I can see it now - the hem of Her gown, so I know She's standing on our right side. But Jesus is now coming down, and He is about - about seven feet about Our Lady's statue. Now He's looking about Him, and He is blessing us again: In the name of the Father, and of the Son, and of the Holy Ghost.

Now He's motioning to me, and placing His first finger to His lips, which means to listen and repeat.

Clergy: driving away vocations

Jesus - "My child and My children, I come once more with an urgent and pleading message to the hierarchy in the Church, My Church upon earth. I want you to know now that We look upon you and find many that do not fall into grace. They are falling out of grace and misleading many of Our sheep.

"Therefore, I warn you now as your God: You will stop your intricacies within My Church. You will stop experimenting. I gave you the rules to follow many years ago, two thousand years approximately. And why now, two thousand years later, do you deem it necessary to change My Church upon earth? I, your God, say to you, you will be judged accordingly. You will return My Church to its former glory, and in that manner you will have more vocations and more entering the seminaries, and not fleeing from them as they hear the heresies and all other innovations that are going on within My Church. This is My last and final word to My clergy: Change now or suffer a just punishment and banishment.

"My child, that message must go out strictly without change. You must not be worried nor affrighted by any of the message because it is a dire necessity. I can no longer stand by and watch, day by day without change, what is happening in My Father's palace upon earth. I say it in glory to the Father and the Holy Spirit: it is His Church on earth.

"Now, My child, you will retire, and I will be speaking with you tomorrow in the A.M., but it will be very privately in your home. Ah, don't be excited now, My child; you will know by tomorrow."

Veronica - Now it's growing very dark in the sky. The light seems to be closing in about Jesus, but He's now touching His lips. He says:

Jesus - "I am not leaving the grounds, My child. My Mother and I will stay here as long a one soul remains upon it, or comes here."

Veronica - And now Our Lady - I happen to notice now Our Lady is coming across the sky from where She was standing by the trees. And They're standing directly over the statue. Now They're going much higher in the sky, very much higher. In fact, now They appear as small - as small figurines; They look almost like figurines in the sky. But I can see that They are both smiling. Now Jesus is touching His lips, like this, and He's saying:

Jesus - "Remember what I said, My child, tomorrow in the A.M."

322

Sex education in the schools
"A debauchery of young souls"

In honor of SS. Michael, Gabriel, Raphael, the Archangels -
September 27, 1986

Veronica - All about the trees there are beautiful cascading color of pink and blue. Oh, they're so beautiful, that I feel strong already. I didn't think I would be here this evening, but Heaven said you must. It is urgent because I have, Our Lady said, a must urgent message for the world. Well now, the - oh, the lights are cascading. They're not rounded blue as usual, but they are streaming, just like streamers, down from the top of the sky, up high above Our Lady's statue.

I can't judge the distance in height, but They're coming slowly down; Our Lady and Jesus are together. Oh, They look so beautiful! Our Lady is extending Her Rosary. She has Her beautiful Rosary with the golden Our Father and the white Hail Marys that cascade off the lights. The streamers of light are still going up. They seem to originate from the trees, but I can't be sure because I notice now, I'm looking at Jesus' hands, and I never saw anything so beautiful. He has these streaming lights of pink, a delicate pastel pink, coming down and parting. And not only that, they seem to be coming in this direction. And I can feel them all about us, and I can feel them on my chest. I feel much better already.

Oh, Our Lady is so beautiful! But oh, look what She's standing on! Our Lady is coming forward, but She's riding on the ball; it's the same ball I saw in 1970. Our Lady is smiling. She has Her Rosary extended, like this, in Her hands; in front of Her, and She's smiling; but there is a sad smile. Jesus is whispering something to Our Lady: I can't hear Him. I imagine I'm not supposed to hear Him. But He's whispering. And He's standing now in place. He's quite high above the statue. But Our Lady is coming down. She is standing on top of the ball. Now She's taking Her crucifix of Her Rosary, and making the sign of the cross, like

323

this: In the name of the Father, and of the Son, and of the Holy Ghost.

Now Our Lady is looking all about Her. She has on Her beautiful white mantle with the trimming of gold. The gold is about a half an inch all about the outside of Her mantle. Now the strange thing this evening is Our Lady does not have sandals on Her feet; they're quite bare, as She stands on top of the ball. But I notice at Her feet though, there are all roses; they look like fresh fragrant roses, all about Her feet. Oh, and Our Lady is so beautiful! She has on a pure white gown, and it's belted with a gold belting, that - Our Lady usually takes Her Rosary and attaches it to Her belting.

Now She is looking up at Jesus, and Jesus is nodding. Now Our Lady ... the ball is moving over, and I think Our Lady is nodding that She wants to come from the ball. Now Our Lady is stepping out ... and She has actual balance, but yet, to us, it would seem that She's suspended in midair. But She has actual balance. And the ball is now passing over on our left side into the trees. And Our Lady now is standing there; She's coming slowly down over Her statue. She's about now, I would say, about ten feet above the statue's crown.

Oh, Our Lady is so beautiful that ... Just the feeling of joy and peace and happiness that She gives to you when She smiles! Our Lady is smiling, but She has a very sad smile. Now She's looking up to Jesus and motioning, and He's coming forward. And He's standing now, He's going over to Our Lady's right side. Now Our Lady is taking up Her crucifix again from the Rosary, and making the sign of the cross: In the name of the Father, and of the Son, and of the Holy Ghost.

Now Jesus is nodding, and Our Lady now is placing Her first finger to Her lips, like this; which means to listen and repeat.

Our Lady - "My child and My children, and especially Veronica, My child, I brought you here this evening because it was urgent that you come from your sickbed and be here this evening. No matter what the struggle, I will sustain you.

"Tell the world, My child, in great haste that the Red Bear is planning to kill Our Holy Father, your Vicar on earth, John Paul II, when he meets with the nations in common prayer. You will not fully understand what I say to you, My child, but I repeat it again: Shout! Shout from the rooftops, until your words, the words from Heaven, reach the Holy Father in Rome. The Red Bear is planning to kill your Vicar, your Holy Father upon earth, John Paul II, when he meets with the nations in common prayer.

"Yes, My child, the evil is accelerating. In fact I understand, from hearing My children in their prayers, that it boggles their minds how the evil continues to accelerate, as we pray and do penance and seek for the repatriation of souls upon earth. We have extended the time far beyond what the Eternal Father wishes, My children. But it is those who are good that must not slacken in their pace to save their brothers and sisters.

"Many of the good have become complacent. They have now brought themselves down from a pinnacle to wallow, we will say, in their self - exaltation of being saved. However, I repeat again to all My children, that to those who have received much, much is expected of them. They cannot sit back and with a smile not consider what goes on beyond their sight. They must work in the world and not retire from it, self - satisfied with their own salvation. They must go out among the nations, because, My children, everyone now cries for peace and security where there is no peace and security. There are more murders: the abortions continue, accelerating at a higher rate.

Terrorism to come to North America

"And your country, My child, the United States, and Canada also, will receive the heavy hand of the Father soon upon them. We can no longer protect them from what is to come about within the next several months. Yes, My child, there will be blood flowing in the streets of the United States. There will be carnage such as has never been seen before in the United States and Canada. Do not take lightly the threats of those murderers in the European states that have felt this carnage. They are now setting up their plans to bring destruction to the heart of the Americas.

"My child and My children, how long can I go about your earth going from place to place, hinder and yon, as your Mother, praying with you, solacing the nations that suffer from their own laxity. We ask for prayer, atonement, and sacrifice. And what do We get? We have theologians who now consider themselves as gods upon earth. They are setting up a new world religion, a one world religion based on humanism and modernism. This will not continue much longer, My children. It has taken many earth - years to develop these theories. And those who have their heads in the clouds (though they wear the purple hats and the red hats), those who have become blinded from the excessive love of luxury and materialism, shall be lost in the chaos.

Annulments without due cause

"Each and every soul shall be held accountable for his soul and the souls of those about him. Families are disintegrating. I must tell you now, My children, the family must be returned to the holy state it was constructed for. We shall never approve nor accept marriage and cohabitation without marriage. We shall not accept the annulments that are being given now to so many without due cause.

"It has become a most distressing situation for the Eternal Father. Many He would remove from the See of Peter, but it seems, My children, that the only way they can be removed is from force; for they do not hearken to the threats, nor even the advice and counsel of the Holy Father in Rome.

Pope well chosen for task

"Your successor to Peter has been chosen well. We sat him upon the Throne of Peter for the principal reason to return My Son's Church to its original state. Understand well, My children, that he is also a human being subject to error. But this does not mean that he is to be subjected to

326

derision and hate, until you build up a fire within the hearts of those who are seeking to destroy him. Better that you pray for the Holy Father than to deride him. Do not question him at this time, because I assure you, My children - as he will tell you in due time - I, too have appeared to the Holy Father.

"Yes, My child, there is much that I have not told you or the world. But there are other seers throughout the world at this time. And I promise you, My child, through all the excessive suffering that you are doing, and as you offer it up to the priesthood, you are gathering some souls for Heaven. Remember, My child, and you will find your suffering much easier to take if you will remember that each pain and each sorrow means that you will offer it up for the priesthood. The prayers that you have conducted for the priesthood on the Sundays of your years upon earth shall be counted at the time when all of you shall go over the veil. Then you will rejoice with all Heaven for the number of priestly souls that you have brought back to the fold.

"We do not want division within the Church. That will solve nothing. You cannot separate yourself from the Holy Father in Rome. And once you are baptized as a Roman Catholic, you must die within the fold; you cannot reject it. There are many false prophets going throughout the world now seeking to take your soul to satan. They come as angels of light.

Jehovah's Witnesses: false prophets

"And now, My child, it has not been My policy to put down in strict perfect order those who are going throughout the world as deceivers, but I warn you now to beware and protect your children from the groups that are forming that are false prophets and will take you from the true religions. One must be named now and it is called the Jehovah Witnesses. My children, they are not a church. They were not founded in the time of My Son's placement upon earth. They were founded approximately fifty - five years ago by a group of so - called learned seminarians, not of the true

327

Christian Faith, but seeking to rewrite the Bible of God to suit their own human frailties and needs. It took a great deal of courage to come away from the true Faith and establish themselves, but this courage will be brought to naught. Except, My children, that there are many now souls that come also from the fold of the Eternal Father, the Roman Catholics, that are being taken in by this group of false prophets.

"I do not wish to seek merriment on this, My child, but We, too, in Heaven must smile as they go about the world saying, that Jesus was not upon earth as a Savior, nor is He the Son of God; no, He is Saint Michael the Archangel! My child, I see this brings a smile to your lips."

Veronica - Oh, yes Blessed Mother, that sounds very funny!

Our Lady - "Yes, My child, to the ordinary human being, or those at least that have a little light of the Holy Spirit with them, they could not actually fall into the web of this organization. So you must do what you can, My child, to enlighten these poor souls. They are gathering the Roman Catholics who have not been attending Mass, or getting the light from Heaven by receiving Holy Communion daily, or at least, My child, on Sunday.

"Now I want you to listen to Me as I repeat for you one of the long discourses you had with Saint Theresa. And I do it for a reason, that it goes to the world because this dear Holy Father is the one in Rome who is suffering now at the hands of his own. His Bishops will fight Bishop against Bishop; there will be Cardinals against Cardinals; and satan has set himself in the midst. But you will all remember the 'Exhortation' and recite it well to those who wish to affront you. Repeat, My child:

Dear Holy Father, worried and wan
Will struggle with Jesus to gather the sheep.
The pastures are rich, but the sheep grow thin;
For the souls have succumbed to the sickness of sin.
You'll need reinforcements from heavenly shores,

328

So deep is the darkness of earth's shallow mores.
All hearts must ascend in true supplication
To avoid the sad fate of divine devastation.
Dear Holy Mother, your Mother of love,
Does beg you to heed these dire words from above:
His heart is torn by careless surrender
Of too many souls who don't try to remember
The Father, the Son, the Spirit of life -
Smite in the heart with the human knife
Of hate, greed, avarice, vanity:
All indications that sin is insanity.
What more must you do but place the full load
Of saving all souls on the few who are bold;
Who'll stand up and fight for all Heaven's glory,
And meet with Pope Paul at the end of life's story.

Our Lady - "My child, you must never forget those words and pray on them daily, for they have true meaning for the world.

"Now, My child, I wish that you will say a full Act of Contrition, for it has been forgotten in many of My Son's churches, His House upon earth.

The Act of Contrition

Veronica -
O my God, I'm heartily sorry for having offended Thee. And I confess to all my sins, because I dread the loss of Heaven and the pains of hell. But, most of all, because I love Thee, my God, who art all good and deserving of all my love. I firmly resolve, with the help of Thy grace, to confess my sins, to do penance, and to amend my life. Amen.

Our Lady - "My child Veronica, it does Our hearts well, and We feel very comforted to know that that has not been lost upon earth. We have watched now the teachings of the children in most of the houses upon earth of My Son, and I must say: I shed tears of pity for the parents, for it is best now if the parents look well into the teaching of their children in the schools, the Catholic schools of the world. Because they will find that the theologians have crept in now with modernism and humanism. And your children must be protected.

Sex Education in schools

"A foul situation has come about in the schools, both public and private. They are now teaching sex education, My children. And this is a debauchery of your young souls. Parents, are you so blind that you do not investigate, or ask your children what has happened in their classes today at school? Show you no interest as you go about the world gathering materialism, and seeking to break your home apart by husband and wife going in both directions; neither do they work together to hold the home together, but they work apart, many leaving the children astray by not having counsel over them.

"My child and My children, I tell you now: All that I have told you in the past will come to pass. There will be great punishments set upon earth. The United States and Canada shall not escape. They have been actually sentenced by the Eternal Father to many calamities that will befall them very shortly. The Father in Heaven feels in this manner shall they bring many back to the fold. It is not an angry God Who speaks to you, My children, but a sorrowful One. All of our hearts in Heaven, and the hearts of the saints, are saddened at what is to come upon mankind.

"Have you forgotten My counsel of all of the years of My appearances upon earth? I have gone to little children and big children, but they are all little children in our eyes. There is no age counted in Heaven. You are all the children of God, and as such, you must be a pride and a joy to Him. And when you hurt Him, He is hurt most deeply. And therefore, He allows satan to go about in his reign. Satan knows that his time is growing short; therefore, he is acting in full fury.

"You will watch as the days go by - I say not years, because this will all happen in days, My child and My children - you will watch as the days go by, the unfolding of the messages, dating from 1970. That is why I have asked you to publish them, My children, again, right from the beginning. In your closet you will find the 1970 messages, the missing ones without the tapes.

"You will see, My child, that all of these messages are renewed. They must be read over because much has been missed and forgotten. But soon, like the steps of a ladder, you will find each prophecy come true. And it will accelerate as we hit the end of time, My children.

"You cannot count your earth - years as being long any longer. If only I could show you, the prideful and boastful United States and Canada - if I could show you what the enemy has in store for you now, you would grovel on your knees to make restitution to the Eternal Father. But now this must be taught to you in a most sorrowful way.

U.S.: another tremendous earthquake

"Your country, My child, the United States, shall know of another tremendous earthquake. I know this grips your heart with fear, My child, but you will see and understand. There will be more floods, more famine, more blood in the streets. The enemy will come from foreign nations now to try to shed this blood. Do not take their words to you lightly. They will enter the United States for one purpose - to destroy the morale.

"Your country and Canada has been surrounded by the Red Bear for many years. They fear the finger upon the first missile, because they know that it will be the end for the human race. But, My children, do not misunderstand, and do not discalculate the power of satan. Because if he is allowed to by the Eternal Father, he will see that someone does put their hand on the wrong button.

"My child and My children, and especially you, My child Veronica, I know you felt that We were asking the impossible of you, to come to the grounds this evening, having spent your life bedridden and in torturous suffering, My child, I cry for you because I experience your pain as your Mother,

331

and I know that the cross one day will be lightened for you. But do this for Us, My children; you will do this for My Son and I, will you not, My child?"

Veronica - Yes, Mother.

Our Lady - "Remember, My child, life is not eternal upon earth. One day you will all have your rest. I know, My child, you do not have much rest, but one day you will come over the veil. It will not be much longer, My child, but We ask you to continue to be a voice - box for My Son and Myself.

"Now My Son has a few words to speak to you, My child."

Veronica - Now Jesus is coming forward. He looks so beautiful! Oh, He has on a burgundy cape, and there is also about a half an inch of gold all about the burgundy cape. Now He has it tied at His neck by a golden belting, sort of. He looks so beautiful. Jesus' hair is blowing a little. And I think it's from the reflection of the light from His robe, but His hair looks like a reddish brown.

Our Lord's Crown of Thorns

And now He's tapping His forehead. Oh, He wants me to tell you, as He told me this afternoon, that I must tell the world that when He was crucified ... they have a false notion about His crown of thorns. The crown of thorns were placed in a basket - weave cap and then placed on His head, and He was pummeled and hammered with sticks and a sledge hammer to get it down on His head; and that drove the terrible spikes of the thorns into His head. It seems that His murderers could not find gloves at the time to handle the thorns. So they thought to take their implements and place these terrible thorn weeds inside of the basket - weave hat. And that is what Jesus wore when He was crucified.

Jesus - "My child, I had you repeat that because you have difficulties in finding the photograph, the picture that I had you draw in 1969. But you will find it if you go out to your garage and in the middle you will find boxes; empty boxes and you will find the photograph.

332

"Now, My child, you will continue with your prayers of atonement. I did not wish to bring you here in your terrible suffering, but I assure you, My child, the rewards that you will know of at the end of time will make full payment upon your suffering, My child. There is only one way that I can explain it. What you suffer on earth is not important. It's how you are laying up your merits to enter into the Kingdom.

"And I repeat again, My child, as I say to you, that it will be easier for a camel to go through a needle's eye than it will be for a rich man to enter Heaven. I say this for a reason, and to those to whom it is directed, they will fully understand. What does it profit a man if he goes about the world gathering all the riches of the world and loses his soul? Think of it well, O men of the Kingdom of God, who have lost their way while they seek the riches. Think of it well for many of you shall be passing over the veil within a few short months.

"Now, My children and My child, I wish that you all continue with the prayers of atonement, that are necessary for the repatriation of the many souls in the world."

Veronica - Now Jesus is moving over to the trees. He's standing above the highest tree on our right side, and He's extending His hands like this, and making the sign of the cross: In the name of the Father, and of the Son, and of the Holy Ghost.

Our Lady has remained above the statue and She's softly smiling; but I notice that She is wiping Her eyes. She's very sad.

Now Jesus is coming across back from the trees. He's coming over to our left side, that would be His right side, and He's almost next to Our Lady. And He's standing out now and placing His hand, like this: In the name of the Father, and of the Son, and of the Holy Ghost.

Now both Our Lady and Jesus are looking over to Their right, our left, and They're moving now. I have to follow Them above the sky there; They are high above the trees. Now Jesus is bending over, like this, and making the sign of

333

the cross: In the name of the Father, and of the Son, and of the Holy Ghost.

Now Our Lady is looking about Her. She had placed Her Rosary beads back in Her belting, but now She's taking it out and She's extending the crucifix, like this, and making the sign of the cross: In the name of the Father, and of the Son, and of the Holy Ghost.

Our Lady - "My child and My children, now continue with your prayers of atonement; We are not leaving. My Son and I will be upon the grounds until the last person leaves. And should anyone come here to pray during the weekdays before the Vigils or the Holy Hours, We will come."

Veronica - Oh!

Our Lady - "Yes, My child, one day these grounds, also will be renown. These grounds shall be a holy place of visitation, as shall also be the Shrine at Bayside.

"Now, My child, you will take three photographs, and these you will not divulge the contents. But take three photographs and read them well, but not a word must be said, My child."

Surrogate motherhood . . .
Manufacturing children as though you were machines

Eve of Pentecost Sunday - June 6, 1987

Veronica - All about the trees now there are cascading
the most beautiful blue lights. They're the call lights of Our
Lady. And directly above the trees, there is a circlet of light
that's opening up. It almost started like a pinpoint... and then
it's opening up until, I would say, it's about the size of a
quarter now. But it's in a great distance away. And while
I'm watching this, I notice that the trees are beginning to,
also, be tinged with pink about them. Oh, that would mean,
that is Jesus' color.

Oh, now I see Our Lady out of the circlet of light, which
has grown very large up above the trees. Our Lady is coming forward. Oh, She's dressed so beautifully this evening.
She has on Her white gown, but it's very iridescent, very
brilliant and difficult to watch; because it seems to set your
eyes in such a way that there are no human words to
describe the way... the colors of Our Lady's gown. There
are two major colors-gold and white.

All about Our Lady's mantle She has this border of gold.
It's about-about a half inch, I would say, wide. And Our
Lady has on this evening Her golden slippers, with the tiny
rosettes right at the toe. Oh, She looks so beautiful and fragile.

Our Lady has Her hands together, like this, with Her
Rosary about Her fingers. And She's coming forward very
slowly. And now She's coming down. And all of a sudden,
there are lights, pink lights, glowing all about Our Lady. It's
not the shimmering type of long vertical lights that I'm so
used to seeing, but these are pink glowing lights, similar to
the blue ones.

And there is Jesus. Oh, He looks so powerful and strong.
The feeling you get is beyond any human intelligence to
understand, unless you experience it yourself. Jesus is wearing His rose - colored gown. And He is placing His hand

out, like this, and rays are coming forward; and as I am looking up, I can feel them. I am beginning to feel something
radiating right through me. And now Jesus has approached
Our Lady, and He is talking to Her very softly. I can't hear.
It's almost like the murmur of the trees. And He is nodding,
"yes " to Our Lady.

Now Our Lady is coming forward, and She is taking Her
crucifix, the golden crucifix, on Her Rosary beads and making the sign of the cross: In the name of the Father, and of
the Son, and of the Holy Ghost.

And now Jesus is looking over. And Our Lady is turning
to Her right, which would be our left side, and She is going
over, closer to the trees on the left. Our Lady now is standing forth with Her Rosary in Her hands, and the golden crucifix in Her right hand. And it seems to have enlarged since
I've been looking at it, the crucifix. It's beautiful, a golden
crucifix. Our Lady is making the sign of the cross: In the
name of the Father, and of the Son, and of the Holy Ghost.

Now Jesus is taking His hand-oh, He is over next to Our
Lady, on Her left side; that would be directly over the large
tree on our left side, by the statue-and Jesus is putting His
hands out, like this, and making the sign of the cross: In the
name of the Father, and of the Son, and of the Holy Ghost.

Now Jesus is murmuring to Our Lady, and They are both
floating over. They don't walk. They're like weightless.
And yet They look so solid-not transparent like some of the
saints that I've seen-but so solid, like you and I, that you feel
that you have something very close in tie to Him and Our
Lady. And They are coming over now, above the statue, and
They are both looking all about. And Jesus is murmuring to
Our Lady. I say murmuring, because I cannot catch His
words. And Our Lady is smiling. Now She is motioning to
me, and putting Her first finger to Her lips; which means to
listen and repeat.

Our Lady - "My child and My children, how happy and
joyful I am this day for the many Rosaries that have ascended to Heaven from among you. I know that all hearts rose,
also, with the prayers. How many shall be used to save

those in purgatory, you will find out in due time.

Abrogate the union of Rome with Russia

"For peace, My child... there is much asked for peace upon earth. I must tell you this: There will be no peace, My children, until what has happened in the past with My visit to Fatima is consummated. Now this has to be done, My children: I repeat this anew-as I have repeated it, as I have gone hinder and yon, across the earth to try to enlighten My children as to the road to true peace-you must now cast aside, abrogate, the union of Rome with Russia. For Russia must be consecrated to My Immaculate Heart for a true peace.

"My child, Veronica, your road has not been easy. You will have much more suffering, My child; but know that your seclusion, and your suffering, has been for a great reason. I asked you in the past, and you said 'yes,' My child; will you continue to do what I have asked of you?"

Veronica - "Yes, dear Mother, I will."

Our Lady - "My child, do you wish to repeat what we had between us of your mission?"

Veronica - "If it will save souls, I will."

Our Lady - "Well then, My child, repeat what I have asked of you."

Veronica - "I must accept my sufferings and offer it for the priesthood. There are not many prayers rising to Heaven for the priesthood, for many believe that the priesthood has a special passport to Heaven."

Our Lady - "My child, I have to tell you in all truth, that there are many priests who have gone to hell because too few prayed for them; and they did not accept the road to penance, dedication and truth.

"I know, My child, this comes as great shock to you, but you must understand that We did caution the world, and the pastors, to mend their ways now; for even many mitres have fallen into hell. Do not be shocked, My child. I know this puts great strain on your weakened heart, but you must make it known to the world that many must offer themselves in

337

compensation, we will say, for those who have not received the grace to enter even into purgatory. Perhaps, at the end of time, My children, when the world meets with the great Chastisement-and the gates of hell then are opened for all to see, and the gates of purgatory opened for all to come out-then you will understand what has happened in the past, and what is coming in the future, as you ponder My words tonight.

"My child, I want you now, for it is greatly urgent for your country, that you take three photographs; but they must remain a great secret, that will be given to the Pope in due times. Not one word must be uttered when these pictures are given, My child; for they will give you the road of mankind."

(Veronica then sees vision of the destruction that is to come upon us. She coughs deeply from the inhalation of the smoke from the fires.)

Veronica - Oh, Mother, I see the fires. I see the fires. I'm choked by the smoke! It's terrible! Save us! Don't have this come upon us, dear Mother, please!
Veronica sighs) It's terrible. (Veronica sighs heavily.)

Greater loss of life in Persian Gulf

Our Lady - "My child, the road to peace has been given to the world. You must write and implore your Holy Father in Rome to make known the full message of Fatima. There is no time to be wasted! Your country, My child, is in great distress, though your medias have camouflaged this from you. Your country will meet with a greater distress and loss of life in the Gulf, the Persian Gulf. No, My child, you cannot accept as full knowledge all that the media impart to you; for they, too, are under control.

"Now, My child, take those three photographs, and you must be silent."

[Pause]

Veronica - Jesus and Our Lady are still standing, about, I would say, about twelve feet above the statue. They've been there the whole time. Jesus directed His pink lights on to me, for I would surely have perished from the sight of seeing the great destruction that is ahead for mankind. It would have taken my very heart from out of my chest. The fright was so bad.

Now Jesus is standing there. It's quite windy, because His cape is blowing back and forth, very slowly though. It's a mild wind. And the cape that Jesus wears is beautiful. It's a burgundy color. And it has a gold tie at the neck, where He has it tied in loop-like shape. And Jesus has nothing on His feet this evening. Nothing. He's barefooted. I can see beyond His gown. Now, His gown is a linen-like quality. It's made like very coarse weave. And it's quite full, and belted by a piece of-it looks like brownish hide, of some animal. Ivory belted about His waist.

Now Jesus is touching His lips with His finger, like this. I feel, as I place my finger out, that Jesus has come down now, and with some way, I felt a kiss upon my finger. It's so difficult to explain. I feel that He's kissed this finger that has often pointed to Our Lady. I feel much stronger now. Now Jesus has touched His lips for the second time, and nodded His head downward.

Jesus - "Veronica, My child, and all the children of the world, I do not this evening intend to go through a long discourse on all of the sins that are rising to Heaven, with the saints crying out for retribution because of them. They cry out, 'When, O when, dear Lord, shall You give fair retribution to mankind upon earth, who put the saints to death?

"My child, you do not understand the full meaning of that message, but in due time I will make it known to you.

No relief for those with AIDS

"I want you, My child, to tell the world, that, as your God, there shall be great suffering placed upon mankind in the near future; more so than the plague that was allowed to be sent down upon you-AIDS. We warned you over and over again, through years of visitations upon earth-My Mother going to and fro to warn you, that those who have given themselves over to debasement, by the practice of homosex-

339

uality, birth control, abortion and all other aberrations that bring sorrow to My Mother's heart-this must be stopped now. There shall be no excuse accepted in Heaven by the saints, nor by My Mother and I, or the Eternal Father and the Holy Ghost, for what you are doing upon earth now.

"AIDS was a plague, and is a plague, and shall continue to be a plague, as long as you will not change your course of destruction. What else must We allow to come upon you? No, My children, there will be no relief for those suffering from AIDS; for it is a penance from a just God. For their punishment will be greater, the suffering that they incur will save many from hell, and give them the chance to enter upon a penance in purgatory.

No sex education in schools

"My child, I know much of this discourse distresses your heart, but you can imagine well-and I know you do, My child Veronica-the sorrow My Mother feels now that sex education has entered upon the school system. We say unto you, and I say to you, as your God, My children: Mothers and fathers of the world, you will not give over your children to be taught by demons! Satan has many loosed upon earth now. They enter into the bodies of any man, woman or child who has fallen out of grace; and they enter into the bodies of those who teach your children error.

"It is the place and the will of the Eternal Father that the home shall be the safeguard for the children's souls-the mother, the father. But what can We expect, My children, when even the state of marriage, the sacrament of Marriage, is being destroyed slowly? We know all that is going on upon earth-living together without unions under God. No, My children, that shall also be destroyed in time; if not by sickness and death of the body, it will also be by sickness and death of the soul.

"My children, it was never deemed by Heaven, nor the Eternal Father-as written in the good Book of life and love, your Bible, that man shall not cohort with man; man shall not cohabit with man; and man shall not seek diversion from his home by setting out to seduce another.

"My child, and My children, are there many strong homes left in the United States, Canada, and many homes of the world? No, My children, the standards have been lowered. And when the standards are lowered, satan takes over.

Far worse plague to come

"You have your chance now, as My Mother pleads for your cause, to stop what you are doing now, that displeases the Eternal Father; or you shall be sent, within the next year, a far worse plague upon mankind, if the great Chastisement hasn't already overcome you.

"Yes, My child, as I told you before you left for the grounds, this would not be a message of great solace but of truth. We expect you, My child, to get this message, also, to the Holy Father, Pope John Paul II in Rome, that he must put aside the Treaty he has accepted from others, to keep from giving My Mother the necessary ammunition, We will say, My child-I will use your term as used upon earth-to fight satan. You must consecrate Russia to the Immaculate Heart of My Mother, or there will be no peace, if but for a time.

"My child, and My children, look all about you. Do not become blinded by the things of your world. They are only material, and all that is material shall pass. All is passing, My children. Look back and count: how many do you know that are still upon earth who have passed over the veil? One day, you too, will be heading down that road-and We don't want to say down, We want to say up, My children!

"Yes, My child, We do have humor in Heaven, but so little in these dire times.

"I want you now to take three more pictures. The other three must be retained for your examination; but three more you are free to give to those about you.

Besiege Pope with letters

"Remember, My child, the Pope, John Paul II in Rome,

he must be besieged by letters to stop now the carnage going throughout the world; or Russia shall enter upon your nation and Canada.

"You are surrounded, My children, as My Mother has told you for years, with submarines. They come closer to your shores by countries, one after another-boots stomping forward, killing, death, licentiousness; father against son, mother against daughter, cousin against cousin; nothing but murders and abominations. Is this what you want within your country, My children?

"You must now, not later-but now before it is too late-you must gather the armor about you that Heaven has given you. Make it known to the world, that they must all, every single individual on earth, must at this time, wear a sacramental: the St. Benedict medal, the brown Scapular; a crucifix, blessed by a holy priest. And I say, holy, my children, for I'm certain I do not have to go into further detail on the other kind. By their fruits will you know them.

"My child, do not be despaired. One day all the world will be restored anew, but there will be few left upon earth to start this. That is why you must all desire in your hearts, and put to work the knowledge given to you by Heaven, to save your soul, and the souls of those all about you. Time is growing short.

Your sons to die on foreign shores?

"Remember, My child, I have already told you, as My Mother did sometime ago, that the enemy is closing in fast upon you. You are being tempted now to bring your sons to the foreign shores of foreign nations to fight and lose their lives. Is this what you want? How many hearts of parents will be torn by the carnage of receiving greetings from the United States or Canada, from the Army, the Navy, the Marines, saying: 'Your son is dead or missing in action.'

"Is this what you want? Cannot you do a slight penance for your God, for your neighbors? Love your neighbors, even if they malign you, even if they make fun of you. Remember, you hold the truth in your hearts and in your hands; for you carry the Rosary, you carry your Scapular about your necks, and you also wear the St. Benedict medal. Satan must run at the sight of the St. Benedict medal, as well as he will when you cast the waters of truth upon him-your holy waters, gathered from the many holy churches left upon earth. Use them all, My children. All! Your armor cannot be strong enough; that is how strong the enemy has become in your country and many nations of the world.

"Now, My child, you will - I hear these anxious voices saying, when are we going to get the three photographs? Now, My child, you will take the time to read the three photographs when you take them. We're not leaving, We have something else to tell you, My child; but bear with Us while you take the photographs."

Veronica - There are pink lights all about the green trees. That means that Jesus is stepping forward. Oh, He was over Our Lady's statue, directly over...but now He stepped down, and He is down almost on the tip of the tree, the pine tree. I guess it's a pine tree. I don't know my trees too well, but it looks like a pine tree; and Jesus is just above it, about a foot. Now Our Lady has remained over by, directly over the statue, high in the sky. But Jesus came down while I was talking to you. And now He must have, because He got there awfully fast, down to the tree on the right side there. And now He is-oh, He is going to give us a blessing first: In the name of the Father, and of the Son, and of the Holy Ghost. Amen. Now Jesus is touching His finger to His lips:

Surrogate motherhood not to be tolerated

"My child, there is also one thing I wish to discuss with you for the world, for all of the world's children to know, how Heaven feels about their diabolical search for life in a test tube. Yes, My child, I know this shocks you, but you are fully aware of what is going on. Your news medias seem to enjoy putting these evils before your eyes and your ears and your readings. Yes, We frown upon surrogate mothers. We shall not tolerate the making of children from one to the other.

343

"The sacrament of Marriage was given for the union of man and woman in love and godliness. There is nothing godly about a man who sets himself up to play God and starts revolving innocent - I prefer to call My children innocent, because in that way I do not refuse them even penance for their sins-but they must know that you cannot bring life in a test tube. This will not be accepted by Heaven.

"These children are not conceived by the Holy Ghost, the spirit within them at the moment of conception, because their conception is from a test tube, and an instrument of a so-called doctor upon earth. He is a doctor, not of divinity but of sin.

"Doctors now are profaning their profession; those who have given themselves over to destroying human life in abortions. Doctors also pretend, or hope to seek far above the Eternal Father. Just as the angels did many years ago. They sought to outshine the Eternal Father, and they were cast forever out of Heaven. But they took many with them.

Test tube babies born without soul

"Therefore, My children, I must tell you this, there will be a major war between the right and the wrong side, the left and the right, over this issue. We will not have test tube babies, for they are not born with a soul. They can only, then, be called a 'thing,' a 'creature' unknown. Is this what you want, My children? Is this what you want of these children you bear for another? To give them as though you were machines, manufacturing them for another?

"My children, you grieve all Heaven, because your sin is becoming more perverse upon earth, crying out to Heaven for retribution. If it were not for My Mother, you would have received the Ball of Redemption last year, My children. That is the knowledge that you have kept, My child, within your heart all this time, but the reprieve was given because of those who offered themselves up in sacrifice for their errant brothers and sisters.

"Now, My children, you will all continue with your prayers of atonement. They are sorely needed. We find great happiness in the millions, the thousands, the hundreds-any number of prayers that was said today by all of those throughout the world. Link to link the Rosary went, which makes Our hearts light. However, shall this be a permanent thing, or shall it pass, as all things of Heaven have, into a darkness?

"My child, and My children, remember now, I have asked you to contact Pope John Paul II, and tell him he must rescind the Treaty, the Pact made with Russia; for only in that way shall you have a true peace.

"Now, My child, I called you quickly. You have not had the opportunity to read the three photographs taken for the fellows who are in the center. I call them fellows, though you may call that a common term; but they are in a fellowship with God, and they will also know that their time upon earth has been used in the best cause of all: to save souls and to bring God to mankind.

"I bless you all, My children, those within the circle, and those without; for you have come here this evening at a time when Our hearts have been lifted for a short period of time, and We wish to spread among you graces, graces by the thousands. All of this will be known to you in time, My children. All will come through the mailing system. You will know the results of these prayers today, and the prayers that continue in the hearts and upon the fingers of the Rosary chains going throughout the world. In the name of the Father, and of the Son, and of the Holy Ghost.

"Now continue, My child, with the photographs. We are not leaving; We do not leave until the last person has left the area.

"Remember always, My child, that these are sacred grounds, and in no way must anyone profane them by coming here with ulterior purposes.

"I must tell you this, My child, too, I do not want you to, in any way, or any manner or measure, to be together with one who has come from Australia; for you shall not unite with him. There is good reason for this. We sit not in judgment of him at this time; however, time will bear witness to what he has been up to, My children.

"Now, My child, you will read the photographs."

Through Mexico to U. S. with missiles
Red invasion from Nicaragua

17th Anniversary of Our Lady's Apparitions at Bayside
- June 18, 1987

Veronica - Now just about the trees there are the most beautiful blue lights. I thought before, when I saw them in the past, that they were beautiful, but tonight they're sparkling and radiant. And now the lights, which were circular in form, are starting to shrink and they're becoming beams of light going high up into the sky, over above the statue. I couldn't even judge the number of feet over the statue.

But there is Our Lady. Oh, I'm sure that the people must see Her. She is so beautiful, and so lifelike-like...whereas other times when I saw the people from Heaven, like St. Theresa, she was quite transparent, and so was Padre Pio. But Our Lady is as solid as you and I, yet She is so beautiful. She's coming down slowly. And now there is a cloud-like formation up there in front of Her so that She's covered, I think, temporarily, because I see something coming out where Her feet should be.

Oh, Our Lady now...the cloud-like formation is turning into rainbow colors. It's so beautiful. And they're separating like wings on both sides of Our Lady. And She's coming down slowly. Oh, the reason She looks so high into the clouds is because She is riding on a ball, a round ball, like I saw Her many years ago. And Our Lady now is descending very slowly, but She is quite near now to the top of Her statue, just above the trees. Now the ball has stopped, and I can see Our Lady very clearly this evening, just as in 1970. It's so clear.

Oh, I'm so happy to see You! Oh! Oh, She is so beautiful. Our Lady has on a sparkling white gown. Oh, it's even more sparkling than Her past gowns. It's as though it was very festive. And She has a border of-about, I would say about, three quarters of an inch of gold around Her gown, even at the border near Her feet; and also the mantle. The mantle still covers Our Lady's hair. I cannot see Her hair, but Her mantle is down on Her forehead. And Our Lady is looking about Her now. And She has on the golden slippers. They're like sandals, with the little golden rosettes on them. Oh, She is so beautiful. Now Our Lady-Her face is very radiant, so radiant that I can actually see Her eyes this evening. They are a blue, a very deep blue. And now Our Lady is taking from about Her belting, Her Rosary, the beautiful Rosary with the large crucifix, made, I know, of solid gold; and also the golden Our Fathers and the translucent white Hail Marys that, as Our Lady is turning, they sparkle and become all the colors of the rainbow.

Now Our Lady is stepping down from the ball. This time I saw Her foot go out, which surprised me because I never saw Her move Her feet, really, up or down, in any direction in the past several years. But She stepped down, actually, from the ball, and the ball is floating away now and going behind a cloud that is just at our right side, over the top of the first tall tree. Now Our Lady is floating; She's not walking. She is carried by the wind, it seems. It's so beautiful to watch. She seems absolutely weightless. Now Our Lady is floating over to Her right side, which is our left side, and She is making the sign of the cross, like this, with Her crucifix: In the name of the Father, and of the Son, and of the Holy Ghost.

Now Our Lady is smiling...so wonderfully warm and heart-rending. I can't explain it to you. You have to see it with your own eyes. There is nothing so beautiful! Not even the rose, the flower, as Our Lady when She smiles.

Our Lady now is turning over towards Her left side, that's our right side, and She is going back, floating very, very easily, over the statue. Now Our Lady is standing, only about, maybe, four feet over Her statue, and She is making the sign of the cross with Her crucifix: In the name of the Father, and of the Son, and of the Holy Ghost.

Now Our Lady is looking over towards Her left side, our right side, and She is floating over now between the trees,

348

and She is making the sign of the cross to the people down below: In the name of the Father, and of the Son, and of the Holy Ghost.

Now Our Lady wants to get closer-I can see Her motioning; She is making a sign to me-closer to the trees over there. There must be many people over on the right side of the grounds. And Our Lady is now extending quite a bit over, almost bent over in two, to go past the trees and make the sign of the cross: In the name of the Father, and of the Son, and of the Holy Ghost.

Now Our Lady is motioning that She's returning-I know She means She's going to return now to the statue's area, because Our Lady is saying very quietly:

Our Lady - "There is a most urgent message for this evening, My child."

Veronica - Now Our Lady is floating back, and She is looking all about Her. She has, both a smile now-it's cheerful, but there's sadness behind Her face now, too. It must have something to do with the message, because She looks awfully sad now.

Our Lady is going over and She is standing now just about six feet above the statue. Now Our Lady is putting Her Rosary into Her left hand, like this, and motioning to Her lips. That means that I am to listen very carefully and repeat:

Our Lady - "My child and My children, how wonderful it is to see you all here this evening. It lightens My heavy heart. I cannot say this evening that My tears fall on you as I did in 1970, because with your persistence in coming this evening-and I know that many of My children had to sacrifice to come here this evening-with your persistence you have lightened Our hearts; and with your prayers and acts of atonement, you have, also, lightened the hearts of those in purgatory. For I promise on My next visit to purgatory, I will be taking out one thousand five hundred souls, whom you have saved, My children. Just the people I am looking at now, all throughout the grounds- your prayers have saved that many souls this evening.

"My child, there is a message I have for you of great urgency. You understand that I have gone throughout the world with the same message-the one about the Treaty of Russia and the Vatican. I have asked that this be put aside by Pope John Paul II.

Write to Cardinal Casaroli

"And now, My child, I must ask that you write, that you all write, to Cardinal Casaroli, who is influencing the Holy Father to not listen to this message. His influence shall bring great penance to his soul if he does not come from his course of appeasement, which shall lead to enslavement for many.

"My child and My children, I do not have to go into a long discourse to tell you of the evils of Communism. The world, and its condition, speaks for itself.

Invasion from Nicaragua through Mexico

"My child, let the world know that Nicaragua is a center point for the capitulation of the United States of America and Canada. Already there are plans afoot, and in the making, with missiles and all dire instruments of destruction. These plans are being formulated from Nicaragua, to go into Mexico, and thereupon into the United States.

"You see, My child and My children, I am sure that with My attempts to approach your President of the United States.... Yes, My child, though he is not of the Faith, I have approached him. He heard My voice. He heard My voice but cannot speak of it. He does not understand the fully supernatural.

Supplies not to be cut off in Persian Gulf

"I asked him to be sure that he does not let the evil go from the shores of Nicaragua, and also cut off all the supplies in the Persian Gulf.

"You understand, My children, that what you read in your newspapers are not fully the truth. They are, also, guarded well by a group named the illuminati. They are active, My children, in the United States, and all the nations of the world, especially in France.

Children brutalized by satanic cults

"Now, My child, I have one more thing to tell you. There has been much publicity afoot in your country and the world about the existence of satanic cults. I must tell you they do exist. They worship satan, and they are the opposite of all Christianity. They will do the opposite of what is asked in the Bible. Therefore, they kill with no remorse. They steal your children and brutalize them.

"How can they do this, My child, you ask Me? How can they be so hard, so cruel, so merciless? Well, My child, the enemies of your country and the world have done their work good. They are using an infiltration with drugs. Your children are being educated for the use of these drugs.

"My dear parents-please!-listen to your Mother. Listen to what I have to say to you, for I tell you the truth. The Eternal Father sees all, and makes us knowledgeable as to what is happening upon earth that will bring its eventual destruction. Your children are being educated in the schools, to take all Christianity from their lives, and believe not in the supernatural things of God, but the diabolical processes of satan, in cults.

Nine thousand satanic cults

"My child and My children, at this time in the United States of America and Canada, there can be counted, at least, nine thousand satanic cults.

"My children, I see you are shivering. You are frightened. Yes, you have reason to be, My child. But do not be affrighted, My child; they will not harm you. They will not harm you, My child; remember that. You must remain calm in the face of adversity.

"I ask you to be retired from the world, for they will come as angels of light and try to approach you, also. Bar

351

your doors to all but your immediate family and your closest Shrine workers. That you will do. The one whom you have met now, My child, will be sufficient. She will help you where there is need.

Write to Pope: Stop policy of appeasement

"Now, My child, I ask for the good of all humanity, that they approach Pope Paul by letter, by ear, by mail-anyway possible, by human means and supernatural means of prayer, to turn back from the present course of appeasement with Russia. For Russia has one thing in mind; that is, to take over the United States, Canada, and all nations of the world.

"My child, you can well understand that they have been doing well lately. That is because, though We cry for prayers, atonement and sacrifice, and the First Saturdays-which I've asked of you since Fatima-they have not been acceded to.

"O My child, how heavy is My heart! See the heart that is pierced by daggers of hate and remorse. And then I must tell you, My child, I can weep now."

Veronica - Our Lady is crying. Our Lady is crying. And the tears are coming down Her face. And I feel that they are so large, and with so much power-supernatural power-that these are falling upon us now. I can feel them...

Our Lady - "I cry, My child, because upon earth, your people-and all the peoples of the world-in their various languages, they cannot talk without abusing My Son's name. They must curse and rebel against My Son. Why must this be so, My child? My Son is all goodness and purity. Why must His name be defiled, just as it is being defiled-His Body-in the Tabernacles throughout the world.

"I do not, at this time, intend to point out any individual, but My voice goes out to you, as My Mother; you know if you are guilty of any sins against the Sacraments.

"There are seven Sacraments commanded of you by Heaven, My children, and you will keep them. You shall not take them apart by using rationality, and modernism, and humanism. This cannot be.

"My children, I do not come this evening to be a bearer of ill tidings, but I must caution you because each day the carnage grows worse. If it continues, My children, you will see your children disappearing from the streets again.

"There is now a plan in the national and international seat of satan...It is a group, My child, that is united with other groups throughout the world: They have one plan in mind-to bring about the fall of all nations and the introduction of Communism to all nations, by destroying the young with drugs and all manners of debasity.

"All the holiness of Marriage has been cast aside. We see now children growing up into sin, as they go forth into life unprepared by their parents.

"O My children, how many parents shall be held accountable for the fall of their children's souls!"

Veronica - Our Lady now is wiping the tears from Her eyes. It is so sad, that I cannot help but cry for Her.

Our Lady - "My child, I wish as penance for the world now, that you ask them to daily repeat the Acts of Faith, Hope and Charity. I ask that all pray with you at this time the Acts of Faith, Hope and Charity.

Veronica - O my God, I firmly believe that Thou are one God in three Divine Persons: the Father, the Son, and the Holy Ghost. I believe that Thy Divine Son became man and died for our sins, and that He shall come to judge the living and the dead. I believe in the Holy Ghost, the Holy Catholic Church, the Communion of Saints, the forgiveness of sins, the resurrection of the life, and-the resurrection of the body, and life everlasting. Amen.

Thank you, Blessed Mother! (Veronica gratefully acknowledges Our Lady's correcting her in the ending of this prayer.)

The Act of Hope: O My God, relying on Thy infinite goodness and promises, I hope to obtain pardon of my sins, with the help of Thy grace, and life everlasting, through the merits of Jesus Christ, Our Lord and Our Redeemer.

Charity: O My God, I love Thee above all, with my whole heart and soul, because Thou art all-good and deserving of all my love. I love my neighbor as myself for the love of Thee. I forgive all who have injured me, and ask pardon of all whom I have injured.

Our Lady - "My child now, you will proceed to take three photographs. You will find that two of them are most frightening. And should you choose to make them known, I give you My permission, My child. I realize the ones at your last visit with Me, I gave you, made terror strike your heart. But these you must have, My children. But remember: I do not wish that you get embroiled in any satanic case that comes along, even if they contact you by telephone.

"I want you, My child, to read them now very carefully, and I will be speaking with you again. I am not leaving. I shall remain right here; in fact, My child, I shall move over to My right side for the present, for My Son shall be coming very shortly."

Veronica - Now about the trees there is a beautiful pink glow. I'm sure if all of you will look at it carefully, you just cannot miss this. It is such a beautiful shade of pink, that I don't believe it has ever been matched on any type of pastel color that we have in our world today. It is just created from Heaven for Jesus, I know, because it is beautiful.

Now the lights, the pink lights, are beginning to go upwards into the sky, high up over Our Lady's statue. And now the sky...there is a circle of light, a pinpoint of light that's growing larger and larger. Now it's about the size of a dime. And it's-oh, I can see now, there is a figure in the light. Oh, now I recognize it...It's Jesus. He's coming forward, and the light is now opening very fast. It looks like a circle now, all around us. Now it's opening so fast, the light, that it's going even behind us with its volume. It is beautiful! It's a clear white, translucent light, like-not looking through a painted glass...There is no way to explain it, not even a magnifying glass. There's an illusion about it, there is no way to explain in human language. You would have to see this for yourself.

Now Jesus is coming forward slowly. He is now looking over to Our Lady and nodding, and Our Lady nodded back.

And Our Lady is coming closer to the-our left side of the
statue; that would be our left side, and Her right side. Now
Our Lady is going to stand with Her-She's standing now
with Her left side to the statue, and Jesus is coming over
now. And He's taking His place right at the other side of the
statue.

Now He's standing about-Our Lady is rising a little high-
er-He's standing, I would say, about six and a half to seven
feet over the statue. And now Jesus is looking about, and
He's whispering something to Our Lady. I don't believe I'm
supposed to hear it, because it's like the rustling of the leaves
in the trees. I can't understand what He's saying. But Our
Lady is nodding, and They're both turning now to Their
right, our left side. And now They're going over to the center, between the statue and the trees.

Now Jesus is extending His hand out, like this, with three
fingers, like this- I'm trying to do it exactly as He has it,
because it's something I've never saw, so beautifully done-
Jesus goes like this: In the name of the Father, and of the
Son, and of the Holy Ghost.

Now Our Lady and Jesus are turning toward Their left
side, our right side, and They're floating now. Our Lady has
to go behind the statue to come up to Jesus, and They're
both floating over, very slowly, to our right side. Now
They're stopping now, and looking about Them. They're
between the statue and the first long leaf from the tree. And
Jesus now is extending His hand out, again, and making the
sign of the cross: In the name of the Father, and of the Son,
and of the Holy Ghost.

Now They're both turning to the right, and They're moving slowly over towards the statue. Now Our Lady is moving faster. They float-They just don't walk. It's really something so fantastic, to see the way They move about there, as
though They are weightless. Yet They look as solid as you
and I.

So They're going across now...and Jesus is now standing
alone, by Himself. Our Lady has gone between the statue
and the trees over there, on the left side. And She is just-

now She has turned to Her left side so She can watch Jesus. Now He's looking about Him. And it's a little windy up there this evening, because I can see Jesus's feet now. He does have on sandals. They're made of a brown leather-like quality. I can't explain it. It looks almost like a thong, just one piece of strapping down through His toes, and one across His instep. And His feet are bare. He has no socks on, or anything; His feet are really bare. But...He is smiling. He thinks this is funny.

But Jesus is smiling now, and He's getting my attention, because He is putting His first finger to His lips. That means to listen and repeat:

Jesus - "My child and My children, I greet you all tonight in the name of My Mother, and the Eternal Father, and the Holy Ghost.

"I ask all to listen to My Mother. She has gone throughout the world through countless earthly-countless years of earth suffering. Why? Because of Her children who do not listen to Her counsel.

False seers confusing the devout

"There are a few seers upon earth, My child and My children. I am saying this, at this time, because We are much disturbed at what is taking place. There is confusion among the realms of the devout, because there are false seers among you. I shall not go into detail at this time, because by their fruits will they be known.

"You understand, My child, that in countless earth-years, My Mother has wandered, and never has She come upon the evil that is taking place now throughout the world. It has accelerated since She first came to you, My child, in 1970. That is why it was most urgent that you be here this evening, even with your illness.

"Now, My children, My Mother has given you the way to peace. It is a way of prayer, atonement and sacrifice. You must love your brothers. It is a faction to say that you must hate the sin, but love the sinner. I have heard that, My children, from many lips upon earth, but they really don't understand the meaning of love. We hear the word 'love', 'love' being expounded throughout the world, and as they cry for love and peace and happiness, it evades them. And why? Because they have taken a wide road, and made it wider, as they ran from the truth, as expressed by My Mother to them.

"It is not only here in New York, My child, that My Mother has appeared. She has tried to make Her presence known in other places, but has been rejected. I cannot say how this hurts My heart; for I love My Mother as the Queen of Heaven-that She is, and also the Queen of all hearts. And most of all, She wishes to have the hearts of Her children upon earth, each and every one of them. For all that is lost, She cries constantly. Were it not for My Mother, and your Mother, you would have received the Ball of Redemption much sooner than you expected. But My Mother held My heavy hand back, as the Eternal Father listened to the saints crying out from Heaven. 'When, O when, My Lord, shall a just punishment come upon the evil ones upon earth, who are sacrificing the saints?'

"My children, this may be a riddle to you, but I warn you all: I have asked you all to retire from a world that has been given over to satan for a short time. You must bar your doors to all but your immediate family and closest associates, for the souls of whom come to knock upon your doors are most likely evil. And you cannot say, in pride, that you have the grace to immediately convert them. Many times, My child and My children, we have seen others who only had a weak grace to sustain them, fall into the clutches of the unknown monster, roaming about the earth, taking away My Catholic children.

The evil sect of Jehovah's Witnesses

"I say the true Church upon earth -My Church, My children-which has been defamed, even by some of My clergy. They have been taken away by crude-and zealots-people who go about posing as witnesses to God. You understand, My children; I am talking to you now about the Jehovah

Witnesses. They must be cast aside, for they are false prophets in these end days. But many-how many tears My Mother has shed upon the earth, as She sees how many have been... capitulated to this evil sect.

"My child and My children, My Mother many years ago came to Fatima. Her story has not changed much through the years. She repeats the same message to all, for it has not been fulfilled.

"I will repeat again for My Mother, that We wish that you all write to Cardinal Casaroli in Rome and beg him, if necessary, to put aside his false pride, and not mislead Pope John Paul II any longer. If necessary, if he does not listen to this counsel ,We will be forced to remove him.

"My child and My children, We ask of all of you, prayer, atonement and sacrifice. Is this too much to ask for the salvation of your soul, and of all the souls in your family?

"I say families must be strong in this age of sorrow, this age of darkness. It is the family, within the family, that the children must be taught. Do not depend upon your schools, for they have been infiltrated with evil. Do not depend upon your neighbors, for they are often caught up in the world of satan.

"You will all keep a constant vigilance of prayer going throughout your nation and the world. Pray that the world does not descend upon you in the form of the Bear. For he is roaming throughout the world, and gradually the nations are falling. He has a plan for the capitulation of the United States and Canada A bit of this, My child and My children, was given to you by My Mother. The rest shall be told to you in due time.

Illuminati control much of media

"I ask that you keep abreast of your times by your radios, and also your newspapers. But remember, My children: keep abreast of your times with an open heart, and eyes, because much is kept from you. It is the way of the medias today. They are controlled, My children. Yes, they are. There is in your country an institution rising, called the

Illuminati. They will control much of the media. So, My children, you will have to depend on the graces received from Heaven.

"I ask that you all read, and re-read the messages given from Heaven from 1970 up. It is important, My children, because I do not wish to put stress on My Mother to constantly repeat to you the same message over and over, while you like indulgent children, go about with your own cares and life upon earth, neither caring nor wishing to hear the Message from Heaven.

"Many of you will wait until it is too late, and then what will you say, as in Noe's time, the Ark was closed and the waters descended upon the earth? So it will be in the end days, My children: the Ark of graces, the Ark of knowledge, the Ark of your God, will close upon those who will be saved, but others will be destroyed by the Ball of Redemption.

Wear your sacramentals

"Keep a constant vigilance of prayer, I beg of you, My children; for you have now an escalating evil upon earth, and without it, without the grace that My Mother gives to you, through Her Appearances here upon your earth, you will not be able to keep from the clutches of satan, I assure you. Wear your sacramentals. Do not go out without them, or you will fall.

"I know, My child, this disturbs you greatly, because you have only so many sacramentals to give to the multitudes. But the words must be heard throughout the world. And the other people, My children and My child, must make haste to obtain their sacramentals. They will find them. There is enough upon earth for all who want them, My children.

"Remember, keep your sacramentals constantly upon you: your brown Scapular, your Saint Benedict medal, the Miraculous Medal, and also the medal of Our Lady of the Roses. You must keep them upon you, with a crucifix. We demand a crucifix, because demons-many of the highest ones in the realms of hell cannot stand the sight of a crucifix.

They will not approach your door. I give you this knowledge, My children, though it is not common knowledge, upon earth, that the crucifix has great power against satan. .

"Now, My children, I want you all to make a firm Act of Contrition, for those who die now in the outer world about you. An Act of Contrition for all those who are unable to say it, for themselves:

Veronica -

O My God, I am heartily sorry for having offended Thee, and I confess to all my sins, because I dread the loss of Heaven and the pains of hell; but most of all because I love Thee, my God, who art all good and deserving of all my love. I firmly resolve, with the help of Thy grace, to confess my sins, to do penance and to amend my life. Amen.

Jesus - "Now, My child, you will take more photographs. These I would be most careful about deciphering to others. I leave that at your discretion when you view them. You will sit back now, My child.

"And I caution you again: Do not be affrighted by what My Mother told you this evening, about the Illuminati and its rise of satanism. You will not be accosted by the ungraced again, My child, to go through what you did several years ago.

"Now you will sit back, My children, and you will take the time to read very carefully, the photographs.

**Pope and bishops all together one day this year
Consecrate Russia, or else . . .**

Vigil of St. Theresa & Feast of the Guardian Angels
- October 2, 1987

Veronica - There are blue lights cascading from the trees,
all about the trees, high up into the sky until they become
like slivers of light. There is no human way I can express
the way these lights are cascading through the trees and up
into the sky, high - high up into the sky. Now over the first
tree that's behind Our Lady's statue, if you'll look closely,
it's so brilliant you can see the blue light that is shining up to
the center of the sky directly over Our Lady's statue.

Now the sky is becoming a very pale blue. The night
was dark; but yet the sky is a beautiful pale blue, and it's
opening up in a circular motion. And now in the center of
the blue sky, the beautiful pale blue sky. I see a pinpoint of
light. It's circling and it's even twirling now. I can't understand why the light is twirling. But now it's stopped the
turning, and it's getting larger as it comes towards us. And
oh! I see now coming out of the sky, Our Lady is directly
descending on top of what appears to be a very large white
ball. Now Our Lady is standing on the ball, and it's coming
down very slowly over Her statue. The ball is very large. I
know it stands for the outline of the world, because I have
seen that ball before with Our Lady standing on it, back in
1970.

Now Our Lady is dressed all in white. She looks so
beautiful. And all about Her cape is the most beautiful gold-
en type of lace work. Our Lady has no- nothing on Her feet
tonight as She's standing on the ball; but then again, though I
can't see sandals and Her gown is quite long, I can see
between Her two toes, on both feet, little rosettes, golden
rosettes. Our Lady has on Her white cape, the one She usually does appear in here; however, at this time Our Lady has
on that beautiful crown that I've always known to be the
Fatima crown. Our Lady is smiling now. She has been com-

ing down with hands drawn together, like this in prayer, with Her beads folded over Her fingers.

And now Our Lady is standing...The ball has stopped turning now. It was turning slightly from the right to the left on Her feet, and I was so afraid perhaps Our Lady would fall off the ball; however She's suspended there now. The ball is being-wafted is the only way I can explain it to you, turned over towards the left and it's going beyond the trees. It looks like the type of globe we would find in the homes where they have the countries on-a globe, like of the world. Now Our Lady is coming down closer to Her statue, and She's just about, I would say, about sixteen feet above Her statue. Our Lady has on the Fatima crown. And She looks very upset about something this evening. That is why I was brought here, I know; because at home Our Lady did say that I must appear because it is very urgent, that I will be taken care of, with the inflammation in my chest.

Now Our Lady is taking out Her Rosary, Her beautiful Rosary with the golden Our Fathers and the white Hail Marys, and She's making the sign of the cross blessing everyone: In the name of the Father, and of the Son, and of the Holy Ghost. Now Our Lady is turning towards Her right and making the blessing to the people: In the name of the Father, and of the Son, and of the Holy Ghost. Now Our Lady is looking over to Her left, that would be our right, and She's extending Her crucifix again: In the name of the Father, and of the Son, and of the Holy Ghost. Now Our Lady is placing Her hands together, but She's doing pitifully like this, as though She has a grave concern over something: She's holding her hands like this, with the Rosary enclosed in them. Now Our Lady has taken the time to place Her finger over Her lips, which means that I must listen and repeat.

Our Lady - "My child and My children, I welcome you all on this great feast day for one little soul who has become a huge soul throughout the world, My children. I say this as a Mother, because she was once upon earth with you and her example should be followed by all. Though she had a hidden life, she has been known to the world."

Veronica - Our Lady is pointing up now to Her right side, high in the sky, and directly at Her right side I see coming through the sky-I know who it is from her habit. It's Saint Theresa, the Little Flower. Now she's carrying...this is wonderful-oh, she's carrying in her arms all roses: different colored roses, pink and red and yellow and white. And now she's taking her hands like this, and she's throwing the roses out, like we do here. She is throwing the roses out to the people. Our Lady is smiling, She's very pleased at this, and She's motioning for Theresa to come closer to Her at the right side, Her right side.

Now Theresa looks different than Our Lady. Our Lady looks very solid, just as solid as you and I; but Theresa has a misty look about her. The light is tremendous around what would be her face. I can't see her face too clearly because the light is so great, but I know she is smiling. I sense the smile on her face. And also it must be quite windy there too, because she does have on a cape, a cream-colored cape, and a brown gown underneath it. Now Theresa is pointing up to the sky, high up to the sky, and I see the sky is opening up again. And oh, coming forward this evening, oh so soon! I see now the rays coming from His hands. Jesus is coming forward to be with Our Lady and Theresa. Jesus is coming forward now and He's coming down very slowly...but He's standing now at Our Lady's left side. And Our Lady is whispering to Him. I can't hear what They're saying: it's almost like the rustling of the leaves. I can't make out what They're saying. But Our Lady now nods Her head. Yes, to Jesus, and He stands there. Now Theresa is going back into what appears to be a cloud-like formation in the sky on the left-hand side. These clouds are very heavy, and they seem to be carrying her back into the sky. And Our Lady now is touching Her fingers to Her lips, like this; that means that you must listen and repeat what She has to say.

Our Lady - "My child and My children, and especially you, My child Veronica, I brought you here this evening because your country is in great strain; it is a though there was just a single vote that is keeping your country from plunging into a war with Iran.

"Now, My child, I want you carefully to listen to what I am about to tell you. It is urgent and the reason I took you from your sickbed to be here this evening. Many years ago in Fatima, My child and My children, I gave a message to the children. Lucy still remains upon earth. She will be here but for a short while longer. Therefore, it is urgent that you help her now, for she also is as greatly concerned about what has been omitted as We are in Heaven about it.

Consecrate Russia, not world

"When I came to Fatima many years ago, I knew that communism would go throughout the world destroying many nations and attacking My Son's Church. Therefore, I made a promise that if the Pope, the Pope of those days and the Pope today, would unite with all the bishops of the world, all together on one day-not the world-but the bishops and the Pope will unite and pray for the consecration of Russia. I do not mean the world, My children; I mean Russia-Russia, the scourge of mankind. You will pray for Russia. One day must be allotted in which Pope John Paul II and, also, all the bishops of the world must unite on one day, I repeat, and pray for Russia; or Russia will continue to be the scourge from God. Russia will continue to go throughout the world annihilating people and places and countries.

"My child and My children, do you not know that death is very close upon many. You are all afraid of going across the veil if you do not have the Faith. However, I am telling you this now as your Mother: you must listen to Me. There is another force rampant in your country, the United States of America: it is a satanic cult that has taken precedence over all cults in the world. The major institution for satan is right here in the United States, with its subsidiary in Canada.

Guard your children

"My child and My children, can you not understand what

364

I am trying to tell you as your Mother: you must guard your children. Warn them against strangers. Don't be taken up with things of the world, so that your children must go and find their pleasures elsewhere; for they will fall into the hands of the walking demons. They prowl the highways. They go through the streets of the cities, looking for the young and the gullible, and those who have no homes. Your country, the United States, has been graced with much prosperity, My children. Therefore, you must take it upon yourselves to guard your children by having proper education for them, and also homes for those without a proper home. There is much money in your country and Canada that can be usefully used for the salvation of these children.

"O My children, how I wanted to caress you and tell you good news, for I am not the bearer of bad news always. I am your Mother and must tell you the truth. I repeat again. My child Veronica, you repeat now in your weakened state, again: the Pope, John Paul II, and all the bishops of the world must allot one day on which they will pray for the conversion of Russia. Not one day for the world, but one day for Russia; or else, I tell you now, Russia will go about and annihilate, destroy many countries. Nations shall disappear from the face of the earth in the twinkling of an eye. That is how desperate the situation is now throughout your world, My children.

Communism from bowels of hell

"The word of Russia is not good, for what communism means is liars, and murderers, deceivers straight from the bowels of hell.

"My child and My children, listen to Me carefully. Guard your children and those in your family with your sacramentals: the Rosary, if you have no other sacramental; until you receive a brown scapular and a crucifix, place a Rosary about your children's necks. They must be guarded in these dire times. How urgent is it? All you have to do, My children, is hear the daily news and you know of the murders of the young and innocent that are being perpetrated

365

by the agents of satan.

"My child and My children, prayer has not become a way of life for many. That is why communism has got such a foothold in your country and in other countries of the world. The prayers given to you in your childhood will be remembered always, I know, My children; but there are those who have not received these prayers in their schools, for prayer has been outlawed in many areas of your country and the world. It took but a few without faith to bring down the flag, for even your country's flag is being defiled, My children. I speak both of the United States and Canada, for when the great Tribulation falls upon them, they will have to hold each other up; for they cannot escape through the waters to get help. They will not escape through the skies, but the number of dead will be counted in the millions.

"Must I go any farther, My child and My children, to bring this urgent message to you? Satan did everything he could to keep you from coming, My child. Everything he could because he knew that this message had to go out.

The brutality of communism

"You do not know, My poor children, what Our eyes have seen as We looked into the dungeons of the communist organizations: the beatings, the scaldings, the torturings. It is beyond all human reasoning that a human being could try to destroy the whole faith of an individual by beatings, by torturings, even by cutting out the tongues of those who had dared to speak against them. And who are these people, My children, who are doing these vile things? In those days when communism enters your country, it will be your own family and your neighbors.

"Yes, My child, I know you are shocked at this, but this is what is going to happen unless the bishops and Pope John Paul II listen to My plea. We have approached them many times; however, I do not understand their fear of Russia. There is nothing to fear but fear itself, for fear is a tool of the devil.

"We know what is right under your God. The Eternal

Father has given you the way to Heaven. It is not an easy road; it is a narrow road, long and narrow for many. Others have reached it early through the grace of their God. I know the removal of children from the earth at early ages brings great sorrow to a parent's heart; however, when they are removed, they go into Heaven.

"And what, My children, are We going to do with all the aborted babies? O My child, I know you feel as I do, for I can see the great distress on your face. What are We going to do, My child? Do you understand when they come to Us, they must go to Limbo? They are in Heaven, a happy place, but they cannot see God. I know you cannot understand fully this, My child, and I know it hurts you to the heart; but it is the ways of the Eternal Father to know just how a soul shall ascend or descend.

Butchery of millions of babies

"The murders must be stopped in your country. That is another reason why communism is getting a foothold in your government and all the governments of the world: because they have given themselves over to sin. Murders and butchery. Millions of babies have been aborted in the United States of America and Canada, and millions more throughout the world. This is murder, and no different than what the communists do to those who dissent from them.

Russia six times the armaments

"My child and My children, keep a constant vigilance of prayer going throughout your nation and the nations of the world. You do not know how close you are to being one of the nations to be annihilated. I speak this of the United States of America, because they are being deluded by Russia. Russia has in armaments six times the number of missiles that we store. While they say they deploy them, and take them out of existence-that is not true. They are increasing and increasing; for they have only one thought in mind-that is to take over the whole world.

"My child and My children, do not be affrighted by this, for there is still time to stop them. But you must do that now! You must get first in touch with the Holy Father, Pope John Paul II. Now this will be most difficult, because he has many agents who work with him that are not in the light. They are in his Secretarial Department-the Secretariat. They do not tell him of his messages. It is difficult-unless you can place it straight into the hands of the Holy Father-it is difficult for him to receive a message. But he must, I repeat again, receive this message.

"He must take one day of this year-this year, not next year, this year-one day, and with all the bishops of the world, he must consecrate Russia to My Immaculate Heart.

"It can be done, My children, with your prayers and your efforts. Your Pope, he is a good man, but he is weak also, having human frailties; and he has great undue pressures upon him. Help him, My children, by writing, by trying to send through the blockade that they have set up in front of him in Rome: send a message of grace from Heaven to Holy Father Pope John Paul II. He must consecrate Russia to My Immaculate Heart; or else Russia shall go throughout the whole world, destroying nation upon nation, even the United States and Canada.

"I leave you now, My children, to pray; and Veronica, you will take three photographs, but you must not allow any reading of them publicly for the time being. It is most urgent. Take three photographs, but be very quiet, My child."

Veronica - Now Our Lady is making the sign of the cross again, with Her crucifix: In the Name of the Father, and of the Son, and of the Holy Ghost. Amen.

Our Lady - "Three photographs, My child, and Jesus will speak with you shortly."

Veronica - All about the trees there are cascading pink lights, and there- oh, is Jesus. He must have gone beyond the trees, looking down at the crowds of people gathered this evening, because He is coming slowly over from our right side, above the trees. He was over in the infirm area, I believe; that is over that way. And now He is coming across the sky, and Our Lady now is standing up...She's still there. She's never left. Our Lady has been standing at the left side of the statue, up about sixteen feet. And it's a little windy up there too, because Her gown is blowing. Our Lady has on a beautiful white gown, and Her mantle is covered, with the-as I told you before, with the beautiful golden trim. And Our Lady looks so delicate, but very sorrowful. She's terribly upset.

Now Our Lady is pointing over, like this, with Her hand to Jesus, and now He is touching with His first finger to His lips.

Jesus - "My child, I shall not repeat the urgent message of My Mother again. You will hear, and read over and over, until you receive the full import of this message from Heaven. And you must act upon it. Each and every individual who knows of this message must act upon it for all Heaven, for there will be a great measure of responsibility given to those who do not make any action to help My Mother.

"My Mother has gone throughout the world to try to stop the carnage that man is making upon other nations. Brother against brother, sister against sister. For what? What is there to gain if you lose your soul? Murder is a sin that is not condoned in Heaven nor upon earth; therefore, why must you murder and kill your brothers? For what? For money? For social standing? For gain? And what is that but a passing fancy. For this is a world where man passes through but for a short duration. Your real life is over the veil. That is when your life begins. You are all pilgrims upon earth, going forward to honor your God; and I should say, that many dishonor Him now, even in His own Church upon earth.

No women on altar

"I ask this of you as your God: in the Holy Sacrifice that I left with you, I did not ask for women to be upon the altar, nor try to be a high priestess. They carry this on in the churches of satan; therefore, it shall not be carried on in My Church.

"When I had the Last Supper with the Apostles, My Mother was not present. If I had it in My power from the Eternal Father to make a priestess, I would surely have chosen My Mother, but, no, there were no women present at the first Dedication.

"My child and My children, I do not have to go through the long list of carnage that is taking place in My Church upon earth. It will suffer a great chastisement soon-very soon-for the communism that is spreading throughout your country, the United States, is entering upon the churches. You can see what they have already did, My child, to your church, and understand why We are so desperately in need of those who are willing to sacrifice their lives for the hereafter. I say the hereafter, for the reward in Heaven shall be great for those who will be willing to stand up and fight for the truth, for their God, to keep the Church as I asked it to be: One, Holy and Apostolic.

"I cannot say that in My visits upon earth, I cannot say that I find much holiness left within the portals of My churches, My children. This has to be regained. There is a force restraining you in these efforts. That is satan. He does not wish to see My Church come back to its true standards. He wishes to demolish it, and to stand and stomp on it with his feet.

"Yes, My child and My children, there is an evil force loosed in the world today. Satan knows that his time is growing short; therefore he will do all he can to capture each and every soul. His bait is very appetizing to some, but they find later on that they throw up at the results. This may be a puzzle to you, My children, but think it over, and you'll understand what I mean.

Jesus only child of Mary

"I come to you as your God, and I also want to make this clear: I did not have any brothers or sisters in My family. My Mother was Mary Ever Virgin. This was a supernatural manifestation from Heaven; and only those who are in the light, they fully understand the existence of My Mother and the role She played in establishing the One, True Church upon earth.

"My child and My children, and My child Veronica, I do not wish to strain your overly burdened heart now, but in that picture one of which I gave was for you; I want you to know the second picture is for you, My child, and you will be guided by it.

"Now I bless you all, My children, with a special grace from Heaven."

Veronica - Now Jesus is taking His hands-and He wants me to take my crucifix and hold it just the way He is, with His fingers-Jesus is blessing with His fingers, but I must do it with my crucifix.

Jesus - "I bless you in the Name of the Father, and of the Son, and of the Holy Ghost."

Veronica - Now Jesus is going over to His right side, our left side, and He is making now the sign of the cross, like this; He said to emulate Him: In the name of the Father, and of the Son, and of the Holy Ghost.

Now Jesus is looking over towards His left side, and He is coming across the clouds. It is beginning to cloud again, and the clouds are covering Our Lady; and I can see the hem of Saint Theresa's gown still up there. But now Jesus is coming over to the right side, and He is standing just by the top of the limb, the highest limb on the tree over on our right side. Now he is looking down at the people, and He is making the sign of the cross: In the Name of the Father, and of the Son, and of the Holy Ghost.

Now He is coming over. It's very windy. Jesus has on His beautiful burgundy-colored cape, and it does have like, I think He called it once a cowl; C - O - W - L, I believe it's spelled. It's like a hat, a headpiece, that comes with His cloak. And he has on a gown, and nothing on His feet. Jesus has nothing on His feet, like Out Lady but the rosettes, Our Lady has. But Jesus has nothing on His feet. And He is going across the sky now, and He's motioning towards

Our Lady. Our Lady is going up into the clouds. Now Jesus is turning back and He's touching His lips.

Sex education-obligation of parents

Jesus - "My child, I do not wish to burden you any longer with the miseries upon earth. I wish to talk only a while, a little bit, about the children of earth, the young children. The parents must be very careful, My children, who you send your children to be taught from. Much evil is being developed in the schools in the name of sexuality. Why cannot we have our children pure of thought and mind? How can we, My children, when the teachers there are being taught to bring in sex education to your children? This belongs not in the schools, but in the homes. This is an obligation of the parents. It will only lead to much greater disaster by having this sex education in the school system.

"I know, My children, you are all heartbroken, but there are many families are heartbroken because of the entrance of AIDS upon the world. Can I not say that you were not warned of this, My children?

"I tell you this now, there will come within a short time a greater plague.
Yes, My child, I know that you have feelings of shivering, but it must be.

Earthquake only the beginning

"And, also, I wish to tell you, as your God, that that was only the beginning-the earthquake in California, only the beginning.

"Do not try, My child, to understand all that is given to you this evening. You cannot fully understand the ways of the Eternal Father. He is most merciful, but there are times when errant children must be shook up to take them back to the fold."

Veronica - Now Jesus is making the sign of the cross again: In the Name of the Father, and of the Son, and of the Holy Ghost.

Jesus - "I bless you all, My children. Now continue with your prayers of atonement. They are sorely needed.

"I will not be dismissed from the grounds. I will not be by individuals who have come to mock Me, as I see two standing over to the right. No, My child, it's no use trying to throw them off the grounds. They will come back. They bounce like a bad ball. Yes, My children, they have caused much discord within your circle, also; but they will not be back. I think, My child, you are beginning to understand whom one is.

"Now, My children, continue with your prayers. All the others cannot count but your prayers this evening. And remember the Pope-as My Mother sought to put in your mind, as though She was branding it in your conscience-to get in touch with Pope John Paul II and ask him-plead with him! -to please do what My Mother asked back at Fatima. Do what She asked; otherwise the world will find itself ablaze."

Veronica - Now Jesus is rising up high in the sky. He is pulling His cape about Him, and He is standing there. He's nodding; He means that He's not leaving. He stays every evening until the last soul has left the grounds, and so does Our Lady and Theresa.

And this evening there will be those who have taken the photographs, and they have been able to capture on photograph Jesus and Our Lady, and possibly the hemline of Saint Theresa. That is what Jesus said. The pictures were taken this evening.

Invalid walks out of wheelchair
"Two massive cures this evening"

18th Anniversary of Our Lady's Apparitions at Bayside -
June 18, 1988

Veronica - All about the trees the lights are flickering off
and on. That's the most urgent indication that Our Lady is
hurrying here. I remember Our Lady said that She would be
here for two specific reasons this evening, and that I had to
be here no matter how ill I am I feel very weak but I'm certain with Heaven's grace and Our Lady helping me I will be
able to bring Her message to the world.

Over on the left side now, Our Lady is appearing. There
are blue lights all cascading around Her. She is so beautiful!
Oh, Our Blessed Mother is dressed in the most beautiful
white robe, with gold trim on Her mantle. And now She is
turning to the right and to the left, looking at people. And
Our Lady is taking the rosary from about Her waist, and
making the sign of the cross: In the name of the Father, and
of the Son, and of the Holy Ghost.

Now Our Lady is pointing upwards to the sky, and directly above our heads there is a large circle of light over the
whole circle here that we are in. And there are cascading
lights coming from beyond the trees straight ahead, down
upon us. I can almost feel the electrical impulse, it feels like;
it's the only way I can explain it, of Jesus and Our Lady
now, with the light pouring down. I feel much stronger,
though when I came I felt that I couldn't make it to the chair.
But I feel much stronger.

And Our Lady now is smiling. I notice as She's floating
gently across the sky - I say gently, because They don't
walk as we do; They seem to glide, just glide along on the
air. It must be just wonderful to be in Heaven, or come from
Heaven. Our Lady is shaking Her head, yes. Now Our
Lady is taking Her crucifix and she's kissing it, like this, on
Her rosary; and She's extending it out now to make the sign
of the cross: In the name of the Father, and of the Son, and

374

of the Holy Ghost.

Now Jesus has wandered over by the tree on the right side. I saw His lights as He went over, cascading from the sky - beams of long, and very pale pink lights. Beautiful! I don't think I have seen upon earth any color like this color that Jesus has coming from His hands now.

Jesus is extending His hands out, like this, in front of Him; and He's moving over towards Our Lady Who has been standing and holding Her Rosary to the left side of the statue, at about, I would say, at about sixteen to eighteen feet up into the sky.

Now Jesus and Our Lady are coming together, and Our Lady is still holding Her Rosary, the beautiful Rosary with the golden Our Fathers and the white Hail Marys. And Our Lady now is specially coming over to the center of Her statue. Now She is coming down much closer, and Jesus, Who has been standing over by the trees, is coming over to Her. Very slowly He is looking about at the crowds.

Now Our Lady is taking Her finger and going like this.

Our Lady - "Look up, My Child, straight up to the sky!"

Veronica - Oh, up in the sky over us there are roses, beautiful roses are held by the angels. I notice they're the three major angels in Heaven: Michael, Raphael, and the third angel. But Michael - oh, Michael is coming through the trees on the left side. Oh, he's massive! His head looks quite big, too; he covers the whole sky. He's truly a warrior of Heaven. And Our Lady now is coming over. Now She is going toward the trees, and She is now touching Her finger to Her lips again:

Our Lady - "My child, listen to what I have to say, and carefully give it to Our wandering sheep.

"I, as your Mother, I am terribly depressed in knowing what is fast coming upon mankind. I see beyond me a ball, a large ball. Were it placed next to the sun, this ball would be like two suns in the sky. But it is a ball of destruction, and I tell you, My children, We have been attempting to hold this back with all manner of graces and fasting and suffering. But the Eternal Father says, 'Look up, My child'; He said to look far up into the sky. Your human eyes cannot perceive yet what is up there, but there is a ball to mankind known as 'unknown origin.' But it is not unknown: it is the Ball of Redemption.

Comet within this century

"Do not be affrighted, My child; you must see this, for it is important. Within this century this Ball will be sent upon mankind.

"My child, I took you from your bed of pain and illness to bring you here to tell the world to prepare now. It is almost too late. We have asked also, urgently, and have had great cooperation from the earth's masses of people - to Rome to tell them, 'Look up, and see what lies beyond your windows: a Ball that is fast hurtling towards earth! It will be here within this century, if not sooner.' For even the scientists have failed to recognize the speed of this Ball."

Veronica - I see a terrible globe, it looks like a globe of fire. It's frightening! It's now bouncing around, like it has no control; as though it's not in a general place to be. It has bounced off another, what looks like a comet, and has actually destroyed the comet to the left.

Our Lady - "This one will not be destroyed; for mankind has listened but has not followed a schedule, as We would say, placed upon mankind by Heaven, a schedule for prayers and repentance. This has not been done to the satisfaction of the Eternal Father. All must get down on their knees, and beg for repentance of mankind. It is mankind's balance."

Veronica - And I see now, over on the right side, there's Michael; and he is holding a balance in his hands. He has on one of the balances, there seems to be gold and silver; but on the other, it seems to be heaped with rocks!

And Our Lady is now touching Her lips again, like this, with Her crucifix and then Her finger, like this:

Our Lady - "My child, I also have to tell you: look up and see, and repeat what you see."

Veronica - I see a large crowd of people in Rome. No,

it's not Rome, because I can't see the...I know the city. It looks like it may be in Russia. I am not familiar, Blessed Mother, with Russia or the buildings.

Dissident plans to kill Pope

Our Lady - "You will understand, My Child, because at this very moment there is a dissident under the number five of communism that is planning to kill the Pope. His words We hear are, "This time we will not fail to destroy him!"

"Please, My children, pray for your Holy Father, the Pope. You must not lose him, for the one who comes after him will destroy if he can - he will attempt to destroy, I should say, My child and My children; he will attempt to destroy Pope John Paul II.

"I know, My child, how this has both affrightened you, and also made you feel weak from terror. I did not want to bring you here at first, My child, as I know how weak and ill you have become; but you see, you must help Our children upon earth.

"Also, they are so lacking in interest in many places. Children are disappearing by the thousands, and where do they go? They go straight to the pits of hell, as they become pawns in the hands of the satanists.

"Yes, My child and My children - and My child, Veronica you must be very careful. I have warned you not to go out alone, not even to your roadway; for you heard the music, My child. They were gathered beneath your windowsill.

"I know, My child, I kept this from you at our last meeting, but it is urgent that you must know this. They are also going to try to murder you on your stoop. Do not be afraid, My child; your destiny is with Jesus and the Father.

"Now, My child, I want you to look up, and look far into the sky. What do you see?"

Veronica - I see a group of people, talking outside a building. The building looks like it may be in Russia. That's the only place I saw spires like they have there. Now coming out of this building are two sinister - looking men.

377

They're looking at shotguns. And they're also whispering. I can't hear what they're saying, but they are mentioning the Pope. They keep repeating, 'the Pope.' Now both of them are laughing, like they have accomplished something bad; but they are laughing because they are demons!

Our Lady - "My child, when We talk of demons, I also mentioned to you that you must be very careful and warn all, that satan was trying, and accomplished his mission, to go into the workrooms of the White Berets and the Blue Berets.

"What is he going to do? He will bring discord and dissatisfaction. And what are you going to do, My child? You are going to pray more, and make a decision; for We are not allowing you to be alone. But you must gain wisdom by making a decision.

"I leave that up to you, My child, as you will follow the rules of charity, holiness, and, also, faith. The greatest is faith. Faith in your fellowman, not only accepting the sorrows of earth..

Market crash within two years

"But do not search, My children, for wealth. Within two years or less, there will be a great crash of the market. The whole world's monetary systems will be paralyzed. That, My child, is why you had to come this evening to the grounds.

"I know you find it difficult to sit up, or stand up; but I will be right next to you, My child, while you do what I asked you to do two days ago."

Veronica - You mean, Blessed Mother, to give out the roses to the infirm?

Our Lady - "Yes, My child."

Veronica - And the Rosaries?

Our Lady - "Yes, My child.

Two massive cures

"You are going to witness two massive cures this evening, after you have given the roses and the Rosaries to the infirm,

378

the suffering.

"My child, since you came late in earth's time, We must now try to put into the time left the path for all mankind to follow in these dangerous days ahead. Many will die in the great flame of the Ball of Redemption! I have told you that for years, My Children, but so many of you will not be ready!

"Keep your waters clean in your bottles.

"Do not accept strangers into your home at this time, for the souls who knock upon your doors will be found to be evil; and they can also destroy the souls of the young.

"There are many groups formed upon earth now that do not bring the words of My Son, but have built among themselves what they call a 'church.' We have many churches, My children and My child. Look up and tell me what you see.

Veronica - I see a church. It's white clapboard. It looks like a church. Yes it is. And it has a bell. It looks quite old - fashioned, like it's been there for years. But I see coming from the back...oh, my goodness! There are people, they look terrible. They're in hoods and cloaks, red on the inside, black on the white. And there's a man behind them.

Our Lady - "This is the leader of the satanic cult which is on Long Island!"

Veronica - Oh, my goodness! This satanic master, or what he calls himself, has two horns! They look like they're coming out of his head - not a costume, but actually out of his head! And he's laughing!

"Blessed Mother, he's so evil! Must I look at him?"

Missing children - pawns of satanic cults

Our Lady - "Do not be affrighted, My child; I placed a veil between him and you at the time. But they are conducting their services this evening, so the prayers that you will say, My child, when you return home tomorrow, you will say it for this group. There are children among them that have been missing now for months, for years. They are all pawns of the satanic cults! "You ask, My child, what can be done about them. First, you must go to the supernatural. You must also read your Bible and place before these obnoxious, self - satisfied demons from hell, that have entered into the bodies of these individuals ... They have been under full control; therefore, they have no conscience. They have no holiness. They are everything the opposite to Christianity, and their goal is to take the Catholic children of the world, through nationwide cults. Already, there are five thousand or more now in the United States and Canada, and people ask: 'Where have my children disappeared to?'"

Veronica - Jesus is nodding His head. He's next to Our Lady. He's nodding His head, and He's touching His lips:

Jesus - "My child, Veronica, listen well to Me. I know there is discord, great discord among the workers. I say this to you now: no decision shall be given at this time."

Our Lady - "Veronica, My child, you will pray, and pray more often to the Infant Jesus."

Veronica - Yes, I do love the infant Jesus. That I have a big Infant Jesus, Blessed Mother, right in my home.

Our Lady - "I know that, My child. I know because I have been in your home many times. No, you do not always see Me, but you do hear Me."

Veronica - Oh, Blessed Mother, I'm so thankful. Now I do not have to be afraid to go to sleep at night, and hear the terrible goings on at my windows, going below the windows...They're most frightening. I have to spend half of the night praying, and I get very little sleep. They think they are going to destroy me with the chanting and the terrible noises coming up. And yet the neighbors are so far apart that no one seems to note these goings on. I don't know, Blessed Mother...

Our Lady - "You will pray, My child. It will be the most difficult task that you have ever had, for they will not be victorious. You will destroy that coven in the end, My child."

Veronica - Now Jesus is coming down closer. He's coming down, down to the top of the statue; and He's taking His hands out, like this, and the rays of light are coming down, right on us! Oh, I feel so much stronger now.

There's something in the beautiful lights. Oh!

Our Lady - "You see, My child, graces are given in abundance when asked for. I know, My child that you do not ask for much, but I did ask you several years ago, with earth's time, if you would be willing to suffer for your Pope, and for the Mission, and you did say 'yes,' My child, didn't you?"

Veronica - Yes, Blessed Mother, I did.

Our Lady - "Well, My child, what We ask of you is not easy, but you will continue; and when there is an urgent message, I will be here. You may call Me at any time, My child, and I will come to you.

"You do not have to weep at night for all the sinners of the world. Many have been saved because of the prayers, My children. There were many in purgatory that had no way to get out of purgatory without your prayers. When you do this, My children, you gain many graces also for yourselves.

"Always remember, call Me, My children. I am your Mother, your Mother of peace, your Mother of grace. I am always your Mother, now and in the hereafter. When you come across the veil, My children, you will fully understand how your works of mercy and caring have brought you across the veil to Heaven."

Jesus - "My child and My children, offer this lesson, My child. You, I repeat from My Mother just told you: you will have to make some decisions yourselves, because on that way of testing, My child - We must test you at all times to help you should you fall out of grace in anger. Anything that is being said with anger shall never be accepted in Heaven.

"I know, My child. You take now - you did not bring the canister that I told you to bring along. Now I want you to take a deep breath."

[Veronica inhales deeply]

Veronica - I can't breathe out!

Jesus - "Yes, you will, My child. Push!"

[Veronica exhales deeply and coughs]

Jesus - "All right, My child, now: you sit back and I will talk to you when you do what you said you promised Us, that you would take the Rosaries and the rose petals to the ill and infirm. They come, My child, with great heart, knowing in their hearts that some will be cured miraculously this evening. And shall We find the individual in the wheelchair, that person is going to walk out of his or her wheelchair. So be sure that someone follows you about. We are going to stand, My child and My children, directly over the statue."

Veronica - They're about fifteen feet, I guess - I'm not good at counting feet, or how high - but I would say about fifteen feet from the statue. And Jesus and Our Lady - it's a little windy, Their capes are blowing, Our Lady's mantle. Our Lady is smiling. She has such a beautiful, soft smile, so compassionate loving.

Our Lady - "My child now, you will gather the rose petals, and the Rosaries that are at hand, and take them now while they are fresh, to the ill and infirm."

[Pause]

Veronica - Oh, now all about the trees, you can see the pink lights. They're cascading down, not in rivulets like Our Lady's used to come down, but like straight lines, actually very powerful lines. And they look like the lines that Jesus sends out to contact the ill and infirm, because the lights are going directly over to the area of the ill and infirm.

Now Jesus is looking down. He has on His burgundy - colored cape, with the tie, a golden tie, on it. But He has on the slippers. I'm trying to look at them. They're made of an animal - type of skin. Yes, that's what they are. Jesus nodded His head. They're made like leather, a leather.

Now Jesus is pointing over, that way! And He's going like this now:

Jesus - "My child and My children, I wish to stress this evening....Look up, My child, and see what this will be about, as you receive a clearer picture."

Veronica - I see what looks to be a school of some kind; and it's a boy's school, and it has them all sitting at desks.

382

But who is the teacher? Oh! I can see that. Oh, it's Frank! Yes! Now Jesus is touching His lips:

Jesus - "My child, there are lessons to be learned from that picture. I am going to ask you to seek the wisdom that is necessary for the present crisis. Now I want you to know, My child, that this has not been solved yet. We will depend on you to do what is necessary."

Veronica - Yes. Jesus said that He does not want me to repeat what He is telling me at this moment.

[Pause]

Right. Yes. Oh, now I may speak. What Jesus is stressing - is that right, Jesus? Yes. Do you want me to speak? All right. Jesus will say it Himself, She said; I don't have to. Just repeat.

Jesus - "My child and My children, We have a great crisis going on in the world, and even among ourselves. This will be solved with humility, charity, prayer and graces. That is all that I will say at this time, but think upon that, and pray upon that; and I assure you, My child, things will not that chaotic.

"Now you will continue, My child; look forward and find the other wheelchair, My child. It seems to be hidden. It is very necessary that you find that invalid, because we must have their name and address."

Veronica - Yes.

Jesus - "Look up!"

Veronica - That individual is in a wheelchair. He has no legs. Oh, no, they're covered by a shawl. I assumed Jesus said that he had no legs; the legs are there, but He is paralyzed.

Jesus - "Now find that individual and place the rose petals about his head and his legs. Can you do that, My child?

Veronica - Oh, yes, Jesus, I will.

Jesus - "Thank you!"

Veronica - Now Jesus is going back into the sky. He's not very far up. Oh, there's Our Lady on the left hand side. Now Jesus is extending His hand, like this - like He does all the time, like this. It's so wonderful to watch Him. It's just so beautiful! The lights are coming out from His hands, and He's making the sign of the cross: In the name of the Father, and of the Son, and of the Holy Ghost.

And now He's over on our left side, that would be His right side, and He's making the sign of the cross again: In the name of the Father, and of the Son, and of the Holy Ghost.

Now Jesus is touching His lips:
Yes?

Now, He is going across the sky now. He changed his mind about something; He had stopped short and was looking down this way, and then He just turned over to the left, and said: "Follow Me!"

Now Jesus is over by the tree, over there. And - yes, it's quite windy up there. We're not getting that much air tonight ourselves; but it's quite windy up there, and comfortable - looking for Jesus and Our Lady.

Now Jesus is bending over and making the sign of the cross: In the name of the Father, and of the Son, and of the Holy Ghost. It's so beautiful!

Now Jesus is placing out both of His hands, like this; and all of these beautiful - oh, Heaven must be so beautiful, beyond anything we could ever conceive of! Those lights, those beautiful, brilliant lights! And they're coming from Jesus' hands. They're just radiating down, over there. Oh, and He is smiling. He said to go over there. Yes, Jesus. We need the roses.

Jesus - "We're standing here, My children, We're not leaving you; but We do want you to find the person for Us this evening. It will make it much easier when they write out their cure."

New York City targeted for destruction
Bombs to be placed in strategic places

Eve of the Guardian Angels and in honor of St. Theresa-
October 1, 1988

Veronica - There are blue lights now coming down from
the sky, high overhead. Oh, the lights are so beautiful! Oh,
I've seen lights before, but there is something different about
these lights. They're magnificent. They're blue. And, also,
now beyond the blue, on the right side of each rivulet of
blue, there are pink cascading lights coming down now.
They're actually lights because they flow out from the blue.
I never saw anything like it before.

And - oh, there they are: all about the lights now are coming out - I know they're angels. They're all different ages
and different sizes, but I do believe it registers their age.
These are all, I know, guardian angels. They are dressed in
the most beautiful pastel shades of blue and pink and white.
And I feel that the blue stands for the masculine angel, if
there is such a thing; and the pink also for the feminine
angels; and the whites are for babies. They are - there are
hundreds of them all about the trees. Oh, I'm sure you must
see them. They are so clear, they're almost human - like in
appearance, except for the translucency of their faces. They
are so beautiful.

Now high up into the sky - oh, about maybe twenty feet
beyond the statue up into the sky, there is now a very white
light. The light is opening up; it's as though it's piercing the
sky. And there coming through the light is Jesus. Oh He's
just beautiful! He has on the most magnificent robe. It's cut
quite differently than He wore the last apparition time. But it
is a beautiful robe, all of a classic type of weave. It's - it
almost looks like it comes from the foreign country, the robe.

But it is so beautiful!

Now - oh, right behind Him now, as the light is opening
up, I can see Our Lady coming with someone else. Oh! It's
Saint Theresa! I'd know her anywhere, since she was practi-
cally living with me in 1968 and '69. She has on a habit

385

now. It's white and black. However she has a cape; the cape is a cream color.

Now they're all together, side by side. Jesus is on our right side; Our Lady is right next to Him on His right side, and Saint Theresa is also standing on Our Lady's right side. Now Jesus is touching His lips, which means He's going to talk. Oh no, He's pointing over to Saint Theresa; she's going to talk. But I can't speak French!

Jesus - "You will understand, My child."

Veronica - Oh, Jesus said that I will understand.

Saint Theresa - "My sister, my dear sister Veronica, how happy I am to see you again after all these years. I have been around, but not permitted by the Eternal Father to appear before you as I did in the early years. But I have been guiding you. I wish at this time that you will recite for me, Veronica, the poem message. This is for Our dear Jesus here."

Veronica - And she is pointing over, and Jesus is smiling. He has such a beautiful warm smile. Oh, it's just beautiful. Now He's touching His lips and He's saying:

Jesus - "Repeat what Theresa has asked".

Veronica - Oh!

Spiritual Childhood.

Dear Jesus, all I can do is just love You,
for my riches are here in my heart;
They're not locked or chained against stealing,
They're always free to depart!
I offer this gift to you, Jesus;
Accept it with your precious joy.
I'm there to hold in Your Kingdom:
Just treat me as your little toy!

Now Theresa is pointing over. She's pointing over to all the angels that are in the sky.

Saint Theresa - "You know, my sister, many of the names. Will you give some this evening to others?"

Veronica - Yes. There's Tomdarius, Tusazeri.... He is my guardian angel, but he's quite a clown. He likes to circle

386

around. And right now he's turning and spinning again. He always does that when he sees me; he turns and spins. And now also, there's Razene and Nadina and many others.

Saint Theresa - "Yes, my sister, that is the happy message for this evening, but I must also come to you as a voice box from Heaven. Many will deride you, my child at these messages."

Veronica - Now Jesus is touching His lips.

Jesus - "My child, I want you to know that you must not be affected by the derision and writings of those who are non - believers. Remember in my time, I also suffered the same for the cause, My child. The Eternal Father had Me within His arms always, and I tell you, My child Veronica, that you are always in My arms. I allow many things to happen to you.

"Look up, My child; I want you to look high into the sky and you will understand why you are being persecuted."

Nuns dancing in leotards

Veronica - I'm looking into what appears to be a convent, but - oh, my goodness!- this is a convent? There's a room there now off the chapel, and I know they're nuns; but what are they doing? They're dancing. And they're dressed, not like nuns, but in leotards! What are they doing?

Now Jesus is pointing over, and I see in the distance - looking far up into the sky, I see in the distance a steeple. The steeple looks like the type you would find on most churches in the United States, with the crucifix - the cross, not a crucifix - but the cross on the top. Now Jesus is pointing down, and I see coming out of the door, three or four men.

Jesus - "They, My child, are priests!"

Veronica - Well...they are? Dear Jesus, I don't understand. What are they doing? They don't look like priests.

Nuns having abortions

Jesus - "That is what makes My Heart ache, My child.

387

That is one of the reasons Theresa is crying constantly when she looks into the convents and sees what is going on. Many now believe in abortion, the murders of the children; and many have committed this act upon themselves.

"You ask, My child, how could this happen to those with a vocation? How can they ever seek an abortion, no matter what the cause? I will tell you, My child: it is because they have given themselves over to immodesty. They have also given up their lives of prayer. They seek the pleasures of the world. They cannot be condemned at this time, My child, because there are too few that pray for the clergy and the nuns. They need your prayers, all the Rosaries that can be said for their repatriation.

"My child, I wish that you will now take three photographs. They are most important, but this I must warn you: I will tell you part of the message when you receive the photographs; but the first part with the date - a very important date, My child - you will hold that to yourself and keep that within yourself.

"Theresa has the permission of the Eternal Father to remain here for the rest of the evening. She will also move about and look upon the ill and infirm, because on her feast day and the feast day of the guardian angels there will be many cures.

"My child, you will question those about you and see if all of the rose petals have been distributed as I asked of you early this morning. If not, they must go out immediately. All Rosaries that can be spared shall be given to the ill and infirm. And should there be others left over, My children, you will please pass them out to all visiting souls. You are in the most dangerous times now."

Veronica - And Jesus seems to be putting His hand, like this, to His brow, as though He's been through some terrible times. It is so pathetic to see Jesus with tears in his eyes. I understand... I understand, Jesus. I will... I will. No, I won't reveal the three pictures, but I understand...

Jesus - "Now, My child, you will sit back and take three photographs or more; whatever you can. But we must have at least three. You will read them in the order in which they are taken; and do not be upset, My child, at what you see. There is much that must be told to the world, as the time is growing very short.

"The Warning will soon be upon mankind. You ask Me, My child, can it be stopped? Only by prayers and sacrifice shall it be held back, but the time is long overdue. If it was not for My Mother Who steadily holds Her hand upon mine in sorrow, I would let My hand fall and the Warning come upon mankind. It is not to be asked for, because you know it is coming, My children. It is to be prayed against, for there will be those who will die in this Warning.

"Now My child, take the three photographs."

[Pause]

Veronica - Jesus is now making the sign of the Cross, and He's standing there right above the trees, about - oh, about, I would say twenty or thirty feet above the trees. Now Jesus is touching His fingers to His lips.

Earthquake because of abortions

Jesus - "My child and My children, I refer to you always as My children because every single soul that is upon the earth today alive and those who have also been aborted, were brought into the world through the intercession of the Holy Spirit; therefore, they are creations of your God, and as such, for the United States, a measure of punishment: there will be a great earthquake. This earthquake will be in a most unusual place, My child; but when it happens they will know that they are facing now an angry God.

"My child and My children, We have gone throughout the world, in various places for many earth - years, trying to warn mankind that unless he changed his ways great chastisements shall fall upon all mankind. There have been wars and rumors of war going now throughout the world. There will be a great war, but first you will receive the Warning, the great Warning. Many hearts shall stop with fear.

"Those who do not listen to Our pleading voices now throughout the world, your time is growing short. We say

389

that to all. For those with the grace and knowledge of what is going to transpass - trespass I should say, because, My child, in My mind I hear all of the trespasses of mankind against the laws of his God.... That is why I cannot hold My Father's hand nor Mine back any longer.

"I know, My child, this frightens you, but I want you to look high into the sky and describe the scene that you see."

Veronica - I see a road. It looks like a normal country road, but it leads to a city, a great city. I would say from the buildings that the city looks like New York. But I see there are very sinister - looking characters walking down the road nonchalantly but carrying bags. Within those bags there are submachine guns.

Jesus - "Yes, My child!"

Veronica - Jesus is pointing in anger at what He sees.

Many in New York to be mowed down

Jesus - "I see murder ahead now, My child, in your city of New York. Many shall be mowed down. It is an attack by a communist nation.

"No, My child, you do not need to know at this time the name of this nation, for it will soon be known when the captors are picked up. The Federal Bureau of Investigation will hear of this, My child, and they will try to stop them.

Bombs in strategic places

"These interlopers upon the serenity of the United States have dark skins. They are not from this nation, but they come from a presently warring nation. It is their object to destroy all and cause chaos in the city of New York. With their plans there will be bombs placed in strategic places and many shall die at the hands of these ruffians.

"My child and My children, and My child Veronica, I brought you here this evening and relieved you of your major suffering the last few days in order for you to be upon your feet. There is much that has to be said.

"One big reason for permitting this disaster in New York

would be the abortion mills throughout the city and the country.

"Much of your money from the world's capitals arrive in New York. These monies are being gathered to start another war. There is a group in your nation called the Illuminati. They are made up of the major money holders, and for money they have sold their souls and the souls of thousands.

A planned great depression

"My child and My children, pray a constant vigilance of prayer. Keep this going throughout the United States and all of the nations of the world, for there is little time left. Soon, in the plans of the Eternal Father, He shall set forth and allow to come upon mankind a great money disaster. In this way it will prove to you that the disaster back in the 1920's, My children, was as nothing compared to what will happen now. I talk of a great depression coming upon mankind. This is well planned by those in control and should hit your country, the United States, and Canada within the next two years.

"Can this be stopped, My child? Anything can be if we can reach the people in time. However, I am not optimistic, My child, at the murders and the two men in particular that are now over here in the United States and using expressions like 'casing the places'. That, My child, means to look and see and report."

Veronica - Oh!

Jesus - "Look up there, My child. You have to look. Look closely, and repeat what you see."

Veronica - Well, I see two men. I don't know if they're Moslems. They have a different - colored skin, but they're not exactly black. Now they are walking through a building, and they're carrying with them, now, bags; but the bags are extra large, which makes it most suspicious.

Jesus - "In those bags they are carrying all the implements of destruction."

Veronica - Oh! I can see now; they're pointing across the street, and I recognize the Empire State Building. Oh, no!

One target: Empire State Bldg.

Jesus - My child, they will choose the Empire State Building to bring more notoriety to the world.

"We have other things to discuss, My child, before the evening is over. I want the world to know now that: We will no longer tolerate the murders of the unborn. The Eternal Father finds that children He had great plans for to bring the true Faith to the world and to save His Son's Church, they have been murdered in the womb. Satan is the father of all liars and many reasons are given for abortion. And even now, in Our convents they are going about consoling women who are about to have abortions; whereas they do not tell them the truth that they are murderers, and they are mothers who will murder their own children.

Women to be with head of household

"The Eternal Father set up women not to be priests and not to be murderers, but to be with the head of a household a guiding light for their children. Each child to the Eternal Father is a pure blessing upon mankind, but all this has been lost in the name of modernism. Immodesty reigns in your country. There are many reasons why the Eternal Father feels that it is now time to do something about all of these abnormalities.

"My child and My children, you will keep a constant vigilance of prayer going throughout your country, and Canada, and the world; for soon you will understand that at the helm of all this disaster shall stand the Eternal Father. Warning and warning, sending throughout the world warnings for many years and what good did it do? But a handful - according to Heaven's estimate only a handful have accepted the messages from Heaven.

"My child and My children, My Mother has been going throughout the world. She is crying tears of pity upon mankind, for She knows the whole program ahead.

392

"You, My child Veronica, will continue to gain strength, and you will be here at the next Vigil; because at that time you are going to have many fleeing from their homes. The Eternal Father feels that it is only in this way that He can save the souls of the children and the unborn.

"Now, My child, you will sit back and take three more photographs. These you can reveal."

[Pause]

Veronica - While we gave out the rosaries and the rose petals, Our Lady and Jesus and Saint Theresa were standing by the trees all this time. I noted them while as we were talking here and examining the pictures. But Our Lady now is - I must say that Our Lady is beautiful this evening, too. Among all the beauties that we've seen this evening, Our Lady's gown is just exquisite. And **Our Lady** - many people ask, you know, what does She look like. How can I describe Her? She has features that are - are just not of this world. The beauty and the light that comes from Her face and Her eyes, and the light that seems to just exude from Her body all throughout the sky, it lights up the sky over us for - oh, a large area of, I would say at least 20 feet extending way behind us there.

Now Our Lady is pointing up. Now She's coming closer to the trees now, and **Our Lady** - and I see Jesus. He's standing over there still by the trees on our right side, and Saint Theresa is directly over the statue. Saint Theresa is standing there and her gown, she has a long gown on; it goes beyond her shoes. I can't see her shoes. Her gown is very modest, and she has on a beautiful cream - colored cape. And it's quite windy. And they actually are floating. Now Our Lady is floating over next to Theresa, and she is touching now Her finger to Her lips.

Our Lady - "My child and My children, I must ask you this evening to remember that there are many messages that have not been read by all. It has been eighteen earth - years since I first appeared here, and much has been given and much has been forgotten. Therefore, We ask all of Our chil-

393

dren to obtain copies of the back messages from Heaven, because we are now in repetition. Because what can We say, My children and My child? If I could show you what is in store for mankind, you too would be shedding tears of sorrow."

Veronica - Our Lady is crying; it must be very serious. Our Lady is crying. And Saint Theresa now is - is going over now and placing her hand upon Our Lady's shoulder. And Theresa is crying too. Now Theresa is turning and touching her fingers to her lips.

Saint Theresa - "Veronica, we will be here for the rest of the evening, until the last person leaves the grounds. There is no time in Heaven as you calculate it upon earth; therefore, everyone who has come this evening shall leave with grace. There will be many cures this evening."

Our Lady - "I understand, My child, what you are thinking, of the complications you fall into when trying to prove to the world the truth. Those who do not have the courage to keep their grace - for graces are given and graces can be taken back - therefore, it is most important, My child, that you will pray for the two individuals that have made it most difficult to get their cures together.

"Right now, My child, I ask you now to hasten back to where you came from because We had much work to do to prepare the grounds for your safe arrival, My child. As I told you at home, you had no doubts that you would be protected; I knew that, but you also had to be warned of what to avoid.

"Yes, My child, there will always be others who will try to destroy you; but they cannot destroy the eighteen years of messages from Heaven, for they will go throughout the world, My child, far after you have been taken from the earth. Do not be alarmed; I am not saying that you are leaving the earth now. Oh no, My child, you will not be given much rest; but there is much that you have to do. I will keep you informed myself, My child. As I repeat: you do not see Me always, but you will always hear My voice."

Veronica - Now Jesus is coming over and He's extending His hand, like this, and making the sign of the Cross: In the Name of the Father, and of the Son, and of the Holy Ghost. Now Our Lady is taking Her beautiful Rosary from about Her waist and She's making the sign of the cross, like this. In the Name of the Father and of the Son and of the Holy Ghost.

Now She's going over... Our Lady, Jesus and Theresa now - Theresa has come from behind the trees. She's standing next to Our Lady, and they're all going over to our left side. And now both in unison, Jesus and Our lady are both making the sign of the Cross. In the Name of the Father and of the Son and of the Holy Ghost.

Now Jesus is placing His first finger to His lips.

Jesus - "Now, My child, you will continue with the prayers of atonement; they are sorely needed. You will not be affrighted at the message this evening, for it must be told to the world, My children. Many will die unless they listen to Us now and follow Our direction.

"Yes, My child, now you will sit back and take two more photographs; three if possible, but most likely two. And as We said, We will not leave the grounds until the last child has left the grounds."

Aids: no cure ever!
Blood supply grossly contaminated

Feast of Our Lady, Queen of the Most Holy Rosary
- October 6, 1988

Veronica - All about the trees now there are blue lights
and pink lights. This is most unusual because usually the
blue lights either show, or the pink lights, but here we have
them both cascading together all about the trees. I'm certain
if you'll look very closely you can't miss the effect they
have on the statue, and everything that is so beautiful on the
excedra. They cascade right down on to the excedra. They
are so beautiful.

Now high up in the sky - I can't judge by feet - there's a
light, a most beautiful light. Now it's opening up. It started
about the size of, I would say, a quarter; but now it's opening
up, and becoming much larger about.

Now as I'm watching, I hear voices in the background,
and they're singing: "Alleluia! Alleluia! Alleluia! Alleluia!
They sound like angels, hundreds of angels now. And there
coming forward through the light is Jesus. Oh, He looks
magnificent. Oh, the lights are coming down all about Him
now. They're blue and they're pink. And He's smiling; I
can see the smile upon His face. It is so soothing and so
invigorating. There is no way I can humanly explain it.

Now if you look high up into the sky, Jesus now has
moved over to His left side, over in that direction. Now
He's pointing up to the sky, that I should look farther up into
the sky. Now there, high over our heads, is another light.
Now this looks about the size of a fifty - cent piece, but it's
getting larger and larger around as it's coming forward.
Now within the light I can see Our Lady.

Oh, She is so beautiful. She is just so beautiful! Words
cannot describe Her beauty. All I can say is, this is something that is not earthly; It's the most heavenly sight that anyone could see. Our Lady has on Her white gown, with the
gold trim all about the edge. And She has the mantle over

Her head. I very seldom have even seen a wisp of Our Lady's hair. It is so beautiful!

Now Our Lady is coming down. She's floating now. And She seems to be standing on the light now. It's created a ball - like effect under Her feet. And it's floating Her over to Jesus' right side; now that would be our left side.

Now as I'm looking over, I notice that Jesus is in deep conversation with Our Lady. I cannot hear it, just what it is They are saying at this time. It must be confidential. But I will say this, that over on one side I see a most beautiful light, and in that light there comes forward a book - a book, a very large book. But it is a Bible.

Now Jesus is touching His finger, His first finger to His lips, and making the sign of the cross: In the Name of the Father, and of the Son, and of the Holy Ghost. Amen. And as I'm watching, I notice the pages are turning in the Bible. And Jesus has nodded "yes"; that is in observing the Bible.

Now Jesus is coming forward. He's about sixteen to twenty feet over the statue. He's looking down all about Him. He's seems very pleased this evening. And now He's touching His lips.

Jesus - "Veronica My child, look up and see, and tell Me what you see; and tell the world what you see, high above your head".

The Eternal Father

Veronica - Oh, I see a most beautiful Being, but He's all of light. I know it's the Eternal Father; but I cannot see Him in form as Jesus and Our Lady are appearing. He seems to be a beam of all light, but the light itself is so beautiful. It gives you a great feeling of warmth and also a feeling of comfort.

Now Jesus is asking me to come down now with Him closer to the crowds about, and look about Him. Yes, I can see it, Jesus. Yes, we do have many infirm this evening.

Jesus - "You will cure two".

Veronica - Oh, That is just wonderful! I know they'll be very happy.

Now Jesus is pointing back up to the circle of light, and He's saying:

Jesus - "Repeat after Me, My child, the words given on the Mount. This is the way you must pray to the Eternal Father:

Our Father, Who art in Heaven,
Hallowed be Thy name;
Thy Kingdom come, Thy will be done,
On earth as it is in Heaven.
Give us this day our daily bread,
And forgive us our trespasses,
As we forgive those who trespass against us;
And lead us not into temptation,
But deliver us from all evil. Amen.

"My child, I had you repeat this even though I know you are having difficulties with your throat this evening. You will be taken care of, My child. Do not be concerned.

Modernists seek to remove the Our Father

Jesus - "Now I asked you to say that prayer because it soon will be forgotten upon earth. The modernists seek to remove it now from the books in the schools. You, My child, will see that this prayer to the Eternal Father is printed up, and given out to all the children within your means.

"Mothers must now take full precedence for their children. In other words, My child, they must be the teachers now; for those who were teachers have given themselves over now to all forms of Modernism, and pacifying those that are evil in their teachings. They do not stand on their two feet solidly before their bishops, who are doing wrong in the teaching of their children. It will be up to the parents, at this time, to go forward, and be a true parent in the eyes of God by teaching their children at home.

"And one more prayer must not be forgotten. But our Modernists are casting it aside. Repeat this, My child: an Act of Contrition.

398

O, my God,
I'm heartily sorry for having offended Thee,
And I confess to all my sins,
Because I dread the loss of Heaven and the
pains of hell;
But most of all because I love Thee, my God,
Who art all good and deserving of all of my love.
I firmly resolve, with the help of Thy grace,
To confess my sins,
To do penance,
And to amend my life. Amen.

Jesus - "You see, My child, that also will be cast from the books this coming year. The children are being taught unity, but world unity. The world is striving and fast heading, for a one - world religion, and also a one - world government. But this will not be a godly government; it will be one of communistic nature.

"My child and My children, listen to Me now. I brought forth Veronica to you this evening even though she is not well. I tell you, My child, it is urgent, to make this sacrifice for mankind. As you well understand from what has transpired the past two days that We were not talking idly in the past message through you.

"We want the world to know again that there was a locution given to My child, Veronica, and it talks of this: Sodom and Gomorrah. Does this seem similar to you, My children: are you not living now among the realms of Sodom and Gomorrah? And what happened to that adulterous city? It was destroyed, just as Babylon the Great shall be destroyed, also.

Two will be cured this evening

Jesus - "Now, My child, there are two who will be cured this evening. To avoid all confusion, I will lead you directly to those whom I wish that you will bless with the crucifix of the Shrine of Our Blessed Mother.

399

"Pray, My child and My children, a constant vigilance of prayer. The world is in it's most dire times, and subject to bad punishments, My children. I say 'bad' because many will die in the great flame of the Ball of Redemption. And many will also die when they see what lies ahead of them, as fear will grip their hearts as they run to and fro from their homes looking for a place of solace - a human word that will give them the courage to face what lies ahead. And that will often be death of the body.

"My child and My children, accept the words of My Mother and My counsel to you throughout the past years. Everything that has been given to you has been given for a reason and will come true. Were it not so I would tell you this now.

"Remember, My children, a constant vigilance of prayer. Use no excuses to relieve your family of this obligation to the Eternal Father. And remember again, My children, the two prayers that makes the heart rise to Heaven. Teach your children, for they will not be taught any longer in the schools.

"Now, My child, I wish that you take any rose petals available and go to the infirm circle and give out also any available Rosaries. My Mother and I will stand to the side while you do this. It will be necessary for the cures, My child".

[Pause]

Veronica - Now all about the trees there are great lights. These are all light lights, summoning the fact that Jesus and Our Lady have been standing over the trees, waiting for us to finish with the infirm circle.

Now Our Lady is pointing over to the sky, and as I look over to where She's pointing, I see great multitudes of people; but they're fighting. I know it's some kind of a war going on. Now their skin is darker, though not black like in Africa. But they are actually killing each other. And I hear a voice from beyond the sky, saying:

Eternal Father - "Father against son, mother against daughter. It will be one of the greatest catastrophes that the

400

world has ever seen."

Veronica - That voice came far beyond the sky, as though it was coming from the Eternal Father Himself. Jesus is nodding, "yes." And Our Lady is coming over to Him. She looks very sad at this time; something must have happened drastically this evening, which we will probably find out about in time.

Now Our Lady is placing Her fingers to Her lips, like this:

Our Lady - "My child and My children, there is not much more that I can say to you. My words have gone throughout the world, and how many have acted upon them? I come to you as a Mother of peace, a Mother of love. My tears have been shed upon you all. I will not give up the incentive to want to save every child upon earth. I shall wander to and fro wherever My voice can be heard, and bring to the world the final message before the end of the age.

"My Son has made it known to you about the reasons the world shall suffer. But, My child and My children, if you will go back to all the past messages I am certain you will find due reasons for the world's suffering.

I tell you now that there shall not be a cure found for the disease of AIDS. It is a punishment from the Eternal Father. Unfortunately, My children, there are many young innocents and those that are older who have come in with the plan of God for the salvation of their souls, but they, too, have fell victim to the AIDS plague. It is a plague, My child, as other plagues shall also follow this one.

Blood supply grossly contaminated by Aids

Our Lady - "Do not be affrighted, My child; I realize that this has given you a feeling of terror, for the AIDS plague has hit many: all the known and unknown, and children as well. I would suggest, My children, that you guard yourselves well against this plague. If you must have a form of operation requiring transfusions, I would suggest that you have a member of your family donate this blood; for the

401

other has been grossly - I say grossly - contaminated and will cause many deaths.

"My child and My children, I repeat as My Son has just said to you, that you must keep a constant vigilance of prayer going throughout the world and your nation. Your nation - all the eyes of the world are upon your nation - but We also watch as they try to fly high into the heavens. Were as much effort put into bringing God the Father to the world, I am sure, My children, much of the evil of the world would disappear. This, of course, is beyond doing, for man has now a proud status - one in which he finds himself king of the world. And for honor, and glory, and money, man will sell his soul. Many have sold their souls to get to the head.

"My child and My children, listen to this well: guard your children. Do not let them be influenced by their teachers today, for modernism has set in, and also immodesty. There are many teachers whose examples are poor to the children; therefore, it is now the duty of each parent to guard their children's souls. Otherwise, the day will come when they will shed great tears of sorrow, not knowing in what realm their children lie, now that they have passed over the veil.

"My child and My children, I call to you now and say again: a constant vigilance of prayer must be made throughout the world - not just the United States and Canada, but throughout the world. And this can only be done and done rightly if you follow the directions from Heaven given to you in the past years.

Read all the past messages or perish

Our Lady - "That is why I say, and I say again: you must read all of the messages given from Heaven through the past years, or you will not be saved. Much is being overlooked due to the quantity of messages. Therefore, you will start from the beginning, and go forward up to the present date. This will also be in the printing, My children. You will start from the beginning, and go forward up to the present date."

Veronica - Now Our Lady is taking the beautiful crucifix on Her Rosary - She's taking it from about Her waist, and She's making the sign of the cross: In the Name of the Father, and of the Son, and of the Holy Ghost.

Now Our Lady is coming forward closer to Her statue, going over on Jesus' right side. Jesus has moved while Our Lady was speaking; He went over closer to the trees on our right side. And now Jesus is extending His hands like this, and making the sign of the cross: In the Name of the Father, and of the Son, and of the Holy Ghost.

Now Jesus is touching His lips, and He's saying:

Jesus - "My child, I want you at this time, to take three photographs. They may be interpreted upon the grounds".

Children being taught to kill!
Parents prime targets

Eve of Palm Sunday - March 18, 1989

Veronica - ... all of the trees about the exedra. They are the most beautiful blue that you could ever see upon this earth. The lights now are becoming like streamers, going high up into the sky. There is no way to explain the translucency of them and the manner in which they are penetrating the sky above us.

Now directly in the center of the streamers I see an opening in the sky. And as I watch, it's becoming round in shape and quite large. I can't see if Our Lady is coming forward. I know it's Our Lady's light because the blue cascading lights are always the symbol for Our Blessed Mother.

Now - yes, now there She is. Oh, Our Blessed Mother is coming now through the sky. She seems to be hurrying; She is most anxious to give Her message to the world. I know that from the conversation I had with Her this morning in my home.

Our Blessed Mother now is coming down. And I see now coming from the right side of us a large ball; it's globe - like in circumference, almost like the ball of the world.

Now Our Lady is watching, and She has a smile on Her face. It's a sad smile, but one that makes you feel like it's just wrenching your heart to look at Her. I know that She is most distressed this evening because of what was told to me this morning at home. Our Lady now is floating over - She's not walking, She's floating over, directly over our heads now. The ball is joining Her, and Our Lady is floating onto the top of the ball.

Now high up in the sky - I can't judge the difference - it's hard to describe Our Lady on the ball; She's a picture of such beauty that it's not earthly. Our Lady - Her face is very radiant, but I do see tears upon Her cheeks. Our Lady has been sobbing, so that as She came through the sky I could hear the gasps of Our Lady as She was sobbing. I can't understand why, except perhaps it has something to do with the message this morning, which at this time I cannot reveal to the world. However, I know that Our Lady will tell you most of this Herself in Her own words.

Now Our Lady is taking Her crucifix from Her Rosary. As I was describing Her appearance, Our Lady was taking Her Rosary from about Her waist; and She's taking the crucifix now and making the sign of the cross: In the name of the Father, and of the Son, and of the Holy Ghost. Our Lady is looking all about Her, and She's smiling.

Now the ball is coming closer down to the tree areas. And now there is a cascading of light up into the sky, and these lights now are turning from the blue to a pink. And I know that signifies that Jesus will be coming through to join Our Lady this evening. Now the lights are becoming dimmer, and the sky is opening up. And I can see Jesus now; He's coming forward. He has on a beautiful burgundy cape, and He has sandal - like slippers. They're made of a skin, an animal skin.

Now Our Lady and the ball are moving farther over our heads. And Our Lady now is motioning with Her hand to Jesus, and He's joining Her on Her left side, our right side. Now Jesus is nodding to Our Lady. And Our Lady now is placing Her first finger to Her lips, which means to listen and repeat.

Our Lady - "My child and My children, I have a most desperate message for you tonight, one which will affect most of the world. But I say now, as your Mother of light, that there is great darkness upon the world. And as this has been allowed to continue, regardless of all the messages from Heaven through various seers throughout the world from the beginning of time, you constantly ignored Our counsel to you, and now the fruits of your evil ways have come to pass. Already you have been found wanting of all the graces necessary to prevent what I am to tell you will happen now in the near future.

405

Earthquake

"My child, as I told you this morning, there will be a great earthquake in the area of New York. When I give you the dates, you will not venture from the island, or you, too, will be caught up in the chaos. There will be much flooding of the highways, so do not try to make your way forth into the areas. Your son, in his work, My child, shall escape the carnage. There will be great fear in the hearts of men, but it will be too late to do anything about this, for the Eternal Father has waited many years.

"My counsel to the world and My Son's word to you have gone throughout the world now for over nineteen years. Now that may seem a long time to you, My children, but nineteen years in Heaven is as a day.

"We do not sleep in Heaven. We must go forth now to plead with Our children upon earth to forsake their evil ways. They now are being guided by satan throughout the world. This cannot be accepted by Heaven. There is only one thing that you can do with an errant child when they do not listen, and that is to shake them up, My child. I realize this is not something for jest; it is but a reality that is coming upon mankind.

"Another area that shall be shaken will be California, My child. There is a great split in the earth that is widening. This is not generally being given to you in your news tabloids. They are trying to lull you to complacency. We have given you the road away from these disasters; and that road is only guided by prayers, penance, and atonement.

"We have asked you to pray for sinners; for you who have been given the grace to come upon these sacred grounds, you must go forward and try and save your brothers and sisters. I say brothers and sisters, My child and My children, because you are all brothers and sisters as you were created by the Eternal Father. Due to man's humility in the beginning - except, My child, for the sin of Adam and Eve - the world was not in such great chaos. Life was far simpler. As man goes forward and tries to seek all of the earth's paradise by way of fortunes and gold and silver, they have sold their souls to get to the head.

A hotbed of fighting

"My child and My children, you must listen well, as I say this also unto you: Latin America shall be a hotbed of fighting, and the United States shall be the prime candidate to enter and have their sons slaughtered upon the lands there. I beg you, as your Mother, to listen to Me. You must not go into Latin America! That is what the plan from Russia is: for you to enter into Latin America.

"My child and My children, listen well while I have My child Veronica repeat to you:

The end is not as far as you can see;
Already there is apostasy.
Man cast his lot and gathered the coals
To stoke the fires that burn the souls.
The days are numbered, your hours are few;
So work and pray and try to do
The work that's given in the light,
Until that sad time when all is night.

The Aurora Borealis

"My children, I wish you to know that you ignored a sign of a short few days ago. We sent from the heavens the Aurora Borealis to shine unto men and let them know that when this happened before, there was a war.

"My child and My children, the United States of America now is in dire conflict with its conscience. But you must remember: Without My Son they cannot succeed. Slowly but surely, against all the counsel from Heaven of the past nineteen years, man has become more scurrilous and more antagonistic towards My Son until he has even entered My Son's Church, seeking to cast aside all tradition and all knowledge of the supernatural, bringing a mode of modernism and humanism into My Son's Church. This has forced many a good soul to lose his way and leave the

407

Church.

"My children, I beg of you, as your Mother, do not leave My Son's Church. Do not allow the rodents to come in and burrow and underground My Son's Church. You can save it if you will only pray more. Pray for sinners, that they will seek the light and be given the knowledge of the errors of their ways, so that they can turn back before it is too late.

Ignore other apparitions

"My child and My children, I want to tell you also at this time: You are not to concern yourself with other words and writings of apparitions in various places. I can tell you, My children, unfortunately there are those who are caught up in the excitement of the times and My appearance at your site. However, you cannot become involved, My child or My children, with any of these apparitions; it is best to ignore them.

Two stupendous cures

"Now, My child, I wish that you go at this time, after three pictures are taken - I wish that you go among the sick and the elderly and give out the blessed rose petals and Rosaries, for there will be two very stupendous cures this evening. It is not necessary at this time, My child, to be told the full details, because before the evening is over, you will have them from the mouth of those that are cured.

"Now, My child, Jesus will speak to you - He is not leaving the grounds - when you return from this mission. First, you will take three photographs, and then proceed to the infirm circle.

A correct decision

"My child, there is much that I told you this morning, but I say at this time: You will stop being concerned of the situation in California. You made a correct decision, guided by My instinct to you. Therefore, you will no longer be concerned with the person. I do not say the name, because I do not, My child, wish him to be ostracized; however, he must listen to Our counsel and proceed to Canada, or he will suffer a dire punishment. He will bring this punishment on upon himself in human ways. It is not the hand of God that will strike him down; it will be his own foolishness and pride.

"You will understand, My child, what I am talking about in time, but this is a semi - private message that can go out to the world. They will ask questions of this message; however, it is not for all to know. You understand that, My child.

"Now take three photographs, and then proceed to the infirm circle."

Veronica - Jesus is standing over by the right side of the statue, high up into the sky. And now before I leave, He is making the sign of the cross with His hands, like this: In the name of the Father, and of the Son, and of the Holy Ghost. Now He's nodding "Yes", He wants me to proceed.

[Pause]

Veronica - The sky is becoming a very bright pink. I'm sure if you could look beyond the trees you can't miss it. Pink is Jesus's color. And I know we spent quite a bit of time with the infirm circle, but now the sky is starting to open up above Our Lady's statue, maybe about forty feet in the air, and it's just beautiful! It feels - looking at the lights you feel so warm inside and so peaceful . I could sit here and just watch this light all day and I'm sure that I would be as buoyant later, after, seeing such a beautiful sight.

And Jesus now is coming through the light. Oh, He has on His burgundy cape. And He is very patient while we were at the infirm circle. He's smiling; He thought that was kind of funny.

Now Jesus is placing His first finger to His lips:

Jesus - "My child and My children, there is one thing I wish to bring to you this evening: that is the word of Russia. You do not understand the great threat she is to the world. I say `she' because We have nothing else that exemplative of explaining the necessity to convert Russia. Now My Mother in the past has told you through countless earth - years of visits upon earth how to do this. I repeat from My Mother Her words to the world some time ago - and I believe, My child, you have been a voice - box before and a means for Heaven to transport this message to the world - that is, that the Holy Father in Rome, in unison with all of the bishops of the world, must consecrate Russia to the Immaculate Heart of My Mother.

Russia plans to take over Sweden

"You do not understand, My children. Already Russia has plans to take over Sweden. I know this shocks you, My child, but it is the truth. Russia now plans to take over Sweden, and they are surveilling the place constantly. You will tell this to the world as an example, that if they could do that to Sweden, it can happen anywhere, My child. Yes, We tell you this because We have great hope that they will not be successful.

Wheel of misfortune

"Now, My children, I speak to the mothers of the world: You must make a firm effort to be a righteous mother and a godly mother, following the rules from Heaven. For eventually every one of you will come over the veil, and you must make an accounting for your actions upon earth. We find that you are all lacking at this time, because as parents, you have been caught up in the wheel of misfortune for your children. They are being ignored, and also, their religious upbringing is nil.

TV teaching children to kill

"My parents of the world, I say unto you, as your God: This will not be tolerated much longer. For if you parents will not raise your children in the light, you will raise them in darkness, and they will eventually rise up and even kill you. There are many satanic institutions throughout the world now that are waiting for your children. Are you going

410

to allow them to fall into their hands because you are too busy elsewhere to watch your children? Are you turning them over to the satanic tube, the television? Yes, My children, they are learning to kill by the television. They are learning disrespect for the parents. They laugh at you when you are not watching. That, My children of the world - parents, your children are to be lost."

Veronica - Now I see a picture forming in the sky. It shows a terrible scene on a television. It shows a young child butchering a cat. The child watching this goes to the kitchen, takes out a large bread knife, and - oh, My God! He's plunging it into the back of his mother! Now the scene is becoming very dark; I don't see anything else. It's ghastly!

Jesus - "That, My child, is what is happening now throughout the world. The children are taken over by satan through this instrument of satan. Much good could be gained if many will monitor their television sets, for their children's minds are being seduced by satan. I repeat again: Your own children will rise up against you and destroy your household. Murders are abounding.

"And also, I say at this time, My children, I will not tolerate much longer the infamous actions of some of My representatives upon earth. Yes, My child and My children, much has happened that has saddened the hearts of all in Heaven. We watch, and we asked you to pray for your brethren, to pray for your priests upon earth, for they, too, are human and are susceptible to attacks from satan.

Stay in your parish church

"Already there is much discord in My Church upon earth. It saddens everyone in Heaven. And We are out in force now, going throughout the world seeking to set up armies of good children who will fight, to the bitter end if necessary, to save My Church upon earth. It is being destroyed. Just as rodents will burrow into a house, those who have evil natures are burrowing into My Church. We find it almost unrecognizable, My children. However, I will say this: I

411

asked you to remain in your parish churches, not to judge by the actions of man.

"The institution itself, as set by Me, remains to be true; however, the cavorting and the banjos and the guitars and the musical interludes and the dancing are all created by satan. So you can understand that satan has entered now with his armies in full regalia, appearing as humans. However, they are demons in disguise, and they have one ultimate aim: to try to destroy My Church, the Roman Catholic Church, with the seat of Peter as the head.

Pope to die?

"You will all pray for your Holy Father, Pope (John) Paul, for there will be very soon another attempt upon his life. Only you can save him now, because, My children, in all factuality, We tell you: Without your prayers you will lose him within the next year.

"I know this frightens you, My child, but you, too, must make many acts of reparation. You will suffer much in the days ahead. This We ask of you because We cannot promise you everything upon earth, for your reward will be great in the afterlife, My child. Accept your suffering, and offer it always for the priesthood.

"Now, My child, you will continue with the prayers of atonement. The Rosary must be kept going throughout the world, even if you have to go about knocking on doors."

Veronica - Now Jesus is stand - placing His hands out like this, and making the sign of the cross : In the Name of the Father, and of the Son, and of the Holy Ghost.

Now He - Our Lady is coming down from Jesus' right side. I didn't see Her over by the tree, but She's coming over slowly, and She's joining Jesus on His right side, our left side. And They are both going over now to the top of the first tree on the right there, and They're making the sign of the cross: In the Name of the Father, and of the Son, and of the Holy Ghost.

Now Our Lady is turning to the right, and They're float-ing over. There is no way to explain it. They don't walk,

They just glide. It's as though They were weightless, yet They look as human and as solid as you and I, going across the sky.

Now They're over on our left side, and Jesus is extending His hand out again, with His fingers like this, and making the sign of the cross: In the Name of the Father, and of the Son, and of the Holy Ghost.

Now Jesus is nodding, and He is touching His lips with His hand:

Jesus - "Continue now with your prayers of atonement."

Besiege the Pope and Bishops
With letters, calls and visits

19th Anniversary of Our Lady's Apparitions at Bayside
- June 17, 1989

Veronica - ... about the trees now, streamers of pink light, going from the trees high into the sky. And directly overhead in the sky I see an opening of light; the light is circular. And coming through the opening - oh, I recognized Him right away from the distance, even, because of His cloak. Jesus is coming through the opening, and He seems to be hurrying down fast because He's moving at a great speed forward. I can see Him very clearly now. He looks so beautiful! He has long flowing hair. His hair looks much longer now - it could be the cape that He has on. The cape is quite shallow around His shoulders; it doesn't have like a cuff, like His last cape that I saw.

Now Jesus is looking all about Him and smiling, and He's pointing high up into the sky. Oh! There - Our Lady is coming! She's directly over Jesus, but to His - to the front of His vision; and He's pointing. And Our Lady is coming forward now. But She's not traveling alone; She has a ball under Her feet. It looks like a globe of the world. And She's coming down slowly.

Oh! And now I can see Jesus; He's smiling. His cape is blowing a bit in the wind up there. And I don't know if it's raining, but it looks so glistening, His cape. And He has a border of gold around the cape now, the mantle part, and down to His feet. And I can see Jesus' feet very closely. He's quite close to us this evening, near the upper tree, directly over Our Lady's statue. And He has on brown, leather - like slippers - sandals really.

And Jesus is pointing now with His hand, like this, to the Blessed Mother, Who is now directly at His right side. That would be Her left side Jesus is standing, but it's Jesus' right side. And now Our Lady is placing Her fingers to Her lips, like this, which means to listen and repeat.

Our Lady - " My dear child, Veronica, it was most urgent that you be here this evening because the evil in your world has accelerated greatly since you were here some time ago.

"My child and My children of the world, I want you to know this: for the perseverance in the fight ahead to stop the satanists in their quest to take your children from your homes, I ask all parents at this time to be a steady guardian of their children and not to become obsessed with the things of this world, the pleasures and the monetary gain.

"I wish that all parents who hear My voice tonight be alerted to the fact that there are over 10,000, now, cults in the United States and Canada alone. Many children have been slain by them in sacrifice to satan. Is this what you want, My children?

"Parents, keep a close watch on your children. Be sure that they do not leave your home without your knowing where they are going, for many will not return.

"This adulation of satanism shall not be prevalent when the Eternal Father gives Us the means to reach all humanity with this plea from Heaven to save your children from the satanists."

Veronica - Now Our Lady is moving over, and She's going to Jesus' right side - that would Her left side. The ball has disappeared, and She's now whispering something I cannot hear to Jesus.

And Jesus now is looking straight down at me. His eyes are very beautiful, but boring. They seem to be a light that goes right through you; there's no way to explain it. But I feel so much better now. Yes, Jesus, I do feel much stronger and better now. I was certain I would not be able to be on the grounds this evening; but I knew that You wanted me here, and Our Lady, for reason; and I knew that You would get me here.

Now Jesus is touching His lips again, like this, and He is making the sign of the cross with His hand, like this: In the name of the Father, and of the Son, and of the Holy Ghost.

Jesus - "My child, Veronica, I have a mission for you

that may not be pleasant. You can reject it when you hear Me out, or you can answer yes. What I want I want you to do, My child, is to reach your bishop. And you will write to him, if not a personal visit - that I will leave up to you, My child. But you will tell your bishop that We in Heaven are much distressed by his current action of allowing the Lutheran groups to enter upon the Cathedral, My Church upon earth, the Cathedral of St. Agnes. You will tell him that all Heaven is distressed by his mistake.

"You, My child, will pray much for your bishop and all of the bishops of the world.

"There are so many errors now abounding that it seems almost hopeless to recover those who have lost their faith. Many have left My Church upon earth, and this disagrees with the heavenly plan to save all mankind.

Prayer life of clergy almost nil

"I become agitated, My child, when speaking of this, because the fault lies mainly with My clergy. The sheep are wandering now, and so few have taken to prayer to save them. The prayer life of the clergy has almost become nil. That means, My child, that they must return to meditation and constant prayer, or much more shall happen to the earth.

Great earthquake in L. A. and New York

" There will be pestilence anew. There will be earthquakes in many places. The present ones have been nothing compared to what will happen next. There will be a great earthquake in the Los Angeles area, and also New York. I told you this before, My children and My child, but I must repeat to you: Many prayers are needed now, for the balance is most uneasy.

"Look up, My child, and tell Me what you see over the farthest tree."

Veronica - Oh, I see Saint Michael! I'd know him any place, but oh, he is so large he covers the whole sky. He has a balance in his hand. It looks like there are gold bars on the right side of the balance, and over on the left it looks like nothing. And yet with that nothing, the balance is heavily to the left.

Jesus - "Yes, My child."

Veronica - Jesus is pointing.

Jesus - "Look up and you will see why."

Veronica - I look high into the sky and I see all kinds of merriment - dancing and drinking and carrying on, and I see things that cannot be holy because it offends God very much. I cannot repeat them, but I see scenes of carnage.

Jesus - "My child, you are only looking upon earth. Should I show you much more that is taking place at this very hour, you would most certainly pass out from the shock. Because, My child, through the years I have given you knowledge of the evil of the world, but to experience them would be too much for your weak heart.

"My child and My children, there is another matter that I brought you here this evening for, My child, Veronica. I want you to tell the world again, and remind them that they must all make it an issue among their cardinals and their bishops that in order to save the world from communism and its fast gallop of the war - like Mongols down after those who are innocent of heart - the fast trod of these hoofs come from, My child, the Apocalypse!

Red horse

"The red horse is war! And war is in the balance, next, My child. And what can you do about this? This is My direction from Heaven - and We hope My children, that you will get this out to the world: Unless the bishops and the Holy Father in unity with all the bishops of the world, unless they consecrate Russia to My Mother's Immaculate Heart, the world will be doomed! Because Russia will continue to spread her errors throughout the world, rising up wars and carnage and pestilence and famine. Is this what you want, My children?

417

Besiege the Holy Father and bishops for consecration

"Every single soul upon earth that hears My voice this evening has an obligation, for the sanctification of their own souls and the souls of those they love, to listen to Me and follow the direction. I wish that all who hear My words this evening will go forward and besiege, if necessary, the Holy Father and the bishops with a request for this consecration of Russia. We do not mean the world, My children, We mean Russia!

Two - legged demon

"Now also the United States of America, that allowed a two - legged demon to walk through this nation with smiles upon his face, as he counted the next victim - yes, My children, his visit to you was not one of solidarity or ecumenism or anything else. Be they not mortals, I would say that they are demons in human form. Do not listen to them, My children, because Russia has not been converted. As I told you before, Russia is planning to take over Sweden.

"Yes, My child, I know this disturbed you, but the truth must be made known.

"You will receive much aggravation and also much discord from some clergy because of the message I give to you this evening, My child, but I know that you in your heart will do as We have directed you."

Veronica - Yes.

Jesus to help many infirm

Jesus - "That, My child, is the answer We expected. Now, My child, there are others outside who are waiting to see you with the blessed cross, the crucifix of My Mother. Will you not go to them in your weakened state? I will support you. Will you not go to them and bless them? For many have traveled many miles to reach here this evening, and I will help many of them.

Veronica - Now Our Lady is looking at Jesus. And Jesus is placing His hands out again, like this, and making

418

the sign of the cross: In the name of the Father, and of the Son, and of the Holy Ghost.

Now Our Lady is turning to Her right - that's our left. And Jesus and Our Lady are both going over to Jesus' right side - that would be our left side of the trees - and He's extending His hands and making the sign of the cross: In the name of the Father, and of the Son, and of the Holy Ghost.

Now Our Lady is pointing over to Her left, and They're coming across the sky. They're not stopping over the statue, but They're continuing on to the first tall tree. And They're bending over now, and Jesus is making the sign of the cross again: In the name of the Father, and of the Son, and of the Holy Ghost.

As They're moving back, I can see Our Lady so closely now. She has on Her beautiful white mantle with the gold trim all around the edging, and Her belting is golden. And on Her delicate feet - oh, She's so beautiful that it absolutely takes my breath away - on Her feet are golden rosettes. They look like pure spun gold, and little rosettes to the right of them. I'm counting, one, two, three, four, five rosettes - how beautiful! Our Lady has them on a slipper. She has on white slippers with the rosettes, made almost like a sandal, but with more of a closed toe.

Now Our Lady is touching Her lips.

Our Lady - "My child, you will go immediately to the infirm and the ill, and bring them the Rosaries and the rose petals as I directed you."

[Pause]

Veronica - ...looking down and Jesus is over on the right side. He's standing over the tall limb there on the right side - the tall limb. He's higher up in the sky than Our Lady, and He's watching everything that's going on.

Oh, Jesus is putting His hand to His mouth. Oh, and He's shaking "yes," I know what He means. He's coming over now; Jesus is coming over.

Jesus - "My child, I did not wish to weaken your condition any more, before than necessary, before the blessing of the infirm and the ill. However, I feel that at this time you

must include the prayers and the admonitions given by
Heaven throughout the years for those who do not choose to
read but to listen:

The end is not as far as you can see;
Already there is apostasy.
Man cast his lot and gathered the coals
To stoke the fires that burn the souls.
The days are numbered, the hours are few;
So work and pray and try to do
The work that's given in the light,
Until that sad time when all is night.

Veronica - Jesus is saying:
Jesus - "For Our dear Holy Father, Pope John Paul II,
you will repeat:

Dear Holy Father, John Paul II,
Dear Holy Father, worried and wan,
Will struggle with Jesus to gather the sheep.
The pastures are rich, but the sheep grow thin;
For the souls have succumbed to the sickness of sin.
You'll need reinforcements from heavenly shores,
So deep is the darkness of earth's shallow mores.
All hearts must ascend in true supplication
To avoid the sad fate of divine devastation.
Dear holy Mother, your Mother of love,
Does beg you to heed these dire words from above:
His Heart -

Veronica - And She's motioning over with Her face
towards Jesus and Her hand pointing.
Jesus -

His Heart is torn by careless surrender
Of too many souls that don't try to remember
The Father, the Son, the Spirit of life -
Cast upon the earth a world of strife.

420

What more must you do now but place the full load
Of saving all souls on the few who are bold;
Who'll stand up and fight for all Heaven's glory,
And meet with John Paul II at the end,
the end of life's story.

Veronica - Now Jesus is mentioning "Yes." Oh, yes. Jesus says repeat:

Jesus - "I wish that all mothers and fathers bring this simple prayer to the hearts of their children. For in the future, with the raging wars and pestilence and famine that will come upon mankind, many will pass over the veil at a young age. You must teach them, parents, to say this simple prayer to Heaven:

Now I lay me down to sleep,
I pray the Lord my soul to keep.
If I should die before I wake,
I pray the Lord my soul to take.

Veronica - Now Jesus is nodding, and - yes. Oh, I can't repeat it. Yes. When? [Veronica gasps.] Really? Oh. Yes, I do. I understand. Right.

Jesus and Our Lady are still standing there. Jesus has His head down low; He looks like He's very upset. I know why. And He's pointing over to Our Lady, and Our Lady is crying. It's like a repetition of many years ago when She said, "My tears fall upon you." And I know in 1970 She cried and cried, just as She's doing tonight. And I know from a discourse with Our Lady earlier that these tears are caused by the abominations that are taking place in the world against Her Son, Jesus. Our Lady feels that for all He did for us upon earth that we could never turn in such violence against Him and His Church.

Our Lady is touching her lips now.

Stay in your parish church

Our Lady - "Remember, My child and My children, no

matter how rough the road gets, you will stay within your parish church. And by good example and many prayers you will bring the priesthood back into the light. Many have lost their way because there are so few who pray for them. Remember, My children, to pray for your clergy, for they are human also and subject to error, mistakes, influence, and sometimes, pure evil. Pray for your priest daily, My children.

"Now you will sit back, My child, or proceed into the infirm circle again."

[Pause]

Veronica - ... statue head, over, over by the trees on the left - hand side. And Jesus is standing, and Our Lady is extending - oh, Our Lady is extending Her Rosary which She has taken from around Her belting, and She's making the sign of the cross upon the people: In the name of the Father, and of the Son, and of the Holy Ghost. And She's looking over, and She's nodding and turning to Her left, which gives Her more room to come over on our right side. Our Lady is floating quite close now to where Jesus is standing, and She's still extending Her Rosary, like this, and making the sign of the cross: In the name of the Father, and of the Son, and of the Holy Ghost.

Oh, there are many blessings here tonight, many. And Our Lady said that - just said there are many blessings here tonight. Oh, it's wonderful!

Now Jesus is extending His hands, like this, and making the sign of the cross: In the name of the Father, and of the Son, and of the Holy Ghost.

And They're both smiling, you know, and They're just standing there now looking at everyone.

Our Lady is looking to Her right and to Her left. She's looking over the whole grounds. And Jesus seems to be following Her, because He's also looking, and it's making His hair come across His shoulders, you know. It's quite long, His hair. And - oh, there's something that He wants to say. Jesus is pointing to His lips. Jesus says this:

Crucified through palms - wrists tied

Jesus - "I want the people to know that when I was crucified the nails were placed through My palms, but I was also tied by skin - like rope about My wrists to the cross. And as I walked to My death, I carried not the full cross but only a cross - beam across My shoulders, and I found at the edge of town on a high hill the other part of what was to be My crucifixion plank."

Veronica - That is what He was told by the people in the shop that were making the spikes that were going through His hands. So Jesus wants that known, that He was not only tied but He was nailed through the palms of His hands. The palms right here, and right here. No, He was tied by the wrists. And also in His feet there was one large, spike - like nail, it was a spike, that went through both His ankles. But He also, at the feet, at His instep, He was tied also by this skin - like rope that was made from animal skin - that was their rope. He wants everyone to know this, because through history, He often says that, you know, the truth has been lost. But He wants everyone to know just how He went to His crucifixion.

Now Jesus and Our Lady - They look like They're getting ready to just - to now stay... Our Lady has gone over to our left side, and She's standing by the upper branch of the fir tree. And Jesus is still over on the right hand side, and He's standing over the small branches now. He's come down, because if you look there and you can see - past Our Lady's statue, you can see Him just standing there with one of the boughs of the fir tree almost on His shoulder. And They're just smiling now; They're remaining there. You see, I don't know if Jesus ever mentioned it before, that when They come during the evening They stay until the last person leaves. They always stay.

423

Pope under Domination of Bishops
Antichrist into mitres

Feast of the Guardian Angels and Eve of the Feast of St.
Theresa - October 2, 1989

Veronica - ... all about the trees now. Oh, they are so
beautiful! They're cascading. I'm certain if you look up at
the top of the leaves section on the trees, you can't help but
notice the beautiful blue lights of Our Lady. Now there are
also streamers of pink coming forward from the top of the
sky. That means that Jesus and Our Lady are both going to
come together.

Oh, the sky is opening up. It is so beautiful! It's like a
clear summer's night with all the stars shining. And I hear
voices in the background, of music; I know they're angelical
voices. It is absolutely beautiful! I feel suspended in such
beauty - it's not of this earth; it is obviously not of this earth,
but from Heaven.

Now Our Lady and Jesus are coming down together.
Our Lady is smiling very sweetly, and Jesus is motioning to
His lips, like this, now. They're still coming down, but He's
telling me to be ready to repeat.

Now Jesus and Our Lady are stopping over the first
streamer of light there. The lights are now cascading from
Their feet downward into the trees. Our Lady and Jesus are
standing there.

Oh, Our Lady looks so beautiful! She has on a pure
white mantle and a white gown, and about Her waist there is
a gold cinch. Our Lady calls it a "cinch" for a reason. But it
looks like - I would call it a belt. And Our Lady has on Her
feet the most beautiful slippers - golden, and there are two
small rosettes on Her feet. Oh, Our Lady has such delicate
feet. This evening, too - I can see Our Lady's face very
clearly this evening, and I would say She doesn't look over,
more than twenty years old. Our Lady looks so young and
radiant.

Now Our Lady is turning towards Jesus. And Jesus is

nodding, and He is placing His first fingers to His lips, like this, which means to repeat.

Jesus - "My child and My children, and especially you, My child, Veronica, I called you here this evening, though I am fully aware of your disabilities. However, it will be not necessary to hear all about you, My child. Be it sufficient that you can bring My message to the world. [Veronica has been suffering from tinnitus, which impairs her hearing.]

"Now, this My child, will bring much consternation from the clergy. Look upward, My child, and tell the world what you see."

Veronica - I see the picture of "Jacinta 1972."

Jesus - "And what is in this picture, My child? Repeat."

Antichrist into mitres

Veronica - I see the letters very heavily penciled over by Jacinta when she wrote this message. It says - one part of the message - there are five parts to the "Jacinta 1972" picture, but one part says: "A - C into, I - N - T - O, mitres 1972."

Jesus - "Repeat that well, My child."

Veronica - "Antichrist into mitres 1972."

Jesus - "That, My child - I know you were much affrighted at that message when you first received it from Jacinta several years ago. But nothing that We give you is to remain hidden. It is necessary for the battle ahead.

"Be it known to all men upon earth that the antichrist has entered now among you. Be it known to Our bishops and cardinals: (I do not include Pope John Paul II at this time, because he is under the domination of his bishops and cardinals.) I look upon My Church at this time and I find gross errors. I tell you now, all bishops and cardinals of the world: My Church shall not be defaced. You shall not defame My Name. I will allow this to continue but for a short time. If you do not acknowledge Me properly before the world, I assure you, I will not acknowledge you before the Father; and you will not have eternal rest with my Father in Heaven.

Disciples of the latter days

"My child and My children, We have looked upon the world now and find that We are fast approaching the latter days. This will be a time of toil for all. Those who will work with Me shall be called now disciples of the latter days. Already, My children, you have gathered for some time. You all know who I am speaking to at this time. I say again, all those who have been picked from among Our vineyard of souls upon earth to come forward as disciples in the latter days to defend the Faith, to remain faithful and true under siege, shall gain Heaven and immortal life. You will find life everlasting with the Father.

"However, I acknowledge the fact that, My child, I have taken you from your home in a weak state; but you know how urgent it was from Our discourse with you all day today, My child, that you get here this evening. For the evil is accelerating in the world. We cannot hold back the Chastisement much longer. The Father has at the foot of His throne the Ball of Redemption. Look up and describe what you see, My child."

Eternal Father - ball at His Feet

Veronica - I see a very wonderful Man. He is so grandfatherly, with a long white beard. And He is sitting with the most beautiful cape on Him; He looks like a regal King. He's smiling. There is no way to explain Him. And He is so translucent and shining. I know It is the Eternal Father. But He has at the foot of His throne a large ball; it's like a ball of fire. I know quite a number of years ago I saw this ball in a photograph taken by the people from Canada. I did not know what it meant then, but now I understand the photograph.

Now Jesus is motioning to His Mother, at His side. Our Lady is standing at the right side of Jesus. I see that She is brushing the tears from Her eyes. Now Jesus is backing up; He's backing up and going higher into the sky. And Our Lady hasn't moved. She is looking all about Her. She looks so very sad. And now She's placing Her fingers to Her lips, like this.

Our Lady - "My child, I implore you to love your brothers, even those that will persecute you. Love them as My Son loved those who even crucified Him. That is the only way you can reach eternity in Heaven.

"My child and My children, I, too, have watched - the Eternal Father made it known that I must see what is going on in the world today. And, I, as your Mother, have given My decision to the Eternal Father to go forward throughout the world, appearing in numerous places now, to awaken the world to the reality of everlasting life.

"How many have sold their souls to satan to get to the head for a temporary time upon earth? My children, do you not realize that you are only a short distance from paradise? Your years upon earth are so few. Isn't it futile, My children, to soil your souls and avoid following the road to Heaven?

"All those who think that life is forever upon earth are making a serious error, and they are defeating the reasons they were placed upon earth. There is no way other than straight through to Heaven, hell, or purgatory. There isn't a soul upon earth that can say, 'I will be here forever.' For the only place that exists, My children, forever, is Heaven, hell, or purgatory.* When My Son returns to earth - when the persecution to the enlightened grows stronger, when all the world is fighting, that My Son shall deem it necessary to return.

*On October 8, 1989, in a locution, Our Lady directed Veronica to write in her own words a clarification, which follows:

When Our Lady spoke about Heaven, hell, and purgatory in the message, She was especially addressing the clergy, as some have lost the reality of the existence of hell. But they have especially lost the reality of the existence of purgatory. Thus She chose to use the word "forever," as this is earth's time, meaning till the end of time, or till the day of the final judgment. The intention being to impress upon the clergy the fact that purgatory does exist, and there are souls who will be in purgatory till the end of time. Naturally, at the end of the world there will no longer be a need for purgatory, and it will cease to exist. "Heaven and hell are forever" in the sense of the eternal, so naturally, they shall exist without end.

The impostor pope

"My child and My children, I ask you in the name of the Father, and My Son, and the Holy Ghost, to listen to Me now: The course you are on is a course to destruction. Satan has entered into My Son's Church. You remember, My children, Pope Paul VI, Our good Vicar, said to the world, `I know that the smoke of satan has entered into the Church.' But who listens to him, and who did listen to him? But they laid him low, and put another in his place.

"I know, My child, the derision and the scoffing that comes your way because of this message. But you will go forward, My child, and not listening to the scoffers, you will succeed one day in bringing forward to Us many wandering sheep.

"There are many souls upon earth that shall not be held accountable for their sins, for they have been led and misled by their elders.

"I say unto the cardinals and bishops in My Son's Church: I am much grieved at your conduct. You will be accountable to the Eternal Father for the destruction of souls. And the abuses that go forward against My Son cannot be tolerated by the Eternal Father. My Son suffers greatly upon earth. Have you forgotten so soon how He sacrificed His very Being for you all? And what are you doing in return?

"Oh, My children, I close My ears. I cannot listen to this painful episodes upon your earth. It appears that there are those who cannot talk without defaming the name of My Son. They use it with cursing and abuse. This is not to be in the eyes of the Eternal Father. This will not be tolerated.

"Do not re-crucify My Son upon earth, because you will all be held accountable. None shall come to the Father except from My Son: For My Son is in the Father, and the Father is in My Son, and the Holy Ghost. I know full well

428

that it is not understandable to many the existence of a Father, the Son, and the Holy Ghost. They are all one, in one God. I repeat again: God the Father, God the Son, and God the Holy Ghost.

Unbelievable: satanic cults

"My child and My children, I implore you to go forward and bring the knowledge of the existence of these terrible satanic cults in your country. There are so many now, My children, that you would find it unbelievable if I could take you and show you throughout your country what is going on this very night while you are here.

"We also are distressed because of Theresa. She has been watching the carnage in the convents. And as such, she finds that her mission upon earth was not fulfilled to the fullest, that so much evil can now be corrupting the convents.

"My child and My children, I promise you after, My child, you bless the ill and infirm I will bring Theresa to you; because I know she made a promise to you to appear here this evening. That will be, My child, after you bless the ill and infirm. There are many who have come a long way to be here this evening.

"And, My child, I wish that you bring a message to D.M. of California, that We accept him in these latter days as a new disciple. That, My child, is all that We will say at this moment.

"We wish that you take three photographs, which you can divulge the contents of to the workers, and then you will proceed to the ill and infirm. And after you visit them, you will meet with Theresa."

[Pause]

Veronica - Oh, Our Lady hadn't left at all. She's coming from behind one of the boughs of the tall fir tree there in front of us, directly over to Her statue on the right side. And right behind Her, I see her - it's Theresa; I'd know her anywhere. Oh, now Theresa is floating over to Our Lady's right side. She was standing behind Her; I don't know why she

429

was standing behind Our Lady. And Our Lady is whispering something to her, but I can't hear them. Now just as I'm looking, St. Theresa is smiling; and she's placing her first finger to her lips, like this.

St. Theresa - "My sister, Veronica, I know that you are much surprised to see me this evening, as I have not made many appearances on your Shrine grounds. However, due to the urgency of the times, and what is happening upon the earth, I come this evening to bring to you a word of good news that the road to Heaven is very simple. All you have to do is be like a young child in your love of Jesus, never questioning, never casting aside, but loving Him fully with your heart.

"My life upon earth was not always easy, my sister, just as all of my sisters and brothers upon earth realize this as time goes on. However, I do say I am much disquieted of spirit by what I see taking place in many of the convents today. My life was always a life of solitude and prayer; therefore, I never lost contact with the Holy Spirit. Now my sisters in the convents are enjoying - as they think they are enjoying - all of the modern diversions that take them away from meditation and prayer.

No TV should be in a holy place

"I come this evening to ask my sisters who hear my message not to be taken over by worldly pursuits. I agree fully with the nuns in the convent that object to the television. No television should be in a holy place.

"Yes, my sister, there is much evil in the world. I always promised when I was upon earth that I would never be lackadaisical or disquiet of spirit while I was in Heaven. I will go forward to the very end of time bringing my roses to you along with Our Lady - graces in abundance for the asking. All you have to do is say, `Jesus, I love You. Save souls, save the consecrated.' That is very important.

"We are made fully aware in these latter days of all the tribulations of the world, and the convents especially. I make note of the convents, my sister, because it was my home for so many years.

The value of suffering

"Also, you will understand fully when I tell you the value of suffering. You can always offer this for the souls that need the repatriation. Yes, my sister, no suffering is ever wasted. For you must accept it in the right light, knowing that even our dear Jesus suffered upon earth at the hands of those He loved. But one thing you know now is He never gave up loving them, even as they recrucified Him.

"And even now, my sister, there is much grief in Heaven. And I know that Our Blessed Mother sheds many tears daily upon the world because of the present abominable conditions. Man is fast heading for a cataclysm. Soon - we all know of the coming of the Ball of Redemption upon mankind, and it is now heading fast in.

Heaven: work much harder

"It is the will of the Eternal Father that the sheep be gathered by those who have become disciples in the latter days. The sheep must be gathered and separated from the wolves that are roaming now. Therefore, we ask you to even work much harder at your apostleship. All will be on the side of the Eternal Father in the end. But He will allow these persecutions to come upon you. Accept all as Jesus did when He was upon earth."

Veronica - Now, I see Theresa is moving over, and she's whispering to Our Lady. I can't understand what she's saying, but she's whispering. And Our Lady is pointing high up into the sky.

Oh, Jesus is coming down now, again. Oh, He's coming up now, and He's going to be at Our Lady's left side. He's raising His hand now, like this, and making the sign of the cross: In the name of the Father, and of the Son, and of the Holy Ghost. Now Jesus is mentioning - I can't hear it; it's like the rustling of the wind. But Jesus is still extending His hand, and He's going over now to Our Lady's right side.

And Theresa has moved back into the sky. I don't know - she seems to have left the circle of light, and she seems to be moving back into the clouds. I do want to tell you at this time, that as I can see her, Theresa has on a brown gown and a creme - colored cape, and she has a black mantle around the top of her head. Theresa is smiling. I know that I must have described her that she is - as I can see her here. She's very clear. She's stopped now moving, and she's standing there behind Jesus and Our Lady.

Now Jesus has hesitated while I was talking about Theresa, and He's going over now to our left side. He's moving very slowly, and looking down all about Him. Now, He's extending out His hand and making the sign of the cross: In the name of the Father, and of the Son, and of the Holy Ghost.

Now Our Lady is coming over, and She's taking the Rosary from about Her waist, and She's making the sign of the cross: In the name of the Father, and of the Son, and of the Holy Ghost. And Our Lady now is touching the crucifix to Her lips and She says - She's asking me to repeat.

Pray for clergy

Our Lady - "Many prayers are needed for the clergy. Won't you, My children, help them? For many are lost; they are on the road to perdition. Please help them. I ask you as your Mother, in your merciful hearts, for My Son and the good of His Church, pray for your priests, your cardinals, and bishops."

Veronica - "We will."

Now Jesus and Our Lady are moving back into the sky. Theresa has gone into the sky; I can't see her anymore. And Our Lady and Jesus now are moving over to our right side, at the uppermost limb of the fir tree on the right side. And They are standing there, and nodding. Our Lady is saying:

Our Lady - "We will be here the rest of the evening, until the last soul has left."

Veronica - Yes.... Yes.

Our Lady - "Continue, My child, to read the Bible well.

Man is casting it aside or rewriting one to fit his own carnal nature. You must not, My children, rewrite the Bible, for it will be a bible of man and not of God.

"Sit back now, My child, and rest."

Veronica - His gown is a beige color, very rugged; it looks like very rough material. I don't know what it is. I hope it isn't what they call "sackcloth." That's what Our Lady once said that They use when They are doing penance for people. Sackcloth and ashes, or something like that. And that's just what it looks like, that's the only way I can explain what Jesus is wearing there.

A cure for Aids - A promise from God if…

20th Anniversary of Our Lady's Apparitions at Bayside -
June 18, 1990

Veronica - Oh, the blue lights are appearing all about
Our Lady's trees now. You know, it is Her signal that She's
coming.

Oh, there's a bright light - oh, like a ball of light, coming
through the sky at the top. And I can see our Lady is standing on the ball, just like She did twenty years ago! Oh, the
ball seems to represent the earth. And Our Lady now is
looking all about Her; She's coming very close. In fact, now
She is drifting off of the ball, and the ball is going to our left.
And Our Lady is coming down to the top of the tree directly
behind Her statue. Our Lady is looking about Her.

Oh, She has on the most beautiful gown! It's white and
luminous. She has a mantle that extends all about Her head
and down to Her feet. And now as I look at Our Lady's feet,
I can see She has delicate petals of roses now coming from
Her feet and coming down our way; they must be special
graces.

Oh, Our Lady is so beautiful! I don't know - I want, I
wish She would appear to everyone to see Her like She is.
It's the most beautiful sight in the world!

"I love You Blessed Mother! Yes."

Now Our Lady is looking, and She's putting Her first
finger to Her lips, like this. That means to listen and repeat.

Our Lady - "My child and My children of the world, I
am very elated at the response from which the workers for
Our Lady of the Roses responded, and have brought in
many new souls. Before the evening is over, you will understand what I am telling you, My child.

"But first of all, I come also for this reason: there is much
going on in the world now that is evil. As I tried to make
you understand several years ago, that satan has entered now
into My Son's Church upon earth, and satan has control now
of all the medias. Therefore, it is up to the parents now to

434

see that their children do not become polluted and lose their souls.

"We're all aware in Heaven of the drug epidemics, the volcanoes erupting; but you see, it was to come about. Now I hear, I hear the prayers of many who call out for mercy because they have the disease called AIDS. My child, make it known to them, in writing, that this was a direct admonition by the Eternal Father for their performing terrible acts of indecency upon earth that destroys the young souls who follow them. I am talking, My child, about homosexuality. It is rampant all over the earth.

"You have to understand, the Eternal Father is not a punishing God. However, He is most interested in the children; and it appears now that the sins of the parents are being placed upon the shoulders of the children. And, O My children, if I could only show you the list that the Eternal Father has for Him to go through the world and bring these souls back. The sins of the parents shall be visited upon the children.

"O My children, I hear your cries because of the AIDS epidemic in your country and the world. I plead for you to the Eternal Father, to remove this plague from among mankind. And I have great news for you this evening, My children. The Eternal Father and My Son have made it clear to Me that if man will repent of his ways that have given - been given to him by satan, We will see that you do have a cure for AIDS.

"A certain length of time has been set about by the Eternal Father. It is the time for you to repent and to do penance for the sins of the world. There are many who are willing to help Us now. We watch you all, My children, and We will guide you to an eventual victory. All who suffer upon earth because of satan's battle with them will know that through Our mercy not all will be lost.

"I want you to stress, My child, the existence of hell and purgatory. It has been forgotten by many. Even the priests in My Son's churches have overlooked this essential knowledge. In fact, some now mock it as being untrue. My child

435

and My children of the world, please believe Me. I have been through purgatory. I have been through hell. And I tell you all: please, do penance for your brothers and sisters who do not have the way.

Man created by the Holy Spirit

"The way to Heaven is really led by a scene of love. The Eternal Father is not One to punish you, for He wishes to save all mankind. He has created you. Even that, My child, is being discarded. I hear the voices that cry out that you were not created by the Holy Spirit. But I say unto you, men of the cloth, too, that you do not follow your religious beliefs. You've given them up, and you work among precepts for man.

"Do not make My Son's Church a place just for man. It was, through the Eternal Father's plan, to be a place of honor and direction to set you on the road to Heaven and not lose your road and wind up in hell or purgatory. You see, the enemies of your God believe that if they can confuse you and make you believe errors, they will take over completely. But I know, My children, if you listen to Our direction, that will not happen.

"I say again: if man will repent of his sin and discard the homosexual life they're living, I will give them a cure for AIDS.

"Now also, My child and My children, there is another fact to be known to mankind, and shouted from the rooftops: the murders of the unborn will not be tolerated. You will read Job, chapter 33, verse 4: *The Holy Spirit made me, and the breath of the Almighty gave me life.* Do not listen to those disciples of satan that are trying to take this knowledge from you. All mankind has been created by the Eternal Father, in the Son and the Holy Ghost.

Change now or suffer another plague

"The existence of the Trinity, too, is being attacked. We are fully aware of what is going on. And I can tell you, My children, if there are not immediate changes, another plague shall be sent upon your country and other countries of the world. Eventually the suffering will be so great, if man does not repent, that there will be few souls left on earth.

"You are in great danger at this time, the United States of America. I tried to warn you some time ago that you allowed a two-legged demon to enter into your country. Do not believe an atheist, because they do not hold the truth.

"O, My children, I know that you had struggled through the years to bring this message from Heaven. And I know, My child, Veronica - I relieve you of one cross; but you cannot be free of all suffering, because it is needed. You will understand this, My child, when you enter through the golden doors.

"Yes, My child. Yes."

Veronica - "You don't want me to repeat it? Am I going that soon? Oh, yes. Yes. Yes."

Our Lady - "Now, My child, one more message to mankind, and I will let you rest, because My Son wants to speak to you. He has grave concern of what is happening to the earth."

Veronica - "Yes. You don't want me to repeat it? I understand. Yes. Yes, I will."

Now, Our Lady is going over to Her left side, our right side, directly over the trees. Oh, She's so luminous, I'm sure everyone could see Her. She's so beautiful! And She, She is so loving that I can feel it; it's just like having another mother.

Now our Lady is going over and making - taking Her Rosary like this. She has the golden Our Fathers and the white, luminous Hail Marys, and She's making the sign of the cross: In the name of the Father, and of the Son, and of the Holy Ghost.

Now Our Lady is looking over, and She's saying:

Our Lady - "Is that a nun I see over there? Where are her garments?"

Veronica - "I don't know, Blessed Mother."

437

Convents must be free of TV/radios

Our Lady - "My child, you will also make it known that We are not happy to see the world enter all of Our convents. They discard the habits; they're no longer maidens of purity. And I tell you, My children, that cannot be tolerated. Modernism must not be a way of life for Our dedicated. Our nuns must have discipline, My children. Do not bring the world into the convents. I ask that the convents remain free of all television and radios, and return to their prayer life.

"Also, My Son wants it known that He is fully aware of the prayer life, the lack of prayer life, in His dedicated. They have become men of the world, and no longer men of God. I know this shocks you, My child, but it cannot be avoided. There has to be a change.

"Satan is working now throughout the world. 666 is upon mankind, and it cannot be denied. There will be murders abounding, and the abortions shall continue until mankind receives a just chastisement.

"I have wandered throughout the world all these earth years, trying to warn mankind that if they love My Son, they will honor Him. But now many are dishonoring Him. The Eternal Father will only put up with this for a short time, and man shall receive a just punishment.

"Now, My child, you go forward now, and My Son will await you. But I wish that you enter by the circle, the infirm circle, because there are some asking Me now, and praying that you come over to them.

"Yes, My child, you go, and My Son shall speak to you when you return."

Veronica - Now - oh, over the tree right there, Jesus is coming through the trees! I didn't notice that, I was so busy watching Our Lady and the ball rolling away.

He looks just beautiful! Jesus has on a red velvet gown, with gold trim all around the edging. And I can see His sandals, like He has brown sandals, but they are tinged in gold around the sides of the strap. And Jesus is looking all about Him. It's kind of windy up there, because His hair is blowing back and forth.

438

Our Lady now has motioned to Him, and She's pointing towards the infirm circle. Now Our Lady is saying - She has placed Her fingers to Her lips - to listen and repeat.

Our Lady - "My Son is going with you, My child, this evening."

Veronica - Oh!

"Yes. Yes, I'll go there right away."

Oh! Oh! Oh! Oh, Jesus is following me; He's coming with me to the circle. That means there's going to be cures.

[Pause]

Veronica - Now Jesus is standing directly over the tall tree by Her statue. He's been there quite awhile. I looked back a couple of times when I was by the infirm circle, and I noticed Him standing there very patiently. He had followed me over, but then returned to the center of the exedra.

Now Jesus is looking all about Him. He is extending His hand, like this, and making the sign of the cross: In the name of the Father, and of the Son, and of the Holy Ghost.

Now Jesus is going over towards His left, our right. He's going farther over to the edge of the trees, and He's looking down. Now He's motioning over to the right side, and I see a map. There's a map forming in the sky; it looks like the East Coast of the United States. I can see Florida, I can even see Long Island. But then I see something very ominous. Looks like a big red bear, like in that bear picture. But you know - I know that country. It's in Cuba!

"What is the bear doing in Cuba, Blessed Mother?"

Now Our Lady is coming back. She was also watching at the infirm circle, although Jesus accompanied me over there. But now They're pointing up, and I see another country that goes across the other side of the world, it looks like. I don't know to - I'm not too familiar with the areas of the nations. But I believe it's U.S.S.R. - the Russians, you know. And Jesus is shaking His head yes. So in the meantime, He's placed His finger to His lips, like this, which means that He wants me to repeat.

Jesus - "My child and My children, I have very little to say that could solace Me for the evil I see prevalent upon the earth. Your generation have become perverse and indoctrinated by satan, until the cults of satan now are well stacked in your country. Your children will be the victims.

"Yes, My child and My children, I know it is difficult for you to understand, without having an actual meeting with these satanists, to see how vile they are, how they desecrate everything, and how they torment the souls of the children and those they have in their grasp.

"Protect your children! All the mothers and fathers of the world, protect your children, or they will disappear from your homes forever. Even human sacrifice is taking place at this very hour that I am here with you. How can We do anything but beg with you to listen now, before it is too late!

"There will come another great chastisement to the United States. Look, My child, and tell Me what you see."

Soviet subs going to Cuba

Veronica - Oh, I don't, I don't know where it's at, but I see a lot of boats. Oh, they're submarines; they're just coming to the surface. And they look like they're off the coast. There's a map; Our Lady's pointing towards the map of the United States. Hmm. I live on Long Island, and that sure look like they're coming off the Long Island area.

Now, as though they have been alerted to something, they're going now down into the water. But they are going now under - I can see; Jesus has me watching them - under sea, and they are going to Cuba. I know it's Cuba. Now what they're doing in Cuba I don't know, but it appears that the Soviets are arming them.

Jesus - "Yes, My child, you have spoken well and directed it as I wanted you to. Now this has to be known.

Warn President of two - legged demon

"My child and My children, make it known to your Senate and your President that the two - legged demon, as We address him, has entered upon your country; and they are not to be deceived, for he has a major plan against the

United States.

"Yes, My children, many prayers are being said at this time throughout the world. The nations are suffering. So therefore, We expect you to understand what may be a riddle, but easy to understand. The United States must not give up its forces in Europe, or the other nations, for they will be disarmed and We will be attacked."

Veronica - Oh! Oh, that's terrible! Oh, yes, I see it - houses just coming down. It's awful! They're shooting! Oh, my goodness!

Jesus - "My child, at this moment, because of the perversity of the world - the world's children - We see it necessary to stand back and watch a just punishment upon mankind.

"I do not want you to think that We are a punishing God. We love Our children, but sometimes, with - the Eternal Father knows the hearts, and they have them hardened. Man has given himself over to pursuits of the flesh, and as such, he condemns his soul to hell or purgatory.

"Pray, My children! Pray for the souls in purgatory. Many shall be there until the end of the world."

Veronica - "Yes, I did see hell already, Jesus. Yes, Our Lady took me down. I really - yes. You want me to go down there again? If You want me to, I will."

Jesus - "Well, don't be affrighted, My child; just look. I am holding your hand."

Jesus and Veronica visit hell

Veronica - Oh, my goodness! I see we're, we're drifting into a hole - like, it's like a large hole in the ground. And I hear, I hear people screaming - they're screaming at the top of their lungs! But I look down now; Jesus said to look down. I want to look up, the heat was so great, I don't want to look down. But I will. All right.

Oh, my! Oh, I see - I know they're demons, hanging on the walls of the cave - like place where - that Jesus says is part one of hell. And all these souls - there must be thousands of them - are screaming! They're screaming and crying, and they're like burning embers! Their bodies are float-

441

ing all around; they have no weight. It looks like bodies, and yet it looks like coals burning!

"Oh, Blessed Mother and Jesus please bring me out of here!"

Oh! Oh, it's terrible!

"Yes."

Jesus - "My child and My children, if I could show this to everyone, you would be on your knees every day. I ask you now to pray for the souls in purgatory, and even pray for those who are in hell.* But of course, My children, unfortunately, hell is eternal."

Veronica - Yes.

Jesus - "Now, My child, My Mother made it known to you about the AIDS epidemic. There will be a cure for mankind as soon as We see the legislative bodies and those politicians of the world, who are at this time causing the abortions with their monies and their funding, especially in the United States - abortion is murder, and as such you shall all be condemned as murderers at the time of your death unless you repent now of your sin! The Eternal Father sends each and every soul upon earth.

Increase your Rosaries

"Repeat again, My children, to those hardened hearts and deaf ears that will not listen, no matter what. They must be then attacked by prayer. They have to be - prayers so numerous that I would advise that the Rosary be upped in every home. Parents, your children - please, have them pray!"

Veronica - "Oh, yes. Oh, yes. Oh, yes."

Jesus says the Eternal Father wants you to remember what His Mother said, that you will read Job, chapter 33, verse 4. And it says - Yes. It says: *I am the Almighty. I am the Almighty.*

Jesus - "But first, the Spirit of life made me, and the breath of the Almighty gave me life."

Veronica - Therefore, you shall not destroy a creation of the Eternal Father! Penance will be great upon mankind for

442

anyone who condones these heinous acts! [abortion]

Priest becoming men of the state, not men of God

Jesus - "Veronica, My child, I repeat again, though My Mother had been throughout your country for years now, with Her messages: We ask that the priests take themselves out of this world. They are becoming men of the state, not men of God. I accept the degradation and the present confusion in My Church upon earth, but I want a change back to normal. Man is building a church without the Eternal Father.

"Please, My children, pray much, for there will be another great chastisement upon mankind. My Mother had been able to hold it back, but I am sad to say that it is the will of the Eternal Father. During this chastisement, many souls will go into Purgatory.

"The road to Heaven is a narrow road. So many never go on it. They become seeped in the pleasures of the world, not thinking that one day they will come over the veil. There isn't a creation upon earth that doesn't have to appear before the Eternal Father at the end of his time."

Veronica - "Yes. I'm to go back?"

Jesus - "Yes."

Veronica - "On the, on the left side?"

Jesus - "Yes."

Veronica - "Yes, I will."

Jesus wants me to go back on the left side. There is somebody over there that He wants to cure. I, I'll do what He says. But He said to go to the left side, over there, and to continue blessing the infirm, because He has His reasons. There is going to be a cure there.

[Pause]

Veronica - ...maybe around four or five feet high up there, and They are looking at everyone.

Now, Our Lady is taking Her Rosary, which was about Her waist, and She's making the sign of the cross: In the name of the Father, and of the Son, and of the Holy Ghost. Now Our Lady is nodding towards Jesus, and He's moving

over to our right side. Now He is putting His hand out - let's
see if I can do it - like this, and saying:

Jesus - "In the name of the Father, and of the Son, and of
the Holy Ghost."

Veronica - Now Our Lady is moving over towards Jesus,
and there's whispering. It feels like - it sounds like the whispering of the trees. I can feel it, but I can't hear the words.

Oh, it wasn't meant to be. Oh! Oh, Our Lady - yes.
Our Lady says:

Our Lady - "You can expect much difference of opinion
on Our message this evening. However, you are to give it
out exactly as I gave it to you.

"We're not going to leave the grounds until the last soul
has left, so don't be afraid. We're watching."

Veronica - "Yes. Thank you."

Oh, **Our Lady** - that light is so brilliant about Her. I'm
sure if it wasn't God's will it would blind me, it's so bright!
And now Our Lady is going back up on the ball, and She's
standing there. But all around Her head now - it looks like
the stars have come out. There are stars! I almost feel like
counting them, the way they're around Her head. One, two,
three, four, five, six, seven, eight, nine, ten, eleven, twelve.
Twelve stars around Her head. I never saw that before on
Our Lady. Our Lady is smiling.

Now She's pointing over to the infirm circle. Oh, my
goodness! Do you know She's holding Her hands down
like this - like this, but the rays are going over our head;
they're going back over our head. I don't know what Our
Lady is doing there, but She certainly has something very
mystical going on because those rays are still radiating from
Her fingers, and going over our head. And now I can see
part of them; they look like little slivers of glass - I can't
explain it, little slivers of glass, like, coming from the rays.
And they're, they're falling down all about us. Our Lady
calls it "graces". Oh!

"Yes. Yes. I will. When? Oh, all right. Yes. Yes. Oh, all
right. I won't mention it."

Hmm. My! Hmm. Our Lady is standing right there. She's going to remain with Jesus until the last soul leaves the grounds you know. She looks so beautiful. She has on Her - you know, Her white gown. Oh, It, it is so beautiful, it almost makes my heart stop. It's such a wonderful feeling, you know, of love. Our Lady, Our Lady acts just like a Mother for everyone, you know. And yet She looks very young.

In a series of locutions to Veronica, Our Lady, thankfully, enlightened us on this matter. The following is a summation. The majority of the wording and terminology is that of Our Lady.

In the principal locution on Wednesday night, June 20 at 9:15 P.M., we were told to remember the Apostles Creed:
I believe in God the Father Almighty, Creator of heaven and earth; and in Jesus Christ, His only Son, our Lord; who was conceived by the Holy Ghost, born of the Virgin Mary suffered under Pontius Pilate, was crucified, died, and was buried. He descended into Hell: the third day He arose again from the dead; He ascended into Heaven, sitteth at the right hand of God the Father Almighty; from thence He shall come to judge the living and the dead. I believe in the Holy Ghost, the Holy Catholic Church, the Communion of Saints, the forgiveness of sins, the resurrection of the body, and life everlasting. Amen.

When Our Lord descended into hell, He was releasing the penitent souls from purgatory, or Part II of hell.

In the description above, Jesus explains to Veronica that she is in Part I of hell. Part I of hell is the abode of the damned, hell eternal. Part II of hell - what we on earth call purgatory, and theologians often refer to as stage two - is the abode of the penitents. It is these souls, the souls of the purgatorians, that we are to pray for.

Our Lady lamented that there are too many false opinions on hell and purgatory coupled with mankind not even being interested in our preparing for eternal life.

In another locution on June 21, 1990, Our Lady reminded us again: "There will be differences of opinion; however, you will be enlightened to combat them." She recalled, also, that many saints have been enlightened on this subject.

By repeating Himself in this sentence, Our Lord is emphasizing, underscoring the fact that purgatory is in hell. St. Thomas Aquinas, in his Summa Theologica, actually articulates the same truth: "Therefore the fire of purgatory is the same as the fire of hell, and hence they are in the same place." (App. 2 Q. 1 Art. 2).

No doubt, Our Lord's intent is to raise our consciousness and stimulate additional discussion, research, and prayer on this very important doctrine.

"A Great War will erupt suddenly"

The Guardian Angels & Eve of Saint Theresa - October 2, 1990

This morning at 10:12 a.m. the Virgin Mary, bathed in a bright, luminous light, appeared to Veronica in her bedroom.

Our Lady wore a very beautiful white dress, made of what appeared to be fine silk. The dress was so long Veronica couldn't see Our Lady's feet, and the sleeves reached down to Her wrist. In addition, Our Lady wore a blue sash around her waist. Overall, the dress was loose - fitting and very billowing.

Our Lady's head covering was white. It fell below her shoulders, and it matched the material of Her dress. Veronica saw only a little bit of Our Lady's hair, which was a light brown color.

Veronica noted Our Lady's extreme modesty of dress and the similarity of Her attire as that shown in the famous and outstanding miraculous photograph: *Our Lady in the Sky*.

Our Lady - "Dear child, you will write just as you receive it from Me. You will be unable to go to the holy grounds this evening; hence, you will disseminate this message to the world as soon as possible!

"I, your Mother, and Protectress of the world's children, do beg you now to repent of your sins against the teachings of the Eternal Father - sins of the flesh and the intellect.

"A great war will erupt suddenly, such as has not been seen from the beginning of creation. Countries shall disappear in moments from the face of the earth. Will you not listen to Me before it is too late? You all do not have much time left.

"I come to you as a Protectress of Peace. Unless you repent of your abortions, the murders of the unborn, and return to lives of prayer and contemplation of the mysteries of the Eternal Father, given by writings - the Bible, the Book of life and love - I cannot save you from the conflagration that lies ahead.

"Prayer, penance and atonement.

My tears fall upon all mankind. Will you not solace Me, My children?"

Comet to collide with earth

21st Anniversary of Our Lady's Apparitions at Bayside -
June 18, 1991

Veronica - All about the sky now, if you look far up
beyond the trees, you can see the beautiful blue lights that
always come before Our Lady and Jesus. Now the whole
sky is opening up. There is a tremendous white light. Oh,
it's so beautiful! There's no way to explain it. It's beyond
anything I have ever seen in my life. It is so beautiful! Now
at the center of the light, I can see Jesus and Our Lady. Oh,
They're coming down together.

They're very small figures now. I can't see the clothes
that well, the light is so bright. But They seem to be stepping out from the circle of light, and coming down through a
clear sky. It's very clear; a light blue tinged in a, sort of red,
a very beautiful, satiny red. Now Our Lady and Jesus are
floating. They don't walk, They're carried like on the wind.
There is no way to explain it. They are so beautiful.

Now Jesus and Our Lady are close enough, I can see
what They're wearing. Our Lady has on the most beautiful
white luminous gown. It's shining! It's all made of light.
And I can't see Our Lady's arms, though I can see Her fingers; they are covered with voluminous sleeves. And Our
Lady's gown goes way beyond Her feet now. I cannot see
any of Her feet, no sandals or anything yet. It's the way the
gown is draped about Her feet.

Now Jesus is nodding, and He's motioning to Our Lady
to go forward on His right side. Now Our Lady is coming
down much closer to the ground than I've ever seen Her
before, and She's nodding yes. She's standing there now,
and Her left hand is motioning up, like this, into the sky.
And Jesus is following Her fingers of light; there's light pro-
truding from all of Her fingers now as She holds them up.
And Jesus is coming down; I can see Him very clearly now.
He's almost standing on the tip of the highest tree there in
front of us. If He goes any farther down, He's going to stand

449

right on top of the tree!

Oh, Jesus has on a most beautiful red velvet gown, tinged in gold all about the edging. And I can see Jesus' slippers; His are a tan. It looks like some type of an animal skin, but they're tan, and they're open. His feet are very evident in His slippers. And Jesus is nodding His head yes, and He's smiling.

Now He's motioning to Our Lady, and She is coming closer to Him. She's just drifting over, as though She's carried on a slight breeze. I can hear the rustling of Her gown. It is so beautiful. I feel that I can reach up and touch Our Lady, but that's not to be, just now.

But Jesus now is looking at me, and He's placing His first finger to His lips, like this:

Jesus - "Listen, My child, and repeat after Me, word for word what I have told you you would be enlightened upon this evening. I want you to know, My children of the world and My child, Veronica, that no evil is ever triumphant; I will turn all evil to good.

Communists seek to assassinate Pope

"Listen, My child, and repeat after Me: the Brown Bear of communism, of red orientation, will seek to devour the Holy Father, your Vicar the Pope, by assassination, and place on the seat of Peter a communist puppet known by all as the White Bear.

"My child and My children of the world, disaster lies ahead in Rome if this happens. Will you not, in your goodness of heart, go forward and give this message to the world. Approach your clergy. Write to Rome! Beg them to listen before it is too late. Your Holy Father, the Pope, is in great danger.

"They cannot outwit the Eternal Father in Heaven. He knows their hearts, and they will not succeed if you will act upon this and keep a constant vigilance of prayer going throughout the world for your Pope, the Holy Vicar in Rome.

Man has become obsessed with sin

"O My children, I have great news for you this evening, but it is not one to bring a smile to your face. The world has not progressed as the Eternal Father has asked. Man has become obsessed with sin. I tell you now, in the Trinity, that unless you listen now, your world will be planet-struck.

"I know, My child, this frightens you, but it cannot be held back much longer. The world has become polluted with all forms of "ism:" communism, atheism, humanism, all destructors of the soul. Man has not progressed as the Eternal Father has deemed them to be. They are now agents of hell. Many have sold their souls to get to the head. Souls are falling into the abyss as fast as the snowflakes that come from the heavens.

TV not to be in homes of the just

"Parents, I ask you now to get rid of the infernal machines in your homes! I warned you through many earth years that this will be a point of destruction for your children. If you at least—I ask at least, which is the least you can do, is to monitor what your children are seeing. Satan has created the infernal tube. Heaven did not deem it to be in the homes of the just.

Comet in our atmosphere

"My child and My children, you will keep a constant vigilance of prayer going throughout your world, because, I repeat again, near the throne of the Eternal Father, He views a ball so immense, so beyond all man's speculation, that it will destroy over three-quarters of the earth. It is in your atmosphere. It has been noticed by few, but the few seek not to bring fear to the hearts of mankind. They do not know that it is the Eternal Father who now will guide that Ball.

"As in Sodom and Gomorrah, mankind had gone down and given itself over to satan. I ask you now, My children, to turn back from your road to destruction, for you will be surely destroyed as was the time of Sodom and Gomorrah.

Homosexuality shall not be condoned. It is an abomination in the eyes of the Eternal Father, and as such, is condemning many to hell.

"Guard your children, mothers of the world, guard them against the forces that are loosed upon earth. It is truly the final battle raging with Lucifer.

"You ask Me, My child, why does this have to come about? I say with sadness—I say this for Myself and My Mother: We have used every means possible to bring mankind back onto the right road, but he has chosen his own path, one built on pride, arrogance, and lust.

"My child and My children, you must awaken now before it is too late."

Veronica - Now Jesus is looking over to Our Lady. Oh, She's crying. I never saw Our Lady cry before. She's crying.

"What's the matter, Mother?"

Our Lady - "My child, My tears fall upon you all. If it weren't for My pleading constantly for you before the throne of the Eternal Father, this would have come upon mankind sooner. But now I can tell you that those who will be saved will be counted in the few. Those who will be saved will be counted in the few.

I come to you as a Mother of peace

"My child and My children, I come to you as a Mother of peace, a Mother of love. And above all, I want you to turn to My Son and have courage in the days ahead. Many will fall from the Ball of Redemption.

"Now, My child, I know that this has been a time of great stress for you. It is urgent that the message from My Son be given to the world."

Veronica - Now Our Lady is taking the most beautiful crucifix from within Her gown. It's made of solid gold, and She's holding it out like this, and She's making the sign of the cross: In the name of the Father, and of the Son, and of the Holy Ghost.

A refuge in Our Lady's heart

"I bless you all, My children. I seek in My heart to find a refuge for you all. I am not despairing at this time at the knowledge that was given to Me by the Eternal Father. I have great hopes for rescuing most of My children. But the Eternal Father makes it known that the numbers saved will be counted in the few."

Veronica - Now Jesus is putting His hand out, and He's making the sign of the cross, like this: In the name of the Father, and of the Son, and of the Holy Ghost. Now Jesus is touching His lips, which means to listen and repeat:

Jesus -
The end is not as far as you can see;
Already there is apostasy.
Man cast his lot and gathered the coals
To stoke the fires that burn the souls.
The days are numbered the hours are few;
So work and pray and try to do
The work that's given in the light
Until that sad time when all is night.

"My child, I asked you once, for the knowledge of the world, to repeat what I now give you, the Exhortation:

Dear Holy Father, worried and wan,
Will struggle with Jesus to gather the sheep.
The pastures are rich but the sheep grow thin;
For the souls have succumbed to the sickness of sin.
You'll need reinforcements from Heavenly shores,
So deep is the darkness of earth's shallow mores.
All hearts must ascend in true supplication
To avoid the sad fate of divine devastation.
Dear Holy Mother, your Mother of love,
Does beg you to heed these dire words from above:
His heart is torn by careless surrender
Of too many souls that don't try to remember,
The Father, the Son, the Spirit of life
Smite in the heart with the human knife,

453

Of hate, greed, avarice, vanity:
All indications that sin is insanity.
What more must you do but place the full load
Of saving all souls on the few who are bold;
Who'll stand up and fight for all Heaven's glory,
And meet with Pope Paul at the end of life's story.

"Now My child, you will sit back and remember what I have told you now. This cannot be revealed at this moment, but listen to Me carefully."

Veronica - Yes…. No…. Yes…. It's very frightful…. Yes…. I will. I can't stand it.

Jesus is looking all about Him at the people. Our Lady is wiping the tears from Her eyes. Now I can see Her much closer, and She's happy. I know how She felt. Our Lady cried the whole time that Jesus was talking. Our Lady still—though She's smiling She still looks very sad.

Our Lady– "My child and My children, I will not elaborate on My Son's discourse with you tonight. All I can say is I stand before the Eternal Father and continuously plead your cause before Him. If this was not to be, you would have received the Ball of Redemption already. I do not know, My children, how long I can hold the hand of the Eternal Father back. I can say at this time, that when the Ball of Redemption hits the earth, only a few will be saved."

Veronica - I see a…I see a—it's a huge ball. [Veronica speaks with great distress.] It's covering the whole sky; it's going into the trees too. It's huge, it's smothering! And there's fire, too, there's fire all around it. It is huge! As far as I can see, it's a whole mountain, like, falling on us—a rock, with fire. Oh! Oh, no!

Now it's becoming dark. The darkness is covering the horrible sky; it was all afire. It was huge!

Now Our Lady is coming forward. She's by Herself. I don't see Jesus, but Our Lady is standing now over the tree directly in front of us, and She's touching Her fingers to Her lips:

Our Lady - "My child, We did not seek to make you affrighted. However, it was necessary to bring to the world

454

the dire consequences if man does not make an immediate reparation to the Eternal Father for his offenses against the Father. I could go on, My child, for hours of earth time, giving to you these offenses, for throughout the earth-years they have multiplied.

"Man has not progressed on the course that the Eternal Father placed him on earth to follow. Therefore, it's in due time, in time known to the Eternal Father in His will, there will be sent upon mankind a Ball of cleansing. I cannot remove His hand near the Ball, My child.

Pray for poor sinners

"Pray for poor sinners who are falling into hell now as numerous as the raindrops or the snow fall upon earth. Hell is overflowing, and hell is eternal. I weep for these poor souls, for they had too few who prayed for them.

A monstrous machine

"Mothers must exercise great care over those placed in their trust by the Eternal Father. The abomination that hits the very Heart of the Eternal Father committed on the earth is the murders of the unborn. At the time of conception, the Holy Spirit makes the child, and the breath of the Almighty gives it life. Therefore, you shall not create a monstrous machine throughout your world! That is what it's become: a machine! No human could conceive, but satan, of this act of the sacrifice of the unborn! Murder in the eyes of the Eternal Father!

"My child, I understand how this has made you ill. However, We depend on you and others to actually help during this crisis. One of the final warnings are being given throughout the world to mankind. I ask you here this evening, My child, because of the short time that is being given for mankind by the Eternal Father."

Veronica - Our Lady now is backing up into the sky, and She's pointing up with Her hand, like this. And over on the right side of the trees, I see Theresa! Oh, Theresa! Saint

Theresa! Oh, she's smiling; she knows me. And now she's touching her fingers to her lips.

St. Theresa - "You will try, my sister, to send the poem messages throughout the world. They will fall into the hands of those who are deemed to receive them.

"Mankind has already been marked by the cross of the Savior, or the sign of the horn. Yes, my sister, man has created a monster upon earth, and the Eternal Father will seek to remove it.

Homosexuality an abomination

"As in the time of Sodom and Gomorrah, the Eternal Father was most merciful until His mercy could no longer be contained. So will it be for those who partake of the abominable acts of what you call upon earth, homosexuality. It is an abomination in the eyes of the Eternal Father.

"Parents must guard their children, even from their teachers. Many are now direct agents of hell, though they walk in human bodies. Protect your children with their sacramentals. Teach them!

"My children, I ask you, please—I call you my children because I have looked down upon earth for many years, and I feel that I have a firm attachment to the souls upon earth.

Parents to be held accountable

"Please, I ask you mothers, monitor your children's lives. Do not be an escapist, running from home and finding pleasures of the world. Bring a prayer life back to your children before it is too late. You will be held accountable for the fall of the souls of the children. Therefore, I ask parents throughout the world—with love, and good leadership in the household, your children will not fall as prey to satan."

Veronica - Now Theresa is backing up. I can see now her habit more fully. It was blowing behind the tree before. But she's smiling; she's still smiling. Now she's taking her hand and she's pointing over to right side of the sky. Our Lady is standing there, and She's reaching out now....I can

456

feel Her fingers. They were so soft, so beautiful. But there's an electricity—I can't explain. It just comes from Her fingers and it radiates right down your arm. It's so beautiful.

Now Our Lady is smiling, and She's pointing upwards. And I notice, I hadn't noticed that Theresa—I'm sorry Jesus, I didn't notice your were standing over there between Our Lady—Jesus is between Our Lady and Theresa. And He's whispering something, but I can't hear; I guess I'm not supposed to hear it. He's saying something to Our Lady. And now He's turned to Theresa. Oh, I see. I think He's telling them to mover farther back into the sky.

Now Jesus is touching His lips:

We have made Our home upon these grounds

Jesus - "We are not leaving, My children. We have made Our home upon these grounds. Therefore, all who come here to be solaced, I will be here. My Mother and I shall stay here even unto the conflagration.

"Now My child, you will sit back and continue with the photographs. Three will be taken, the first will remain silent, and the others you may look into."

A momentous Fatima breakthrough
Jacinta told Mother Godinho famous Third Secret

Feast of St. Thérèse of the Child Jesus - October 3, 1991

Early this afternoon at 12:12 p.m., as Veronica lay on her living room couch resting from her debilitating health problems that have plagued her for years, St. Thérèse the Little Flower suddenly appeared to her.

The popular French Carmelite nun, who was declared a saint by the Roman Catholic Church in 1925, and whose feast day is traditionally celebrated today, revealed only her face to Veronica. She was bathed in a brilliant light, with a youthful, contented, yet serious appearance about her.

"Honor the Salutation at all times: Glory be to the Father, the Son, and the Holy Ghost.

"The peoples of the earth have not progressed satisfactorily in the plan for the salvation of their souls. Prayer, penance, atonement we ask of all. The time grows short.

"All honor and glory must be given to the Trinity. Hasten, hearken, and listen, for I shall not repeat this call again."

St. Thérèse then proceeded to reveal a great secret to Veronica

Now as we are in the latter days, when many things hidden are to be revealed, St. Thérèse has made known through Veronica an astonishing revelation: little Jacinta actually confided the famous Third Secret of Fatima to Mother Godinho, a pious lady who was caring for her during her final illness. Mother Godinho was instructed by Jacinta to pass a message on to a certain priest designated by Our Lady, but tragically failed in the mission entrusted to her for reasons disclosed by St. Thérèse to Veronica. (Actually, Veronica is not permitted to release all that St. Thérèse revealed to her, but the report below represents a significant portion.)

Two nights later, restless and unable to sleep, Veronica

was pondering the startling facts which St. Thérèse had brought to light, when she was inspired to seek out Brother Michael of the Holy Trinity's monumental and authoritative work on Fatima, The Whole Truth About Fatima.

Canon Formigao

Volume II contains a detailed account of the little seer's painful illness and her death. Much of the information that follows is taken from this source.

In Appendix II of Chapter IV is the text of a message given to Canon Manuel Formigao by Mother Godinho at Jacinta's request. Canon Formigao was Jacinta's confessor, a very holy priest, and he believed wholeheartedly in the apparitions.

Appendix III lists what the author calls an "apocryphal message," one which he and other Fatima experts believe may not be authentic. It is in the form of a letter sent by Mother Godinho to Pope Pius XII in 1954. The letter does exist, and was actually sent to the Holy Father, but Brother Michael in his commentary lists several reasons for doubting the truth of the message.

St. Thérèse sheds new light

The clarification given by St. Thérèse sheds new light on both of these messages from Mother Godinho, and shows that instead of two separate messages, there was really only one message and it was to have been given in its entirety to Canon Formigao, who would then pass it on to the Holy Father.

Maria of the Purification Godinho was the directress and foundress—hence referred to as Mother—of the orphanage of Our Lady of Miracles in Lisbon, where Jacinta stayed for some time during her final illness prior to entering the hospital for surgery. Mother Godinho had gathered a community of women around her who lived as religious but without the habit and without official recognition.

Mother Godinho's dream

She had hoped to found an order of nuns; a dream she
clung to with tenacity all her life, despite the fact that her
bishop repeatedly refused to grant her the necessary authorization. Apparently, he felt that despite her obvious good
intentions, she did not possess the qualities needed to carry
out such an undertaking.

Shortly before her death, Jacinta had asked repeatedly
that Canon Formigao be called to her bedside, explaining
that Our Lady had appeared to her and given a message to
be related to him. Unfortunately, the good priest was unable
to come at once, and arrived a few days after her death.

Meanwhile, Jacinta, knowing she was to die, gave the
message to Mother Godinho, asking her to relate it to the
Canon.

Upon the arrival of Canon Formigao, Mother Godinho
met with him and repeated to him the first part of little
Jacinta's message. It concerned a chastisement predicted for
Portugal, especially the city of Lisbon, in punishment for the
sins and crimes committed in that country.

As Mother Godinho later testified, Jacinta explained that
the prophecy of the Blessed Mother was conditional: "If
there were souls who would do penance and make reparation for the offenses done to God, and works of reparation
were instituted to make satisfaction for crimes, the chastisement would be prevented."

Burning ambition

How these words must have rung in her ears, and fueled
her burning ambition to found a religious order! There
would be no problem with Mother Godinho in relaying the
first part, as it fit neatly into her plans. However, the remaining part of the message would be a different story. She kept
that part as her own secret, seeking all the while her bishop's
approval.

Finally, in 1954, at the age of seventy-six, she wrote to
the Holy Father, Pope Pius XII, daring to present her pro-

posed order of Franciscan nuns as the express wish of the Blessed Virgin Mary, tailoring the remainder of the secret message to fit her dreams.

The first two paragraphs of her letter were devoted as an ardent appeal to the Holy Father for the authorization she so anxiously sought. When we omit all of the many references to herself and her proposed religious order, what remains— from what we have learned now—is a distorted message undoubtedly mingled with truths, but definitely devoid of the heart of the Third Secret.

A critical omission

We know that the little seers of Fatima were subjected to all sorts of ridicule and disbelief, as well as endless questioning from the authorities. Mother Godinho realized this and knew to make public all of the very startling message Our Lady gave to Jacinta might make her the object of similar scrutiny, jeopardizing her goal of founding an order of nuns. Therefore, according to St. Thérèse, she omitted the most crucial part of the message.

We all know that the famous Third Secret of Fatima was supposed to be publicly revealed in 1960, but to this day lies buried in the Vatican archives. Unknown until now is the fact that it was also buried in the ground in 1960 when Mother Godinho went to her grave!

Yes, according to the revelation of St. Thérèse, the Third Secret was an integral part of the final message Our Lady gave to Jacinta for Canon Formigao. Knowing she would die soon, Jacinta related it to Mother Godinho to pass on to Canon Formigao.

Mother Godinho was only an intermediary; the message was not intended for her at all. However, grasping at a chance to further her own ambitions, she gave the good priest only the part concerning Portugal and kept the rest to herself.

The antichrist

February 1920, what is really the essence of the Third Secret of Fatima: that 666, satan, the forces of antichrist, would enter the highest realms of the hierarchy in Rome beginning in the year 1972!

Given human weakness and Mother Godinho's obsession, it would seem that this prediction of an event which would unlikely be fulfilled in her lifetime actually served to increase her delusion. Of course, she never did get her order.

Our Lady told Veronica that for this infidelity Mother Godinho suffered in purgatory for eight years, until the year 1968.

Pope Paul VI - a prisoner

Now we know from Our Lady's messages that beginning in 1972, Pope Paul VI was kept a virtual prisoner in the Vatican. Some ecclesiastics in the highest positions of the hierarchy, being infiltrators or having fallen from grace, drugged the good Pope, censored his mail, forged his documents, and finally staged an impostor to complete their sinister plan.

Pope Paul himself gave the world an indication of this terrible situation on June 29, 1972, when he said: "From some fissure the smoke of satan entered into the Temple of God." Though it was generally unknown at the time, he truly had much to suffer. While Fatima watchers were waiting to see a great catastrophe in the world in the year 1972, as predicted in Mother Godinho's letter, Pope Paul was beginning his silent, heroic martyrdom as he watched Jesus' beloved Church being demolished from within.

More prayers for priests

It is precisely a horrible situation like this that underscores the importance and necessity of prayer and more prayer for cardinals, bishops, and clergy of all ranks. And so it is since September 1972—not coincidentally—we have conducted a Holy Hour for priests every Sunday.

In conclusion, one can only wonder what the scenario would be today if only Mother Godinho had followed through correctly. Would the Third Secret have been publicly released by now? Would this knowledge have thwarted or at least hampered the evil designs of those who sought to destroy the Church—a Church today which lies in shambles? Would the Second Vatican Council been even considered, much less convened? Or if it was, with a different agenda?

The story of Fatima

During World War I, on May 13, 1917, in the first of six apparitions, a beautiful Lady who said She came from Heaven appeared to three shepherd children, Jacinta, Francisco, and Lucy in Fatima, Portugal.

Two months later, the Lady gave the heart of Her message to the three children, in what is known as the great Secret of Fatima. This Secret is composed of three distinct parts. The first two parts have been released by the Church as related to Lucy:

"As Our Lady spoke these last words, She opened Her hands once more, as She had done during the two previous months. The rays of light seemed to penetrate the earth, and we saw as it were a sea of fire. Plunged in this fire were demons and souls in human form.... Terrified and as if to plead for succor, we looked up at Our Lady, who said to us, so kindly and so sadly:

"You have seen hell, where the souls of poor sinners go. To save them, God wishes to establish in the world devotion to My Immaculate Heart.

"If what I say to you is done, many souls will be saved and there will be peace. The war is going to end, but if people do not cease offending God, a worse one will break out in the reign of Pius XI.

"When you see a night illumined by an unknown light, know that it is the great sign given you by God that He is about to punish the world for its crimes, by means of war, famine and persecutions of the Church and the Holy Father.

"To prevent this, I shall come to ask for the consecration of Russia to My Immaculate Heart, and the Communion of reparation on the First Saturdays.

"If My requests are heeded, Russia will be converted and there will be peace; if not, she will spread her errors throughout the world, causing wars and persecutions of the Church. The good will be martyred, the Holy Father will have much to suffer, various nations will be annihilated.

"In Portugal, the dogma of the Faith will always be preserved…"

(The Third Secret enters here.)

"In the end, My Immaculate Heart will triumph. The Holy Father will consecrate Russia to Me, and she will be converted, and a certain period of peace will be granted to the world."

However, it is the never-released Third Secret of Fatima* which has long been the subject of great intrigue, wonderment, and speculation...until now.

The Lady had promised that on October 13, She would perform a great public miracle so all would believe. Secular newspapers from around the world reported that while 70,000 people stood in the pouring rain, what appeared to be the sun suddenly came out, whirled madly like a pinwheel, casting all shades of color on land and people. It then plunged three separate times directly over the astonished crowd, many of whom threw themselves on their knees pleading for God's mercy.

"After about twelve minutes of this phenomenon, the sun returned to its natural place and appearance in a clear sky. The people were completely dry, as well as the ground around them. During this miracle, the beautiful Lady identified Herself: "I AM THE LADY OF THE ROSARY."

The apparitions, which are now formally approved by the Catholic Church, were an appeal for prayer, sacrifice, reparation, consecration, and especially the daily recitation of the Rosary.

*Lucy, the only living seer, now a Carmelite nun, has been silenced by her superiors on this subject.

Communism death: a ruse*

Yeltsin, Gorbachev, agents of satan, executing master plan

22nd Anniversary of Our Lady's Apparitions at Bayside - June 18, 1992

Veronica - ...left side. Over on our left side, directly over the trees, there is the most beautiful flashing of lights. They're all colors of the rainbow. And a rainbow is forming across the sky, from the left to the right side. Oh, it's so beautiful! It's something that's not of this world. The colors are absolutely fantastic! And there now, within the rainbow, I see Our Lady coming forward.

Oh, Our Lady is so beautifully dressed! I've never seen anything so beautiful. And for the first time now in many years, I see that Our Lady has Her hair showing. Our Lady's hair is a dark brown - not black, like mine, but a dark brown.

And Our Lady has on the most brilliant white gown, covering right down to Her fingers; I can barely see Her fingers. The gown is very long. It's two-piece like a cape, over a long gown that covers Her feet. I can see that Our Lady is wearing this evening, gold slippers. They're like a sandal - not a full slipper, but a sandal.

And Our Lady is smiling now. Oh, and do you know! Oh, Our Lady has on Her wonderful crown! The roses are forming all about now; there are roses falling all about the rainbow. And Our Lady has this beautiful crown. It's all gold, golden, and it sits so squarely on the top of Her head. You see, Her head is covered with a mantle on Her head, and the, the crown is set right on top of that.

But I notice now, I see two beautiful angels. One is standing now over - coming to Her right, our left side, and the other is now standing beside Her on Her left side, our right side. And high up into the sky Our Lady is pointing. And I see the most huge person! I think you'd call him a person. I know who it is by his size, but he's an angel. But

465

he's tremendous! He's covering the whole sky. That is Michael! Oh, Oh he's nodding his head. Oh, yes.

Now he's pointing down, now, to Our Lady, and he's moving across the sky without even a rustle. I hear no rustle about me; all has become very still.

Now there is gathering of angels on the right side. They seem to be of all sizes. And they go up steps now - I see steps rising high into the sky. It's like an open portal to Heaven. They are - the steps are luminous. They are of a material that is not of this world. They're formed of a light formation, but solid. And they are going up these steps now and standing and watching Our Lady; they're watching Her there. I have never seen such a guardian of angels for Our Lady. I wonder.

Now Our Lady is smiling. She looks sad, but She's trying to smile. And now She's stepping off what must have been a pedestal. I didn't notice that before because of Her gown. But She's stepping off now and coming down and over to our left, right over the tall tree, the right side of Her statue.

But up above the tree now, Our Lady is stopping; She's looking. Even in the sky it's windy, because Our Lady's cape is blowing to the right and to the left. Now Our Lady is smiling, but She has a look that's very pensive. And though She's trying to smile I can see that there is a heavy sadness hanging over Her. I can feel it.

Now Our Lady is coming forward. She's closer now to the top of the trees, and She's placing Her first finger to Her lips, like this, which means to listen and repeat.

Our Lady - "My child and My children, I come to you with a Mothers sad heart this evening. And I brought you forth, Veronica, to make it known to the world that there are dire events heading towards your country and the world. As I tried to instruct you all in the past: that you must pray much for the leaders of your country and the leaders of the nations of the world, because if you do not, this will bring on the most disastrous war to mankind. It is coming in steps, My children.

"Now I want this known to all mankind: Man does not seem to learn from his past. He goes on still making the same mistakes to his own destruction.

This Is a ruse

"As I counseled you all in the past, I said to you as quote: 'This is a ruse,' I repeat again. This is the visit to your country, the once great and illustrious United States of the world, the nation, the United States of America, the illustrious country that now is leading into a path of darkness. This has been allowed because of the dire straits of your nation. The morality has now been cast aside. Darkness has fallen upon mankind.

"Mothers and fathers, how often have I counseled you to protect your children in these days. You will find that many of those that you entrust to teach your children are bringing them into a world of unrealistic atheism. Already, My child, it saddens My heart to know that you are not, as a nation, allowed any longer to pray in your schools.

Yeltsin: The man of sin

"Do you know who is in your nation now? The man of sin. I counseled you in the past and I will warn you all for the last time that you have allowed to come in upon your nation a man who is a counterpart, an identical figure to his past successors.

"I tell you now, and I will not tell you again. This is the last time you will receive this counsel.

"As in the past, Lenin; as in the past, Stalin; and Khrushchev; and many others had tried to deceive the United States. They all felt that by trying to ensnare you with delusions of casting aside their communistic aspirations, that they had become as you, a free nation for all.

"I assure you, My children, there is no freedom in Russia. It is all a delusion.

"They seek the monies of the world from the nations of the world. And why do you not learn a lesson? It happened in the time of Lenin; it happened in the time of Stalin. And there you are all on the same road, ready to give billions of monies that should be given to those of your nation and the free nations of the world.

"Do not be deceived, My children, Russia is not free. It is a cosmetic act to delude you. Lenin and Stalin used the same tactics, My children. Why do you not learn from your errors?"

Veronica - Our Lady now, Our Lady is crying. Now She is looking up and She says:

Lenin and Stalin in hell

Our Lady - "My tears fall on you, My children. And I must give you also the conclusion to what I have spoken to you of. Lenin and Stalin are not with Us. They were cast off to meet with their god, the prince of darkness, satan.

"It behooves Me to say, and it tears My heart in anguish, that they did not seek to be saved. For those who approach them, as they will approach you in your nation and try to convince you that their way of life without the Eternal Father was a way that should be adopted by all - no, My children!

"I repeat again, because this will be My last discourse to the world on this subject: This man, these two men are of the same creed, color, spirituality - or should I say, My children, lack of spirituality. They have a father who is the father of all liars, so what does it make them, My children - Lenin, Stalin, Khrushchev, Yeltsin, Gorbachev?

"That is the same old plan, My children, and those leaders of your nation are as blind as they were in the past. I tell you for your own good, My children of the United States of America, that once was a nation under God and indivisible, that you will fall! If you do not come out of your slumber now, you will fall!

Storing armaments in other nations

"For it is their plan to subdue you, once they get the billions that they need in aid, to bring up the economy and buy more armaments. They have not disposed of their armaments, My child and My children. They store them in other nations. They have the same goals as their forefathers.

"Now, My child, I know it has distressed you much to hear this. It is not easy to have to tell you this, My child, because it places a great burden upon you.

"And I must also warn you that you must be very cautious of how you guard your home in the future. Do not be affrighted, My child. I will be with you always. My Son will not abandon you.

"But you must remember, My child, for all the suffering that is received, think and read your Book of life and love, the Bible. Know that all who followed My Son had suffering, whether of mind, spirit, or body. It is not an easy road, My child, to Heaven. It will never be an easy road."

Veronica - ...Now Our Lady is pointing up to the sky, high into the sky. And I see, I don't know what it looks like; it's some kind of a bomb or.-.no, no, it's not a bomb. It's a submarine.

Now Our Lady is coming. She had gone over to the right side by the trees, but She's coming over, and She's pointing again. She says:

Our Lady - ..."My child, I'm showing this to you. Your country is not free of submarines. They're planning their attacks. They're guarding you, so that you do not receive the truth, as they will try to destroy you now, My child."

Yeltsin and Gorbachev: Agents of satan

"You will see that you keep a constant vigilance of prayer going throughout your nation and the free nations of the world. We say free nations, because they are the ones that are being planned to fall and capitulate to satan's consort. And I say it in plural: consorts, Yeltsin and Gorbachev.

Veronica - Now Our Lady is placing Her hand down on Her chest, and She's looking very upset. I don't think I have ever seen Our Lady so upset. And now She's touching her lips, which means She wants to speak.

Our Lady - "My child, I did not bring you here for an

469

easy mission, as I tried to explain to you before you left. However, it had to be.

"You see, My children, as long as there is someone praying the rosary in your country, We will be here to guide you. But accept Our counsel now. Do not wait until it is too late. America the beautiful will fall!

"Sit back, My child, and wait. My Son wants to counsel you on a very urgent matter."

Veronica - Now Our Lady is going over to our right side, that's Her left side. And She's going high into the sky now, and standing over on the side. I can barely see Her because of the trees. I can see through the trees that She's standing over on our right side, and She's pointing over now to our left side. Oh! Oh, there - Jesus is now coming through the sky. He's moving very fast across the sky, over to Our Lady. Now He's reached Her side, and He's whispering something to Her. I can't hear it.

Now Our Lady is touching Her lips; She means for me to listen. And Jesus has moved over, outside the tree range. Our Lady is now between the trees and the sky, but Jesus is outside the range of the trees. And He's now touching His lips.

Jesus has on a beautiful red cape. Oh, it looks like it's made of velvet. It's a velvet cape and a beige gown underneath. And His feet look quite bare, except that I can see the two straps of a sandal, a beige-colored sandal. It looks like some kind of animal skin. I can see Him very clearly. Now He has no covering on His head. And Jesus' hair is quite long, quite long, and it's quite caught up in the wind now, blowing back and forth. Now Jesus is smiling, and He's now touching His lips, which means to listen.

Jesus - "My child and My children of the world, as My Mother counseled you in the past, We will not abandon you. We will be with you as long as there is a Rosary recited in your country. I say now, My children, these Rosaries must reach throughout your country and the world, for the world is fast hurtling towards a great catastrophe for mankind.

"I assure you, My children, that those minds that have

reached beyond the clouds seeking the impossible have now grasped the atoms from the heavens, that were once given to the Eternal Father. They were His possessions, and now they are using them to destroy the earth.

"In time, My child and My children, you will understand what I mean, if We cannot turn Our beloved children of the earth. And I say, no matter how dark the souls now, you, My children of the earth, are beloved to Us, and We do not want to lose one to satan.

"My child Veronica, you have seen many photographs miraculous taken on the grounds, the sacred grounds. They may guide you in what I have to say.

Stratosphere covered by Demons

"As I discoursed with you in the past, I told you that satan and his legion of demons are loosed upon the earth. If you go up to your stratosphere now, there is hardly an inch that is not covered by the demons.

No life on other planets

"Do not look for land, do not look on another planet for life, for there is none. Only those who delude you tell you this. What you saw, My child, in the past, called a flying saucer by mankind, We have allowed many to see this. They are transports from hell. However, We have never seen a demon, My child, who has taken on a human form, except through the spirit.

"No, My child, We did not allow you to see any formation of any nature on this celestial object that you saw many years ago by the doors of St. Robert Bellarmine church. Therefore, do not be deluded that there are beings coming from other planets. This is not true, My children.

"What you have now, because of the sins of mankind, all hell is loosed upon earth. Satan now knows that his time in growing short. That is the truth, My children, I tell you all: your time is growing short.

"All that is written in the Apocalypse of St. John - the

471

Apocalypse must be read by everyone who is knowledgeable enough to understand.

Parents must take responsibility

"And as for your children, I say this as your God: every parent that does not take the responsibility of teaching and raising his children, and giving them to others who are possessed by these demons that are loosed now upon your earth - I say possessed, and that is only a kind word. I could discourse with you much farther, but I'm afraid, My child, your heart would not be able to accept this."

Veronica - Now Jesus is telling me something, but He doesn't want me to repeat it.

"Yes. I will. I will."

Now Our Lady is coming over to Jesus, and She's standing there and looking all about Her. Now there's an angel coming over to Our Lady, a beautiful angel. I don't think it's Saint Michael. This angel is not as large as Michael, but the angel has a huge bouquet of red roses in its arms. It looks quite human in a gown. I don't know its substance, because I can't see any feet and whatever it's holding the roses by. Its arms are just filled with red roses.

And now Our Lady is motioning to the angel, and he's coming right over the trees here, and he's throwing these red roses all about here at the Shrine, all about, and to the left, and to the right. Now he's being joined by another grouping of angels high above Our Lady's head, and they have an assortment of yellow roses! And now they are starting to throw them down on us. I can feel them on my head.

Oh! And now the beautiful whites are showing up, and they look like little children. These angels look like little children. They're very, very tiny; they look like infants. And they also are throwing the roses. And for their strength they're throwing them very far! Oh, they are falling all the way down outside the circle. Oh, it's beautiful! They look like cascading stars. That's the only way I can explain it. I have never seen anything so beautiful in my life! And if that is Heaven - is what Heaven is like, that's for me and for everyone.

Our Lady is smiling. And now She says to continue with the Rosary.

Our Lady - "And I will speak to you once more this evening, My child. It's more in counsel to mothers.

"Now sit back and join the prayers. We're not leaving, We're going to stand right there. If you look up, you will see Us."

Veronica - Our Lady wants the Rosary said. Join the Rosary.

[Pause]

Our Lady is coming back over the trees.

"I'm sorry, Our Lady. I had almost forgotten that You were coming back. I was so engrossed with the people in the infirm circle. However, I know that You 're not crying so badly now. There's much more - pleasant I was very upset, seeing how badly You felt before."

But Our Lady now is touching Her lips, to listen and repeat.

Directives from Heaven

Our Lady - "My child and My children, We are very pleased at the manner in which you are getting out the Directives from Heaven. Do not slacken your pace. There are many souls to be reached. They must understand the signs of the times.

"The biggest threshold for the United States and other countries of the world is if they are willing to go forth and overcome the evils within their own countries. The morality has fallen in most nations of the world now, and this cries to Heaven for either repentance or punishment.

"Know, My children, that We do not wish to see disaster come upon mankind, but the Eternal Father wills and operates sometimes, My child, in most mysterious manners.

"However, I say at this time that all parents will be held responsible for the fall of their children's souls. Do not expect them to leave your homes and to be taught in light and truth, for the demons are raging now all about you. All

473

hell is opened wide now, and you know that that means that the onslaught is at hand.

"Therefore, We ask all parents to keep a steady hand on their children. Bar them from all the insensitive acts being committed on the diabolical tube of satan, your television. I ask if you cannot monitor your sets, to remove it immediately from your homes, for your children will even resort to murder if they continue to watch the programming.

"I, as your Mother, understand the difficulties of the world. You must remember, My children, I was also among you and one of you, and I understand all that is going on.

"And through the countless years that I've overlooked everyone from Heaven with My Son, this is not unusual to find a country in the state such as yours is, My child.

Pray the Rosary always

"For We have great hope that if the peoples of the world and the United States will say the Rosary in their homes, and also to reach out to their brothers and bring them the light in truth of the nature of God the Father in the Trinity - that is, the Father, the Son, and the Holy Spirit, also known as the Holy Ghost.

"My child and My children, you understand it is a known fact that when the morals of a country fall, that country will be destroyed in one way or another. Wars are always a punishment for man's sins.

"So I ask you, My children, to keep a constant vigilance of prayer going throughout your world and through your churches, and even if you have to approach your pastors.

"Many pastors have fallen away from the truth, and they are like black sheep now among the white sheep. However, I say to you, prayer can overrule all evil. Keep a constant vigilance of prayer going throughout your country and the world. It is the only resort now that you have against the evil.

"Do not remember these things that happen that will drive you to absolute despair in your world. Think over this, My children, and know that things are allowed upon earth by the Eternal Father for a reason, for the eventual good of all. I know that you cannot understand this fully, My child, but you will in time.

> "Therefore, when you despair, say:
> O My Jesus, forgive us our sins,
> Save us from the fires of hell.
> Lead all souls to Heaven,
> Especially those most in need of Your mercy.

"Now, My child, you will all continue with the prayers of atonement. I will be with you always, as will My Son."

Veronica - Now it's growing very cloudy, and it seems like Jesus and Our Lady - Jesus was standing there while Our Lady was talking, and I didn't have the opportunity to tell you this, but They're both carried now back up into the sky in a series of clouds, beautiful white clouds. Now I can't see Them anymore, though I can see the clouds in a distance.

*Trick; stratagem; wile

The Antichrist ready to emerge
U.S. to fall to one-world tyranny

Vigil in Honor of Our Lady of the Rosary -October 6, 1992

Veronica -... directly over Our Lady's statue, up to the tree on the right. The branch is extending out. I can see Our Lady coming through the sky. Oh, She's just beautiful! There is no way I can explain the brilliance and the beauty of our Blessed Mother. And She - I, I was quite weak when I arrived here, but I feel stronger already. I feel that Our Lady - oh Our Lady is smiling now, and She's nodding Her head. She's looking all about Her, and She's pointing down to the crucifix.

Now Our Lady said to extend the crucifix high up into the air, that She is going to place upon this crucifix the power of cures and conversions: cures of the body and cures of the spirit. Now Our Lady is extending Her hands out, like this. I can see Her very clearly.

People have asked me in the past how young or how old does Our Blessed Mother look. She looks really young, and I, couldn't put an age upon Her.

The light is touching my left hand for some reason, the light from Our Lady's fingers. They're coming down through my fingers now, and I feel the rays now from Her left hand - that's on our right side - coming down now onto the grounds. But they seem to go beyond us here over into the rope I can see - though my back is to it, I can see, Our Lady is showing me the rope behind us. I do believe it's the infirm circle.

Yes. Our Lady is nodding, yes.

Now Our Lady is looking all about Her. And She's extending Her hands out, and She's saying:

Our Lady - "Pray a firm Act of Contrition, one Our Father, and One Hail Mary.* And you will look up again, My child, as I will stay here. This is for reason."

Veronica - In the name of the Father, and of the Son, and of the Holy Ghost. Amen.

Our Father Who art in Heaven, hallowed be Thy name; Thy Kingdom come; Thy will be done on earth as it is in Heaven. Give us this day our daily bread; and forgive us our trespasses as we forgive those who trespass against us. Lead us not into temptation, but deliver us from all evil. Amen.

A firm Act of Contrition: O my God, I am heartily sorry for having offended Thee, and I confess to all my sins, because I dread the loss of Heaven and the pains of hell, but most of all because I love Thee, my God, Who art all good and deserving of all my love. I firmly resolve with the help of Thy grace, to confess my sins, to do penance, and to amend my life. Amen.

O Mary, conceived without sin, pray for us who have recourse to Thee. O Mary, conceived without sin, pray for us who have recourse to Thee. O Mary, conceived without sin, pray for us who have recourse to Thee.

Our Lady is smiling, Oh, I only wish we could get a portrait of Our Lady as She's smiling now. You feel - the feeling is beyond human words to describe. She's so beautiful and you feel so relaxed, as though you don't have a problem in the world. Our Lady has an aura about Her, and I'm certain that this aura is encircling many upon the grounds.

Now Our Lady is looking about Her, and She's touching Her fingers to Her lips like this, which means to listen and repeat.

Our Lady - "My child and My children, and especially you, My child, Veronica, I brought you here this evening because I have a dire and urgent message for the world at this time. The Eternal Father, His hand now is getting ready for a chastisement upon mankind. I say this to you all: do not be afeared, for all who have remained faithful and true shall escape this punishment.

"My child and My children, as it was in the past, so it shall be. There are many now foul deeds being committed upon the earth that cry to Heaven for retribution. The leaders of your country have lost their way, My child and My children. They are now making sin a way of life.

"In My past, My own experiences, My child and My

children, I went through great sorrow, and saw the persecution set upon My Son by the world. Now He is made to suffer anew, and I join Him on His new cross.

"Yes, My child and My children, mankind is recrucifying My Son. They have forgotten; they have lost their way.

Study your bible

"My child and My children, the pages are turning fast in the Apocalypse. Have you listened to My counsel in the past, My children? Are you making an effort to study the book of life and love, your Bible?

Sodom and Gomorrah destroyed by fire

"There is not much time left. Many will be taken from the earth. I will not at this time, My child and My children, go into full detail. However, I want you to stress the knowledge of Sodom and Gomorrah. You saw in the story of Sodom and Gomorrah, its obliteration by fire and brimstone. Can you expect less of a trial? My children, you do not listen; you do not learn from your past. You are on the same road to perdition!

"The Eternal Father has watched with hope. And with His convictions now coming to the point of great knowledge to Him, He finds that at this time many must be taken from the earth.

"Your word of homosexuality can be explained by the story of Sodom and Gomorrah. Read in your Bibles or consult your clergy. Find yourselves, My children, a humble, pious clergy. Many have fallen away from the Faith. Many have sold their souls to get to the head. And this, My children, I say of all denominations!"

Veronica - Our Lady is looking about Her, and now She's taking...I, it's very sad. She's taking the coverlet around Her shoulders, the cape, and She's wiping Her eyes. Now I can see Our Lady is struggling very hard for composure. This is very hard upon Her. Now She's looking at me, and Her eyes are boring right into my eyes.

Not one shred of paper

Our Lady - "My child, you must bring all past messages to the fore. Soon you will be unable to deliver them upon the grounds. Therefore, I ask that not one shred of paper be discarded, for it will be needed.

"My child and My children, your children are leading lives without direction or knowledge of eternal life in Heaven. Sin has become a way of life in your country and many countries of the world, little children led astray by their elders.

Secret conference being held to exterminate Pope

"My child and My children, you will continue to pray for your Vicar in Rome, Pope John Paul II. At this very moment, there is now being held a conference, in secret to the world for his extermination, and to place upon the Seat of Peter the despot.

"Yes, My child, you've heard that word before, the 'despot.' I say it for reason.

The Antichrist

"You will continue to pray a vigil of prayers for the clergy of the world. Darkness has descended upon My Son's Churches upon earth. Whatever shall become of you all in the chaos that is fast coming to your country and other nations of the world! There will soon enter upon your world a despot. Number two, I call him. But many have named him, and the Book of life refers to him as the Antichrist.

"Yes, My children, you will recognize him by his deeds. Many will sell their souls to him to get to the head, but all that is rotten will fall eventually. No matter what the struggle to keep the light in your country and the world, you will go forward as soldiers of light, carrying your banner Faithful and True, in the face of adversity.

"My child and My children, I had promised you relief from the suffering now being inflicted even on little children, of AIDS. This will come in due time. This is actually based, My child and My children, on the acceptance of mankind of the Eternal Father and My Son as their leaders.

Find bibles published before '64

"You must all obtain a copy of the Book of life and love, the Bible. Do not accept the new mods. Try to find in your bookstores the old Bibles, My children, for many are being changed to suit the carnal natures of man. I repeat, sin has become a way of life.

"My child and My children, if I could open up the sky above Me and show you a picture of the tears that fall upon you! It's truly raining teardrops from heaven. For many of you are blind to what lies ahead. There will come a time of great tribulation upon mankind. Will you be able to persevere during this time?

Sacramentals never to be removed

"My child and My children, I have given you - I should say, My Son and The Eternal Father, have given you your armor. You must keep about you at all times - at no cost you must remove from your bodies your crucifix, the St. Benedict medal, and your Scapulars. I say this for reason.

"Now, My child, this week you were placed in great trial. I want you at this time to explain to others just what transpired when you removed your protection."

Veronica - I do? It's embarrassing.

Our Lady - Yes, My child, reach out to the world. You were allowed to go through this crucible for a reason."

A lesson learned

Veronica - Well, last week on Monday, I had to go to St. Charles Hospital for tests - seven different tests. Blood tests, EKG, everything you could think of, I went through there.

However, when I first arrived, they said to me, "Take off your medals and your Scapular." The lady seemed to know the Scapular. I said to her, "I really don't want to take off my protection". She said, "We're here to protect you. Here, let me have them and I'll put them in your bag." So off she took them.

Now I was at a terrible position of either losing my tests and giving her an argument because she was a very stern individual. So I said nothing at that time and she went forward and made her tests.

All right. Now I was there quite a while in the hospital, as you understand when you go through those tests and wait, and wait, and wait. Now at that time then, when I was finished, I was quite hungry, and so was Arthur. So we took off for a McDonald's along the highway for breakfast.

Well fortunately, Our Lady and Jesus held back what was to happen until we at least had finished our breakfast. But unfortunately for the others, who had just arrived, they were at a disadvantage. Because as we finished the cup of coffee a man ran to us and said, "Leave here in an instant. The place is going to blow up!" I said, "What?" And then I smelled gas. I knew there was something wrong.

Well, everyone started running, and I mean they ran out of that building with me fast ahead, and Arthur, and my bag, and we jumped in the car and took off. Because you could smell the gas exuding out of that pipe.

Well, I found out later - but this was only the beginning - I found out later that these men who had a big crane had chopped up the gas pipe and out came the fumes. And if somebody had lit a match in that place, because the fumes were all around us, we would have went Boom! So I got outside in the car and I said, "Oh, thank you Jesus, Blessed Mother."

Well, I guess the old boy figured I'll still get her so I arrived home thinking now I'm safe. O yeah?

I noticed that my dog had been eating a lot of bones and things and left little slivers on the floor. But they were only tiny little slivers. I say this for a reason. But my dog liked these milk bones. They were a sort of a pinkish brown color, if you know your dog . He's a poodle and he loved milk bones . So he gets those.

However, I was sweeping up the floor, with some popcorn that Arthur had dropped, when all of a sudden I said, "Gee, what in the world am I eating? What am I eating?" But in the beginning, I had a feeling I was going to choke, so I opened my mouth. There - what was in my mouth, what was in my mouth but two large chunks of dog biscuit! Now, I'm not eating dog biscuits. So I said, "Ah-hah! He's still after me." And I said, "And I know what it is."

Because you see, Our Lady let me go through this so I'd learn a stern lesson. And She wants everyone to know about this. And anyone that doubts this, I'll prove it to them.

Because my husband came running in, and I said, "They're trying to choke me or something". "So what is it?" says Arthur. I said, "Dog biscuits in my mouth, big pieces!" "How did they get there?" "I don't know", I said, "but then I think I know."

So I ran right in, got my St. Benedict medal out of my purse that I had forgotten to put on in all the excitement, and also the Scapular. And I assure you I don't care if they have to tack it to my nose the next time! I'm not taking off my Scapular and my St. Benedict medal for anyone, including your crucifix, also.

So you can see Our Lady allowed this for reason. And I feel that - you know it was a little embarrassing to come forward, but Our Lady said She wants others to know this because there will be others who will have this experience if they are not protected with their Scapular, the St. Benedict medal, and a crucifix.

Now Our Lady is smiling.

Our Lady - "You see, My child, the world would have nothing if man was not free to speak out."

Veronica - Now Our Lady is looking about Her, and She said to listen carefully.

Our Lady - "My child, you understand the Eternal Father is most merciful, and My Son does not want the world to be destroyed. However, great tribulations shall be set upon mankind. Sodom and Gomorrah were destroyed, destroyed by fire and brimstone.

Leaders going direction of satan

"What can you expect upon your country which allows homosexuality to flourish and become the way of life which now your leaders under a banner of truthfulness and faithfulness to his God, have now torn down that banner and is going in the direction of satan.

"Laws are being made now to protect the offenders of God, the homosexuals. Mankind will have a banner ahead. There will be tribulations set upon the world before My Son returns to gather His own. Yes, in time many will be removed from the earth. However, there will be a tribulation before that moment.

"My child and My children, keep a constant vigilance of prayer going throughout your country and the world.

"And My children of the earth and the once-beautiful United States of America, do not sell your souls to get to the head! Money has been called the root of all evil. Already the young are being tarnished, their souls corrupted by their elders.

Enslaved by despot

"What, O what, My children, can you expect from the Eternal Father? My Son constantly pleads your cause before the Eternal Father. However, the time is growing short. That's why, My child, I brought you here this evening in your debilitated state, as an act of mercy to the world, to turn from their path of destruction. Your nation, the United States, shall fall to the despot, and you will be all enslaved by him!

"I know, My children, many of you who hear My voice or My words will say, 'How can this happen to us?' But We heard that, the Eternal Father has said Himself that He heard that many years ago when He sent prophets to warn Sodom and Gomorrah, and they, too, did not listen.

If you swerve . . .

"So now, My children, you will go forth as soldiers for

Christ, My Son. If you swerve in your course of dedication, you can lose your eternal soul. Is this not worth fighting for, My children. Go out as soldiers of Christ! Carry the banner called Faithful and True!

"And do not be swerved by the works of mankind. Because what is coming out in your press is controlled, My children, throughout your country and the world. You must pray to be enlightened, so that you will not be deluded by the forces of evil loosed in your country and other nations of the world.

"Now, My child, you will sit back, and I want you to take several photographs of light."

Veronica - "May I decipher them publicly?"

Our Lady - "Yes, My child, you may. It will save time."

Veronica -... is going back into the sky. Oh, She looks so beautiful. Our Lady is smiling, She's looking all about Her. It must be quite windy up there, because Her cape - I didn't tell you, She has on a beautiful blue cape. I guess you'd call it a cape; it goes all around Her head and down the sides. And She has a cream-colored gown on with a blue sash. I don't think I have ever seen Our Lady in a blue, a light blue cape before, but it looks just beautiful.

Now Our Lady is touching Her lips.

Our Lady - "I am not leaving, My child; I will stay here. And if I interrupt you, you will understand that there is a mistake in the deciphering. If I do not interrupt you, you will go ahead."

*Veronica explains that the Blessed Mother requested (something Veronica knew intuitively) that she not recite this prayer outwardly in Her presence, hence the omission. She prayed it internally, while repeating out loud the ejaculation O Mary, conceived...Through God's providence, Our Lady is demonstrating the absolute necessity of knowing and praying these fundamental prayers, but as Veronica looked on, Our Lady characteristically asked that she not recite the Hail Mary outwardly, a prayer that rightfully exalts Her.

Upon deeper reflection, the reason for Our Lady's modest

behavior becomes even more apparent: the preeminence of Her virtue of humility, a sublime example for all to imitate. This point is reinforced later in the ecstasy when Our Lady would state privately to Veronica: "I am the Mediatrix between God and man." This also explains the curious absence of Our Lord this evening, Who clearly wanted to defer to His Mother, to Whom He has entrusted this special Mission in these latter days(Genesis 3:15).

Clergy in dire need of prayers
Falling into purgatory, hell

23rd Anniversary of Our Lady's Apparitions at Bayside -
June 18, 1993

Veronica - Oh, I can see the Blessed Mother coming
through the sky. Her figure was very dark, as though She is
coming through a great darkness. I have a sensitivity about
the darkness around us-are we really surrounded, as a globe,
in darkness now?

Our Lady is coming forward. And I saw Jesus, but He
has sort of gone back into the dark clouds there to remain,
for reason. Now Our Lady is coming forward. Oh, She is
so beautiful! Oh, She absolutely sparkles tonight. She's
looking about Her.

And Our Lady has on a beautiful white cape; it's bordered
in gold. I never saw that before. It's very beautiful. And of
course, Lady has on Her long cream colored gown. Oh, She
looks absolutely beautiful! Our Lady appears to be very tall
tonight. Maybe it's the way She's standing. And I can't see
Jesus anymore. He seems to be like in a haze on Her left
side, our right side.

Our Lady is looking all about Her, and Her mantle on Her
head has slipped a little back where I can see Her hair. Her
hair appears to be quite dark. And Our Lady is smiling now,
and placing Her finger to her lips, which means to listen and
repeat.

Our Lady - "My child and My children, I come to you as
a Mother of Grace; and as a mother, I cannot evade the truth
with you. I must give it to you for your own protection.

"The Eternal Father - I have had to go before Him and
plead your cause time and again, for He wishes to bring the
great Ball upon mankind. In His reasoning, His all-knowing
reasoning, He feels that too many souls are now falling into
hell, driven there even by some of the clergy.

If you neglect your children...

"My child and My children, I have often admonished you to guard your children in this world of darkness. You are responsible for your children's souls. As such, if you neglect them in this lifetime you cannot enter the Kingdom of Heaven, but could spend an eternity in hell or a long session in the other place of banishment, Purgatory.

"Do not laugh, O you who cannot understand the truth nor seek the truth. I say now that if you will look, My child, for Me, look into what I show you-the realm of the suffering."

Veronica - "Purgatory?"

Our Lady - "Yes, purgatory."

Vision of purgatory

Veronica - Oh my goodness! I have never heard such a din- the screaming and the wailing. And I see people; they're clothed, but they're floating. I don't know, it seems to be endless. They're being tossed back and forth, and all I can hear is screams and moans. Oh my goodness!

"Oh, Blessed Mother, don't make me look. My heart will stop, it's so frightening!"

Our Lady - "My child, come closer to Me. You understand there are three realms: Heaven, purgatory, and hell. I allowed you to look upon purgatory, and I understand your . Because-tell, My child, fully what you have seen."

Veronica - "I have seen miters: bishops, and even several cardinals. And then I see a whole score of priests with their cassocks- they're still dressed in their garments-that they are moaning and pleading. Now Our Lady is placing Her hand before my eyes. It is frightening. It's one of the most frightening things I have ever witnessed."

Our Lady is touching Her lips, which means to repeat.

Bishops and priests in purgatory, hell

Our Lady - "My child, I want you to understand and bring to the world the absolute truth and reality of this realm. There are miters and there are cassocks there. I want you to tell the world that there are clergy who are now going into purgatory, if not some in hell, because they are misguiding the sheep.

"The Eternal Father wants to set upon the world the Ball of Redemption. How long, My children of the world, can I beg for your reprieve? Why don't you listen to My voice? I have traveled throughout your world through many earth-years, pleading with you to turn back from your ways of destruction.

"Clergy in My Son's houses, you must show more honor to My Son. There are some who are a disgrace to their profession, leading others into ways of sin. Oh ye of little faith, why do you debase the young? You who have given themselves over to worldly pleasures and defamed their profession shall not enter the Kingdom of Heaven.

No special passport

"My child and My children, We have asked you on numerous occasions to pray for the clergy. They do not have a special passport from Heaven. They fight the influence of satan and his agents upon earth, but they need your prayers. You have forgotten them. They need your prayers, I ask of you all to pray for your parish priests. Temptation is great upon them; however, they are being put to the test by the Eternal Father, and all who are rotten will fall."

Frolicking down the aisle

Veronica - Our Lady is placing Her hands upon Her eyes, and She's pointing over to the left side, Her right side. I see the inside of a church. There is a service going on. But however, what are they doing? They are skipping, like frolicking down the aisle. As I watch, I see-it is the priest, I believe, behind the altar.

He's motioning to two children to come out of the pews and go to the rear of the church. The children are hastily-almost running to the back of the church, and I see they are picking up something. Oh, it is the ciborium and the plate.

Oh!

Our Lady - "Now what are they doing, My child?"

Veronica - They are taking it up to the altar. Now the priest and the other man-

Our Lady - "The deacon, he is called, My child, the deacon."

Wearing shorts at Mass

Veronica - They are giving these over to them and the priest is now going back to his station behind the altar. Now all of a sudden he raises his hand, and a young- oh, a young woman is coming out of the pew. But oh, my goodness me! She has on a pair of shorts, and she's heading for the altar.

Now Our Lady is pointing. The woman starts to sing. Her music is not one of the church, or those accepted by God. And as she sings, the priest stands behind the altar. And in his eyes -

"Is he admiring her or admonishing her?"

Our Lady - "It looks, My child, like he is admiring her."

Veronica - The shorts she is wearing is most revealing and immodest, Our Lady said. Now that woman is now going to sit at the side of the altar, and as she crosses her legs it is a most horrible infringement on the sacred rite, for it-

"It is almost embarrassing, Blessed Mother, for me to look. Must I see it?"

Our Lady - "Yes."

Veronica - The shorts are no longer shorts. They're almost gone! And, and I can see the expression on the priest's face as he's observing this. Now also, there are two young girls about fourteen years of age sitting at the side of the altar as the priest goes forward to consecrate the host.

Our Lady - "My Son's Body."

Veronica - Now as I watch I notice now after the consecration that the priest is now taking his place on the right side in the altar at the last pew over to the right, and the deacon is going over to the left. And now-I don't believe it!

"Oh, I see it Blessed Mother! There are two young girls. Our Lady, how old are they?"

Our Lady - "Fourteen years old."

Veronica - And Our Lady is saying:

Our Lady - "Veronica, don't close your eyes. Open them and tell Me what you see."

Two young girls distributing communion

Veronica - I see people streaming forward from the pews, and they're now being given the Hosts by the two young girls. Now the woman who's standing off to the side, very friendly but immodest, Our Lady said, immodest you must say, is observing all this with a smile on her face.

Now I see a man sitting in the aisle. He's crying. He has his rosary beads in his right hand, and he's crying.

I know, Blessed Mother, how he feels. He's not of this generation which has fallen to satan. I know just how he feels. The only thing that he has to hold onto is the rosary. "

Our Lady is looking all about Her, and as I watch. She's taking Her hand and She's placing it over her eyes. I think She's been crying.

Our Lady - "My child-"

Veronica - Our Lady, I can hear Her gasping.

Our Lady - "You see what is going on. Less and less honor is given to My Son. Whatever shall become of My children upon earth? I have wandered through earth-though timeless earth-years trying to warn My children of the coming punishment to mankind.

"Now also, We give fair warning to all clergy. Should you not turn from your path of self-seeking riches and think of the souls that you have in your care to bring to Heaven, you, too, shall vanish with the fires of the Ball of Redemption."

Veronica - Now I see coming across the sky a huge ball of some kind, but it's shooting out flames. It looks huge! I've never seen anything so big. And I see what looks like a globe on the left-hand side of the world. And this globe is heading for us, and as it gets closer, it appears that this ball is larger than the earth. I don't think this has ever been seen before. I've never seen anything so large.

Now as I'm watching it's getting very dark up there. But

the light is very bright about Our Blessed Mother. She's standing there now, and She has in Her hands a large crucifix. And She's holding it up now. It's a crucifix without the body of Christ on it for some reason. And She's making the sign of the cross: In the name of the Father and of the Son and of the Holy Ghost.

Now Our Lady is looking to the right and looking to the left, and I have a feeling that She can see just about every soul that's standing on the grounds. Now She's turning and with the cross- I knew when I originally saw it, it had a corpus on it, the body of Christ. But now She has turned. When She came closer, it had disappeared and just was a cross.

Now Our Lady is turning to Her right side, and She is extending the cross up again and making the sign of the cross: In the name of the Father, and of the Son, and of the Holy Ghost. She's repeating it, Our Lady, in sort of a singing manner- almost like being in church.

Now Our Lady is crossing over to Her left side, our right side, and She's pausing and looking about Her. It's quite windy up there. I don't know if I told you that Our Lady has a white cape on, like a mantilla. But it looks like it my be woolen; it looks heavy. She has that over her head. Now She's extending the cross and making the sign of the cross: In the name of the Father, and of the Son, and of the Holy Ghost, Amen.

Now Our Lady is still terribly upset. I can see it in the expression on Her face. And She's moving back to be between the trees directly above us. Now She's touching Her lips, which means to listen and repeat.

Our Lady - "My children, it is almost too late to reach the multitudes. My heart is torn by the knowledge that many will die in the flame of the Ball of Redemption. Many will not be prepared. I have come to you through many earth-years, and how many have listened to My counsel? How many have tried to mend their ways that offend their God?

"My child and My children, especially you, Veronica, My child, make it known that your country will soon receive a just punishment for the slaughter of the young, for the abomination to their God- given bodies- will receive a just punishment. I repeat, I repeat this three times in warnings to you all who are the ones, the culprits of the world now who have been instrumental in the destruction of the young.

Bishops: despoilers of the human race

"Cardinals, bishops, priests of the order of God, if you are guilty, turn from your ways. I make no accusations by name, though the list is growing long, to the Eternal Father. You who were given the God-given grace to be leaders of the flock have now scattered Our sheep! Bishops, what has become of your vocation? You are becoming despoilers of the human race. You cannot hide your sin from the Eternal Father. Turn back while there is still time!"

Veronica - Now Our Lady is touching Her lips and She is going like this, which means to listen but don't repeat.

"Oh no!… Mercy! Mercy!… Yes… I understand. But I can't repeat it? No. No, I won't. Oh my goodness!"

Our Lady - "Now, My child, you will sit back and wait for My Son."

[Pause]

Veronica - I see a huge ball now coming through the sky. It looks like a globe of the earth. But like pinpoints, I see fires springing up. I don't understand it. It looks like the globe is on fire. And now I hear a voice saying:

Angelic voice - "The Owl have eyes fore and aft, ever watching the eagle. When the world cries peace, then shall he strike." [Veronica understood it to be angelic]

Our Lady - "Do you understand what I am trying to tell you, My child?"

Veronica - Yes. How much of this can I repeat.

In 1968 and '69 Our Lady talked to me about a great chastisement to the United States. As the leader of the world, the eyes of the world have been upon the United States, so Heaven holds the United States under bondage, in a way, for leading the world onto the path of destruction of the souls.

Yes … Must I? … All right. If you say so, Blessed

Mother. But I'm scar - I'm afraid."

Our Lady - I want you to look, My child, and tell Me
what you see."

Vision of hell

Veronica - I see a hole. It's very deep, and there seems,
to be fire all over. But in the fire I see bodies floating up and
down, and they seem to be alive. In fact ,I can see some
men and some women. I don't see little children, but I see
many men and women.

And they're floating like they have no weight, yet I can
see the outline of their figures. And the fire burns and burns
but doesn't consume them. They seem to float up and
down, up and down, but there's a din of noise that's hurting
my ears- the screaming, the pleading. But it's like they're in
a huge hole someplace beyond where I've seen on earth.

Blessed Mother, please take me out of here. It's terrible."

Now I hear the voices pleading for mercy, but a loud
voice booms back: "Too late, too late. You had your
chance!"

Now Our Lady is touching Her lips and it's growing
darker. I don't have to look there anymore. Our Lady said to
touch Her lip-

Our Lady - "Your lip, and repeat.

"What you have just seen, My child, is hell. Many have
taken away the knowledge of the existence of this abode.
Remember, My children, the truth in fact that there is purgatory and hell, perpetual torment in Hell."

Veronica - Now Our Lady is looking up to Her left and I
see, I only see wings and two angels coming down by Her.
They don't seem to have a body. I see like beautiful children's faces- what they look like, sort of like cheruby, very
pleasant looking. And I do see wings behind them but no
body. They're coming now up beside Our Blessed Mother.
Now Our Blessed Mother is touching Her lips.

Our Lady - "You will sit back now, My child and wait
for My Son. He has an urgent message for mankind."

Veronica - Now it's growing quite hazy. I can still see

493

Our Blessed Mother up there, but the darkness is closing in. Although I see a pinpoint of light on Her left side- that's our right side-and I'm going to watch the light. Now I can hear Our Lady's voice still, Her sweet voice, and She's saying:

Our Lady - "Sit back, My child, and rest."

Veronica - The light has become stationary now. It doesn't seem to be moving forward. It seems to have stopped for a reason. Now the light is moving to the center of the sky, and it's opening up. Oh. It's getting very large now very fast.

Oh, and I can see Jesus. I recognize Him now; I can see now. I haven't- it hadn't opened up enough, the light, to show me His chest or His face, but I can see His feet- He has sandals on- and His gown, which is golden cream color, and He has on a beautiful red robe with gold trim around the outside.

Now Jesus is coming forward. I can see Him fully now. He's coming to the middle tree. There are three trees right before us. In the middle Jesus is standing over it, up in the sky, high in the sky. Now He's looking about Him. And it seems to be quite windy up there, because His hair is moving.

Now there's a brilliance about Him I can't explain. He absolutely shines in the sky. It's so dark up there, but He lights up the whole sky. Now I can notice He's looking down, and now He is touching His fingers to His lips.

Jesus - "My child and My children, what more can I add to My Mother's discourse with you? She has said it all at this time. She has spent many earth years going throughout your world trying to warn mankind of the coming chastisement.

"There have been many miracles set forth upon the earth by My Mother. This We have allowed as a grace to mankind, but many have been forgotten and rejected. My Mother has at this time gone throughout all corners of the world seeking salvation for mankind. How many have listened to Her counsel?

494

"The prayer life of the clergy has fallen. Unless they return to prayer and sacrifice, give up the worldly cravings of mankind, and agree to a life of piety and dedication and fortitude, even while under attack-you will get nowhere, My clergy, by following the modes of the world. You must lead a disciplined life and give to Our children of the earth the knowledge of Heaven, hell, and purgatory. Not

"Man can defame Me very easily, but I will allow him to defame My Mother!"

Veronica - Jesus looks very upset, very upset.

Jesus - "My child, Veronica, I do not mean to frighten you. But I am in dire suffering for the abuse to My Mother. I will not accept this much longer. Unless man makes a complete change from his ways that offend the Eternal Father, We will no longer try to keep His heavy hand from upon you.

"Your country, the United States, have been graced; but your country has fallen from the pedestal that she had been placed on by mankind. Spirituality has been cast aside. Prayer life has fallen, even in the convents.

"How can you, My clergy, lead others when you have adopted a mode of humanism catering to mankind? You do not feed the spirits of My children upon earth. As such, you cannot enter the Kingdom!

"The Eternal Father never changes, My children. You cannot build a paradise upon earth. That point shall never be reached, because you are doing this without your God.

"My child and My children, I ask you all from the mercy of your hearts to pray for your clergy. They are human and as such, they can fall into error and sin. Unless you pray for them many more shall be in the hell you have seen, My child.

"Veronica, I feel your weakness. You will sit back now. And My Mother is not leaving. She'll stay over on My right side."

A killer comet hovers
At least a billion people will perish

24th Anniversary of Our Lady's Appearance at Bayside
- June 18,1994

Veronica - The sky above us is becoming very lighted.
Oh, it's in the - the light is very, very mysterious. And as it's
coming forward, it's forming a huge, brilliant, diamond,
glowing star, a beautiful star.

Now the star itself is opening up and there, as though
coming from a picture portrait - I can't place it in words
exactly, how to describe this to you - a tremendous star. And
right in the center of it - it's covering now the whole sky
above us, over our heads, and I would say also to the rear of
our heads.

Oh, and Our Lady is coming directly through that star.
She's stepping down as though She was held up on the
pedestal there. Our Lady is stepping down and She's looking all about Her. It's not still up there; there seems to be a
wind because it's blowing Her skirt back and forth.

Our Lady looks so fragile and so beautiful. And there's a
light emanating from Her. There's a light shining that makes
Her look so beautiful that there are no human words to
describe.

Now Our Lady is looking up and smiling. I, I understand
She is looking at what just went overhead and making quite
a bit of noise [an airplane]. Now Our Lady is smiling, and
She's coming down to almost now - very close to us. And
Our Lady touches Her finger to Her mouth.

Our Lady - "My child, I am coming this close because
of the multitudes. I do not in any way wish to be disturbed
by their seeing Me en masse, My child.

Five see Our Blessed Mother

"I know you have often asked Me to appear to others to
make your mission shorter. However, My child, I must go
under the direction of the Eternal Father, and He wills it at

496

this time that no more than five be given this sighting. You will explain everything that I tell you, My child, of this visit."

Veronica - Now Our Lady is turning to Her right and looking over. And now I see something that Our Lady has in Her hand that I never noticed before during all the years of the apparitions. She has a crucifix - no, not exactly a crucifix, but a cross like mine. But there's no corpus on the cross. Our Lady is smiling.

Now She is placing the cross right next to Her, and the strange thing about it, I don't see the cross setting on anything like a table. It's just suspended next to Our Lady by the air. That's the only way I can explain it. Our Lady is shaking Her head, yes. Now Our Lady is placing Her finger to Her lips.

Our Lady - "My child and My children, and especially you, My child Veronica, I wish to explain to you the urgency of calling you upon the grounds this evening.

"Your strength is not as proficient for you as in the past, My child. I would advise you to not try to do too much at one time. I know, My child, what you are saying interiorly to Me, that I do not feel that I am losing any strength. That is because what you will and what you can suffer do not coincide, My child. I will ask you in your own language to take it a bit easy. We do wish to keep you upon the earth for some time.

U.S. embroiled in another war

"Now, My child, you will tell mankind that there is a terrible punishment scheduled for the earth. If you, My child and My children, all who hear My words, will go forward as soldiers of peace this time, because - I say peace, because your country will soon be embroiled in another war.

A war to the finish

"Your prayers must rise to Heaven, and I will accompany them before the Eternal Father. Perhaps, My child and My children, there is hope for mankind. The next war will embroil many nations. It will be a war to the finish. Man has gained much knowledge, not to prevent destruction, but to maintain it for their own gluttony, their own loss of face, and for the belittlement of his fellow man.

"Know, My children, the Eternal Father watches, and We in Heaven are all knowledgeable of what is in store for mankind. The Ball of Redemption hovers now in your atmosphere. It is through the will of the Eternal Father that I come to you this evening to warn you that the Eternal Father grows weary of your reasoning, of your lack of faith, of the despoiling of your children.

"Parents, your children will one day scorn you if you do not show them a true expression of love and give them the seeds of the Faith. Without these seeds, they will be lost to mankind and to Heaven.

"My child and My children, do not be afeared at My words. I do not come to punish nor to make you grieve. I come as a Mother of truth. Heaven cannot allow the despoilment of the young souls. All parents who do not guard their children's souls as well as their bodies shall be held accountable in their last days.

"My child and My children, I often cry in My time and My trip throughout the world. I know what is in store for mankind. Several years ago I brought you the knowledge of the Ball of Redemption. Though you cannot see it now, it still hovers over the world. I ask you now, can you not turn from your ways of despoilment? Your children are suffering as they are left to roam, to make their own decisions without the guidance of the family.

Ball of Redemption sent unless

"My child and My children, please, the Ball of Redemption shall be sent upon mankind if he does not heed the measures that I have given you tonight to save your country and other countries of the world. Little children are left to roam, to make their own decisions while the parents go merrily on their way, not thinking of the souls that they

498

had to guide. Many parents have now lost their way. They have become embroiled with mankind and not God.

"Parents, teach your children the words of the Bible. Make the Bible a necessary book in your home, not something that may be given to you as a gift by mankind, but as a gift from the Eternal Father. Read this Book to your children. They are thirsting for the knowledge from God. Only you as parents can save them.

Parents must discipline children

"Do not feel, parents, that you are doing unjustment to your children when you reprimand them when they do wrong. You must keep a stern attitude also toward the rearment of your children. Many will die in the great flame of the Ball of Redemption. How many will be saved, the count is only known by the Eternal Father.

"My child and My children, please, I ask - I'm willing to beg you as your Mother to save your children and also in the end, save your own souls.

"My child, you will sit back and wait, because I have a great surprise for you in a short while, but I am now stepping back as I have a conversation with someone, My child, who you know."

Veronica - Oh, over Our Lady's side, on Her left side, I see the sky opening up and - oh, it's Jesus! He's standing right next to Our Lady on Her left side. And He's wearing a long, sort of an ecru-colored gown and sandals. I can see His feet from down here. He has on brown sandals. They look like leather; I think they're leather.

And He has on a cape, an ecru, almost white-colored cape over His gown. It's quite, it's quite a bit chilly over here. That is why I would assume that Jesus is wearing His cape.

Now Our Lady is placing Her first finger to Her lips.

Our Lady - "My child, sit back and rest. I am not finished with the discourse with you, but now you must read some very important photographs."

[Pause]

Veronica - Right now I see a large star up above the tall tree at the right side of the banner. Now this star is growing very large, an exaggerated form of the star. But oh, I can see why because the star now is covering the whole area of the trees, beyond the trees and down towards us; it seems to be increasing in velocity or whatever you want to call it, this expansion of the star.

Now oh, right in the center I can see Him now - I know who it is because He did say He would come late this evening. I know it's Jesus.

Now He's coming closer, He's coming closer now. I can see Him very clearly now. He has a beautiful golden - tinged robe about Him now. It's pulled very tight, I don't know if it's because of the wind or what, but He's pulling the gown about Him to prevent it from flying up, I guess. It looks very windy there.

And the robe over His gown has - it's tinged in some kind of fur, but it's sort of scintillating, or sort of shining. I never saw anything like that, as though there were some fragments of diamonds in the fur. I never saw anything like that on earth.

Now Jesus has come over by the tallest tree, directly in front of us there. Jesus is standing there. I can see He does have shoes on, some kind of slippers.

Now He's looking all about Him, and He appears to be smiling. That, of course, makes me feel very relieved. I didn't know why He came so late tonight, but He's smiling. And now He's placing his fingers to His lips, like this, which means to listen and repeat.

Jesus - "My child and My children, My Mother* had an urgent message for you, and I come now at this late evening not to enlarge upon it in full. All I can say to you is you must all pray more now, if not for your immediate families, but for those you know who are not in the grace.

Circle of light

"My child and My children, I do not come for a lecture to Our children upon earth. All I can say is I want and I

500

wish that all of you would pray more and by good example bring others to Us. I call all of Our children here this evening the circle of light.

A great trial soon

"There will come upon the earth a great trial soon. Many will be lost. I will not enlarge upon it because you, Veronica, I have told you countless times not to discourse on the punishment.

"Now I want you to listen to Me quietly, My child, I have something to tell you. You will not repeat it until I tell you. "

Veronica - "Yes....No. Real - Oh, no - I don't know....Does it, does it have to happen?... I understand. It is something so horrible that it can't be spoken of."

Jesus said that I must repeat that many have forgotten the warning given through countless earth - years of the coming of the Ball of Redemption. Many will die in the great flame of this Ball of Redemption. Only the prayers of those who cared for their fellow men have prevented this from coming sooner.

Go forth as angels of light

Jesus - "My child and My children, I come as an emissary from God the Father, My Father and the Father of all mankind upon earth. I wish at this time to stress anew to you that many must go forth now as angels of light - angels certainly My children, without wings, but no less an angel."

Veronica - Now Jesus is looking all about Him. He looks very calm; He doesn't seem angry or anything, just very calmly looking about. He said:

Scientists bewildered

Jesus - "You will continue, My children, with the prayers of atonement. And I must tell you the time is, in earth time, growing short. There will be a great Chastisement sent upon mankind. You will recognize this when you find out in the atmosphere a huge, immense ball of light. Do not be

501

affrighted, My child. Your scientists will be bewildered. It is the little people who will know the truth.

"Now, My child, you will sit back and rest. But remember, the message to the world is urgent. I do not want to place upon you, My child, the burden of knowing the full results"

On Wednesday, June 22 at 10:15a.m., Jesus exclaimed to Veronica in locution: "She is the Star of Heaven." In the Litany of the Blessed Virgin Mary, Our Lady is invoked as the Morning Star, symbolic of Her brightness and preeminence in Heaven.

The end of the Bayside Message.

These Last Days Ministries
PO Box 40
Lowell, MI, USA 49331-0040

http://www.tldm.org
E-Mail: tldm@tldm.org
Fax: (616) 698-2260
Phone (616) 698-6448

Religious Items Available

Heaven's Home Protection Packet...

Our Lord stated we must have crucifixes upon the outside of all of our outside doors. In the "Heaven's Home Protection Packet" there are instructions, four crucifixes, and a tube of special cement for wooden or metal crucifixes. Put a light coat of cement on the back of the crucifix and then press it to the outside of the door. *Item # P15 Suggested donation $5.00 each*

Personal Protection Packet

Our Lady tells us to be protected from all evil, we must wear the following sacramentals around our necks: a rosary, a crucifix, the St. Benedict medal, Our Lady of the Roses medal, the Miraculous Medal, and the scapular. We have all of these sacramentals in a packet we call "Heaven's Personal Protection Packet." This packet is available for a donation of $5.00 and is listed in the sacramental section of the order form.

Our Lady of the Roses, Mary Help of Mothers promises to help protect our children. On September 13, 1977, She said, "He has an army of ogres wandering now throughout your country and all of the countries of the world. They are in possession of great power; so wear your sacramentals, and protect your children and your households. Learn the use every day of holy water throughout your household. Insist even with obstructions, insist that your children always wear a sacramental. One day they will understand that they will repel the demons."

On February 1, 1974, Our Lady said, "My children, know the value of these sacramentals. Guard your children well. You must awaken to the knowledge that you will not be protected without the sacramentals. Guard your children's souls. They must be surrounded with an aura of purity. Remove them if necessary from the sources of contamination, be it your schools or even false pastors." *Item # P5 Suggested donation $5.00 each*

Brown Scapular

Our Lady - "I promise you all, when you wear My Brown Scapular, you shall not be condemned to hell. I repeat: if you pass on over the veil and are wearing the Brown Scapular, you shall not see the fires of hell." (9-14-85) We have available a blessed wool scapular which meets all of the requirements Our Lady gave in the message. *Item # S2 Suggested donation $1.00 each*

15 Decade Rosary CD (Compact Disc)

The Joyful, Sorrowful, and Glorious Mysteries are on this CD. You can choose to say one, two, or all three of the mysteries. You can pause saying the Rosary at any time and return to complete it any time later. On September 14, 1984 Our Lady said; "The Rosary must be recited daily, and twice a day, if possible. All others we leave to you to say for added graces." *Item # CD15 Cost $10.00 each*

Bayside Prophecy & Bible CD (Compact Disc)

A personal computer CD is available with all the messages given by Our Lady from 1970 through 1994, along with the Douay Rheims Bible. Included is software that will do instantaneous word searches through the Bayside Prophecies or the Bible. We have had many requests for this and now it is finally available.

This is an excellent way to search the messages and Bible on a given topic, such as the rosary, prayer, sacramentals, heaven, saints, suffering, earthquakes, comets, UFO's, AIDS, test tube babies, warning, and much more. You may want to order it for a family member or a relative that has a computer with Microsoft Windows. Order it today. *Item #CD10 Cost $50.00 each*

15 Decade Rosary on audio cassette tape

This 90-minute audiocassette tape has the 15 decade rosary. On September 14, 1985 Jesus said; "Now, My children, We are not leaving. We wish to hear the prayers of atonement, for it is like music to Our hearts. The Rosary has always been music to Our hearts." *Item #T2 Cost $5.00 each*

Two inch wooden Crucifix

On June 18, 1987 Jesus said; "Remember, keep your sacramentals constantly upon you: your brown Scapular, your Saint Benedict medal, the Miraculous Medal, and also the medal of Our Lady of the Roses. You must keep them upon you, with a crucifix. We demand a crucifix, because demons - many of the highest ones in the realms of hell cannot stand the sight of a crucifix. They will not approach your door. I give you this knowledge, My children, though it is not common knowledge, My children, though it is not common knowledge upon earth, that the crucifix has great power against satan." *Item #C2 Suggested Donation $1.00*

St. Benedict medal

On July 25, 1985 Our Lord said the St. Benedict medal is the indulgenced medal in the Church: "Satan has a plan to eliminate the good. Do not be affrighted, My child or My children. You will wear your sacramentals. Specifically, We have asked you, and My Mother has asked you, to wear the Brown Scapular, and also a crucifix, and with that the highest indulgenced medal in the Church."

"My child remember the St. Benedict medal. Many years ago, We gave unto you through long searching the second hidden meaning of the St. Benedict medal. You will bring that out again, My child, in publication for the salvation of souls." *Item #M4 Suggested Donation $.50 cents each*

Miraculous Medal on a chain

In May 1832, the first Miraculous Medals were distributed, and soon there was a flood of reported cures and conversions. So many, in fact, that the people soon began calling it the "Miraculous Medal." Millions of people worldwide wear the Miraculous Medal as a reminder of the blessing Our Lady had waiting for them to request.

Jesus - "Remember, keep your sacramentals constantly upon you: your brown Scapular, your Saint Benedict medal, the Miraculous Medal, and also the medal of Our Lady of the Roses. You must keep them upon you, with a crucifix." (6-18-87)

The Miraculous Medal is one of the most popular and widely known medals in the world. The Miraculous Medal is 1 3/8" and the stainless steel chain is 24" long. *Item #M14 Suggested Donation $2.00*

Crystal Rosary

On April 14, 1984 Our Lord said; "Now, My children, you will continue with your prayers of atonement. Remember: one Rosary a day at least, at least I say, must be prayed in the home that is to be spared."

This Rosary is 18" long and comes with blue, red, or clear 5mm faceted beads. Please choose the color. *Item #S12 Suggested Donation $10.00*

Prices are subjest to change without notice.

These Last Days Ministries
PO Box 40
Lowell, MI, USA 49331-0040

http://www.tldm.org
E-Mail: tldm@tldm.org
Fax: (616) 698-2260
Phone (616) 698-6448

Order Form

Qty	Description	Price	Amt
____	Home Protection Packet *(P15)*..................	$5.00	____
____	Personal Protection Packet *(P5)*..............	$5.00	____
____	Brown Scapular *(S2)*....................................	$1.00	____
____	15 Decade Rosary CD *(CD15)*................	$10.00	____
____	15 Decade Rosary Audio Tape *(T2)*.........	$5.00	____
____	Bayside Prophecy & Bible CD *(CD10)*..	$50.00	____
____	2" Wooden Crucifix *(C2)*...........................	$1.00	____
____	St. Benedict Medal *(M4)*...........................	$0.50	____
____	Miraculous Medal on a chain *(M14)*..........	$2.00	____
____	Crystal Rosary *(S12)*..................................	$10.00	____
		Subtotal	____

Michigan Residents 6% Sales Tax....................... ____

Shipping & Handling: If your order is:
  $0.00 to $10.00 add $3.00
  $10.00 to $25.00 add $4.50
  $25.00 to $50.00 add $6.00
  Over $50.00 add 10% of Subtotal ____
Rush Order: COD+$5.00, Priority+$3.00 ____
Non-US Order add 30% ____

Total ____

Mr. Mrs. Miss_____

Address_____

City_____**State/Prov**_____**Zip**_____

Bill my: MasterCard Visa **Expiration Date**_____

Card No:_____

Signature:_____

Send all orders to:
  These Last Days Ministries   http://www.tldm.org
  PO Box 40   E-Mail: tldm@tldm.org
  Lowell, MI, USA 49331-0040   Fax: (616) 698-2260
                                         Phone (616) 698-6448

Prayer Request Form

Please write below your prayer requests to Jesus and Mary. We will have it placed at the very spot below where Jesus and Mary appeared to Veronica.

My Dearest Jesus and Mary,
   I humbly and prayerfully ask for these requests:

_____

_____

_____

_____

_____

_____

_____

_____

                              Graciously yours,

                              _____

Mail to: These Last Days Ministries
           PO Box 40, Lowell, MI 49331-0040
Fax: **(616) 698-2260**   **Email: tldm@tldm.org**
Phone: **(616) 698-6448**   **Web: http://www.tldm.org**
Toll Free: (800) 444-6279

Order Form

Qty	Description	Price	Amt
____	Home Protection Packet *(P15)*..................$5.00		____
____	Personal Protection Packet *(P5)*................$5.00		____
____	Brown Scapular *(S2)*....................................$1.00		____
____	15 Decade Rosary CD *(CD15)*................$10.00		____
____	15 Decade Rosary Audio Tape *(T2)*......... $5.00		____
____	Bayside Prophecy & Bible CD *(CD10)*.. $50.00		____
____	2" Wooden Crucifix *(C2)*...........................$1.00		____
____	St. Benedict Medal *(M4)*............................$0.50		____
____	Miraculous Medal on a chain *(M14)*..........$2.00		____
____	Crystal Rosary *(S12)*................................$10.00		____

Subtotal ____

Michigan Residents 6% Sales Tax...................... ____

Shipping & Handling: If your order is:
  $0.00 to $10.00 add $3.00
  $10.00 to $25.00 add $4.50
  $25.00 to $50.00 add $6.00
  Over $50.00 add 10% of Subtotal ____
Rush Order: COD+$5.00, Priority+$3.00 ____
Non-US Order add 30% ____

Total ____

Mr. Mrs. Miss_____

Address_____

City_____State/Prov_____Zip_____

Bill my: MasterCard Visa **Expiration Date**_____

Card No:_____

Signature:_____

Send all orders to:

These Last Days Ministries http://www.tldm.org
PO Box 40 E-Mail: tldm@tldm.org
Lowell, MI, USA 49331-0040 Fax: 1-616-698-2260
  Phone 1-616-698-6448

Prayer Request Form

Please write below your prayer requests to Jesus and Mary. We will have it placed at the very spot below where Jesus and Mary appeared to Veronica.

My Dearest Jesus and Mary,
I humbly and prayerfully ask for these requests:

_____

_____

_____

_____

_____

_____

_____

_____

Graciously yours,

_____

Mail to: These Last Days Ministries
PO Box 40, Lowell, MI 49331-0040
Fax: (616) 698-2260   Email: tldm@tldm.org
Phone: (616) 698-6448   Web: http://www.tldm.org
Toll Free: (800) 444-6279

Index

B

C

172, 175, 176, 177, 182, 188, 189, 190, 191, 202, 203,
208, 209, 212, 213, 218, 220, 229, 230, 232, 239, 246,
247, 251, 269, 273, 275, 282, 283, 287, 291, 296, 298,
318, 323, 324, 333, 336, 342, 348, 359, 362, 365, 368,
371, 374, 376, 387, 399, 402, 405, 418, 432, 452, 476,
480, 482, 491, 497
cruel 284, 351
curative 15, 16, 17
cure 70, 148, 163, 174, 179, 210, 217, 219, 225, 226,
235, 384, 396, 397, 401, 434, 435, 436, 442, 443

D

damnation 34, 156, 157, 200, 244, 277
damned 19, 21, 43, 44, 67, 109, 128, 445
dance 288
daughter 42, 213, 234, 271, 320, 342, 400
deacon 489
debase 488
deceit 8, 12, 56
deceive 22, 23, 186, 248, 302, 467
deceiver 186, 319
deception 20, 266
decision 35, 201, 378, 380, 408, 427
defame 196, 425, 495
defend 71, 179, 426
defense 103
defiling 117, 151
degenerate 7, 12
degradation 443
delude 67, 468, 471
delusion 167, 462, 467
demolish 370
demon 237, 244, 418, 437, 440, 471
denomination 71, 89

doctor 78, 344
dome 197
dream 85, 92, 460
duress 72

E

eagle 8, 118, 147, 492
Earthquake 264, 273, 331, 372, 389, 406, 416
education 323, 330, 340, 365, 372
Egypt 301
elements 124, 126
Empire 391
enemies 5, 42, 63, 102, 103, 118, 123, 141, 143, 175, 196, 223, 229, 233, 283, 351, 436
enemy 5, 21, 56, 59, 86, 105, 117, 125, 129, 144, 174, 184, 194, 234, 238, 277, 331, 342, 343
engulf 223
ensnare 467
envy 20, 41, 187, 266
epidemic 29, 435, 442
errors 7, 124, 204, 258, 259, 408, 416, 417, 425, 436, 464, 468
Eucharist 44, 70, 86, 99, 151
Europe 187, 236, 237, 441
excommunication 23
excuse 85, 175, 287, 340
execution 128, 138
Exorcism 178
explosion 264, 313
extermination 192, 479

F

Faith 13, 27, 35, 43, 48, 63, 93, 95, 96, 97, 105, 133, 176, 200, 237, 241, 242, 254, 256, 301, 304, 320, 328, 350, 353, 364, 366, 378, 392, 416, 426, 464, 478, 488, 498

Faithful and True 13

family 5, 20, 57, 178, 185, 186, 195, 245, 252, 274, 293, 326, 352, 357, 358, 365, 366, 370, 400, 401, 498

famine 28, 43, 148, 265, 331, 417, 421, 463

famous 447, 458, 461

fashion 207

fasting 375

father 40, 42, 213, 242, 259, 271, 320, 340, 342, 392, 468

Fatima 258, 281, 312, 313, 318, 319, 337, 338, 352, 358, 364, 373, 458, 459, 461, 462, 463, 464

feast 20, 77, 78, 81, 95, 97, 362, 388, 458

fight 88, 163, 168, 200, 221, 254, 302, 305, 328, 329, 341, 342, 370, 411, 415, 421, 454, 488

fire 26, 40, 57, 121, 164, 193, 203, 214, 215, 235, 275, 304, 306, 315, 327, 376, 426, 446, 454, 463, 478, 482, 492, 493

Florida 439

folly 257

force 27, 114, 116, 124, 128, 206, 223, 233, 255, 295, 326, 364, 370, 411

foreign 103, 331, 342, 385

Fornication 287

fortitude 495

foul 184, 330, 477

French 386, 458

G

Gabriel 323
Garabandal 81

H

horns 106, 379
horse 417
hospital 459, 480, 481
hourglass 72, 73, 110, 148, 149, 167, 186, 221, 223,
234, 254, 303, 309, 313
household 283, 392, 411, 456
Humanism 8, 12, 49, 70, 95, 110, 167, 247, 276, 326,
330, 352, 407, 451, 495
humility 383, 406, 485
Hunger 27, 43, 75, 76, 236
Hurricane 272, 273
husband 40, 80, 91, 245, 330, 482

|

idols 8, 41
illuminati 351, 358, 359, 360, 391
immodesty 89, 388, 392, 402
immorality 58, 88, 167, 276, 277, 293
impurity 41
Infant 380
intellectual 44
intercession 117, 120, 389
interlopers 20, 23, 274, 390
international 70, 353
intervention 48, 310
invade 112, 117, 185
invasion 116, 133, 134, 143, 144, 184, 347, 350
investigate 291, 330
Iran 364
Italy 103, 128, 294

*** J***

Jesus 6
Job 436, 442

justice 59, 238, 271

K

Khrushchev 467, 468
kill 97, 213, 224, 257, 325, 351, 369, 377, 404, 410, 411

L

lamb 175, 305, 308
Latin 407
laws 195, 278, 293, 301, 302, 303, 390, 483
laxity 326
layman 19
Lenin 467, 468
liars 365, 392, 468
licentiousness 342
lie 81, 207, 402
Limbo 367
Lot 33, 293
Lourdes 247, 258
Lucifer 4, 7, 12, 35, 44, 67, 88, 178, 216, 452
lukewarm 169
luminous 97, 190, 275, 306, 318, 434, 437, 447, 449, 466
lust 41, 56, 452
luxury 27, 48, 326
lying 55, 79, 81, 194, 214

M

maneuver 177
marriage 287, 301, 302, 326, 340, 344, 353
mask 77
master 8, 58, 110, 160, 161, 257, 379, 465

materialism 266, 276, 314, 326, 330
Matthew 93, 94, 308, 309
media 179, 338, 358, 359
Mediterranean 39
meteors 255
Mideast 132, 134
minister 89, 96
miracle 112, 138, 295, 464
missile 116, 125, 331
Mission 2
miters 487
mitres 15, 19, 48, 52, 57, 69, 88, 169, 229, 337, 424, 425
modernism 8, 12, 49, 69, 95, 110, 117, 216, 293, 326, 330, 352, 392, 398, 402, 407, 438
modest 393, 484
money 29, 41, 56, 87, 202, 237, 238, 240, 242, 257, 286, 293, 294, 365, 369, 391, 402, 483
monks 150
monster 89, 357, 456
morality 276, 285, 467, 473
morals 88, 474
Moses 287
Moslems 301, 391
mountain 128, 272, 273, 454
murder 20, 27, 34, 41, 42, 43, 56, 59, 69, 90, 105, 106, 128, 134, 163, 167, 169, 187, 195, 197, 201, 213, 238, 242, 244, 271, 284, 286, 300, 302, 305, 320, 325, 326, 342, 365, 367, 369, 377, 388, 390, 391, 392, 411, 436, 438, 442, 447, 455, 474

pastor 68
Paul 21, 24, 27, 71, 102, 104, 122, 123, 128, 140, 143, 144, 192, 193, 197, 201, 221, 226, 227, 249, 255, 256, 260, 280, 283, 286, 306, 325, 329, 341, 345, 350, 352, 358, 364, 365, 366, 368, 373, 377, 412, 420, 421, 425, 428, 454, 462, 479
paws 21
penetrate 463
Pentecost 298
perdition 85, 133, 173, 196, 216, 226, 432, 478
perfection 142, 177, 254
perish 227, 237, 243, 402, 496
persecution 36, 301, 427, 478
Persian 338, 350
perverse 7, 344, 440
pestilence 43, 416, 417, 421
petals 14, 382, 383, 388, 393, 400, 408, 419, 434
Peter 26, 104, 197, 255, 326, 412, 450, 479
phenomenon 177, 464
physicians 42
pinnacle 138, 325
plague 56, 124, 148, 149, 219, 226, 268, 339, 340, 341, 372, 401, 435, 436, 437
planet 471
plead 35, 41, 223, 303, 312, 313, 373, 406, 435, 454, 463, 486
pleasure 7, 56, 125, 170
Plot 175
plum 126, 136
political 118, 256, 378
Pontius 176, 445
Pope 21, 71, 100, 102, 103, 104, 123, 125, 128, 140, 143, 144, 166, 188, 192, 193, 197, 201, 221, 227, 234, 249, 255, 260, 280, 283, 286, 294, 297, 302, 306, 312, 326, 329, 338, 341, 345, 350, 352, 358, 361, 364, 365,

S

206

third world war 30, 104, 120, 130, 132, 134, 139, 174, 177, 191, 194, 215, 223, 224, 300, 301, 319
Thomas 446
tongues 33, 366
torment 19, 147, 222, 283, 440, 493
tornado 200
Tradition 261, 407, 458
transcend 235, 240
translucent 5
transport 116, 186, 284, 410, 471
treasure 75, 98, 157
treaty 190, 198, 341, 345, 350
tribulation 2, 8
tribulations 12
trumpet 93
tunnel 115, 281
TV 410, 430, 438, 451

U

U.S.S.R. 439
unholy 19, 87

V

vapor 109
Vatican 77, 142, 198, 201, 216, 255, 256, 319, 350, 461, 462, 463
vehicles 186, 283, 284, 293
Veronica 9
Veronica of the Cross 3
volcano 314, 435
vow 88